ACCOUNTING
CANADIAN EDITION

VOLUME 2
FINANCIAL ACCOUNTING

ACCOUNTING
CANADIAN EDITION

Carl S. Warren
University of Georgia, Athens

Philip E. Fess
University of Illinois, Champaign-Urbana

James M. Reeve
University of Tennessee, Knoxville

Sandra M. Felton
Brock University, St. Catharines, Ontario

H. Donald Brown
Brock University, St. Catharines, Ontario

VOLUME 2
FINANCIAL ACCOUNTING

 I(T)P Nelson

an International Thomson Publishing company

Toronto • Albany • Bonn • Boston • Cincinnati • Detroit • London • Madrid • Melbourne
Mexico City • New York • Pacific Grove • Paris • San Francisco • Singapore • Tokyo • Washington

I⊤P® **International Thomson Publishing**
The ITP logo is a trademark under licence.
www.thomson.com

Published in 1999 by
I⊤P® **Nelson**
A division of Thomson Canada Limited
1120 Birchmount Road
Scarborough, Ontario M1K 5G4
www.nelson.com

First published by South-Western Publishing Company, copyright 1996.

Canadian Cataloguing in Publication Data

Main entry under title:

Accounting

Canadian ed.
Includes index.
ISBN 0-17-616638-6 (v. 1)   ISBN 0-17-616748-X (v. 2)   ISBN 0-17-616639-4 (v. 3)

1. Accounting.   I. Warren, Carl S.

HF5635.A365 1998   657   C98-931794-3

Editorial Director: Michael Young
Executive Editor: Tim Sellers
Developmental Editor: Anita Miecznikowski
Production Editor: Valerie Adams
Copy Editor: Anna Garnham
Production Coordinator: Hedy Later
Marketing Manager: David Tonen
Cover Image: Dave Starrett
Cover and Interior Design: Angela Cluer
Composition Analyst: Marnie Benedict
Composition Manager: Dolores Pritchard

Printed and bound in the U.S.A.

1 2 3 4   WCB   02 01 00 99

Contents

v

Preface

When we were first approached by ITP Nelson to consider adapting *Accounting* by Warren, Fess, and Reeve for the Canadian market, we were curious to know why it had been a best-seller in the American market for 18 editions. Upon examining the book, we found that it offered students a superlative learning system—complete with illustrations, real world examples, questions, exercises, problems, cases, and a full set of supplementary materials.

Warren, Fess, and Reeve have produced a truly student-friendly text. *Accounting* provides students with ample material to assist them in understanding accounting concepts, as well as preparing and using accounting information. Chapters are framed by clear sets of objectives, which are referenced throughout the text, and conclude with brief summaries of content related to these objectives. The writing is simple and the presentation well organized. The content is relevant and the context is real.

One of the chronic problems associated with teaching introductory accounting is the errors that are often found in the texts and solutions manuals. These errors confuse the students and aggravate the instructor. We found *Accounting* to be very free from errors and wanted to ensure that the Canadian edition upheld the same standards of accuracy. Consequently we have carefully reviewed the entire book for errors, and the Solutions Manual, which was prepared independently by Betty Wong and Richard Wright, was checked by both ourselves and a research assistant.

THE CANADIAN EDITION

The Canadian edition of *Accounting* is split into three volumes. Volumes 1 and 2 cover financial accounting and Volume 3 is on managerial accounting. The book has been published in three volumes thanks to feedback from the marketplace. The general consensus from reviewers and focus group participants alike was that such a split would make for maximum student benefit and flexibility. The book has been divided as follows:

- Volume 1 (Chapters 1–11) covers financial accounting topics up to and including current liabilities. This volume includes both inventories and payroll.
- Volume 2 (Chapters 12–16) covers the balance of the financial accounting material.
- Volume 3 (Chapters 17–26) covers all of the management accounting material.

Please note that each volume will contain some references to material in the companion volumes.

For those students who require two or three volumes for their courses, affordable shrink-wrapped packages of Volumes 1, 2, and/or 3 will be readily available from ITP Nelson.

This edition provides full integration of accounting concepts and practices within the Canadian context. Included is an introduction to the professional accounting organizations and the development of generally accepted accounting principles in Canada. The text contains numerous examples from the financial reports of Canadian companies and appropriate and up-to-date references to the *CICA Handbook,* including the most recent recommendations related to accounting for income taxes, financial instruments, and the statement of cash flows. We increased the conceptual content of the material, particularly in the early chapters, in order to provide students with a solid basis for preparing and understanding accounting information.

In addition, we compressed and rearranged the coverage of certain topics in the U.S. text. For example, we have included all of the essentials of accounting for corporations in one chapter (which we have completely rewritten from the Canadian perspective). Similarly, we have reorganized the material to group together long-term liabilities arising from various sources such as bonds, notes payable, leases, pensions, and income taxes. We have also revised and restructured the chapter on current liabilities to cover a broader range of items, and have moved some of the details of payroll calculation to an appendix at the end of the chapter.

In addition, we have aimed to improve the clarity of the writing by moving from the more traditional and cumbersome passive style to the active voice. Not only does this improve the readability for students and engage them more directly with the material, but we believe that it provides them with a model of good writing, as recommended by various handbooks on effective writing for accountants.

We believe that the scope and extent of problem, exercise, and case material in this book is unparallelled in any existing text. In keeping with the U.S. edition, we have included an extensive set of "A" and "B" problems at the end of each chapter. However, we have revised the "B" set of problems to increase variation and ensure that they are not an exact mirror of the "A" set. New to the Canadian edition is a selection of challenge problems in each chapter. We have also added several problems which specifically review accounting concepts as we proceed from topic to topic through the text.

Each chapter includes several cases, one or more of which is related to ethical issues in the preparation and use of accounting information. In addition, each chapter includes a case based on the Annual Report of Sears Canada Inc. (reproduced in Appendix C) to introduce the students to the use and analysis of financial statements.

We believe that the structure of the chapters, the writing style, the extensive collection of exercises, problems, and cases, and the balance of conceptual and procedural content set this book apart from other introductory accounting texts.

FEATURES

Perspective

Over the years we have used many different texts in our introductory accounting courses, from those labelled "preparer-oriented," to the "conceptual," to those described as presenting a "user perspective." We have concluded that a sound conceptual foundation is a necessary prerequisite to approaching both the preparation and use of financial reports. In addition, we think that preparation and use belong together (a preparer/user perspective). One of our goals in adapting this text was to ensure an appropriate balance among these three approaches (concepts, preparation, and use). To achieve this we increased and integrated the conceptual matter in the earlier chapters and eliminated the need for the traditional separate chapter on concepts part way through the book.

We believe that *Accounting, Canadian Edition,* can fulfill the needs of both those who wish to take either a more user-oriented, a more conceptual, or a more preparer-oriented approach. The focus can vary depending on the emphasis supplied by the instructor.

From the user's perspective, each chapter begins with an introductory section entitled "You and Accounting" which emphasizes how accounting information relates to so many areas of the student's everyday life. Each chapter also contains a case requiring the student to analyze some aspect of the financial statements of Sears Canada Inc., which appear in Appendix C. We chose Sears because it is a highly visible company with operations across Canada, and one that should be familiar to most students. The text also introduces the student to the various components of the annual report (such as the management report, historical summary, various notes to the financial statements, etc.). Although this material is included in the chapter on financial statement analysis, it could be included earlier in the course. We also introduce some of the more complex items which a user could encounter in the financial statements, such as capital leases, accrued/deferred pension costs, and future income tax assets and liabilities. We have covered these topics lightly, avoiding the excessive detail which might confuse an introductory accounting student. At the same time, we have ensured that our coverage reflects current practice in the area, and is not so overly simplistic as to be misleading.

The book can also be used effectively to emphasize a "preparer perspective." Each chapter contains clear examples of the accounting techniques presented along with journal entries, ledger account examples, and worksheets as appropriate. For example, reviewers have commented that Chapter 15 ("The Statement of Cash Flows") presents a very clear rationale and methodology for preparing the financial statement. With over 20 exercises per chapter, the book offers sufficient single-topic material to provide for mastery of principles and techniques prior to trying problems. A continuing problem built upon successive chapters ties together the basics introduced in the first section of the book. In later chapters, we have included comprehensive problems which review material covered earlier in the text. We were careful to reflect the latest professional accounting pronouncements in all areas and to present all topics in a way which is entirely compatible with a more in-depth study of the material so that, in the future, a student can make a smooth transition into intermediate accounting—without having to "unlearn" anything covered at the introductory level.

For either of the user or preparer approach, the integration of conceptual material provides the basis for understanding accounting. Accounting concepts are emphasized from the very beginning of the book and reinforced as each new topic is introduced. Aside from a comprehensive introduction of concepts in the first few chapters, each chapter contains principles, definitions, and concepts related to particular topics. Many chapters have two problems related to accounting concepts, which encourage the student to focus on the concepts which underlie the treatment of items discussed in that chapter, and many of the cases draw upon a conceptual understanding of what accounting is trying to do. Reviewers have commented that our presentation of present value concepts, effective interest rates, and statement of cash flow material was conceptually much clearer than material contained in other introductory texts.

Class Tested for Accuracy

As stated earlier, we know nothing is more upsetting to both students and instructors than to adopt a text with technical errors. We know the feeling first-hand, having adopted error-filled books ourselves in the past. That is why, in September of 1998, a group of seven instructors and over 500 students at our school used a pre-publication version of Volumes 1 and 2 of this text. The reason? We wanted to be sure the text you consider for adoption has been given a true "test drive"—and we knew the only way to do that was to put it through a rigorous class test. And believe us, we did! With over 500 students using the text, we were able to clean up any (and hopefully all) technical inaccuracies. And most importantly, the students enjoyed the text and performed well.

It's important to note this accuracy check was not limited to the text alone. The solutions manuals for Volumes 1 and 2 were also closely scrutinized at the same time, and corrections made to them as well. We are confident you will be very pleased with the accuracy of both our text and solutions manuals.

Format

Given the visual orientation of today's students, we have carefully integrated the use of colour and type style with the format of the book in order to attract and hold the students' attention.

"You and Accounting"

A short story at the beginning of each chapter relates the chapter's topic to the personal experience of the student. By capturing the student's attention at the beginning of the chapter, we hope to make the material more enjoyable to read and easier to grasp.

Chapter Objectives

A boxed and highlighted listing sets out the objectives to be covered at the beginning of each chapter. Throughout the text, we include the objectives as margin references for each section of text, and summarize them again at the end of the chapter in a "Key Points" recap, which includes brief explanatory notes.

"Using Accounting to Understand Business"

 Each chapter includes one or more informative examples, set apart in highlighted boxes, that clearly connect accounting to the business environment and show how students might use accounting information in their future business careers.

"Computer King"

 Introduced in Chapter 1 and continued throughout most of the text, the statements from this company help students tie together elements of the accounting cycle and more.

Glossary of Key Terms

Each chapter includes a glossary of definitions for terms introduced in the chapter. We have also combined these chapter glossaries into a comprehensive glossary included at the end of the text.

End-of-Chapter Material

We consistently conclude each chapter with the following pedagogy:

- Key Points
- Glossary of Key Terms
- Illustrative Problem
- Self-Examination Questions
- Discussion Questions
- Exercises (cross-referenced to topic and chapter objectives)
- Series A Problems (cross-referenced to topic and chapter objectives)
- Series B Problems (cross-referenced to topic and chapter objectives)
- Challenge Problems
- Cases
- Answers to the Self-Examination Questions

The assignment material encompasses a wide range of levels of difficulty: from straightforward exercises and questions to in-depth problems, conceptual analysis, comprehensive reviews, thought-provoking cases, and analysis of real-world financial data. The abundance and variety of this material is so extensive that it could provide the basis for numerous new assignments from year-to-year, providing for use of the text for an extended period.

Icons you will come across in the end-of-chapter material include:

 This continuing problem offers students the opportunity to practise what is being learned by following the accounting cycle step-by-step for a single company over Chapters 1–4. In addition, Chapters 4, 6, 11, and 14 include comprehensive problems, which integrate and summarize the concepts and principles covered over several chapters.

 "What's Wrong With This?"—We employ these unique exercises to challenge students to analyze and discover what is wrong with a financial statement, report, or management decision. Students will gain practical experience and critical thinking skills that will assist them in the business world.

 We use Ethics cases to stimulate discussion on ethical dilemmas in business.

 To help students develop essential communication skills, we have included communication exercises in the end-of-chapter material.

 "What Do You Think?"—These exercises require analyses beyond the material included in the text. Real companies are presented.

"Real World Examples"—We employ the annual report of Sears Canada Inc., as well as numerous other real world examples, to demonstrate how organizations use accounting and how it affects business in Canada and throughout the world. Integrated throughout the chapters and in the end-of-chapter cases and problems, these examples add concrete meaning to the concepts and principles.

End-of-Text Material

We have included the following appendices at the end of the text:

- **Appendix A: Accounting Concepts**
- **Appendix B: Interest Tables**
- **Appendix C: Annual Report for Sears Canada**
- **Appendix D: The Basics**—a review of basic accounting facts
- **Appendix E: Abbreviations and Acronyms Commonly Used in Business and Accounting**
- **Appendix F: Classification of Accounts**—a handy reference chart of account titles indicating classification, normal balance as debit or credit, and location in financial statements

SUPPLEMENTS

For the Instructor

The following supplements are available for use with the Canadian edition of *Accounting*, Volumes 1, 2, and 3:

- **Solutions Manual**—adapted by the text authors and by Betty Wong of Athabasca University (Volume 1), Richard Wright of Fanshawe College (Volume 2), and Dave Kennedy of Lethbridge Community College (Volume 3). It provides complete written solutions for all exercises, questions, problems, and cases in the end-of-chapter assignment material.
- **Overhead Transparencies**—a complete set of acetates of the Solutions Manual (for adopters only).
- **Instructor's Manual**—adapted by Leo Gallant of St. Francis Xavier University. It provides lecture notes, overhead transparency masters, demonstration problems, group learning activities, and writing exercises.
- **PowerPoint Slides**—adapted by Dennis Wilson of Centennial College. These slides provide graphic presentations of accounting concepts.
- **Test Bank**—adapted by Irene Wiecek of the University of Toronto. It contains true/false questions, multiple-choice questions, and problems that test students' comprehension of the material presented in each chapter.
- **Computerized Test Bank**—adapted by Irene Wiecek of the University of Toronto. This electronic version of the Test Bank allows the instructor to produce customized, computer-generated examinations.

For the Student

The following student supplements are available for use with the Canadian edition of *Accounting*, Volumes 1, 2, and 3:

- **Study Guide** (Volumes 1, 2, and 3)—adapted by Kim Dyck of Red River Community College. These guides include chapter outlines, problems, and solutions to help the student understand the concepts presented in the text.

- **Working Papers** (Volumes 1, 2, and 3)—adapted by Michael Lee of Humber College. These include the forms needed for completing all problems in the end-of-chapter material.

   In addition to the above supplementary materials, you can explore the world of accounting and conveniently access support for this text at

   http://accounting.nelson.com

This resource site includes instructor supplements in a password-protected area, student activities, an accounting education page, a careers section, links to accounting software providers, accounting references and study resources, and a case/question of the month. We will be continually updating this site to keep the information current and to continue to meet your needs.

ACKNOWLEDGEMENTS

We would like to thank the following instructors who acted as consultants, reviewers, and/or participated in focus groups:

CONSULTANTS
- Kim Dyck, Red River Community College
- Robin Hemmingsen, Centennial College
- John Western, Kwantlen University College

FOCUS GROUP PARTICIPANTS
- Ted Carney, Humber College
- Sandy Caven, George Brown College
- Ron Francis, Seneca College
- John Glendenning, Centennial College
- Rob Harvey, Algonquin College
- Marie Madill-Payne, George Brown College
- Winston Marcellin, George Brown College
- Bonnie Martel, Niagara College
- Ann Paterson, Humber College
- Mike Perretta, Sheridan College
- John Varga, George Brown College

REVIEWERS
- Lewis Callahan, Lethbridge Community College
- Patricia Corkum, Acadia University
- Kim Dyck, Red River Community College
- Gordon Farrell, British Columbia Institute of Technology
- Mahlon Harvey, University of Winnipeg
- Rob Harvey, Algonquin College
- Bruce Hazelton, Sheridan College
- Dave Kennedy, Lethbridge Community College
- Guy Penney, College of the North Atlantic
- Ken Smith, College of the North Atlantic
- Ralph Sweet, Durham College
- Dennis Wilson, Centennial College
- Christopher Wright, University of Northern British Columbia
- Richard Wright, Fanshawe College
- Elizabeth Zaleschuk, Douglas College

We offer special thanks to our assistant, Miss Shari Leitch, who assisted us with searching the web for examples and statistics, and assisted with checking the detail of all answers for all of the discussion questions, exercises, problems, and cases. In addition, the enthusiasm, support, and expertise of the ITP Nelson College publishing staff have facilitated the completion of this project in a timely and professional manner.

Sandra M. Felton
H. Donald Brown

CARL S. WARREN

Dr. Carl S. Warren is the Arthur Andersen & Co. Alumni Professor of Accounting at the J.M. Tull School of Accounting at the University of Georgia, Athens. Professor Warren received his Ph.D. from Michigan State University in 1973. Dr. Warren's experience in listening to users of his texts sharpens his keen focus on helping students learn. When he is not teaching classes or writing textbooks, Dr. Warren enjoys golf, racquetball, and fishing.

PHILIP E. FESS

Dr. Philip E. Fess is the Arthur Andersen & Co. Alumni Professor of Accountancy Emeritus at the University of Illinois, Champaign-Urbana. He received his Ph.D. from the University of Illinois. Dr. Fess has been involved in writing textbooks for over twenty-five years, and his knowledge of how to make texts user-friendly is reflected on the pages of this edition. Dr. Fess plays golf and tennis, and he has represented the United States in international tennis competition.

JAMES M. REEVE

Dr. James M. Reeve is Professor of Accounting at the University of Tennessee, Knoxville. He received his Ph.D. from Oklahoma State University in 1980. Dr. Reeve is founder of the Cost Management Institute and a member of the Institute for Productivity Through Quality faculty at the University of Tennessee. In addition to his teaching experience, Dr. Reeve brings to this text a wealth of experience consulting on managerial accounting issues with numerous companies, including Procter and Gamble, AMOCO, Rockwell International, Harris Corporation, and Freddie Mac. Dr. Reeve's interests outside the classroom and the business world include golf, skiing, reading, and travel.

SANDRA M. FELTON

Dr. Sandra M. Felton is Associate Professor of Accounting in the Department of Accounting and Finance in the Faculty of Business at Brock University, St. Catharines, Ontario. She received her C.A. while employed with Clarkson Gordon in 1974, and her Ph.D. from the State University of New York at Buffalo in 1988. She is a Doctoral Fellow of the Institute of Chartered Accountants of Ontario. Dr. Felton has twenty-four years of experience teaching accounting and has published articles in the areas of financial accounting, accounting education, and accounting history.

H. DONALD BROWN

Donald Brown is an Adjunct Professor of Accounting and Academic Advisor for accounting and business students in the Department of Accounting and Finance at Brock University, St. Catharines, Ontario. He holds a Master of Divinity degree from the University of Emmanuel College, Saskatoon, and a Master of Science in Accounting degree from the University of Saskatchewan. He is a Chartered Accountant and Certified Management Accountant with experience in public accounting with national, regional, and local firms. He taught at the University of Lethbridge and the University of Saskatchewan before moving to Brock in 1985. With over twenty years of experience in teaching accounting, he has published and presented papers in the areas of accounting education, thinking skills, and problem solving.

PART FOUR

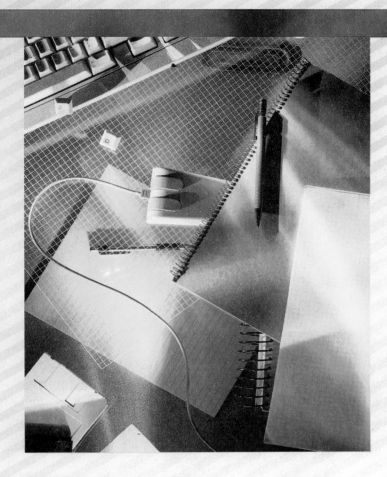

Partnerships

12 Partnership Formation, Income Division, and Liquidation

YOU AND ACCOUNTING

Assume that you and a friend have an idea for starting a part-time business to earn some extra money.

What does it take to start a business operated by two or more individuals? How much money should each individual (you and your friend) contribute to start the business? How will the profits be divided? Can you withdraw money from the business whenever you want, or do you have to have your friend's (partner's) approval? Can your friend bring someone else into the business as a partner without your approval? Could you or your friend quit the business at any time? Will you be liable for commitments made by your partner, even if they were made without your knowledge? Is the amount you can lose in the business, if it's not successful, limited to the amount you initially invested?

The partnership form of business organization allows two or more persons to combine capital, managerial talent, and experience with a minimum of effort. This form is used widely by small businesses. In many cases, the only alternative to the partnership form of business organization is the corporate form. Most provinces, however, do not permit the corporate form for certain types of businesses, especially professionals such as physicians, lawyers, and public accountants. Legal partnerships made up of 20 or more partners are not unusual, and the number of partners in some national CA firms exceeds 500.

The preceding chapters focused on the accounting for sole proprietorships. This chapter describes and illustrates the accounting for the partnership form of business organization, which is the form you and your friend would be using in operating your business. We will address the answers to the questions above, and the accounting for partnerships, throughout this discussion.

After studying this chapter, you should be able to:

Objective 1
Identify and list the basic characteristics of the partnership form of business organization.

Objective 2
Journalize the entries for the formation of partnerships.

Objective 3
Journalize the entries for dividing partnership net income and net loss.

Objective 4
Journalize the entries for partnership dissolution, including admission of new partners and the withdrawal or death of partners.

Objective 5
Journalize the entries for liquidating partnerships.

Characteristics of Partnerships

Objective 1
Identify and list the basic characteristics of the partnership form of business organization.

A partnership is a form of business ownership where two or more persons carry on a business together to earn a profit. Most provinces have legislation that requires partnerships to register the names of the partners and the name under which the business operates. Partnerships have several characteristics with accounting implications. These characteristics are described in the following paragraphs.

A partnership has a limited life. Dissolving a partnership occurs whenever a partner ceases to be a member of the firm. For example, a partnership is dissolved if a partner withdraws due to bankruptcy, incapacity, or death. Likewise, admitting a new partner dissolves the old partnership. When a partnership is dissolved, a new partnership must be formed if operations of the business are to continue. This situation often occurs in professional partnerships, such as medical, legal, and accounting firms. Their membership changes as new partners join the firm and others retire.

Most partnerships are *general partnerships,* in which the partners have **unlimited liability.** Each partner is individually liable to creditors for debts incurred by the partnership. Thus, if a partnership becomes insolvent, the partners must contribute sufficient personal assets to settle the debts of the partnership. For some partnerships (excluding physicians, lawyers, or accountants), this may be avoided by forming a *limited partnership*. In a **limited partnership,** the liability of some partners may be limited to the amount of their capital investment. However, a limited partnership must have at least one general partner who has unlimited liability. This chapter will focus on the general partnership.

Partners have co-ownership of partnership property. The property invested in a partnership by a partner becomes the property of all the partners jointly. When a partnership is dissolved, we measure the partners' claims against the assets by the amount in their capital accounts.

Another characteristic of a partnership is mutual agency. This means that each partner is an agent of the partnership. Thus, each partner has the authority to enter into contracts for the partnership. The acts of each partner bind the entire partnership and become the obligations of all partners.

An important right of partners is participation in income of the partnership. Net income and net loss are distributed among the partners according to their agreement. In the absence of any agreement, all partners share equally. If the agreement indicates a profit distribution but is silent as to losses, partners share the losses in the same manner as profits.

USING ACCOUNTING TO UNDERSTAND BUSINESS

The 10 largest accounting partnerships in Canada, ranked by revenues, are listed below.

Largest Accounting Partnerships in Canada

Rank by revenue 1997	Rank by revenue 1996	1997 revenue '000s	Firm (Year end) (Head office location)	Number of partners (±)	Revenue per partner '000s (±%)	Number of professional staff
1	1	$524,725	KPMG (Feb. 28/97) (Toronto)	680 (–1)	$ 772 (+6.8)	3,678
2	2	499,000	Deloitte & Touche (Aug. 31/96) (Toronto)	540 (–15)	924 (+16)	3,549
3	3	415,000	Ernst & Young (Jan. 31/97) (Toronto)	398 (–48)	1,043 (+22)	2,395
4	4	336,433	Coopers & Lybrand (Dec. 31/96) (Toronto)	283 (–1)	1,189 (+13)	2,111
5	5	300,000	Andersen Worldwide (Dec. 31/96) (Toronto)	169 (+2)	1,775 (+7.4)	1,997
6	6	275,982	Price Waterhouse (Dec. 31/96) (Toronto)	255 (+7)	1,082 (+6.9)	1,848
7	7	202,900	Doane Raymond Grant Thornton (Dec. 31/96) (Ottawa)	366 (–15)	554 (+3.2)	1,691
8	8	132,330	BDO Dunwoody (Dec. 31/96) (Toronto)	254 (–10)	521 (+7.4)	1,116
9	—	62,000	Richter, Usher & Vineberg (Feb. 28/97) (Montreal)	61 —	1,016 —	383
10	9	31,120	Collins Barrow (Jan. 31/97) (Toronto)	97 (+17)	321 (–7.2)	321

Source: *The Bottom Line*, April 1997, p. 15.

A partnership, like a sole proprietorship, is not a **taxable entity** and thus does not pay income taxes. The partners must report their share of partnership income on their personal tax returns.

A partnership is created by a contract. It is not necessary that the contract be in writing, nor even that its terms be specifically expressed. However, good business practice requires that the contract be in writing and that it clearly expresses the intentions of the partners. The contract is known as the partnership agreement or **articles of partnership.** It should include statements regarding such matters as amounts to be invested, limits on withdrawals, distributions of income and losses, and admission and withdrawal of partners.

ADVANTAGES AND DISADVANTAGES OF PARTNERSHIPS

The partnership form of business organization is less widely used than are the sole proprietorship and corporate forms. For many business purposes, however, the advantages of the partnership form are greater than its disadvantages.

A partnership is relatively easy and inexpensive to organize, requiring only an agreement between two or more persons. A partnership has the advantage of bringing together more capital, managerial skills, and experience than does a sole proprietorship. Since a partnership is a nontaxable entity, the combined income taxes paid by the individual partners may be lower than the income taxes that would be paid by a corporation, which is a taxable entity.

A major disadvantage of the partnership form of business organization is the unlimited liability feature for partners. For example, in 1993, some 90 creditors and investors filed close to $1 billion in lawsuits against the accounting firm of Coopers & Lybrand over the failure of one of Cooper's clients, the real estate company,

Castor Holdings Ltd. By 1997, $100 million of the claims had been withdrawn and the remainder were working their way through the court system. Coopers has 283 partners who will have to share in the payment of any settlements beyond amounts covered by insurance. Most professional partnerships have liability insurance to protect the partners from financial hardship in the event that the partnership is sued and found liable for the claim.

Other disadvantages of a partnership are that its life is limited and that one partner can bind the partnership to contracts. Also, raising large amounts of capital is more difficult for a partnership than for a corporation.

ACCOUNTING FOR PARTNERSHIPS

Most of the day-to-day accounting for a partnership is the same as the accounting for any other form of business organization. Partnerships can use the accounting system described in previous chapters with little change. The chart of accounts, with the exception of withdrawals and capital accounts for each partner, does not differ from the chart of accounts of a similar business conducted by a single owner. However, the formation, income distribution, dissolution, and liquidation of partnerships give rise to unique transactions. In the remainder of this chapter, we discuss accounting principles related to these areas.

Formation of a Partnership

Objective 2
Journalize the entries for the formation of partnerships.

We record a separate entry for the investment of each partner in a partnership. The assets contributed by a partner are debited to the partnership asset accounts. If liabilities are assumed by the partnership, the partnership liability accounts are credited. The partner's capital account is credited for the net amount.

To illustrate, assume that Joseph A. Stevens and Earl S. Foster, sole owners of competing hardware stores, agree to combine their businesses in a partnership. Each is to contribute certain amounts of cash and other assets. They also agree that the partnership will assume the liabilities of the separate businesses. The entry to record the assets contributed and the liabilities transferred by Stevens is as follows:

Apr. 1	Cash	7,200	
	Accounts Receivable	16,300	
	Inventory	28,700	
	Store Equipment	5,400	
	Office Equipment	1,500	
	Allowance for Doubtful Accounts		1,500
	Accounts Payable		2,600
	Joseph A. Stevens, Capital		55,000

A similar entry would record the assets contributed and the liabilities transferred by Foster. In each entry, we record the noncash assets at values agreed upon by the partners. These values represent the acquisition cost to the new partnership. The agreed-upon values normally represent current market values and therefore usually differ from the book values of the assets in the records of the separate businesses. For example, the store equipment recorded at $5,400 in the preceding entry may have had a book value of $3,500 in Stevens's ledger (cost of $10,000 less accumulated amortization of $6,500).

We record receivables contributed to the partnership at their face amount, and provide for future bad debts by crediting a contra account. Only accounts that are likely to be collected are normally transferred to the partnership. For example, assume that in the prior example the accounts receivable ledger of Stevens totalled $17,600. Of this total, accounts of $1,300 are considered worthless. The remaining receivables of $16,300 were transferred to the partnership accounts by a debit to the accounts receivable account in the general ledger. The partnership sets up a subsidiary ledger by debiting each customer's individual account. Finally, an allowance for possible uncollectible accounts is recorded by crediting Allowance for Doubtful Accounts for $1,500.

Dividing Net Income or Net Loss

Objective 3
Journalize the entries for dividing partnership net income and net loss.

Many partnerships have been dissolved because partners could not agree on an equitable distribution of income. Therefore, the partners need to state the method of dividing partnership income in the partnership agreement. In the absence of an agreement or if the agreement is silent on dividing net income or net losses, all partners share equally. However, if one partner contributes a larger portion of capital than the others, then net income could be divided to reflect the unequal capital contributions. Likewise, if one partner renders services that are more important than those of the others, net income could be divided to reflect the unequal service contributions. In the following paragraphs, we illustrate partnership agreements that recognize these differences.

An equitable distribution of income among partners is vital to the success of the business. Therefore, the partnership agreement should state a method of dividing partnership income.

INCOME DIVISION—SERVICES OF PARTNERS

One method of recognizing differences in partners' abilities and amount of time devoted to the business is to provide salary allowances to partners. Since partners are legally not employees of the partnership, we treat such salary allowances as divisions of net income (not as an expense of the business) and credit the partners' capital accounts.

To illustrate, assume that the partnership agreement of Jennifer L. Stone and Crystal R. Mills provides for monthly salary allowances. Jennifer Stone is to receive a monthly allowance of $2,500 and Crystal Mills is to receive $2,000 a month. Any net income remaining after the salary allowances is to be divided equally. Assume also that the net income for the year is $75,000.

A report of the division of net income may be presented as a separate statement to accompany the balance sheet and the income statement. Another format is to add the division to the bottom of the income statement. If the latter format is used, the lower part of the income statement would appear as follows:

Net income $75,000

Division of net income:

	J. L. Stone	C. R. Mills	Total
Salary allowance	$30,000	$24,000	$54,000
Remaining income	10,500	10,500	21,000
Net income	$40,500	$34,500	$75,000

The partnership records net income division as a closing entry, even if the partners do not actually withdraw the amounts of their salary allowances. The entry for dividing net income is as follows:

Dec. 31	Income Summary	75,000	
	Jennifer L. Stone, Capital		40,500
	Crystal R. Mills, Capital		34,500

If Stone and Mills had withdrawn their salary allowances monthly, the withdrawals would have been debited to their withdrawals accounts during the year. At the end of the year, the partnership would transfer the debit balances of $30,000 and $24,000 in their withdrawals accounts to reduce their capital accounts.

Accountants should be careful to distinguish between salary allowances and partner withdrawals. The amount of net income distributed to each partner's capital account at the end of the year may differ from the amount the partner withdraws during the year. In some cases, the partnership agreement may limit the amount of withdrawals a partner may make during a period.

INCOME DIVISION—SERVICES OF PARTNERS AND INVESTMENT

Partners may agree that the most equitable plan of dividing income is to provide for (1) salary allowances and (2) interest allowances on capital investments. As with salary allowances, interest allowances are divisions of income among partners, not expenses of the business. Any remaining net income is then divided as agreed. For example, assume that the partnership agreement for Stone and Mills divides income as follows:

1. Monthly salary allowances of $2,500 for Stone and $2,000 for Mills.
2. Interest allowance of 12% on each partner's capital balance on January 1.
3. Any remaining net income divided equally between the partners.

Stone had a credit balance of $80,000 in her capital account on January 1 of the current fiscal year and Mills had a credit balance of $60,000 in her capital account. The $75,000 net income for the year is divided in the schedule below.

Net income $75,000

Division of net income:

	J. L. Stone	C. R. Mills	Total
Salary allowance	$30,000	$24,000	$54,000
Interest allowance	9,600	7,200	16,800
Remaining income	2,100	2,100	4,200
Net income	$41,700	$33,300	$75,000

For the above example, the entry to close the income summary account is shown below.

Dec. 31	Income Summary	75,000	
	Jennifer L. Stone, Capital		41,700
	Crystal R. Mills, Capital		33,300

INCOME DIVISION—ALLOWANCES EXCEED NET INCOME

In the previous examples, net income exceeded the total of the salary and interest allowances. If the net income is less than the total of the allowances, the **remaining balance** will be a negative amount. This amount is divided among the partners as though it were a net loss.

To illustrate, assume the same salary and interest allowances as in the previous example, but assume that net income is $50,000. The salary and interest allowances total $39,600 for Stone and $31,200 for Mills. The sum of these amounts, $70,800, exceeds the net income of $50,000 by $20,800. It is necessary to divide the $20,800 excess between Stone and Mills. Under the partnership agreement, any net income or net loss remaining after deducting the allowances is divided equally between Stone and Mills. Thus, we allocate one-half of the $20,800 to each partner and deduct $10,400 from each partner's share of the allowances. The final division of net income between Stone and Mills is as follows:

Net income $50,000

Division of net income:

	J. L. Stone	C. R. Mills	Total
Salary allowance	$30,000	$24,000	$54,000
Interest allowance	9,600	7,200	16,800
Total	$39,600	$31,200	$70,800
Excess of allowances over income	10,400	10,400	20,800
Net income	$29,200	$20,800	$50,000

In closing Income Summary at the end of the year, we would credit $29,200 to Jennifer L. Stone, Capital, and $20,800 to Crystal R. Mills, Capital.

REPORTING CHANGES IN PARTNERS' EQUITIES

The partnership balance sheet usually reports the balance of the capital account of each partner. In addition, a statement of partners' equity should report the changes in the partners' equity of a partnership during the period. The purpose of this statement is similar to that of the statement of owner's equity for a sole proprietorship.

There are a number of different forms of the statement of partners' equity. One such format is shown below for the Stone and Mills partnership.

EXECUTIVE COMPENSATION—A PARTNERSHIP VS. A CORPORATION

Deloitte, Haskins & Sells (now Deloitte & Touche), a public accounting partnership, described its view of partner compensation and the division of the firm's income as follows:

. . . As a general rule, compensation in major mid-sized corporations (to which we might be compared based on revenue size, number of personnel, etc.) consists of current cash, deferred payments, payments made on behalf of an individual for retirement benefits, and perquisites. In addition, options to purchase stock at potentially favourable prices may also be an attractive compensation component. Unlike a corporation, partners . . . must provide from their own earnings for their own retirement benefits, as well as paying for self-employment taxes, group insurance, and other benefit programs. . . .

Each year the majority of the firm's earnings are distributed to the partners. Some small percentage is usually retained for working capital needs. No amounts are guaranteed, like a "preset" annual salary. If earnings decline, partners'. . . individual earnings also decline. Partners . . . are also required to invest capital in the firm. As such, part of their earnings represent a return on their investment. . . .

The factors mentioned above must be considered in making meaningful comparisons of partners' compensation with other business executives. To simply compare amounts would be misleading.

The average earnings of all of our partners for fiscal year 1985 was approximately $143,000. As to our five most highly compensated partners, their individual earnings ranged from $385,000 to $725,000, and their average was $500,000. . . .

Source: Deloitte, Haskins & Sells, *A Report for Congress and the Public,* September 1985.

Stone and Mills
Statement of Partners' Equity
For the Year Ended December 31, 20—

	Jennifer L. Stone	Crystal R. Mills	Total
Capital, January 1, 20—	$ 80,000	$60,000	$140,000
Additional investment during the year		5,000	5,000
	$ 80,000	$65,000	$145,000
Net income for the year	41,700	33,300	75,000
	$121,700	$98,300	$220,000
Withdrawals during the year	30,000	24,000	54,000
Capital, December 31, 20—	$ 91,700	$74,300	$166,000

Partnership Dissolution

Objective 4
Journalize the entries for partnership dissolution, including admission of new partners and the withdrawal or death of partners.

One of the basic characteristics of the partnership form of business organization is its limited life. Any change in the ownership dissolves the partnership. Thus, admission of a new partner dissolves the old firm. Likewise, death, bankruptcy, or withdrawal of a partner dissolves the partnership.

When a partnership dissolves, its affairs are not necessarily wound up. For example, a partnership of two partners may admit a third partner. Or if one of the partners in a business withdraws, the remaining partners may continue to operate the business. In such cases a new partnership is formed and a new partnership agreement should be prepared. Many partnerships provide for the admission of new partners and partner withdrawals in the partnership agreement so that the partnership may continue operations without executing a new agreement.

ADMISSION OF A PARTNER

A person may be admitted to a partnership only with the consent of all the current partners, through either of two methods:[1]

1. Purchasing an interest from one or more of the current partners.
2. Contributing assets to the partnership.

Under the first method, the capital interest of the incoming partner is obtained from current partners, with no effect on *either the total assets or the total partners' equity of the business.* Under the second method, *both the total assets and the total partners' equity of the business are increased.* In the following paragraphs, we discuss each of these methods.

Purchasing an Interest in a Partnership

A person may be admitted to a partnership by buying an interest from one or more of the existing partners. The purchase and sale of the partnership interest occurs between the new partner and the existing partners acting as individuals. Thus, the purchase price is paid directly to the selling partner(s). Neither the total assets nor

---

[1] Although an individual cannot become a partner without the consent of the other partners, the rights of a partner, such as the right to share in the income of a partnership, may be assigned to others without the consent of the other partners. Such issues are discussed in business law textbooks.

the total partners' equity of the business are affected. The only entry needed is to transfer equity amounts from the capital account(s) of the selling partner(s) to the capital account established for the incoming partner.

As an example, assume that partners Tom Andrews and Nathan Bell have capital balances of $50,000 each. On June 1, each sells one-fifth of his equity to Joe Canter for $10,000 in cash. The exchange of cash is not a partnership transaction and thus is not recorded by the partnership. The only entry required in the partnership accounts is as follows:

June	1	Tom Andrews, Capital	10,000	
		Nathan Bell, Capital	10,000	
		Joe Canter, Capital		20,000

The following diagram presents the effect of the transaction on the partnership accounts:

Partnership Accounts

The preceding entry is not affected by the amount paid by Canter for the one-fifth interest. If the firm had been earning a high rate of return on the investment, Canter might have paid more than $20,000. If the existing partners had been eager to sell, he might have acquired the one-fifth interest for less than $20,000. In either case, the entry to transfer the capital interests is the same as shown above.

After Canter is admitted to the partnership, the total partners' equity of the firm is still $100,000. Canter now has a one-fifth interest, or a $20,000 capital balance. However, Canter may not be entitled to a one-fifth share of the partnership net income. Division of net income or net loss will be made according to the new partnership agreement.

Contributing Assets to a Partnership

Instead of buying an interest from the current partners, the incoming partner may contribute assets to the partnership. In this case, both the assets and the partners' equity of the firm increase. For example, assume that Donald Lewis and Gerald Morton are partners with capital accounts of $35,000 and $25,000 respectively. On June 1, Sharon Nelson invests $20,000 cash in the business for an ownership equity of $20,000. The entry to record this transaction is as follows:

June	1	Cash	20,000	
		Sharon Nelson, Capital		20,000

The major difference between the admission of Nelson and the admission of Canter in the preceding examples may be observed by comparing the following diagram with the preceding diagram.

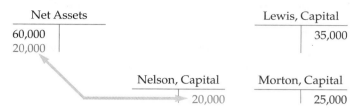

Partnership Accounts

By admitting Nelson, the total equity of the new partnership becomes $80,000, of which Nelson has a one-fourth interest, or $20,000. The extent of Nelson's share in partnership net income will be determined by the partnership agreement.

Revaluation of Assets

A partnership's asset account balances should be stated at current values when a new partner is admitted. If the accounts do not approximate current market values, we adjust the accounts and divide the net adjustment (increase or decrease) in asset values among the capital accounts of the existing partners according to their income-sharing ratio. Failure to adjust the accounts for current values may result in the new partner sharing in asset gains or losses that arose in prior periods.

To illustrate, assume that in the preceding example for the Lewis and Morton partnership, the balance of the inventory account is $14,000 and its current replacement value is $17,000. Assuming that Lewis and Morton share net income equally, we record the revaluation as follows:

June	1	Inventory	3,000	
		Donald Lewis, Capital		1,500
		Gerald Morton, Capital		1,500

If a number of assets are revalued, we may debit or credit the adjustments to a temporary account entitled Asset Revaluations. After all adjustments are made, we close this account to the partner capital accounts.

Partner Bonuses

When a new partner is admitted to a partnership, the incoming partner may pay a bonus to the existing partners for the privilege of joining the partnership. Such a bonus is usually paid in expectation of high partnership profits in the future due to the contributions of the existing partners. Alternatively, the existing partners may pay the incoming partner a bonus to join the partnership. In this case, the bonus is usually paid in recognition of special qualities or skills that the incoming partner is bringing to the partnership. For example, celebrities such as actors, musicians, or sports figures often provide name recognition that is expected to increase partnership profits in the future. We distribute the amount of any bonus paid to the partnership among the partner capital accounts.[2]

To illustrate, assume that on March 1 the partnership of Marsha Jenkins and Helen Kramer is considering admitting a new partner, William Larson. After the

---

[2] Another method is sometimes used to record the admission of partners in situations such as that described in this paragraph. This method attributes goodwill rather than a bonus to the partners. This method is discussed in advanced accounting textbooks.

assets of the partnership have been adjusted to current market values, the capital balance of Jenkins is $20,000 and the capital balance of Kramer is $24,000. Jenkins and Kramer agree to admit Larson to the partnership for $31,000. In return, Larson will receive a one-third equity in the partnership and will share equally with Jenkins and Kramer in partnership income or losses.

In this case Larson is paying Jenkins and Kramer a $6,000 bonus to join the partnership. We compute this bonus as follows:

Equity of Jenkins	$20,000
Equity of Kramer	24,000
Contribution of Larson	31,000
Total equity after admission of Larson	$75,000
Larson's equity interest after admission	$\times$ ⅓
Larson's equity after admission	$25,000
Contribution of Larson	$31,000
Larson's equity after admission	25,000
Bonus paid to Jenkins and Kramer	$ 6,000

We distribute the bonus to Jenkins and Kramer according to their income-sharing ratio. Assuming that Jenkins and Kramer share profits and losses equally, we record the admission of Larson to the partnership as follows:

Mar. 1	Cash	31,000	
	William Larson, Capital		25,000
	Marsha Jenkins, Capital		3,000
	Helen Kramer, Capital		3,000

If a new partner possesses unique qualities or skills, the existing partners may agree to pay the new partner a bonus to join the partnership. To illustrate, assume that after adjustment to market values the capital balance of Janice Cowen is $80,000 and the capital balance of Steve Dodd is $40,000. Cowen and Dodd agree to admit Sandra Ellis to the partnership on June 1 for an investment of $30,000. In return, Ellis will receive a one-fourth equity interest in the partnership and will share in one-fourth of the profits and losses.

In this case Cowen and Dodd are paying Ellis a $7,500 bonus to join the partnership. We compute this bonus as follows:

Equity of Cowen	$ 80,000
Equity of Dodd	40,000
Contribution of Ellis	30,000
Total equity after admission of Ellis	$150,000
Ellis's equity interest after admission	$\times$ 25%
Ellis's equity after admission	$ 37,500
Contribution of Ellis	30,000
Bonus paid to Ellis	$ 7,500

Assuming that the income-sharing ratio of Cowen and Dodd was 2:1 before the admission of Ellis, we record the bonus and admission of Ellis to the partnership as follows:

June 1	Cash	30,000	
	Janice Cowen, Capital	5,000	
	Steve Dodd, Capital	2,500	
	Sandra Ellis, Capital		37,500

WITHDRAWAL OF A PARTNER

When a partner retires or withdraws from a partnership, one or more of the remaining partners may buy the withdrawing partner's interest. The firm may then continue its operations uninterrupted. In such cases the purchase and sale of the partnership interest are between the partners as individuals. The only entry on the partnership's records is to debit the capital account of the partner withdrawing and to credit the capital account of the partner or partners buying the additional interest.

If the withdrawing partner sells the interest directly to the partnership, we reduce both the assets and the partners' equity of the partnership. Before the sale, the partnership should adjust the asset accounts to current values, so that the withdrawing partner's equity may be accurately determined. The net amount of the adjustment should be divided among the capital accounts of the partners according to their income-sharing ratio. If not enough partnership cash or other assets are available to pay the withdrawing partner, a liability may be created (credited) for the amount owed the withdrawing partner.

DEATH OF A PARTNER

The death of a partner dissolves the partnership. In the absence of an agreement, the accounts should be closed as of the date of death. As part of this process, we determine the net income for this part of the current year and divide it among the partners' capital accounts. It is not unusual, however, for the partnership agreement to indicate that the accounts should remain open until the end of the current fiscal year. At that time, the net income of the entire period is divided, as provided by the agreement, between the periods before and after the partner's death.

The business then transfers the balance in the capital account of the deceased partner to a liability account with the deceased's estate. The remaining partner or partners may continue the business, or may terminate its affairs. If the partnership continues in business, the procedures for settling with the estate are the same as those discussed for the withdrawal of a partner.

Liquidating Partnerships

Objective 5

Journalize the entries for liquidating partnerships.

When a partnership goes out of business, it usually sells the assets, pays the creditors, and distributes the remaining cash or other assets to the partners. We call this winding-up process the liquidation of the partnership. Although liquidating refers to the payment of liabilities, it is often used to include the entire winding-up process.

When the partnership goes out of business and normal operations are discontinued, we adjust and close the accounts. The only accounts remaining open will be the asset, contra asset, liability, and partners' equity accounts.

The sale of the assets is called realization. As cash is realized, it is used to pay the claims of creditors. After paying all liabilities, the business distributes the remaining cash to the partners based on the balances in their capital accounts.

The liquidating process may extend over a long period of time as individual assets are sold. This delays the distribution of cash to partners, but does not affect the amount each partner will receive.

As a basis for illustration, assume that Farley, Greene, and Hall share income and losses in a ratio of 5:3:2 ($\frac{5}{10}$, $\frac{3}{10}$, $\frac{2}{10}$). On April 9, after discontinuing business operations of the partnership and closing the accounts, the business prepares the following trial balance in summary form:

Cash	11,000	
Noncash Assets	64,000	
Liabilities		9,000
Jean Farley, Capital		22,000
Brad Greene, Capital		22,000
Alice Hall, Capital		22,000
Total	75,000	75,000

Based on these facts, we will show the accounting for liquidating the partnership by using three different selling prices for the noncash assets. To simplify, we assume that all noncash assets are sold in a single transaction and that all liabilities are paid at one time. In addition, we will use Noncash Assets and Liabilities as account titles in place of the various asset, contra asset, and liability accounts.

GAIN ON REALIZATION

Between April 10 and April 30 of the current year, Farley, Greene, and Hall sell all noncash assets for $72,000 and realize a gain of $8,000 ($72,000 – $64,000). We divide the gain among the capital accounts in the income-sharing ratio of 5:3:2. The liabilities are paid, and the remaining cash is distributed to the partners. *The cash is distributed to the partners based on the balances in their capital accounts.* Exhibit 1 shows a statement of partnership liquidation, which summarizes the liquidation process.

Exhibit 1
Gain on Realization

Farley, Greene, and Hall
Statement of Partnership Liquidation
For Period April 10–30, 20—

	Cash	+	Noncash Assets	=	Liabilities	+	Capital Farley (50%)	+	Greene (30%)	+	Hall (20%)
Balances before realization	$11,000		$64,000		$9,000		$22,000		$22,000		$22,000
Sale of assets and division of gain	+72,000		–64,000		—		+ 4,000		+ 2,400		+ 1,600
Balances after realization	$83,000		$ 0		$9,000		$26,000		$24,400		$23,600
Payment of liabilities	– 9,000		—		–9,000		—		—		—
Balances after payment of liabilities	$74,000		$ 0		$ 0		$26,000		$24,400		$23,600
Cash distributed to partners	–74,000		—		—		–26,000		–24,400		–23,600
Final balances	$ 0		$ 0		$ 0		$ 0		$ 0		$ 0

The entries to record the steps in the liquidating process are as follows:

Sale of assets:	Cash	72,000	
	Noncash Assets		64,000
	Gain on Realization		8,000
Division of gain:	Gain on Realization	8,000	
	Jean Farley, Capital		4,000
	Brad Greene, Capital		2,400
	Alice Hall, Capital		1,600

| **Payment of liabilities:** | Liabilities | 9,000 | |
| | Cash | | 9,000 |

Distribution of cash to partners:	Jean Farley, Capital	26,000	
	Brad Greene, Capital	24,400	
	Alice Hall, Capital	23,600	
	Cash		74,000

As shown in Exhibit 1, the cash is distributed to the partners based on the balances of their capital accounts. We determine these balances after dividing the gain on realization among the partners. *The income-sharing ratio should not be used as a basis for distributing the cash to partners.*

LOSS ON REALIZATION

Assume that in the preceding example, Farley, Greene, and Hall dispose of all noncash assets for $44,000, realizing a loss of $20,000 ($64,000 – $44,000). Exhibit 2 summarizes the steps in liquidating the partnership.

Exhibit 2
Loss on Realization

				Capital		
	Cash +	Noncash Assets	= Liabilities +	Farley (50%)	+ Greene (30%)	+ Hall (20%)
Balances before realization	$11,000	$64,000	$9,000	$22,000	$22,000	$22,000
Sale of assets and division of loss	+44,000	−64,000	—	−10,000	− 6,000	− 4,000
Balances after realization	$55,000	$ 0	$9,000	$12,000	$16,000	$18,000
Payment of liabilities	− 9,000	—	−9,000	—	—	—
Balances after payment of liabilities	$46,000	$ 0	$ 0	$12,000	$16,000	$18,000
Cash distributed to partners	−46,000	—	—	−12,000	−16,000	−18,000
Final balances	$ 0	$ 0	$ 0	$ 0	$ 0	$ 0

Farley, Greene, and Hall
Statement of Partnership Liquidation
For Period April 10–30, 20—

The entries to liquidate the partnership are as follows:

Sale of assets:	Cash	44,000	
	Loss on Realization	20,000	
	Noncash Assets		64,000

Division of loss:	Jean Farley, Capital	10,000	
	Brad Greene, Capital	6,000	
	Alice Hall, Capital	4,000	
	Loss on Realization		20,000

| **Payment of liabilities:** | Liabilities | 9,000 | |
| | Cash | | 9,000 |

Distribution of cash to partners:	Jean Farley, Capital	12,000	
	Brad Greene, Capital	16,000	
	Alice Hall, Capital	18,000	
	Cash		46,000

LOSS ON REALIZATION—CAPITAL DEFICIENCY

In the preceding example the capital account of each partner was large enough to absorb the partner's share of the loss from realization. The partners received cash to the extent of the remaining balances in their capital accounts. However, sometimes the share of loss on realization may exceed the balance in the partners' capital accounts. We call the resulting debit balance in the capital account a deficiency. It represents a claim of the partnership against the partner.

To illustrate, assume that Farley, Greene, and Hall sell all of the noncash assets for $10,000, realizing a loss of $54,000 ($64,000 − $10,000). The share of the loss allocated to Farley, $27,000 (50% of $54,000), exceeds the $22,000 balance in her capital account. This $5,000 deficiency represents an amount that Farley owes the partnership. Assuming that Farley pays the entire deficiency to the partnership, the business will have sufficient cash to distribute to the remaining partners according to their capital balances. Exhibit 3 summarizes the steps in liquidating the partnership in this case.

Exhibit 3

*Loss on Realization—
Capital Deficiency*

**Farley, Greene, and Hall
Statement of Partnership Liquidation
For Period April 10–30, 20—**

	Cash	+	Noncash Assets	=	Liabilities	+	Capital Farley (50%)	+	Greene (30%)	+	Hall (20%)
Balances before realization	$11,000		$64,000		$9,000		$22,000		$22,000		$22,000
Sale of assets and division of loss	+10,000		−64,000		—		−27,000		−16,200		−10,800
Balances after realization	$21,000		$ 0		$9,000		$ 5,000(Dr.)		$ 5,800		$11,200
Payment of liabilities	− 9,000		—		−9,000		—		—		—
Balances after payment of liabilities	$12,000		$ 0		$ 0		$ 5,000(Dr.)		$ 5,800		$11,200
Receipt of deficiency	+ 5,000		—		—		+ 5,000		—		—
Balances	$17,000		$ 0		$ 0		$ 0		$ 5,800		$11,200
Cash distributed to partners	−17,000		—		—		—		− 5,800		−11,200
Final balances	$ 0		$ 0		$ 0		$ 0		$ 0		$ 0

The entries to record the liquidation are as follows:

Sale of assets:	Cash	10,000	
	Loss on Realization	54,000	
	Noncash Assets		64,000
Division of loss:	Jean Farley, Capital	27,000	
	Brad Greene, Capital	16,200	
	Alice Hall, Capital	10,800	
	Loss on Realization		54,000
Payment of liabilities:	Liabilities	9,000	
	Cash		9,000
Receipt of deficiency:	Cash	5,000	
	Jean Farley, Capital		5,000
Distribution of cash to partners:	Brad Greene, Capital	5,800	
	Alice Hall, Capital	11,200	
	Cash		17,000

If cash is not collected from a deficient partner, the partnership cash will not be large enough to pay the other partners in full. Any uncollected deficiency becomes a loss to the partnership to be divided among the remaining partners' capital balances, based on their income-sharing ratio. The cash balance will then equal the sum of the capital account balances. Cash is then distributed to the remaining partners, based on the balances of their capital accounts.[3]

ERRORS IN LIQUIDATION

The type of error that occurs most often in liquidating a partnership is an improper distribution of cash to the partners. Such errors usually occur because the distribution of cash to partners in liquidation is confused with the division of gains and losses on realization.

Gains and losses on realization result from the disposal of assets to outsiders. *Realization gains and losses should be divided among the partner capital accounts in the same manner as net income or net loss from normal business operations—using the income-sharing ratio.* On the other hand, the distribution of cash (or other assets) to the partners in liquidation is not directly related to the income-sharing ratio. The distribution of assets to the partners in liquidation is the exact reverse of the contribution of assets by the partners at the time the partnership was established. *The distribution of assets to partners in liquidation is equal to the credit balances in their capital accounts after all gains and losses on realization have been divided and allowances have been made for any partner deficiencies.*

KEY POINTS

Objective 1. Identify and list the basic characteristics of the partnership form of business organization.

A partnership is a form of business ownership where two or more persons carry on a business together to earn a profit. Partnership characteristics that have accounting implications are limited life, unlimited liability, co-ownership of property, mutual agency, and participation in income.

The principal advantages of a partnership include the ease with which it can be organized, bringing together capital of one or more individuals, and the fact that it is a nontaxable entity. The major disadvantages of a partnership are its limited life, its unlimited liability, and its limitations for raising large amounts of capital.

Objective 2. Journalize the entries for the formation of partnerships.

When a partnership is formed, we debit accounts for the assets contributed, credit accounts for the liabilities assumed, and credit the partners' capital accounts for their respective net amounts. Noncash assets are recorded at amounts agreed upon by the partners.

Objective 3. Journalize the entries for dividing partnership net income or net loss.

We divide the net income (net loss) of a partnership among the partners by debiting (crediting) Income Summary and crediting (debiting) the partners' capital accounts. The net income or net loss may be divided on the basis of services rendered by individual partners and/or on the basis of the investments of the individual partners. In the absence of any agreement, we divide net income equally among the partners.

The division of partnership net income should be disclosed in the partnership financial statements. In addition, changes in the partners' equity during the period should be reported in the statement of partners' equity.

Objective 4. Journalize the entries for partnership dissolution, including admission of new partners and the withdrawal or death of partners.

Any change in the personnel or ownership dissolves the partnership. A partnership may be dissolved by admission of a new partner, withdrawal of a partner, or death of a partner. A

---

[3] The accounting for uncollectible deficiencies of partners is discussed and illustrated in advanced accounting texts.

partnership's asset account balances should be stated at current values at the time of dissolution of the partnership.

A new partner may be admitted to a partnership by buying an interest from one or more of the existing partners. We record the admission of the new partner by debiting the capital accounts of the selling partners and crediting the capital account of the new partner.

A new partner may be admitted to a partnership by contributing assets to the partnership. We record the admission of the new partner by debiting asset accounts for the fair market value of the assets contributed and crediting the capital account of the new partner.

When a new partner is admitted to a partnership, the incoming partner may pay a bonus to the existing partners. Alternatively, the existing partners may pay a bonus to the new partner to join the partnership.

When a partner retires, dies, or withdraws from a partnership, one or more of the remaining partners may buy the withdrawing partner's interest. The only entry for the partnership is to debit the capital account of the withdrawing partner and to credit the capital account of the partner or partners purchasing the additional interest.

Objective 5. Journalize the entries for liquidating partnerships.

When a partnership liquidates, it sells its noncash assets, pays the creditors, and distributes the remaining cash or other assets to the partners. The journal entries for the sale of noncash assets and the payment of liabilities are similar to those illustrated in earlier chapters. Any gain or loss on the sale of the noncash assets should be divided among the partners according to their income-sharing ratio. The final asset distribution to partners is based on the balances of the partners' capital accounts after all noncash assets have been sold and liabilities paid. The journal entry for the final distribution of assets debits the partners' capital accounts and credits the asset accounts.

GLOSSARY OF KEY TERMS

Deficiency. The debit balance in the owner's equity account of a partner. *Objective 5*

Liquidation (of a partnership). The winding-up process when a partnership goes out of business. *Objective 5*

Partnership. An unincorporated business wherein two or more persons carry on a business together for profit. *Objective 1*

Partnership agreement. The formal written contract creating a partnership. *Objective 1*

Realization (of a partnership). The sale of assets when a partnership is being liquidated. *Objective 5*

ILLUSTRATIVE PROBLEM

Radcliffe, Sonders, and Towers, who share in income and losses in the ratio of 2:3:5, decided to discontinue operations as of April 30 and liquidated their partnership. After the accounts were closed on April 30, the following trial balance was prepared:

Cash	5,900	
Noncash Assets	109,900	
Liabilities		26,800
Radcliffe, Capital		14,600
Sonders, Capital		27,900
Towers, Capital		46,500
Total	115,800	115,800

Between May 1 and May 18, the business sold the noncash assets for $27,400 and paid the liabilities.

Instructions

1. Assuming that the partner with the capital deficiency pays the entire amount owed to the partnership, prepare a statement of partnership liquidation.
2. Journalize the entries to record (a) the sale of the assets, (b) the division of loss on the sale of the assets, (c) the payment of the liabilities, (d) the receipt of the deficiency, and (e) the distribution of cash to the partners.

Solution

1.

Radcliff, Sonders, and Towers
Statement of Partnership Liquidation
For Period May 1–18, 20—

	Cash	+	Noncash Assets	=	Liabilities	+	*Capital* Radcliffe (20%)	+	Sonders (30%)	+	Towers (50%)
Balances before realization	$ 5,900		$109,900		$26,800		$14,600		$27,900		$46,500
Sale of assets and division of loss	+27,400		−109,900		—		−16,500		−24,750		−41,250
Balances after realization	$33,300		$ 0		$26,800		$ 1,900 (Dr.)		$ 3,150		$ 5,250
Payment of liabilities	−26,800		—		−26,800		—		—		—
Balances after payment of liabilities	$ 6,500		$ 0		$ 0		$ 1,900 (Dr.)		$ 3,150		$ 5,250
Receipt of deficiency	+ 1,900		—		—		+ 1,900		—		—
Balances	$ 8,400		$ 0		$ 0		$ 0		$ 3,150		$ 5,250
Cash distributed to partners	− 8,400		—		—		—		− 3,150		− 5,250
Final balances	$ 0		$ 0		$ 0		$ 0		$ 0		$ 0

2. a. Cash   27,400
        Loss on Realization   82,500
            Noncash Assets   109,900

    b. Radcliffe, Capital   16,500
        Sonders, Capital   24,750
        Towers, Capital   41,250
            Loss on Realization   82,500

    c. Liabilities   26,800
            Cash   26,800

    d. Cash   1,900
            Radcliffe, Capital   1,900

    e. Sonders, Capital   3,150
        Towers, Capital   5,250
            Cash   8,400

SELF-EXAMINATION QUESTIONS (ANSWERS AT END OF CHAPTER)

1. As part of the initial investment, a partner contributes office equipment that had cost $20,000 and on which accumulated amortization of $12,500 had been recorded. If the partners agree on a valuation of $9,000 for the equipment, what amount should be debited to the office equipment account?
   A. $7,500   C. $12,500
   B. $9,000   D. $20,000

2. X and Y agree to form a partnership. X is to contribute $50,000 in assets and to devote one-half time to the partnership. Y is to contribute $20,000 and to devote full time to the partnership. How will X and Y share in the division of net income or net loss?
   A. 5:2   C. 1:1
   B. 1:2   D. 2.5:1

3. X and Y invest $100,000 and $50,000 respectively in a partnership and agree to a division of net income that provides for an allowance of interest at 10% on original investments, salary allowances of $12,000 and $24,000

respectively, with the remainder divided equally. What would be X's share of a periodic net income of $45,000?
   A. $22,500   C. $19,000
   B. $22,000   D. $10,000

4. X and Y are partners who share income in the ratio of 2:1 and who have capital balances of $65,000 and $35,000 respectively. If P, with the consent of Y, acquired one-half of X's interest for $40,000, for what amount would P's capital account be credited?
   A. $32,500   C. $50,000
   B. $40,000   D. $72,500

5. X and Y share gains and losses in the ratio of 2:1. After the business sold all assets for cash, divided the losses on realization, and paid liabilities, the balances in the capital accounts were as follows: X, $10,000 Cr.; Y, $2,000 Cr. How much of the cash of $12,000 would be distributed to X?
   A. $2,000   C. $10,000
   B. $8,000   D. $12,000

DISCUSSION QUESTIONS

1. In a *general* partnership, what is the liability of the partners?
2. In a *limited* partnership, what is the liability of the partners?
3. Alan Biles and Joan Crandall joined together to form a partnership. Is it possible for them to lose a greater amount than the amount of their investment in the partnership? Explain.
4. Must a partnership file an income tax return or pay income taxes? Explain.
5. The partnership agreement between Roberta Baker and Jose Cruz provides for the sharing of partnership net income in the ratio of 3:2. Since the agreement is silent concerning the sharing of net losses, in what ratio will they be shared?
6. In the absence of an agreement, how will the net income be distributed between Michael Evans and Janice Farr, partners in the firm of E and F Environmental Consultants?
7. Paul Boyer, Fran Carrick, and Ed DiPano are contemplating the formation of a partnership. According to the partnership agreement, Boyer is to invest $60,000 and devote one-half time, Carrick is to invest $40,000 and devote three-fourths time, and DiPano is to make no investment and devote full time. Would DiPano be correct in assuming that, since he is not contributing any assets to the firm, he is risking nothing? Explain.
8. What are the disadvantages of the partnership over the corporation as a form of organization for a profit-making business?
9. As a part of the initial investment, a partner contributes delivery equipment that had originally cost $50,000 and on which accumulated amortization of $37,500 had been recorded. The partners agree on a valuation of $15,000. How should the partnership record the delivery equipment in its accounts?
10. All partners agree that $200,000 of accounts receivable invested by a partner will be collectible to the extent of 90%. How should the partnership record the accounts receivable in its general ledger?
11. Ramon Flores and Jean Vanier are contemplating the formation of a partnership in which Flores is to devote full time and Vanier is to devote one-half time. In the absence of any agreement, will the partners share in net income or net loss in the ratio of 2:1? Explain.
12. During the current year, Helen Bray withdrew $3,000 monthly from the partnership of Bray and Cox Water Management Consultants. Is it possible that her share of partnership net income for the current year might be more or less than $36,000? Explain.
13. a. What accounts are debited and credited to record a partner's cash withdrawal in lieu of salary?
    b. At the end of the fiscal year, what accounts are debited and credited to record the division of net income among partners?
    c. The partnership agreement provides for a salary allowance of $5,000 per month to partner C. If C withdrew only $4,000 per month, would this affect the division of the partnership net income?
14. How can you disclose the division of net income in the financial statements of a partnership?
15. Harry Imes, a partner in the firm of Greene, Herbert, and Imes, sells his investment (capital balance of $75,000) to Agnes Smith. (a) Does the withdrawal of Imes dissolve the partnership? (b) Are Greene and Herbert required to admit Smith as a partner?
16. Explain the difference between the admission of a new partner to a partnership (a) by purchase of an interest from another partner and (b) by contribution of assets to the partnership.
17. Why is it important to state all partnership assets in terms of current prices at the time of the admission of a new partner?
18. When a new partner is admitted to a partnership and agrees to pay a bonus to the original partners, how should the amount of the bonus be allocated to the capital accounts of the original partners?
19. Why might a partnership pay a bonus to a newly admitted partner?
20. a. Differentiate between *dissolution* and *liquidation* of a partnership.
    b. What does *realization* mean when used in connection with liquidation of a partnership?
21. In the liquidation process, (a) how are losses and gains on realization divided among the partners, and (b) how is cash distributed among the partners?

EXERCISES

EXERCISE 12–1
Entry for partner's original investment
Objective 2

Todd Jost and D. Caldwell decide to form a partnership by combining the assets of their separate businesses. Jost contributes the following assets to the partnership: cash, $6,000; accounts receivable with a face amount of $96,000 and an allowance for doubtful accounts of $6,600; inventory with a cost of $85,000; and equipment with a cost of $140,000 and accumulated amortization of $90,000.

The partners agree that $5,000 of the accounts receivable are completely worthless and are not to be accepted by the partnership, that $8,000 is a reasonable allowance for the uncollectibility of the remaining accounts, that the inventory is to be recorded at the current market price of $76,500, and that the equipment is to be valued at $90,000.

Journalize the partnership's entry to record Jost's investment.

EXERCISE 12–2
Dividing partnership income
Objective 3

Dan Moore and T. J. Knell formed a partnership, investing $240,000 and $120,000 respectively. Determine their participation in the year's net income of $120,000 under each of the following independent assumptions: (a) no agreement concerning division of net income; (b) divided in the ratio of original capital investment; (c) interest allowances at the rate of 10% on original investments and the remainder divided in the ratio of 2:3; (d) salary allowances of $40,000 and $50,000 respectively, and the balance divided equally; (e) allowance of interest at the rate of 10% on original investments, salary allowances of $40,000 and $50,000 respectively, and the remainder divided equally.

EXERCISE 12–3
Dividing partnership income
Objective 3

Determine the participation of Moore and Knell in the year's net income of $180,000, according to each of the five assumptions as to income division listed in Exercise 12–2.

EXERCISE 12–4
Dividing partnership net loss
Objective 3

Jane Williams and Y. Osaka formed a partnership in which the partnership agreement provided for salary allowances of $40,000 and $60,000 respectively. Determine the division of a $20,000 net loss for the current year.

EXERCISE 12–5
Negotiating income-sharing ratio
Objective 3

Sixty-year-old Jim Ebers retired from his computer consulting business in Boston and moved to Florida. There he met 27-year-old Ann Bowers, who had just graduated from Eldon Community College with an associate degree in computer science. Jim and Ann formed a partnership called E&B Computer Consultants. Jim contributed $15,000 for startup costs and devoted one-half time to the business. Ann devoted full time to the business. The monthly withdrawals were $1,500 for Jim and $3,000 for Ann.

At the end of the first year of operations, the two partners disagreed on the division of net income. Jim reasoned that the division should be equal. Although he devoted only one-half time to the business, he contributed all of the startup funds. Ann reasoned that the income-sharing ratio should be 2:1 in her favour because she devoted full-time to the business and her monthly withdrawals were twice those of Jim.

Can you identify any flaws in the partners' reasoning regarding the income-sharing ratio?

EXERCISE 12–6
Partnership entries and statement of partners' equity
Objective 3

The capital accounts of Walt Bigney and Dan Harris have balances of $80,000 and $95,000 respectively on January 1, the beginning of the current fiscal year. On April 10, Bigney invested an additional $10,000. During the year, Bigney and Harris withdrew $72,000 and $84,000 respectively, and net income for the year was $160,000. The articles of partnership make no reference to the division of net income.

a. Journalize the entries to close (1) the income summary account and (2) the withdrawals accounts.
b. Prepare a statement of partners' equity for the current year for the partnership of Bigney and Harris.

EXERCISE 12–7
Admitting new partners
Objective 4

Jenny Kirk and Harold Spock are partners who share in the income equally and have capital balances of $90,000 and $62,500, respectively. Kirk, with the consent of Spock, sells one-third of her interest to Benjamin McCoy. What entry is required by the partnership if the sale price is (a) $20,000? (b) $40,000?

EXERCISE 12–8
Admitting new partners who buy an interest and contribute assets
Objective 4

The capital accounts of Susan Yu and Ben Hardy have balances of $100,000 and $90,000 respectively. Ken Mahl and Jeff Wood are to be admitted to the partnership. Mahl buys one-fourth of Yu's interest for $27,500 and one-fifth of Hardy's interest for $20,000. Wood contributes $35,000 cash to the partnership, for which he is to receive a partnership equity of $35,000.

a.　Journalize the entries to record the admission of (1) Mahl and (2) Wood.
b.　What are the capital balances of each partner after the admission of the new partners?

EXERCISE 12–9
Admitting new partner who contributes assets
Objective 4

After the tangible assets have been adjusted to current market prices, the capital accounts of Cecil Jacobs and Maria Estaban have balances of $61,000 and $59,000 respectively. Lee White is to be admitted to the partnership, contributing $45,000 cash to the partnership, for which she is to receive a partnership equity of $55,000. All partners share equally in income.

a.　Journalize the admission of White, who is to receive a bonus of $10,000.
b.　What are the capital balances of each partner after the admission of the new partner?

EXERCISE 12–10
Withdrawal of partner
Objective 4

Glenn Otis is to retire from the partnership of Otis and Associates as of March 31, the end of the current fiscal year. After closing the accounts, the capital balances of the partners are as follows: Glenn Otis, $200,000; Tammie Sawyer, $125,000; and Joe Parrott, $140,000. They have shared net income and net losses in the ratio of 3:2:2. The partners agree that the inventory should be increased by $15,000 and the allowance for doubtful accounts should be increased by $3,100. Otis agrees to accept a note for $150,000 in partial settlement of his partnership equity. The remainder of his claim is to be paid in cash. Sawyer and Parrott are to share equally in the net income or net loss of the new partnership.

Journalize the entries to record (a) the adjustment of the assets to bring them into agreement with current market prices and (b) the withdrawal of Otis from the partnership.

EXERCISE 12–11
Distribution of cash upon liquidation
Objective 5

Hires and Bellman are partners, sharing gains and losses equally. At the time they decide to terminate their partnership, their capital balances are $5,000 and $20,000 respectively. After all noncash assets are sold and all liabilities are paid, there is a cash balance of $20,000.

a.　What is the amount of a gain or loss on realization?
b.　How should the gain or loss be divided between Hires and Bellman?
c.　How should the cash be divided between Hires and Bellman?

EXERCISE 12–12
Distribution of cash upon liquidation
Objective 5

Jacob Goldburg and Harlan Luce, with capital balances of $57,000 and $40,000 respectively, decide to liquidate their partnership. After selling the noncash assets and paying the liabilities, the business has $67,000 of cash remaining. If the partners share income and losses equally, how should the cash be distributed?

EXERCISE 12–13
Liquidating partnerships—capital deficiency
Objective 5

Bakki, Towers, and Nell share equally in net income and net losses. After the partnership sells all assets for cash, divides the losses on realization, and pays the liabilities, the balances in the capital accounts are as follows: Bakki, $20,000 Cr.; Towers, $57,500 Cr.; Nell, $17,500 Dr.

a.　What term is applied to the debit balance in Nell's capital account?
b.　What is the amount of cash on hand?
c.　Journalize the transaction that must take place for Bakki and Towers to receive cash in the liquidation process equal to their capital account balances.

EXERCISE 12–14
Distribution of cash upon liquidation
Objective 5

Allyn Meyer, Jim Ball, and Laura David arranged to import and sell orchid corsages for a university dance. They agreed to share equally the net income or net loss of the venture. Meyer and Ball advanced $175 and $125 of their own respective funds to pay for advertising and other expenses. After collecting for all sales and paying creditors, the partnership has $600 in cash.

a. How should the money be distributed?
b. If the partnership has only $120 instead of $600, do any of the three partners have a capital deficiency? If so, how much?

EXERCISE 12–15
Liquidating partnerships—capital deficiency
Objective 5

Duncan, Tribe, and Ho are partners sharing income in the ratio of 3:2:1. After the firm's loss from liquidation is distributed, the capital account balances were: Duncan, $15,000 Dr.; Tribe, $50,000 Cr.; and Ho, $40,000 Cr. If Duncan is personally bankrupt and unable to pay any of the $15,000, what will be the amount of cash received by Tribe and Ho upon liquidation?

EXERCISE 12–16
Statement of partnership liquidation
Objective 5

After the partnership closed its accounts on July 1, prior to liquidating the partnership, the capital account balances of Gibbs, Hill, and Manson are $24,000, $28,000, and $14,000 respectively. Cash, noncash assets, and liabilities total $11,000, $85,000, and $30,000 respectively. Between July 1 and July 29, the noncash assets are sold for $61,000, the liabilities are paid, and the remaining cash is distributed to the partners. The partners share net income and loss in the ratio of 3:2:1. Prepare a statement of partnership liquidation for the period July 1–29.

PROBLEMS SERIES A

PROBLEM 12–1A
Entries and balance sheet for partnership
Objectives 2, 3

On November 1 of the current year, Elaine Tsao and Mark Ivens form a partnership. Tsao agrees to invest $15,000 cash and inventory valued at $55,000. Ivens invests certain business assets at valuations agreed upon, transfers business liabilities, and contributes sufficient cash to bring his total capital to $85,000. Details regarding the book values of the business assets and liabilities, and the agreed valuations, are as follows:

	Ivens' Ledger Balance	Agreed-Upon Valuation
Accounts Receivable	$33,250	$31,500
Allowance for Doubtful Accounts	500	800
Inventory	42,500	42,900
Equipment	50,000 ⎫	25,000
Accumulated Amortization	29,700 ⎭	
Accounts Payable	9,700	9,700
Notes Payable	10,000	10,000

The partnership agreement includes the following provisions regarding the division of net income: interest allowance of 10% on original investments, salary allowances of $24,000 and $18,000 respectively, and the remainder equally.

Instructions

1. Journalize the entries to record the investments of Tsao and Ivens in the partnership accounts.
2. Prepare a balance sheet as of November 1, the date of formation of the partnership of Tsao and Ivens.
3. After adjustments and the closing of revenue and expense accounts at October 31, the end of the first full year of operations, the income summary account has a credit balance of $75,500, and the withdrawals accounts have debit balances of $26,000 (Tsao) and $17,500 (Ivens). Journalize the entries to close the income summary account and the withdrawals accounts at October 31.

PROBLEM 12–2A
Dividing partnership income
Objective 3

Phil Haddox and Russ French have decided to form a partnership. They have agreed that Haddox is to invest $120,000 and that French is to invest $180,000. Haddox is to devote full time to the business, and French is to devote one-half time. The following plans for the division of income are being considered:

a. Equal division.
b. In the ratio of original investments.
c. In the ratio of time devoted to the business.
d. Interest allowances of 10% on original investments and the remainder in the ratio of 3:2.
e. Interest allowances of 10% on original investments, salary allowances of $60,000 to Haddox and $30,000 to French, and the remainder equally.
f. Plan (e), except that Haddox is also to be allowed a bonus equal to 20% of the amount by which net income exceeds the salary allowances.

Instructions

For each plan, determine the division of the net income under each of the following assumptions: (1) net income of $150,000 and (2) net income of $90,000. Present the data in tabular form, using the following headings:

| | $150,000 | | $90,000 | |
Plan	Haddox	French	Haddox	French

PROBLEM 12–3A
Financial statements for partnerships
Objective 3

The ledger of Dan Reeves and Ron Strange, partners in law, contains the following accounts and balances after adjustments have been recorded on December 31, the end of the current fiscal year:

Cash	$ 24,500
Accounts Receivable	40,500
Supplies	2,400
Land	50,000
Building	150,000
Accumulated Amortization—Building	77,500
Office Equipment	40,000
Accumulated Amortization—Office Equipment	22,400
Accounts Payable	1,000
Salaries Payable	1,500
Dan Reeves, Capital	75,000
Dan Reeves, Withdrawals	50,000
Ron Strange, Capital	55,000
Ron Strange, Withdrawals	60,000
Professional Fees	316,750
Salary Expense	84,500
Amortization Expense—Building	10,500
Property Tax Expense	10,000
Heating and Lighting Expense	9,900
Supplies Expense	5,750
Amortization Expense—Office Equipment	5,000
Miscellaneous Expense	6,100

The balance in Strange's capital account includes an additional investment of $5,000 made on April 5 of the current year.

Instructions

1. Prepare an income statement for the current fiscal year, indicating the division of net income. The articles of partnership provide for salary allowances of $25,000 to Reeves and $35,000 to Strange, allowances of 12% on each partner's capital balance at the beginning of the fiscal year, and equal division of the remaining net income or net loss.
2. Prepare a statement of partners' equity for the current fiscal year.
3. Prepare a balance sheet in report form as of the end of the current fiscal year.

PROBLEM 12–4A
Admitting new partner
Objective 4

Adrian Capps and Lisa Knight have operated a successful firm for many years, sharing net income and net losses equally. Todd Aguero is to be admitted to the partnership on June 1 of the current year, in accordance with the following agreement:

a. Assets and liabilities of the old partnership are to be valued at their book values as of May 31, except for the following:
- Accounts receivable amounting to $3,250 are to be written off and the allowance for doubtful accounts is to be increased to 5% of the remaining accounts.
- Inventory is to be valued at $63,400.
- Equipment is to be valued at $108,000.

b. Aguero is to purchase $25,000 of the partnership interest of Capps for $37,500 cash and to contribute $25,000 cash to the partnership for a total equity of $50,000.

c. The income-sharing ratio of Capps, Knight, and Aguero is to be 2:1:1.

The post-closing trial balance of Capps and Knight as of May 31 is as follows:

Capps and Knight
Post-Closing Trial Balance
May 31, 20—

Cash	9,500	
Accounts Receivable	29,250	
Allowance for Doubtful Accounts		500
Inventory	60,100	
Prepaid Insurance	2,000	
Equipment	162,000	
Accumulated Amortization—Equipment		72,500
Accounts Payable		9,850
Notes Payable		20,000
Adrian Capps, Capital		120,000
Lisa Knight, Capital		40,000
	262,850	262,850

Instructions

1. Journalize the entries as of May 31 to record the revaluations, using a temporary account entitled Asset Revaluations. The balance in the accumulated amortization account is to be eliminated.
2. Journalize the additional entries to record the remaining transactions relating to the formation of the new partnership. Assume that all transactions occur on June 1.
3. Present a balance sheet for the new partnership as of June 1.

PROBLEM 12–5A
Statement of partnership liquidation
Objective 5

After the accounts are closed on May 10, prior to liquidating the partnership, the capital accounts of Mark Wilson, Donna Crowder, and Janice Patel are $27,800, $8,300, and $13,900 respectively. Cash and noncash assets total $6,500 and $89,100 respectively. Amounts owed to creditors total $45,600. The partners share income and losses in the ratio of 2:1:1. Between May 10 and May 30, the noncash assets are sold for $37,500, the partner with the capital deficiency pays his or her deficiency to the partnership, and the liabilities are paid.

Instructions

1. Prepare a statement of partnership liquidation, indicating (a) the sale of assets and division of loss, (b) the receipt of the deficiency (from the appropriate partner), (c) the payment of liabilities, and (d) the distribution of cash.
2. ➤ If the partner with the capital deficiency declares bankruptcy and is unable to pay the deficiency, explain how the deficiency would be divided between the partners.

PROBLEM 12–6A
Statement of partnership liquidation
Objective 5

On May 3, the firm of Imhoff, Baxter, and Wise decided to liquidate their partnership. The partners have capital balances of $30,000, $90,000, and $120,000 respectively. The cash balance is $10,000, the book values of noncash assets total $285,000, and liabilities total $55,000. The partners share income and losses in the ratio of 1:2:2.

Instructions
Prepare a statement of partnership liquidation, covering the period May 3 through May 29 for each of the following independent assumptions:

1. All of the noncash assets are sold for $345,000 in cash, the creditors are paid, and the remaining cash is distributed to the partners.
2. All of the noncash assets are sold for $175,000 in cash, the creditors are paid, and the remaining cash is distributed to the partners.
3. All of the noncash assets are sold for $105,000 in cash, the creditors are paid, the partner with the debit capital balance pays the amount owed to the firm, and the remaining cash is distributed to the partners.

PROBLEMS SERIES B

PROBLEM 12–1B
Entries and balance sheet for partnership
Objectives 2, 3

On May 1 of the current year, Crystal Hall and Doug Tucker form a partnership. Hall agrees to invest $10,500 in cash and inventory valued at $36,500. Tucker invests certain business assets at valuations agreed upon, transfers business liabilities, and contributes sufficient cash to bring his total capital to $40,000. Details regarding the book values of the business assets and liabilities, and the agreed valuations, are as follows:

	Tucker's Ledger Balance	Agreed-Upon Valuation
Accounts Receivable	$20,750	$18,000
Allowance for Doubtful Accounts	950	1,000
Equipment	79,100	40,000
Accumulated Amortization	35,200	
Accounts Payable	14,000	14,000
Notes Payable	15,000	15,000

The partnership agreement includes the following provisions regarding the division of net income: interest allowances on original investments at 10%, salary allowances of $18,000 and $21,000 respectively, and the remainder equally.

Instructions

1. Journalize the entries to record the investments of Hall and Tucker in the partnership accounts.
2. Prepare a balance sheet as of May 1, the date of formation of the partnership of Hall and Tucker.
3. After adjustments and the closing of revenue and expense accounts at April 30, the end of the first full year of operations, the income summary account has a credit balance of $72,700, and the withdrawals accounts have debit balances of $20,000 (Hall) and $26,000 (Tucker). Journalize the entries to close the income summary account and the withdrawals accounts at April 30.

PROBLEM 12–2B
Dividing partnership income
Objective 3

Garland and Driscoe have decided to form a partnership. They have agreed that Garland is to invest $200,000 and that Driscoe is to invest $100,000. Garland is to devote one-half time to the business and Driscoe is to devote full time. The following plans for the division of income are being considered:

a. Equal division.
b. In the ratio of original investments.
c. In the ratio of time devoted to the business.
d. Interest allowances of 12% on original investments and the remainder equally.
e. Interest allowances of 12% on original investments, salary allowances of $30,000 to Garland and $60,000 to Driscoe, and the remainder equally.
f. Plan (e), except that Driscoe is also to be allowed a bonus equal to 20% of the amount by which net income exceeds the salary allowances.

Instructions

For each plan, determine the division of the net income under each of the following assumptions: (1) net income of $90,000 and (2) net income of $240,000. Present the data in tabular form, using the following headings:

	$90,000		$240,000	
Plan	Garland	Driscoe	Garland	Driscoe

PROBLEM 12–3B
Financial statements for partnership
Objective 3

The ledger of Peter Tracy and May Hepburn, partners in law, contains the following accounts and balances after adjustments have been recorded on December 31, the end of the current fiscal year:

Cash	$ 22,000
Accounts Receivable	38,900
Supplies	1,900
Land	25,000
Building	130,000
Accumulated Amortization—Building	69,200
Office Equipment	39,000
Accumulated Amortization—Office Equipment	21,500
Accounts Payable	2,100
Salaries Payable	2,000
Peter Tracy, Capital	75,000
Peter Tracy, Withdrawals	60,000
May Hepburn, Capital	55,000
May Hepburn, Withdrawals	75,000
Professional Fees	285,650
Salary Expense	80,500
Amortization Expense—Building	10,500
Property Tax Expense	8,000
Heating and Lighting Expense	7,900
Supplies Expense	2,850
Amortization Expense—Office Equipment	2,800
Miscellaneous Expense	6,100

The balance in Hepburn's capital account includes an additional investment of $5,000 made on August 10 of the current year.

Instructions

1. Prepare an income statement for the current fiscal year, indicating the division of net income. The articles of partnership provide for salary allowances of $30,000 to Tracy and $40,000 to Hepburn, allowances of 12% on each partner's capital balance at the beginning of the fiscal year, and equal division of the remaining net income or net loss.
2. Prepare a statement of partners' equity for the current fiscal year.
3. Prepare a balance sheet in report form as of the end of the current fiscal year.

PROBLEM 12–4B
Admitting new partner
Objective 4

Tom Denney and Cheryl Burks have operated a successful firm for many years, sharing net income and net losses equally. Sara Wold is to be admitted to the partnership on May 1 of the current year, in accordance with the following agreement:

a. Assets and liabilities of the old partnership are to be valued at their book values as of April 30, except for the following:
    • Accounts receivable amounting to $1,900 are to be written off, and the allowance for doubtful accounts is to be increased to 5% of the remaining accounts.
    • Inventory is to be valued at $53,100.
    • Equipment is to be valued at $100,000.

b. Wold is to purchase $20,000 of the ownership interest of Burks for $25,000 cash and to contribute $20,000 cash to the partnership for a total ownership equity of $40,000.
c. The income-sharing ratio of Denney, Burks, and Wold is to be 2:1:1.

The post-closing trial balance of Denney and Burks as of April 30 is as follows:

Denney and Burks
Post-Closing Trial Balance
April 30, 20—

Cash	7,900	
Accounts Receivable	22,500	
Allowance for Doubtful Accounts		550
Inventory	50,600	
Prepaid Insurance	1,650	
Equipment	145,000	
Accumulated Amortization—Equipment		65,000
Accounts Payable		12,100
Notes Payable		10,000
Tom Denney, Capital		80,000
Cheryl Burks, Capital		60,000
	227,650	227,650

Instructions

1. Journalize the entries as of April 30 to record the revaluations using a temporary account entitled Asset Revaluations. The balance in the accumulated amortization account is to be eliminated.
2. Journalize the additional entries to record the remaining transactions relating to the formation of the new partnership. Assume that all transactions occur on May 1.
3. Present a balance sheet for the new partnership as of May 1.

PROBLEM 12–5B
Statement of partnership liquidation
Objective 5

After the accounts are closed on May 3, prior to liquidating the partnership, the capital accounts of Ann Booth, Harold Owen, and Carla Ramariz are $20,000, $3,900, and $10,000 respectively. Cash and noncash assets total $1,900 and $62,000 respectively. Amounts owed to creditors total $30,000. The partners share income and losses in the ratio of 2:1:1. Between May 3 and May 29, the noncash assets are sold for $26,000, the partner with the capital deficiency pays his or her deficiency to the partnership, and the liabilities are paid.

Instructions

1. Prepare a statement of partnership liquidation, indicating (a) the sale of assets and division of loss, (b) the receipt of the deficiency (from the appropriate partner), (c) the payment of liabilities, and (d) the distribution of cash.
2. ◀━━━▶ If the partner with the capital deficiency declares bankruptcy and is unable to pay the deficiency, explain how the deficiency would be divided between the partners.

PROBLEM 12–6B
Statement of partnership liquidation
Objective 5

On October 1, the firm of Ewing, Johnson, and Landry, decided to liquidate their partnership. The partners have capital balances of $100,000, $90,000, and $30,000 respectively. The cash balance is $20,000, the book values of noncash assets total $250,000, and liabilities total $50,000. The partners share income and losses in the ratio of 2:2:1.

Instructions

Prepare a statement of partnership liquidation, covering the period October 1 through October 30 for each of the following independent assumptions:

1. All of the noncash assets are sold for $330,000 in cash, the creditors are paid, and the remaining cash is distributed to the partners.
2. All of the noncash assets are sold for $120,000 in cash, the creditors are paid, and the remaining cash is distributed to the partners.
3. All of the noncash assets are sold for $50,000 in cash, the creditors are paid, the partner with the debit capital balance pays the amount owed to the firm, and the remaining cash is distributed to the partners.

CASES

CASE 12–1
Miller and Harrison
Partnership agreement

Ted Miller, M.D., and Glen Harrison, M.D., are sole owners of two medical practices that operate in the same medical building. The two doctors agree to combine assets and liabilities of the two businesses to form a partnership. The partnership agreement calls for dividing income equally between the two doctors. After several months, the following conversation takes place between the two doctors:

Miller: I've noticed that your patient load has dropped over the last couple of months. When we formed our partnership, we were seeing about the same number of patients per week. However, now our patient records show that you have been seeing about half as many patients as I have. Are there any issues that I should be aware of?

Harrison: There's nothing going on. When I was working on my own, I was really putting in the hours. One of the reasons I formed this partnership was to enjoy life a little more and scale back a little bit.

Miller: I see. Well, I find that I'm working as hard as I did when I was on my own, yet making less than I did previously. Essentially, you're sharing in half of my billings and I'm sharing in half of yours. Since you are working much less than I am, I end up on the short end of the bargain.

Harrison: Well, I don't know what to say. An agreement is an agreement. The partnership is based on a 50/50 split. That's what a partnership is all about.

Miller: If that's so, then it applies equally well to the effort end of the equation as to the income end.

➤ Discuss whether Harrison is acting in an ethical manner. How could Miller rewrite the partnership agreement to avoid this dispute?

CASE 12–2
Adair and Fontana
Dividing partnership income

John Adair and Raul Fontana decide to form a partnership. Adair will contribute $300,000 to the partnership, while Fontana will contribute only $30,000. However, Fontana will be responsible for running the day-to-day operations of the partnership, which are anticipated to require about 50 hours per week. In contrast, Adair will only work five hours per week for the part-

nership. The two partners are attempting to determine a formula for dividing partnership net income. Adair believes the partners should divide income in the ratio of 7:3, favouring Adair, since Adair provides the majority of the capital. Fontana believes the income should be divided 7:3, favouring Fontana, since Fontana provides the majority of effort in running the partnership business.

➤ How would you advise the partners in developing a method for dividing income?

CASE 12–3
Ellen, Cook, and Cierra
Admitting new partner

Ted Cierra wishes to join the Ellen and Cook partnership. Ellen and Cook share all partnership income equally. Cierra would be admitted as an equal partner. The capital accounts are $50,000 each for Ellen and Cook prior to admitting Cierra. The fair market value of the net assets is $160,000. The following exchange took place during the final negotiations between the partners and Cierra:

Cierra: I'm looking forward to joining the partnership. I've drawn a cheque for my share, which I believe is $50,000.

Ellen: Well, Ted, we're also looking forward to you joining us. How did you arrive at the $50,000 number?

Cierra: Easy. Just look at the partnership books. You each have a capital account of $50,000, which yields a total

partnership value of $100,000. If I'm to be an equal partner, I should contribute as much as each of you did—namely, $50,000. That will bring the total capital to $150,000, with each of us having a ⅓ investment in the partnership. What could be more fair?

Cook: Ted, I'm not very comfortable with that number. We believe you should give us a cheque for $80,000.

Cierra: What? We never talked about any kind of partner bonuses upon my entry into the firm. We all previously agreed that you need me and I need you. That was that. Now you're bringing up some partner bonus scheme at the last minute of negotiations. I'm not too sure I want to be part of a partnership that deals in this way.

➤ Discuss whether Ellen and Cook behaved in an ethical manner.

CASE 12–4
Felix and Diaz
Financial analysis

The partnership of Felix and Diaz, CAs, has 100 partners and 800 staff professionals. Each partner shares equally in partnership income. Assume that the average income for partners in CA firms across the country is $150,000 per year, and the average salary for staff professionals is $45,000 per year. In addition, assume that the prevailing interest allowance rate is 12% per year. The partnership income statement for the year is as follows:

Revenues		$65,000,000
Staff professional salaries	$36,000,000	
Nonprofessional salaries	6,000,000	
Rent, supplies, telephones, etc.	2,000,000	
Travel	2,000,000	
Litigation losses	8,000,000	54,000,000
Net income		$11,000,000

The total partnership capital balance is $10,000,000 for 100 partners or $100,000 per partner.

a. ▄▄▄▶ Evaluate the financial performance of the partnership from a partner's perspective. In other words, if you were a partner in this firm, would you be satisfied or dissatisfied with partnership performance? Support your answer.

b. ▄▄▄▶ What are some explanations for the partnership's performance?

CASE 12–5
Abbott and Martin
Dividing partnership income

Twelve years ago, Chet Abbott and Alicia Martin formed a partnership by each contributing $100,000 in capital. The partnership agreement indicated the following division of net income: salary allowances of $20,000 and $30,000 to Abbott and Martin respectively, and all remaining net income divided equally.

Martin recently expressed concern with the manner in which profits are being divided. Specifically, the income-sharing agreement did not consider changes in the amounts invested by each partner as reflected in the balances of their capital accounts. Over the years, Abbott has consistently withdrawn more from the partnership than Martin, with the result that the capital balances as of January 1, 1999, indicated an investment of $200,000 by Abbott and $362,500 by Martin.

Abbott agreed with Martin that a change in the income-sharing agreement was warranted and accordingly proposed the following two alternatives:

Proposal I:

a. The salary allowances of Abbott and Martin would be increased to $30,000 and $45,000 respectively.
b. Interest of 8% would be allowed on the January 1 balances of the capital accounts.

c. All remaining income would be divided equally.

Proposal II:

a. The salary allowances of Abbott and Martin would not be changed.
b. No interest would be allowed on the capital balances.
c. Martin would be allowed a bonus of 20% of the amount by which net income exceeds salary allowances, and the remainder would be divided equally.

Martin has asked for your advice on which of the two proposals she should accept.

1. For each proposal, prepare an analysis of the distribution of net income between Abbott and Martin for 1999 for net income levels of $90,000, $130,000, and $190,000.
2. ▄▄▄▶ Which proposal would you recommend that Martin accept?
3. Elizabeth Sanford has offered to purchase for $250,000 a one-fourth interest in the partnership capital and net income. Assuming that the net tangible assets of the partnership approximate their fair market values at January 1, 1999, how much bonus is Sanford paying to the partnership?

ANSWERS TO SELF-EXAMINATION QUESTIONS

1. **B** We should record noncash assets contributed to a partnership at the amounts agreed upon by the partners. The preferred practice is to record the office equipment at $9,000 (answer B).

2. **C** Net income and net loss are divided among the partners in accordance with their agreement. In the absence of any agreement, all partners share equally (answer C).

3. **C**   X's share of the $45,000 of net income is $19,000 (answer C), determined as follows:

	X	Y	Total
Interest allowance	$10,000	$ 5,000	$15,000
Salary allowance	12,000	24,000	36,000
Total	$22,000	$29,000	$51,000
Excess of allowances over income	3,000	3,000	6,000
Net income distribution	$19,000	$26,000	$45,000

4. **A**   When an additional person is admitted to a partnership by purchasing an interest from one or more of the partners, the purchase price is paid directly to the selling partner(s). The amount of capital transferred from the capital account(s) of the selling partner(s) to the capital account of the incoming partner is the capital interest acquired from the selling partner(s). In the question, the amount is $32,500 (answer A), which is one-half of X's capital balance of $65,000.

5. **C**   Partnership cash would be distributed in accordance with the credit balances in the partners' capital accounts. Therefore, $10,000 (answer C) would be distributed to X (X's $10,000 capital balance).

PART FIVE

Corporations

13 Corporations: Organization, Equity Rights, and Earnings

YOU AND ACCOUNTING

If you own an investment in shares of a corporation, you are interested in how the stock is performing in the market. If you are considering buying shares, you are interested in what your rights are as a shareholder and what kind of returns you might expect from the shares. In either case, you should be able to interpret stock market quotations, such as the following:

| 52 weeks | | | | | | | | | Net | Vol | | |
Hi	Lo	Stock	Sym	Div	Hi	Lo	Close	Chg	(100s)	Yield	P/E
58.10	43.25	Seagram	VO a	0.66	55.00	53.75	54.50	+0.35	2509	1.7	40.6
1.65	0.67	Search En	SGY		0.85	0.80	0.80	+0.02	182		40.0
25.75	12.50	Sears Cda	SCC	0.24	24.00	22.75	23.50	−0.35	738	1.0	21.4
13.50	9.00	2nd Cup	SKL		13.00	12.90	13.00	+0.50	110		28.9
6.15	1.20	Semafo	SMF		1.80	1.70	1.70	+0.05	72		85.0
4.95	0.61	♣Smi sv	SEM.A		0.70	0.61	0.63	−0.07	2454		
13.00	9.10	Senvest Ca	SEC	0.15	12.85	12.50	12.85	+0.60	12	1.2	5.4
3.00	1.65	Sepp's Go	SGO		2.70	2.70	2.70	−0.10	20		27.0
18.10	8.75	Shw C nv	SCL.B	0.07	17.15	17.00	17.10		834	0.4	71.3
60.00	28.80	Shaw Ind	SHL.A	0.18	46.00	44.50	44.50	−0.25	71	0.4	16.1
59.00	28.00	Shaw Ind	SHL.B	0.17	45.50	44.75	45.50	+0.75	8	0.4	16.5
29.25	17.33	Shell Cda	SHC	0.72	24.00	23.25	23.25	−0.15	1304	3.1	13.8

Although you may not own any share investments, you probably buy services or products from corporations, and you may work for a corporation. Understanding the corporate form of organization will help you in your role as a shareholder, a consumer, or an employee. In this chapter, we discuss the characteristics of corporations, as well as how corporations account for shares.

After studying this chapter, you should be able to:

Objective 1
Describe the nature of the corporate form of organization.

Objective 2
List the two main sources of shareholders' equity.

Objective 3
List the major sources of paid-in capital, including the various classes of shares.

Objective 4
Journalize the entries for issuing shares.

Objective 5
Journalize the entries for transactions when a company acquires its own shares.

Objective 6
Prepare the Paid-In Capital section of a corporate balance sheet.

Objective 7
State the effect of stock splits on corporate financial statements.

Objective 8
Journalize the entries for cash dividends and stock dividends.

Objective 9
Describe the required disclosures for the following income statement items: discontinued operations, extraordinary items, unusual items, and earnings per share.

Objective 10
Journalize adjustments to retained earnings for appropriations, corrections of errors made in prior periods, and retroactive adjustments of accounting changes.

Objective 11
Prepare a retained earnings statement.

Objective 12
Report changes in shareholders' equity.

Nature of a Corporation

Objective 1
Describe the nature of the corporate form of organization.

What is a corporation? A corporation is a separate legal entity, an artificial being created by law.

The concept underlying this definition is the basis for recognizing a corporation as a legal entity, distinct and separate from the individuals who create and operate it. Almost all large businesses in Canada use the corporate form of organization.

CHARACTERISTICS OF CORPORATIONS

As a separate legal entity, a corporation may acquire, own, and dispose of property in its own name. It may also incur liabilities and enter into other types of contracts.

The ownership of a corporation is divided into units called shares or stock. A corporation may have several classes of shares, and each share within a class has the same rights as every other share in its class. The owners of the shares own the corporation and are called shareholders.

Because a corporation has a separate legal existence, shares of stock may be bought and sold without affecting the operations or continued existence of the corporation. This is in contrast to the partnership form of organization, in which changes in the ownership dissolve the partnership. Corporations whose shares are traded in public markets are called **public corporations.** Corporations whose shares are not traded publicly are usually owned by a small group of investors and are referred to as **private corporations.** T. Eaton Company Ltd. is a well-known private corporation.

The shareholders of a corporation have **limited liability.** A corporation is responsible for its own acts and obligations under law. Therefore, a corporation's creditors usually may not go beyond the assets of the corporation to satisfy their claims. Thus, the financial loss that a shareholder may suffer is limited to the amount invested. This limited liability feature contributed to the rapid growth of the corporate form of organization.

Shareholders exercise control over the management of a corporation's operations and activities by electing a **board of directors.** The board of directors meets periodically to establish corporate policies. The board selects the chief executive officer (CEO) and other major officers to manage the day-to-day affairs of the corporation. The board also has responsibility for deciding when and how much corporate income to distribute to shareholders in the form of **dividends.**

Exhibit 1 shows the organizational structure of a corporation.

Exhibit 1
*Organizational Structure
of a Corporate Enterprise*

As separate entities, corporations are subject to **taxes.** Thus, unlike the sole proprietorship and partnership forms of organization, corporations must pay income taxes at both the federal and provincial level. Shareholders must include dividends distributed to them in computing their taxable income. The Income Tax Act allows shareholders to claim a dividend tax credit that minimizes the potential for double taxation.

Corporations may be organized for nonprofit reasons, such as recreational, educational, charitable, or humanitarian purposes. However, most corporations are organized to earn a profit and a fair rate of return for their shareholders. Throughout this chapter, we focus on corporations organized for profit.

FORMING A CORPORATION

A corporation is established under federal or provincial laws by submitting the required documentation to the appropriate government office. Companies that operate in only one province usually decide to incorporate under provincial legislation, whereas companies that operate across the country will typically choose to incorporate federally under the Canada Business Corporations Act (CBCA). Although there is some variation among the provincial corporations acts, most are quite comparable to the CBCA.

Under the CBCA one or more individuals aged 18 or over, of sound mind and not bankrupt, can develop and sign **articles of incorporation** and file them with the Director of the Department of Consumer and Corporate Affairs, who administers the CBCA. The articles of incorporation must include the name of the corporation, the address of its registered head office, the classes and maximum number of shares authorized, and the number of directors. If the application complies with all requirements for incorporation, the Director will issue a **certificate of incorporation**. Thereafter, the Directors will prepare a set of **bylaws,** which are the rules and procedures for conducting the affairs of the corporation.

Significant costs are often incurred in organizing a corporation. These costs include legal fees, taxes, incorporation fees, licence fees, and promotional costs.

The company should debit such costs to an intangible asset account entitled *Organization Costs*. Although such costs have no value upon liquidation, they are accounted for as an asset, since the corporation could not have been created without them.

The organizers of a corporation normally assume that it will continue in existence indefinitely. Thus, we could argue that organization costs should be carried in the accounts as an asset until the corporation ceases its operations and liquidates.

However, generally accepted accounting principles require that a business must amortize all intangible assets. Although the *CICA Handbook* specifies a maximum amortization period of 40 years for intangibles,[1] in practice many businesses amortize incorporation costs over a much shorter period.

The following entries illustrate the recording of organization costs of $8,500 on January 2 and the subsequent amortization (over 10 years) on December 31, the end of the first year of operations:

Jan.	2	Organization Costs	8,500	
		Cash		8,500
		Record organization costs.		
Dec.	31	Amortization Expense—Organization Costs	850	
		Organization Costs		850
		($8,500 ÷ 10 years = $850)		
		Record amortization of organization costs.		

Shareholders' Equity

Objective 2
List the two main sources of shareholders' equity.

The owners' equity in a corporation is commonly called shareholders' equity. In a corporate balance sheet, the owners' equity section is called the Shareholders' Equity section. This section reports the amount of each of the two main sources of shareholders' equity. The first source is capital contributed to the corporation by the shareholders and others, called **paid-in capital** or **contributed capital.** Paid-in capital is sometimes further divided into two categories: (i) share capital, which records the amount assigned to shares when they are issued; and (ii) contributed surplus, which includes other contributions to equity and gains arising from share transactions. The second main source of capital is net income retained in the business, called retained earnings. An example of a Shareholders' Equity section of a corporation balance sheet is shown below.

Shareholders' Equity

Paid-in capital:		
Common shares	$330,000	
Retained earnings	80,000	
Total shareholders' equity		$410,000

The paid-in capital contributed by the shareholders is recorded in separate accounts for each class of shares. If there is only one class of shares, the account is entitled *Common Shares.*

Retained earnings results from transferring the balance in the income summary account (the net income or net loss) to the retained earnings account at the end of each fiscal year. As a result of net losses, a debit balance in Retained Earnings may occur. Such a balance is called a deficit. In the Shareholders' Equity section of the balance sheet, a deficit is deducted from paid-in capital in determining total shareholders' equity. We also close the dividends account, which is similar to the

---

[1] *CICA Handbook*, Section 3060, paragraph 32.

withdrawals account for a sole proprietorship or partnership, to Retained Earnings. Thus, the balance of Retained Earnings represents the corporation's accumulated net income that has not been distributed to shareholders as dividends.

There are a number of alternative terms used for retained earnings, including *earnings retained for use in the business* and *earnings reinvested in the business.* These terms refer to the *use* of retained earnings and not to an amount of *surplus cash* or *cash left over for dividends.* Earnings retained in the business normally are used by management to improve or expand operations. Over time, as the amount of retained earnings from profitable operations increases, the balance recorded as retained earnings will far exceed the amount of cash on hand.

Sources of Paid-in Capital

Objective 3
List the major sources of paid-in capital, including the various classes of shares.

As we mentioned in the preceding section, the two main sources of shareholders' equity are **paid-in capital** (or contributed capital) and retained earnings. The main source of paid-in capital is from issuing shares. In the following paragraphs, we discuss the characteristics of the various classes of shares. We conclude this section with a brief discussion of other sources of paid-in capital.

SHARES

The number of shares that a corporation is authorized to issue is stated in its articles of incorporation. The term *issued* refers to the shares issued to the shareholders. A corporation may, under circumstances we discuss later in this chapter, reacquire some of the shares that it has issued. The shares remaining in the hands of shareholders are called **outstanding shares.**

Sometimes, a nominal amount known as par value will be printed on the face of a share certificate. These are called **par value shares.** As we will discuss in the next chapter, the par value stated on a bond indicates the maturity value of the bond. However, as shares do not have a maturity date, their par value has no such significance. Nor does the par value indicate the proceeds that the corporation will receive for the shares, which are determined by how much investors are willing to pay on the issuance date, and not by the company. Thus, the par value stated on a share has no economic importance.

Most likely it is for this reason that the CBCA requires that all federally incorporated companies issue only **no par value shares.** Most provincial corporation acts also limit firms under their jurisdiction to no par value shares. Thus, although par value shares are still common in the United States, they are only issued in a few jurisdictions in Canada. A 1996 survey of large Canadian public companies indicates that less than 10% of the firms surveyed reported shares with a par value or stated value.[2] Accordingly, in the remainder of this chapter, we will limit our illustration of share transactions to no par shares. The details of accounting for par value shares can be found in more advanced accounting texts.

The major rights that accompany ownership of a share are as follows:

1. The right to vote in matters concerning the corporation.
2. The right to share in distributions of earnings.
3. The **preemptive right,** which is the right to maintain the same fractional interest in the corporation by purchasing shares of any additional issuances of stock.
4. The right to share in the residual assets of the corporation on liquidation.

[2] C. Byrd and I. Chen, *Financial Reporting in Canada,* 22nd edition, CICA, Toronto, 1997, p. 251.

When only one class of shares is issued, it is called **common shares.** In this case, each share of common stock has equal rights. To appeal to a broader investment market, a corporation may issue one or more classes of shares with various preference rights. An example of such a right is the preference to share in distributions of earnings. Such shares are generally called **preferred shares.**

The board of directors has the sole authority to distribute dividends to the shareholders. When taking such action, the directors are said to *declare* a dividend. Since dividends are normally based on earnings, a corporation cannot guarantee dividends to its shareholders.

A corporation with both preferred shares and common shares may declare dividends on the common only after it meets the dividend preference of the preferred shares. The dividend preference of the preferred shares is stated on the share certificate. For example, $4 preferred shares have a prior claim to an annual $4 per share dividend. If the par value of the preferred share were $50, the same claim on dividends could be stated as 8% preferred share.

Nonparticipating and Participating Preferred Shares

The preferred shareholders' dividend preference is usually limited to a certain amount. Such shares are said to be **nonparticipating preferred shares.** To continue the preceding example, assume that a corporation has 1,000 $4 nonparticipating preferred shares and 4,000 common shares outstanding. Also assume that the net income, amount of earnings retained, and the amount of earnings distributed by the board of directors for the first three years of operations are as follows:

	First Year	Second Year	Third Year
Net income	$20,000	$55,000	$100,000
Amount retained	10,000	20,000	40,000
Amount distributed	$10,000	$35,000	$ 60,000

Exhibit 2 shows the distribution of the earnings between the preferred shares and the common shares for each year.

In this example, the preferred shareholders received an annual dividend of $4 per share, compared to the common shareholders' dividends of $1.50, $7.75, and $14.00 per share. The preferred shareholders have a greater chance of receiving regular dividends than do the common shareholders. On the other hand, common shareholders have a greater chance of receiving larger dividends than do the preferred shareholders.

Preferred shares may provide for the possibility of receiving additional dividends if certain conditions are met. These conditions often include reaching a certain level of earnings and distributing a certain amount of dividends to common

Exhibit 2

Dividends to Nonparticipating Preferred Shares

	First Year	Second Year	Third Year
Amount distributed	$10,000	$35,000	$60,000
Preferred dividend (1,000 shares)	4,000	4,000	4,000
Common dividend (4,000 shares)	$ 6,000	$31,000	$56,000
Dividends per share:			
Preferred	$ 4.00	$ 4.00	$ 4.00
Common	$ 1.50	$ 7.75	$ 14.00

shareholders. Such shares are called **participating preferred shares** but are rarely used in today's financial markets.

Cumulative and Noncumulative Preferred Shares

Preferred shares may contain special provisions that apply if the board of directors fail to declare regular preferred dividends. These provisions normally prohibit the payment of any common share dividends if any preferred dividends have not been declared in prior years. Such preferred shares are called cumulative preferred shares, and any preferred dividends that have not been declared are said to be *in arrears*. Preferred shares not having this cumulative right are called **noncumulative preferred shares.**

To illustrate, assume that a corporation has 1,000 $4 preferred shares and 4,000 common shares outstanding. Also assume that no dividends have been paid in the preceding two years. In the third (current) year, the board of directors declare dividends of $22,000. Exhibit 3 shows the distribution of these dividends between the preferred and common shares if the preferred are cumulative or noncumulative.

Exhibit 3
Dividends to Cumulative Preferred Shares

		Cumulative Preferred	Noncumulative Preferred
Amount distributed		$22,000	$22,000
Preferred dividend (1,000 shares):			
First-year dividend in arrears	$4,000		—
Second-year dividend in arrears	4,000		—
Third-year current dividend	4,000	12,000	4,000
Common dividend (4,000 shares)		$10,000	$18,000
Dividends per share:			
Preferred		$ 12.00	$ 4.00
Common		$ 2.50	$ 4.50

Other Preferential Rights

In addition to the preferential rights in dividend distributions, preferred shares usually have preference rights on assets in liquidation of the corporation. However, the company must satisfy claims of creditors first before distributing any assets to shareholders. Any assets remaining after the creditors have been paid are first distributed to preferred shareholders. Any remaining assets are then distributed to common shareholders. Common shareholders of corporations that liquidate rarely get back their full investment.

OTHER SOURCES OF PAID-IN CAPITAL

In addition to the issuance of shares, paid-in capital may arise when shareholders or other parties donate real estate or other properties to a corporation. In such cases, the corporation debits the assets for their fair market value and credits *Donated Capital,* which may be reported as Contributed Surplus on the balance sheet. Sometimes the provincial or federal government will grant land or other assets to a corporation as an incentive to locate or remain in a particular community. Unlike private donations, these government grants cannot be treated as donated capital, but must be recorded through income in accordance with the provisions of *CICA Handbook,* Section 3800. These types of transactions are discussed in more advanced accounting texts.

PREFERRED SHARES—RISKS VS. REWARDS

Preferred shares shield shareholders somewhat from the lows of corporate fortunes. If a company must reduce dividend payments, preferred shareholders receive dividends before common shareholders. However, preferred shareholders often miss out on the highs of corporate fortunes. Because preferred shareholders receive a fixed dividend, and the bulk of any large dividends goes to common shareholders, most preferred shares are nonparticipating. These "safe-but-stodgy" equities can offer dramatic profits, however, as described in the following excerpt from an article in *Business Week*:

. . . In times of grave financial trouble, dividends on preferreds are often suspended and placed in arrears. . . . If and when the company reinstates dividends, current shareholders are entitled to all the back payments, whether or not they owned stock during the arrearage period—if the preferred is cumulative. . . .

The gains [from purchasing preferred stock with dividends in arrears] can be impressive. Bethlehem Steel announced in April that it would pay $22.5 million in arrears and resume the regular quarterly dividend on its two classes of preferred stock. Because Bethlehem had missed four payments, investors receive an extra year's worth of dividends: One class that usually pays $1.25 quarterly will return $6.25—not bad on a stock that traded in the low 30s just a few months ago.

Source: Troy Segal, "Preferred Stock: The Risky Hunt for Hidden Rewards," *Business Week,* June 13, 1988, p. 114.

Issuing Shares

Objective 4
Journalize the entries for issuing shares.

The corporation must use a separate account for recording the amount of each class of shares issued to investors. For example, suppose that a corporation is authorized to issue 10,000 $4 no par preferred shares and 100,000 no par common shares. Assume that the company issues 5,000 common shares for $200 each and 5,000 preferred shares for $100 each. The entry to record the shareholders' investment and the receipt of the cash is as follows:

Cash	1,500,000	
Preferred Shares		500,000
Common Shares		1,000,000
Record issuance of shares for cash.		

The share accounts (Preferred Shares, Common Shares) are control accounts. A record of each shareholder's name, address, and number of shares held is normally kept in a subsidiary ledger. This subsidiary ledger is called the **shareholders' ledger.** It provides the information for issuing dividend cheques, annual meeting notices, and financial reports to individual shareholders.[3]

When a corporation issues no par shares, it must credit the share capital account with the fair value of the shares issued. In those few jurisdictions in Canada that provide for assigning a nominal or par value to each share at the time of incorporation, the rules governing the accounting for the issuing of shares are governed by the corporations acts. With par value shares, share capital is credited for the par value of the shares issued and the difference between the par value and the issue price is credited to contributed surplus on the share issue.

[3] Large public corporations often use a financial institution, such as a bank or trust company, for maintaining shareholder records.

When the company sells shares for cash, the fair value of the transaction is measured by the amount of cash received. What happens if the company issues shares in exchange for non-cash assets, such as capital assets? In this case, the general rule is to record the transaction at the fair market value of what is given up or what is received, whichever is more easily determinable. For a corporation whose shares are traded frequently on a stock exchange, we will usually record the transaction at the fair market value of the shares, which we can ascertain readily from the published stock market quotations.

Acquisitions by a Corporation of Its Own Shares

Objective 5
Journalize the entries for transactions when a corporation acquires its own shares.

The CBCA and provincial corporation acts permit a company to repurchase (buy back) some of its own outstanding shares. There are various reasons why a company would do this, such as the following:

1. to have enough unissued shares to meet employee stock option plans,
2. to reduce shares outstanding to increase earnings per share,
3. to attempt to increase the share price by reducing the supply of shares in the market,
4. to change from public to private corporation status.

Such an action requires a resolution by the board of directors and approval from the stock exchange that lists the shares, and must not result in insolvency. The CBCA generally requires that the acquired shares be cancelled. If the articles of incorpora-

INTERPRETING STOCK QUOTATIONS

The following stock quotation for Sears Canada Inc. is taken from the February 19, 1998 *Globe and Mail:*

THE TORONTO STOCK EXCHANGE

| 52 Weeks | | | | | | | | Net | Vol | | |
Hi	Lo	Stock	Sym	Div	Hi	Lo	Close	Chg	(100's)	Yield	P/E
25.75	12.50	Sears Cda	SCC	.24	24	22.75	23.50	–0.35	738	1.0	21.4

The preceding quotation is interpreted as follows:

Hi	Highest price during the past 52 weeks
Lo	Lowest price during the past 52 weeks
Stock	Name of the company
Sym	Stock exchange symbol (SCC for Sears Canada)
Div	Dividends paid per share during the past year
Hi	Highest price for the day
Lo	Lowest price for the day
Close	Closing price for the day
Net Chg	The net change in price from the previous day
Vol	The volume of shares traded in 100s
Yield	Annual dividend yield per share based on the closing price (Sears Canada's 1.0% yield on common share is computed as $0.24 ÷ $23.50)
P/E	Price-earnings ratio on common shares (discussed in chapter 16)

tion have a limit on the number of shares authorized, the act allows the corporation to restore the repurchased shares to the status of authorized but unissued shares.

When a corporation repurchases and cancels its no par shares, it should (1) credit Cash for the funds expended to acquire the shares and (2) debit Share Capital for their original issuance price (the amount credited to Share Capital when the shares were issued). When share transactions have taken place at different prices over time, we must calculate the average issuance price. But what if the price paid for the shares differs from their original issuance price? Can the company record a gain or loss on repurchasing its own shares? No. Generally accepted accounting principles do not permit a business to record a gain or loss on the income statement for any transactions involving its own shares (known as capital transactions).

If the original issue price exceeds the cost to repurchase the shares, the corporation should credit the excess to Contributed Surplus.[4] To illustrate, assume that on January 1, 2000 Menzies Corporation has Share Capital of $500,000 representing 20,000 outstanding no par common shares (indicating an original issuance price of $500,000/20,000 = $25 per share) and Retained Earnings of $150,000. On February 1, 2000 the company repurchases 500 shares on the open market for $22 each and makes the following entry:

Common Shares (500 × $25)	12,500	
Contributed Surplus from reacquisition of shares		1,500
Cash (500 × $22)		11,000
Record the acquisition of 500 common shares @ $22 per share.		

If the original issue price is less than the cost to repurchase the shares, the corporation should account for the difference as follows:

a. debit Contributed Surplus created by previous acquisitions of the same class of shares,
b. debit any remaining difference to Contributed Surplus created by any other transactions in the same class of shares on a pro rata (proportional) basis,
c. debit any remaining difference to Retained Earnings.[5]

To illustrate, assume that, after repurchasing 400 shares on February 1 and making the entry shown above, Menzies repurchases an additional 500 of its shares on the open market at $30 per share on October 1, 2000. It should record this transaction as follows:

Common Shares (500 × $25)	12,500	
Contributed Surplus from Feb. 1 share reacquisition	1,500	
Retained Earnings ($15,000 – 12,500 – 1,500)	1,000	
Cash (500 × $30)		15,000
Record the acquisition of 500 common shares @ $30 per share.		

Note that Retained Earnings may sometimes be *decreased* by capital transactions, but *never increased*. A corporation must report all gains on capital transactions in Contributed Surplus. The only way to increase Retained Earnings is through the transfer of net income from the income statement.

In contrast to Canadian regulations, many U.S. jurisdictions allow a company to buy back its own shares and hold them for distribution or sale (rather than having to cancel them as in Canada). Such shares are called treasury shares. As in Canada, all transactions related to such shares are of a capital nature. Thus, any gains or losses arising from treasury shares are recorded directly into shareholders' equity accounts and not shown on the income statement. More advanced texts illustrate accounting for treasury shares.

[4] *CICA Handbook*, Section 3240, paragraph 17.
[5] *Ibid.*, paragraph 15.

Reporting Paid-in Capital

Objective 6
Prepare the Paid-In Capital section of a corporate balance sheet.

As with other sections of the balance sheet, a corporation may use alternative terms and formats in reporting paid-in capital. Exhibit 4 illustrates two examples from these alternatives.

Significant changes in paid-in capital during a period should also be disclosed. Such disclosures may be presented either in a *statement of shareholders' equity* or in notes to the financial statements. We describe and illustrate the statement of shareholders' equity later in this chapter.

Exhibit 4
Paid-In Capital Section of Shareholders' Equity

Shareholders' Equity (partial statement)

Paid-in Capital:	
Share Capital:	
Preferred $5 shares, cumulative, 2,000 shares authorized and issued	$ 110,000
Common no par shares, 50,000 shares authorized and 45,000 issued	1,032,000
	$1,142,000
Contributed Surplus:	
From donated land	60,000
Total paid-in capital	$1,202,000

Shareholders' Equity (partial statement)

Contributed Capital:	
Share Capital *(Note x)*	$1,142,000
From donated land	60,000
Total	$1,202,000

Note x.

Share capital consists of 2,000 authorized and issued $5 preferred shares ($110,000) and 50,000 authorized common shares, 45,000 issued ($1,032,00).

Stock Splits

Objective 7
State the effect of stock splits on corporate financial statements.

Corporations will sometimes authorize an event called a stock split by issuing a proportionate number of additional shares to all shareholders of the class of shares affected. A major objective of a stock split is to reduce the market price per share of the corporation's shares. The lower share price encourages more investors to enter the market. This, in turn, tends to increase or broaden the types and numbers of a corporation's shareholders.

To illustrate a stock split, assume that the board of directors of Rojek Corporation, which has 10,000 common shares outstanding with a book value of $1,000,000, authorizes a five-for-one split increasing the number of shares outstanding to 50,000. The book value of common shares outstanding is $1,000,000 both before and after the stock split. Only the number of shares is changed. Since there are no changes in the balances of any of the corporation's accounts, no entry is required to record a stock split. However, the company should disclose the details of stock splits within notes to the financial statements because they significantly change the make-up of the paid-in capital.

Each shareholder in a corporation whose stock is split owns the same proportionate amount of shares before and after the split. For example, a Rojek Corporation shareholder who owned 100 shares before the split would own 500 shares after the split. This shareholder holds 1% of the total shares outstanding both before and after the split.

Accounting for Dividends

Objective 8
Journalize the entries for cash dividends and stock dividends.

A dividend usually represents a distribution of retained earnings. Dividends may be paid in cash, in shares of the company, or in other property. In rare cases, a dividend may also represent a distribution of paid-in capital.

CASH DIVIDENDS

A cash distribution of earnings by a corporation to its shareholders is called a **cash dividend.** Cash dividends are the most common form of dividend.

Can a corporation pay a cash dividend at any time? There are usually three conditions that a corporation must meet to pay a cash dividend:

1. Sufficient retained earnings
2. Sufficient cash
3. Formal action by the board of directors

In addition, corporate laws generally provide certain protections for creditors and others who depend on the continued existence of the corporation. Thus, acts like the CBCA include a solvency test to determine the legality of dividends, such as the following:

> A corporation shall not declare or pay a dividend if there are reasonable grounds for believing that:
> a. the corporation is, or would after the payment be, unable to pay its liabilities as they become due; or
> b. the realizable value of the corporation's assets would thereby be less than the aggregate of its liabilities and stated capital of all classes. (CBCA 1975, Section 40).

A large amount of retained earnings does not always mean that a corporation is able to pay dividends. There must also be enough cash in excess of normal operating needs. A corporation's board of directors is not required by law to declare dividends. This is true even if both retained earnings and cash are large enough to justify a dividend. However, once the directors have *declared* a dividend, it becomes a liability of the corporation.

Most public corporations try to maintain a stable dividend record in order to make their shares attractive to investors. Dividends may be paid once a year or semi-annually or quarterly. The general tendency is to pay quarterly dividends on both common and preferred shares. In periods of high profitability, the board of directors may declare an *extra* dividend on common shares payable at one of the usual dividend dates or at some other date.

You may have seen corporate announcements of dividend declarations in newspapers. Dividend declarations are usually announced and reported in financial newspapers and investor services. Three dates are important in a dividend announcement:

1. The date of declaration
2. The date of record
3. The date of payment

The date of declaration is the date the board of directors takes formal action to declare the dividend. The date of record is the date on which ownership of shares is to be determined. The date of payment is the date on which the dividend is to be paid. For example, a dividend announcement might read:

On June 26, the board of directors of Campbell Soup Co. declared a quarterly cash dividend of $0.33 per common share to stockholders of record as of the close of business on July 8, payable on July 31.

We record the liability for a dividend on the declaration date. No entry is required on the date of record. This date merely sets the date for determining the identity of the shareholders who will receive the dividend. The period of time between the record date and the payment date allows for the preparation of the dividend cheques. During this period, the share price is usually quoted as selling *ex-dividends*. This means that, since the date of record has passed, a new investor will not receive the unpaid dividends. On the date of payment, the corporation pays its dividend liability by mailing the dividend cheques.

To illustrate, assume that on December 1 the board of directors of Hiber Corporation declare both preferred and common share dividends. The preferred dividend is a regular quarterly dividend of $2.50 on the 5,000 shares of $10 preferred shares outstanding (total dividend of $12,500). The common share dividend is a quarterly dividend of $0.30 on the 100,000 shares of no par common shares outstanding (total dividend of $30,000). The record date is December 10, and cheques are to be issued to shareholders on January 2. The entry to record the declaration of the dividends is as follows:

Corporations such as Campbell Soup Co. include the important dates of declaration, record, and payment in their dividend announcements.

Dec.	1	Dividends	42,500	
		Dividends Payable		42,500
		Record declaration of dividends on common and preferred shares.		

We transfer the balance in Dividends to Retained Earnings as a part of the closing process by debiting Retained Earnings and crediting Dividends. The company reports Dividends Payable on its December 31 balance sheet as a current liability. The entry to record the payment of the dividends on January 2 is as follows:

Jan.	2	Dividends Payable	42,500	
		Cash		42,500
		Record payment of dividends.		

Dividends on cumulative preferred shares do not become a liability of the corporation until formal declaration by the board of directors. However, dividends in arrears at a balance sheet date must be disclosed. This disclosure may be made by a footnote or a parenthetical note.

STOCK DIVIDENDS

Sometimes a corporation is unwilling or unable to pay dividends in cash because it needs its cash resources to reinvest in the business. At the same time, management still wishes to give its shareholders a positive signal that the business is doing well. A common way to do this is through the issuance of a small stock dividend. A **stock dividend** is a pro rata distribution of shares to shareholders through a transfer of retained earnings to paid-in capital. Such distributions are usually in common shares and are issued to holders of common shares. It is possible to issue common shares to preferred shareholders or vice versa, but such dividends are rare.

Stock dividends are different from cash dividends in that there is no distribution of cash or other assets to shareholders. Corporations experiencing rapid growth

USING ACCOUNTING TO UNDERSTAND BUSINESS

Potential investors in a corporation often rely on accounting information in assessing the attractiveness of stocks. For example, the existence of dividends in arrears on cumulative preferred shares can serve as a warning that the corporation does not pay dividends every year. Such dividends in arrears must be paid before any dividends are available to common shareholders. Likewise, any liquidation preference of preferred shares ranks ahead of the common shares if the corporation goes out of business. If the ability to earn dividends from investing in the shares is a primary concern, then the size of retained earnings, the dividend history of the corporation, and the amount of cash and cash equivalents as well as cash flows are important pieces of information.

often issue stock dividends. Such corporations use most of the cash generated from operations to acquire new facilities or to expand their operations and do not wish to use cash to pay dividends.

How is a stock dividend different from a stock split? Both entail a pro rata distribution of shares to existing shareholders. In both cases the distribution leaves each shareholder's interest in the firm unchanged and has no effect on the firm's assets, liabilities, and total shareholders' equity. However, there is an *economic* difference between a stock dividend and a stock split that is related to: (1) the relative size of the share distribution, (2) the reason for the distribution, and (3) the impact of the event on the share's market price and shareholder wealth.

A stock split involves the issuance of a much larger proportion of the company's existing shares than a stock dividend. A stock dividend will usually increase the firm's outstanding shares by 5% to 25%, whereas a stock split will often increase them by 100% or more. As we noted earlier, the reason for a stock split is to lower the market price per share so that investors can trade in the shares more easily. Investors anticipate that the future dividends per share will likely drop in proportion to the split and the market price per share generally falls proportionately to the number of new shares being issued. For example, a two-for-one stock split will usually cause the market price to drop to one-half. Thus, a shareholder who owned 1,000 shares with a market value of $20 each before the split will hold 2,000 shares worth $10 each after the split. In total, the split should leave the shareholder's wealth unchanged.

The reason for a stock dividend is to give shareholders a positive signal from management that the company is doing well. Investors may expect that, although the corporation is not distributing a cash dividend this period, future cash dividends per share will not drop as a result of the stock dividend. Because of this, and because of the smaller size of the share distribution, the market price per share does not usually drop proportionately with the number of new shares issued. Consider a shareholder who owns 1,000 shares with a market value of $20 each, for a total investment value of $20,000 ($20 × 1,000 shares). If the market price per share does not drop when the company issues a 5% stock dividend, the shareholder's total wealth has increased, since the investment is now worth $21,000 ($20 × 1,050 shares). Has the market acted irrationally in not revaluing the share price downwards as a result of the stock dividend? Probably not. If the market interprets the stock dividend as a signal of positive management expectations about the firm's future, this "good news" may cause the market's total valuation of the company to increase.

The difference in accounting for stock splits and stock dividends has sometimes been justified on the basis of this *economic* difference between the two. Whereas an issuing corporation makes no journal entry for a stock split, it does make an entry to record a stock dividend.

The effect of a stock dividend on the shareholders' equity of the issuing corporation is to transfer retained earnings to paid-in capital. The CBCA requires that the *fair value* (market price) of the shares issued in a stock dividend is the amount transferred from retained earnings to paid-in capital.

To illustrate a stock dividend for a public corporation, assume that the shareholders' equity accounts of Hendrix Corporation as of December 15 are as follows:

Common Shares, no par value (2,000,000 shares issued)	$49,000,000
Retained Earnings	26,600,000

On December 15, the board of directors declares a stock dividend of 5% or 100,000 shares (2,000,000 shares × 5%), to be issued on January 10. The market price of the stock on the declaration date is $31 a share. The entry to record the declaration is as follows:

Dec. 15	Stock Dividends (100,000 × $31 market price)	3,100,000	
	Stock Dividends Distributable		3,100,000
	Record stock dividend of 5%.		

The following entry records the issuance of the stock on January 10:

Jan. 10	Stock Dividends Distributable	3,100,000	
	Common Shares		3,100,000
	Record issuances of shares for stock dividend.		

We close the $3,100,000 debit to Stock Dividends to Retained Earnings at the end of the period. The effect of the stock dividend is to transfer $3,100,000 of retained earnings to paid-in capital and to increase by 100,000 the number of shares outstanding. There is no change in the assets, liabilities, or total shareholders' equity of the corporation. If the company prepares financial statements between the date of declaration and the date of issuance, it will list the stock dividends distributable account in the Paid-In Capital section of the balance sheet.

Note that, unlike cash dividends payable, a stock dividend distributable is *not* a current liability. By definition a liability will result in a future outflow of the firm's assets. Payment of a stock dividend will not affect the assets of the company.

The issuance of the additional stock dividend shares does not affect the total amount of a shareholder's equity. A stock dividend also does not affect a shareholder's proportionate interest (equity) in the corporation. We illustrate this for a shareholder who is assumed to own 1,000 shares.

The Corporation	Before Stock Dividend	After Stock Dividend
Common shares	$49,000,000	$52,100,000
Retained earnings	26,600,000	23,500,000
Total shareholders' equity	$75,600,000	$75,600,000
Number of shares outstanding	2,000,000	2,100,000
Book value per share	$37.80	$36.00

A Shareholder		
Number of shares owned	1,000	1,050
Total book value of shares owned	$37,800	$37,800
Portion of corporation owned	0.05%	0.05%

LIQUIDATING DIVIDENDS

A liquidating dividend is a distribution to shareholders from paid-in capital. Such dividends are rare and are usually paid when a corporation is permanently reducing its operations or winding up its affairs completely. Since dividends are normally paid from retained earnings, dividends that reduce paid-in capital should be identified as liquidating dividends when paid.

Income and Retained Earnings

THE CORPORATION'S INCOME STATEMENT

Objective 9
Describe the required disclosures for the following income statement items: discontinued operations, extraordinary items, unusual items, and earnings per share.

In earlier chapters we presented the income statement for an unincorporated business. A corporation's income statement follows a similar format, except that the corporation must also report income tax expense, which is not applicable to proprietorships and partnerships. In this chapter we discuss some other special or irregular items that you might find sometimes on the income statement. These include results from discontinued operations, extraordinary items, and unusual items. In addition, we discuss earnings per share, which is a required disclosure for public corporations.

IRREGULAR ITEMS THAT AFFECT THE INCOME STATEMENT

Three types of irregular items that may affect the current year's net income are:

1. Discontinued operations.
2. Extraordinary gains or losses.
3. Unusual items.

A business must report these items separately on the income statement if they are of material amounts. Unusual items are reported in a corporate income statement before the line disclosure of "income from continuing operations before income tax." We then deduct income tax on continuing operations to arrive at "income from continuing operations." After this line, the results of discontinued operations and extraordinary items are each reported separately along with their respective tax effect. Exhibit 5 shows a partial income statement for Jones Corporation illustrating this presentation.

Exhibit 5
Special Items in Income Statement

Jones Corporation
Income Statement
For the Year Ended December 31, 2000

Net sales	$9,600,000
Operating income	$1,390,000
Unusual loss on write-off of obsolete inventory	80,000
Income from continuing operations before income tax	$1,310,000
Income tax	620,000
Income from continuing operations	$ 690,000
Loss on discontinued operations (Note A)	100,000
Income before extraordinary item	$ 590,000
Extraordinary item:	
Gain on expropriation of land, net of applicable income tax of $65,000	150,000
Net income	$ 740,000

Note A.

On July 1 of the current year, the electrical products division of the corporation was sold. Earnings on discontinued operations to July 1 were $150,000 ($290,000 less income tax of $140,000). The loss on disposal was $250,000 (after applicable tax of $125,000). Therefore the net after-tax loss on discontinued operations was $100,000. The net sales of the division for the current year were $2,900,000. The assets sold were composed of inventories, equipment, and plant totalling $2,100,000. The purchaser assumed liabilities of $600,000.

In the following paragraphs, we briefly discuss each of these types of items assuming that the items are material to the financial statements.

DISCONTINUED OPERATIONS

Discontinued operations are "the operations of a business segment that has been sold, abandoned, shut down, or otherwise disposed of, or that is the subject of a formal plan of disposal."[6] A business segment is a distinguishable component of a company, such as a particular line of business that is significant to the entity as a whole.[7]

For example, assume that a company owns newspapers, television stations, and radio stations. If it were to sell its radio stations, it should report separately on its income statement the effects (including the tax effect) of the discontinued operations for the current period. The effects of discontinued operations may be divided into two components: (1) the results of operations of the discontinued segment during the current period, and (2) the gain or loss on disposal of the segment. As shown in Exhibit 5, the income statement should present the income from continuing operations (after tax) followed by the gain or loss from discontinued operations, net of applicable income tax. In addition, we must report the identity of the segment, the disposal date, a description of the segment's assets and liabilities, and the revenue of the discontinued operations for the reporting period. These data are often disclosed in a note to the financial statements. An example from the 1996 financial statements of Shell Canada Ltd. is shown opposite.

EXTRAORDINARY ITEMS

Extraordinary items are gains or losses that possess **all three** of the following characteristics:

1. they are not expected to occur frequently over several years,
2. they do not typify the normal business activities of the entity,
3. they do not depend primarily on decisions or determinations by management or owners.[8]

Examples of transactions and events that have all of the characteristics of extraordinary items include the expropriation of a company's land by a government or the cost of destruction caused by unusual natural disasters, such as a tornado. A company must report extraordinary items, net of applicable income taxes, separately on the income statement immediately before net income.[9]

Gains or losses resulting from the risks inherent in an entity's normal business activities would not be considered extraordinary.[10] For example, gains and losses on the disposal of capital assets or other investments do not qualify as extraordi-

---

[6] *CICA Handbook,* Section 3475, paragraph 02 (a).
[7] *Ibid.,* paragraph 02 (b).
[8] *CICA Handbook,* Section 3480, paragraph 02.
[9] *Ibid.,* paragraph 08.
[10]*Ibid.,* paragraph 04.

Shell Canada Ltd.
Income Statement Disclosure

Year ended December 31 ($ millions)	1996	1995	1994
Earnings from continuing operations	326	302	223
Gain from discontinued operations (Note 2)	269	221	97
Earnings	595	523	320

Notes to Financial Statements

Note 2 Discontinued Operations

The Corporation sold its Chemicals business effective December 31, 1996, to Shell Chemicals Canada Ltd. The sale of the Chemicals business resulted in a gain of $324 million before tax, or $226 million after tax. The results of the Chemicals business have been accounted for as discontinued operations and previously reported financial statements have been restated. The Corporation was able to take advantage of capital losses which it acquired on the amalgamation of a related company, reducing the taxes on the gain. In 1995, the Corporation sold its polypropylene business to a company owned 50 percent by a related party, which resulted in a gain of $144 million before tax or $95 million after tax.

($ millions)	1996	1995	1994
Revenues from discontinued operations	606	740	758
Earnings from discontinued operations before income taxes	66	201	152
Income taxes	23	75	55
Earnings from discontinued operations	43	126	97
Disposals, gain on sale			
Discontinued operations	324	–	–
Polypropylene business	–	144	–
Gain on disposals before income taxes	324	144	–
Income taxes	98	49	–
Gain on disposals after income taxes	226	95	–
Total	269	221	97

Source: C. Byrd and I. Chen, *Financial Reporting in Canada*, 1997, CICA, Toronto, p. 326.

nary items. This is because: (1) they are not unusual, (2) they recur from time to time in the normal operations of a business, and/or (3) they depend on decisions made by management.

An example of the disclosure of an extraordinary item from the 1995 financial statements of Alcan Aluminum Limited is shown on the following page.

UNUSUAL OR ATYPICAL ITEMS

Few items meet all three criteria for designation as extraordinary, yet many gains or losses satisfy one or more of the criteria. These items are either not expected to occur frequently or do not typify normal business activities. Generally accepted accounting principles require that such unusual items be disclosed separately in the income statement.[11] However, unlike extraordinary items, we do not report unusual gains or losses net of their tax effect. They are included on the income statement before the line disclosure of income from continuing operations before taxes.

About one-half of the companies surveyed for the 1997 edition of *Financial Reporting in Canada* reported non-recurring items such as gains or losses on asset

[11] *CICA Handbook*, Section 1520, paragraph .03.

Alcan Aluminum Limited
Income Statement Disclosure

(in thousands of dollars)	1995	1994	1993
Net income (Loss) before extraordinary item	$543	$96	$(104)
Extraordinary loss (Note 4)	280	–	–
Net income (Loss)	$263	$96	$(104)

Notes to Financial Statements

Note 4 Extraordinary Loss – Kemano Completion Project

In the third quarter of 1995, the Company wrote down its investment in Kemano Completion Project (KCP). After estimated disposal proceeds and site restoration costs, the amount of the write-down is $420, resulting in an extraordinary loss of $280 on an after-tax basis or US$1.24 per common share.

In January 1995, the government of British Columbia unilaterally announced that it would not allow KCP to proceed and indicated its preparedness to confirm this prohibition by legislation. This highly unusual action by the government was in breach of longstanding legal agreements with both the Company and the government of Canada under which the Company was carrying out the project.

Shortly after the government's announcement, Alcan and the government began talks for the purpose of attempting to reach a satisfactory resolution of this matter and, in July 1995, the parties announced a framework agreement to govern future negotiations. The Company continues in negotiations with the government with a view to protecting its interests including the supply of energy from alternative sources for possible future smelter expansions in British Columbia.

The write-down of KCP recognizes that the project cannot be completed due to the government's prohibition. Under the terms of the framework agreement, the value of any settlement would be contingent on future events and in accordance with generally accepted accounting principles, the value of such a settlement cannot be recognized in the legal rights nor its determination to seek an equitable result in this matter.

Any future quantifiable benefit received as compensation for the government's rejection of KCP will be treated as an extraordinary gain.

Source: C. Byrd and I. Chen, *Financial Reporting in Canada*, 1997, CICA, Toronto, p. 335.

write-downs, restructuring costs, severance pay, foreign exchange transactions, and investment disposals.[12] The following excerpt from the 1996 financial statements of Oshawa Group Limited illustrates one such disclosure:

Notes to Financial Statements

Note 7 Other Items

	1996 (52 weeks)	1995 (53 weeks)
Gain on sale of real estate	$ 14.3	$ –
Restructuring costs	(11.6)	(7.2)
	$ 2.7	$(7.2)

In 1996 restructuring costs consisted primarily of severance and related expenditures incurred to reduce the Company's operating cost base in its wholesale operations. In 1995 costs related to a staff restructuring program in 53 corporate food stores in Ontario.

Source: C. Byrd and I. Chen, *Financial Reporting in Canada,* 22nd edition, CICA, Toronto, 1997, p. 336

[12]C. Byrd and I. Chen, *Financial Reporting in Canada,* 22nd edition, CICA, Toronto, 1997, p. 334.

EARNINGS PER COMMON SHARE

Investors and creditors use net income in evaluating a company's profitability. However, net income by itself is difficult to use in comparing companies of different sizes. For example, a net income of $750,000 may be acceptable for a small computer software company, but it would be unacceptable for Apple Computer Inc. Moreover, investors might have difficulty evaluating earnings trends using only net income, when there have been significant changes in a company's shareholders' equity.

To address these concerns, we often express the profitability of companies in terms of earnings per share. Earnings per share (EPS) is the net income per common shares outstanding during a period. Public corporations must report earnings per share for the current and preceding period on their income statements or in a note cross-referenced to the income statement.[13]

If a company has only common shares outstanding, it determines the earnings per share by dividing net income by the number of common shares outstanding during the period. When common share transactions have taken place during the year, we determine the weighted average number of common shares outstanding during the year. Such complexities are usually covered in a more advanced text. If preferred shares are outstanding, the net income must be reduced by the amount of any preferred dividend requirements before dividing by the number of common shares outstanding.

The effect of discontinued operations and extraordinary items should be considered in computing earnings per share. Otherwise, a single earnings per share amount based on net income could be misleading. For example, assume that Jones Corporation, whose partial income statement was presented in Exhibit 5, reported net income of $700,000 for 1999. Also assume that no extraordinary or other special items were reported in 1999. The corporation had 200,000 common shares outstanding during 1999 and 2000. The earnings per share is $3.50 ($700,000 ÷ 200,000) for 1999 and $3.70 ($740,000 ÷ 200,000) for 2000. Comparing the two earnings per share amounts for 1999 and 2000 suggests that operations had significantly improved. However, the current year's per share amount that is comparable to $3.50 is $3.45, which is the income from continuing operations of $690,000 divided by 200,000 common shares outstanding. This latter amount indicates a slight downward trend in normal operations.

When such items exist, earnings per share must be reported for the following items:

1. Income from continuing operations before discontinued operations and extraordinary items.
2. Net income.[14]

The reporting of earnings per share for the gain or loss on discontinued operations and for extraordinary items is optional. Earnings per share data may be shown in a footnote cross-referenced to the income statement or added at the bottom of the statement, as shown in Exhibit 6 for Jones Corporation.

In computing the earnings per common share, we must consider all factors that could affect the number of common shares outstanding. For example, an issue of preferred shares or bonds (debt) with the right to convert to common shares may be outstanding. Such securities that are convertible to common shares are considered **dilutive securities,** which could potentially lower (dilute) future earnings per share, if converted.

When dilutive securities exist, a corporation must normally report two amounts for earnings per share. One amount is computed without regard for the conversion privilege. This amount is called basic earnings per share. The second amount is

[13]*CICA Handbook,* Section 3500, paragraph 6.
[14]*CICA Handbook,* Section 3500, paragraph 11.

Exhibit 6
Income Statement with
Earnings per Share

Jones Corporation
Income Statement
For the Year Ended December 31, 2000

Income from continuing operations	$690,000
Net income	$740,000
Earnings per common share:	
Income from continuing operations	$ 3.45
Loss on discontinued operations	.50
Income before extraordinary item	$ 2.95
Extraordinary item	.75
Net income	$ 3.70

based on the assumption that the preferred shares or bonds were converted to common shares, if the conversion would have reduced the earnings per share. This amount is called fully diluted earnings per share.[15] This figure shows shareholders the maximum dilution of current earnings that potential conversions would have caused if they had occurred during the current period. The 1997 edition of *Financial Reporting in Canada* indicates that 38% of the public companies surveyed disclosed fully diluted earnings per share in 1996.[16] Basic, fully diluted, and other earnings per share data are discussed in more detail in advanced accounting texts.

A note accompanying the financial statements normally explains how the earnings per share were computed.

ADJUSTMENTS AND REPORTING OF RETAINED EARNINGS

Objective 10
Journalize adjustments to retained earnings for appropriations, corrections of errors made in prior periods, and retroactive adjustments of accounting changes.

We report the closing balance in retained earnings in the balance sheet as part of shareholders' equity. Changes in retained earnings may be reported in a separate statement, in a combined statement of income and retained earnings, or in the notes to the financial statements. The purpose of such disclosure is to provide a reconciliation from the balance at the beginning of the year to the balance at the end of the year.

The regular entries in the retained earnings account include an increase to record net income for the year (and a decrease for a net loss) and a decrease for dividends declared during the year. The regular pattern is:

Retained earnings, beginning of the year
Add net income for the year   +
Deduct dividends declared   −
Retained earnings, end of the year

In addition, we sometimes find one or more of the following three items in the statement:

1. appropriations of retained earnings,
2. adjustments to the opening balance of retained earnings related to correction of material errors made in a prior period,

[15]*CICA Handbook,* Section 3500, paragraph 30.
[16]C. Byrd and I. Chen, *op. cit.,* p. 343.

3. adjustments to the opening balance of retained earnings for the retroactive effects of a change in accounting principles.

We discuss these items in the following paragraphs.

APPROPRIATIONS

A corporation may voluntarily limit the amount of retained earnings available for use as dividends by action of its board of directors. The amount restricted is called an appropriation. This amount remains a part of retained earnings and is reported as such in the financial statements.

The business journalizes the appropriation by transferring the amount from the retained earnings account to a special account. This special account is identified as an appropriation with a description of its purpose. An example of such an account would be *Appropriation for Plant Expansion.*

Assume that a corporation with retained earnings of $700,000 decides to appropriate $400,000 for plant expansion. An appropriation of $400,000 would be transferred to the account: Appropriation for Plant Expansion. This appropriation would restrict the payment of dividends to not more than $300,000. The entry to record the appropriation is as follows:

Apr. 1	Retained Earnings	400,000	
	Appropriation for Plant Expansion		400,000
	Appropriation for plant expansion per Board of Directors' meeting March 31, 1998.		

When a part or all of an appropriation is no longer needed, it is transferred back to the retained earnings account. In the preceding example, when the corporation decides, in May 1999, that the appropriation is no longer needed, it makes the following entry:

May 31	Appropriation for Plant Expansion	400,000	
	Retained Earnings		400,000

Appropriations may also be required by contract, such as a bank loan or the corporation's cumulative preferred shares with dividends in arrears. For example, when a corporation borrows a large amount of money, the lender may require restrictions on dividends until the debt is paid. The amount restricted is usually equal to the amount of the debt outstanding. The appropriation of retained earnings may be made in total, or an annual buildup of appropriations may be required. Even if the lender does not require the appropriation of retained earnings, the corporation's board of directors might make such an appropriation. In this case, the appropriation is said to be **discretionary** rather than **contractual.**

The board of directors may establish appropriations for other discretionary purposes. For example, a board of directors may appropriate retained earnings for contingencies, such as inventory price declines, a possible settlement of a pending lawsuit, or possible losses from self-insurance.

You should note that an appropriation of retained earnings is not related to any specific assets. Thus, an appropriation does not mean that there is an equivalent amount of cash or other assets set aside in a special fund. *The only purpose of an appropriation is to signal a restriction in dividend distributions to shareholders.* The cash that otherwise might be distributed as dividends could be invested in other assets, such as capital and equipment, or used to reduce liabilities.

The board of directors of a corporation may as a separate action set aside assets such as cash or marketable securities for a specific purpose. This setting aside of assets may also be accompanied by an appropriation of retained earnings. In this case, the appropriation is said to be **funded.**

CORRECTION OF ERRORS MADE IN PRIOR PERIODS

Sometimes during the current year we discover that the company made a significant accounting error in a prior period due to mistakes in calculations, failure to consider some available information, or misinterpretation of information. For example, the accountant may have made an addition error last year when computing ending inventory. The company must correct such errors in the year of discovery by adjusting the opening balance of retained earnings for the amount of the error, net of any tax effect.[17] Exhibit 7 illustrates the format for such a correction in the statement of retained earnings.

Exhibit 7

*Correction of Prior Period
Error in Retained Earnings
Statement*

**Mohawk Corporation
Statement of Retained Earnings
For the year ended December 31, 2000**

Opening retained earnings, as previously reported	$1,500,000
Add: correction for understatement of 1999 ending inventory,	
net of applicable income tax of $20,000	30,000
Opening retained earnings, as restated	$1,530,000
Add current year's net income	300,000
Retained earnings at end of the year	$1,830,000

The company must disclose in the financial statements a description of the error, the effect of the correction on current and prior periods, and the fact that the statements of prior periods have been restated.[18] The following excerpt from the 1995 financial statements of Canadian Airlines Corporation illustrates a note disclosure for correction of an error.

Note 16 Restatement of Prior Year's Results

In 1995, errors relating to the reporting of commissions, which are netted against passenger revenue, were identified. As a result, 1994 passenger revenues were overstated by $15,900,000 and results have been restated to properly report passenger revenue.

On the 1994 consolidated statement of operations passenger revenues and operating income have been reduced by $15,900,000 and the loss has been increased by $15,900,000. On the consolidated balance sheet, accounts payable and accrued liabilities and deficit have been increased by $15,900,000. On the statement of changes in financial position, change in non-cash working capital related to operations increased $15,900,000. Loss per share was increased by $0.39 to $1.39.

Source: C. Byrd and I. Chen, *Financial Reporting in Canada*, 22nd edition, CICA, Toronto, 1997, p. 68.

CHANGES IN ACCOUNTING POLICIES

Sometimes businesses will decide during the current year to change the accounting policy used for a particular item or group of items. For example, a business might decide to change to the average method of assigning cost to inventory rather than using FIFO as it had done in the past, due to an increasing trend towards fluctuating inventory prices. Or it might decide to change from the straight-line to the declining balance method for amortizing its capital assets, in order to conform to industry practice.

[17]*CICA Handbook,* Section 1506, paragraph 29.
[18]*Ibid.,* paragraph 30.

Obviously, it could be difficult for an investor to compare the results of this year's operations with prior years, if the company has changed its accounting policy in the current year. In order to enhance **comparability,** we usually recalculate the income of prior years using the new accounting policy that has been adopted in the current year. We then make a retroactive adjustment to the opening balance of retained earnings to reflect the effect of the change (net of applicable income tax) on the income of all prior periods. Generally accepted accounting principles require that the financial statements disclose both the nature and income effects of the change in accounting policy.[19]

Note that the treatment used for a change in accounting policy is different from the treatment of a change in accounting estimate, which was illustrated in Chapter 10. For a change in accounting estimate, we adjust only the current and future years' statements, but we do *not* adjust the income of prior periods or opening retained earnings. A change in our approximation of the years of useful life or residual value of a capital asset is an example of a change in accounting estimate. A change from straight-line to declining balance method of amortization is a change in accounting principle.

The following example from the 1996 financial statements of the Bannister Foundation, Inc. illustrates the note disclosure for retroactive treatment of a change in accounting policy:

> **Note 18 Change in Accounting Policy**
>
> *Effective January 1, 1996, the Corporation retroactively changed its accounting policy to amortize the $6,973 of pre-1974 Banister Pipeline's excess of cost over net identifiable assets at acquisition over its expected useful life of twenty years. As a result, the Corporation has recorded a $6,973 downward adjustment to the January 1, 1994 opening retained earnings balance and a corresponding downward adjustment to the carrying value of excess of cost over net identifiable assets at acquisition.*

Source: C. Byrd and I. Chen, *Financial Reporting in Canada*, 22nd edition, CICA, Toronto, 1997, p. 67.

Reporting Retained Earnings

Objective 11
Prepare a retained earnings statement.

As we discussed earlier, we report the closing balance of retained earnings in the balance sheet. Changes in retained earnings may be reported in a separate retained earnings statement. In the following paragraphs, we illustrate the reporting of retained earnings and the combining of the retained earnings statement and the income statement.

REPORTING RETAINED EARNINGS IN THE BALANCE SHEET

In the balance sheet, the company should report retained earnings so that readers of the statement can clearly distinguish between the *appropriated* and *unappropriated* portions. An example of such a presentation is shown below.

Retained earnings:
  Appropriated:
    For plant expansion $ 250,000
  Unappropriated   1,800,000
    Total retained earnings $2,050,000

[19]*CICA Handbook,* Section 1506, paragraph 11.

The corporation could use presentations other than the above to report retained earnings in the balance sheet. For example, it could present the preceding data in a note accompanying the balance sheet. Such a presentation, including the note, might appear as follows:

Retained earnings (see note) $2,050,000

Note:
Retained earnings in the amount of $250,000 are appropriated for expansion of plant facilities; the remaining $1,800,000 is unappropriated.

RETAINED EARNINGS STATEMENT

When a company prepares a separate retained earnings statement, it normally divides the statement into two major sections: (1) appropriated and (2) unappropriated. The first section presents for each appropriation account its beginning balance, any additions or deductions during the period, and its ending balance. The second section presents for the unappropriated retained earnings account its beginning balance, adjustments to the opening balance for any correction of prior period errors or retroactive changes in accounting policy, net income or net loss for the period, dividends, transfers to and from the appropriation accounts, and the ending balance. The final figure on the statement is the total retained earnings as of the end of the period. An example of this form of retained earnings statement is shown in Exhibit 8 for Lester Corporation.

Exhibit 8

Retained Earnings Statement with Appropriations

Lester Corporation
Retained Earnings Statement
For the Year Ended December 31, 2000

Appropriated:			
Appropriation for plant expansion, January 1, 2000		$ 180,000	
Additional appropriation (see below)		100,000	
Retained earnings appropriated, December 31, 2000			$ 280,000
Unappropriated:			
Balance, January 1, 2000	$1,414,500		
Net income for the year	580,000	1,994,500	
Cash dividends declared	125,000		
Transfer to approp. for plant expansion	100,000	225,000	
Retained earnings unappropriated, December 31, 2000			1,769,500
Total retained earnings, December 31, 2000			$2,049,500

COMBINED INCOME AND RETAINED EARNINGS STATEMENT

An alternative format for presenting the retained earnings statement is to combine it with the income statement. This combined form was used by approximately 20% of the companies surveyed in the 1997 edition of *Financial Reporting in Canada.*[20] An example of the combined income and retained earnings statement is shown in Exhibit 9 for Dominic Company.

An advantage of the combined format is that it emphasizes net income as the connecting link between the income statement and the retained earnings portion of

[20]C. Byrd and I. Chen, *op. cit.,* p. 76.

Exhibit 9
*Combined Income and
Retained Earnings Statement*

Dominic Company
Combined Income and Retained Earnings Statement
For the Year Ended December 31, 2000

EARNINGS	*In thousands of dollars*
Revenues:	
Net sales	$1,428,504
Investment and other interest income	11,938
Total revenues	1,440,442
Costs and expenses:	
Cost of sales	617,156
Selling, distribution, and general administrative	542,944
Interest	1,507
Total costs and expenses	1,161,607
Earnings before income taxes	278,835
Income taxes	103,944
Net income	174,891
RETAINED EARNINGS	
Retained earnings at beginning of the year	491,481
Dividends declared	(87,301)
Retained earnings at end of the year	$ 404,180

shareholders' equity. A disadvantage of the combined form is that the net income figure is buried in the body of the statement.

Reporting Changes in Shareholders' Equity

Objective 12
Report changes in shareholders' equity.

According to GAAP, we must report significant changes in shareholders' equity during the period in which they occur. Although these changes may be reported in the retained earnings statement or the balance sheet, we often report the changes in share accounts in a note.

The note on shareholders' equity may be prepared in a columnar format, where each column represents a major shareholders' equity classification. The left column describes changes in each classification. Exhibit 10 reports the balance sheet disclosure and related note for CCL Industries.

Exhibit 10
*Statement of Shareholders'
Equity*

Balance Sheet Disclosure

As at December 31, 1996 and 1995 (in thousands of dollars)	1996	1995
Shareholders' Equity		
Capital stock (Note 7)	$146,789	$139,432
Retained earnings	232,436	207,903
Foreign currency translation adjustment	14,879	10,532
	$394,104	$357,867

Notes to Financial Statements

Note 7 Capital Stock

The company's authorized capital consists of an unlimited number of Class A voting shares and an unlimited number of Class B non-voting shares.

Exhibit 10 (concluded)

	Class A		Class B	
	Shares	Amount	Shares	Amount
Balance at January 1, 1995	3,425	$6,517	29,503	$122,004
Issued for cash under employee share plans	–	–	1,243	11,127
Repurchase of shares under Normal Course Issuer Bid process	–	–	(50)	(216)
Conversions from Class A to Class B shares	(916)	(1,743)	916	1,743
Balance at December 31, 1995	2,509	4,774	31,612	134,658
Issued for cash under employee share plans	–	–	854	7,357
Conversions from Class A to Class B shares	(11)	(21)	11	21
Balance at December 31, 1996	2,498	$4,753	32,477	$142,036

Total capital stock at December 31, 1996 was $146,789,000 (1995 – $139,432,000).

(b) Share attributes

Class A
Class A shares carry full voting rights and are convertible at any time into Class B shares. Dividends are currently set at 5 cents per share per annum less than Class B shares.

Class B
Class B shares rank equally in all material respects with the Class A shares, except as follows:
(i)   They are entitled to receive material and attend, but not to vote at, regular shareholder meetings.
(ii) They are entitled to voting privileges when consideration for the Class A shares, under a takeover bid when voting control has been acquired, exceeds 115% of the market price of the Class B shares.
(iii) They are entitled to receive, or have set aside for payment, dividends as declared by the Board of Directors from time to time.

Source: C. Byrd and I. Chen, *Financial Reporting in Canada*, 1997, CICA, Toronto, p. 259.

KEY POINTS

Objective 1. Describe the nature of the corporate form of organization.
Characteristics of corporations that have accounting implications are separate legal existence, transferable share units, and limited liability. Corporations may be either public or private corporations, and they are subject to income taxes.

The documents included in forming a corporation include an application of incorporation, articles of incorporation, and bylaws. Costs often incurred in organizing a corporation include legal fees, taxes, government incorporation fees, and promotional costs. The company may debit such costs to an asset account entitled Organization Costs and amortize them to expense over an appropriate period of time.

Objective 2. List the two main sources of shareholders' equity.
The two main sources of shareholders' equity are (1) capital contributed by the shareholders and others, called paid-in capital, and (2) net income retained in the business, called retained earnings. Shareholders' equity is reported in a corporation balance sheet according to these two sources.

Objective 3. List the major sources of paid-in capital, including the various classes of shares.
The main source of paid-in capital is from the issuance of shares. The two primary classes of shares are common and preferred. Preferred shares are normally nonparticipating and may be cumulative or noncumulative. In addition to the issuance of shares, paid-in capital may arise from the donations of assets and gains on capital transactions.

Objective 4. Journalize the entries for issuing shares.
When a corporation issues no par shares for cash, the cash account is debited, and share capital for the class of shares issued is credited for the same amount. When shares are

issued in exchange for assets other than cash, the company should record the assets acquired at their fair market price.

Objective 5. Journalize the entries for transactions when a corporation acquires its own shares.

When a corporation purchases its own shares, we credit cash for the reacquisition cost and debit share capital for an amount equal to the average issuance price of the shares. Any gain on repurchase is credited to contributed surplus. Any loss is debited first to contributed surplus created by previous acquisitions of the same class of shares or created by other transactions of the same class of shares, with any excess debited to retained earnings.

Objective 6. Prepare the Paid-In Capital section of a corporate balance sheet.

A company may use alternative terms and formats in reporting paid-in capital. Under one format, each class of shares is listed, followed by its related paid-in capital accounts. Other paid-in capital, such as donated capital, is then listed.

Objective 7. State the effect of stock splits on corporate financial statements.

A stock split issues present shareholders a proportionate number of additional shares in order to reduce the market price per share. There are no changes in the balances of any corporation accounts, and no entry is required for a stock split.

Objective 8. Journalize the entries for cash dividends and stock dividends.

The entry to record a declaration of cash dividends is to debit Dividends and credit Dividends Payable. We record the payment of dividends in the normal manner. When the company declares a stock dividend, it debits Dividends for the fair value of the stock to be issued and credits Stock Dividends Distributable. When the shares are issued on the payment date, the company debits Stock Dividends Distributable and credits Share Capital for the value of the stock issued.

Objective 9. Describe the required disclosures for the following income statement items: discontinued operations, extraordinary items, unusual items, and earnings per share.

We report the results of discontinued operations separately and net of their tax effect, immediately following income (after tax) from continuing operations on the income statement. Extraordinary items occur infrequently, do not arise

from normal business operations, and are not the result of management decisions. We report them separately (net of related tax effects) immediately before net income. We report separately material unusual or atypical items prior to the line disclosure for income from continuing operations before tax. Public corporations must disclose earnings per share (net income per common share outstanding). Fully diluted earnings per share is disclosed if convertible securities have the potential to lower basic earnings per share.

Objective 10. Journalize adjustments to retained earnings for appropriations, corrections of errors made in prior periods, and retroactive adjustments of accounting changes.

Retained earnings reflects changes due to net income (or net loss) and dividends declared. The board of directors may restrict the amount of retained earnings available for distribution of dividends by segregating an amount as an appropriation for a specific purpose. This is recorded by debiting Unappropriated Retained Earnings and crediting Appropriated Retained Earnings. If we discover errors in the accounting for prior periods, we correct these by an adjustment to the current year's opening balance of retained earnings. If the company changes an accounting policy, we recalculate the accumulated net income for prior periods using the new policy and adjust the opening balance of retained earnings for the effect of the change on prior periods.

Objective 11. Prepare a retained earnings statement.

A retained earnings statement is normally divided into two major sections: (1) appropriated and (2) unappropriated. The first section presents the beginning balances of any appropriations, any additions or deductions during the period, and an ending balance. The second section presents for the unappropriated retained earnings account its beginning balance, net income or net loss for the period, dividends, and any of the items discussed under Objective 10. The statement concludes with the total retained earnings as of the end of the period. An alternative format for reporting retained earnings is to combine the retained earnings statement and the income statement.

Objective 12. Report changes in shareholders' equity.

Significant changes in shareholders' equity must be reported for the period in which they occur. We may report these changes in the balance sheet and statement of retained earnings. Often we report changes related to the various classes of shares in a note.

GLOSSARY OF KEY TERMS

Appropriation. The amount of a corporation's retained earnings that has been restricted and therefore is not available for distribution to shareholders as dividends. *Objective 10*

Capital transaction. Transaction involving the firm's own shares. *Objective 5*

Cash dividend. A cash distribution of earnings by a corporation to its shareholders. *Objective 8*

Common shares. The basic ownership class of a corporation. *Objective 3*

Contributed surplus. Account(s) where we record contributions to equity arising from capital transactions other than the issuance of shares. *Objective 2*

Cumulative preferred shares. Preferred shares entitled to current and past dividends before dividends may be paid on common shares. *Objective 3*

Deficit. A debit balance in the retained earnings account. *Objective 2*

Discontinued operations. The operations of a business segment that has been sold, abandoned, spun off, or otherwise disposed of, or is the subject of a formal plan for disposal. *Objective 9*

Earnings per share. The net income available to common shareholders divided by the weighted average number of common shares outstanding during the year. *Objective 9*

Extraordinary item. A significant gain or loss that has all of the following characteristics: occurs infrequently, does not arise from normal business operations, and is not the result of management decisions or determinations. *Objective 9*

Fully diluted earnings per share. Earnings per share figure showing maximum dilution of current earnings if potential conversions had taken place during the period. *Objective 9*

Liquidating dividend. A distribution out of paid-in capital when a corporation permanently reduces its operations or winds up its affairs completely. *Objective 8*

No par value share. Share with no monetary amount stated on the share certificate. *Objective 3*

Nonparticipating preferred shares. Preferred shares with a limited dividend preference. *Objective 3*

Outstanding shares. The shares that are in the hands of shareholders. *Objective 3*

Paid-in capital. Share capital plus contributed surplus. *Objective 3*

Par value share. Share with a monetary amount stated on the share certificate. *Objective 3*

Preemptive right. The right of each shareholder to maintain the same fractional interest in the corporation by purchasing shares of any additional issuances. *Objective 3*

Preferred shares. A class of shares with preferential rights over common shares. *Objective 3*

Retained earnings. Net income retained in a corporation. *Objective 2*

Retroactive adjustment. An adjustment to the opening balance of retained earnings reflecting the cumulative effect on prior years' income of a current change in an accounting policy. *Objective 10*

Share capital. Account where we record the amount assigned to shares when they are issued. *Objective 2*

Shareholders. The owners of a corporation. *Objective 1*

Shareholders' equity. The equity of the shareholders in a corporation. *Objective 2*

Stock. Shares of ownership of a corporation. *Objective 1*

Stock dividend. Distribution of a company's own shares as a dividend to its shareholders. *Objective 8*

Stock split. The issuance of a proportionate number of additional shares to existing shareholders in order to reduce the market value per share. *Objective 7*

Treasury shares. Shares repurchased by a company and held for resale. *Objective 5*

Unusual item. Material, atypical, and infrequent gain or loss, which meets some, but not all of the criteria to be classified as an extraordinary item. *Objective 9*

ILLUSTRATIVE PROBLEM

Altenburg Inc. is a lighting fixture wholesaler located in Alberta. During its current fiscal year, ended December 31, 2000, Altenburg Inc. completed the following selected transactions:

On January 1, 2000 Altenburg's balance sheet showed the following:

Shared capital:

No par common shares, 60,000 authorized, 40,000 outstanding	$800,000
No par $2 preferred shares, 10,000 authorized and outstanding	100,000
Contributed surplus (gain on reacquisition of common shares)	5,000
Retained earnings	300,000

Feb. 3. Purchased 2,500 shares of its own common shares at $26.

May 1. Declared a semi-annual dividend of $1 on the preferred shares and a $0.30 dividend on the common shares to shareholders of record on May 15, payable on June 15.

June 15. Paid the cash dividends.

Nov. 1. Declared semi-annual dividends of $1 on the preferred shares and $0.30 on the common shares to shareholders of record on Nov. 15.

Nov. 20 A 5% common stock dividend was declared on the common shares outstanding, to be capitalized at the fair market value of the common shares, estimated at $30.

Dec. 1. Paid the cash dividends and issued the certificates for the common stock dividend.

Dec. 31. The board of directors authorized an appropriation of $50,000 for future plant expansion.

Instructions

Journalize the entries to record the transactions for Altenburg Inc.

Solution

2000

Feb. 3	Common Shares [2,500 × ($800,000 ÷ 40,000)]	50,000	
	Contributed Surplus	5,000	
	Retained Earnings	10,000	
	Cash		65,000
	Repurchase 2,500 common shares at $26.		
May 1	Dividends	21,250	
	Cash Dividends Payable		21,250*
	Declare $1 dividend on preferred and $0.30 dividend on		
	common shares. *(10,000 × $1) + [(40,000 − 2,500) × $0.30]		
June 15	Dividends Payable	21,250	
	Cash		21,250
	Payment of dividends.		
Nov. 1	Dividends	21,250*	
	Cash Dividends Payable		21,250
	Declare $1 dividend on preferred and $0.30 dividend on		
	common shares. *(10,000 × $1) + [(40,000 − 2,500) × $0.30]		
Nov. 20	Stock Dividends	56,250*	
	Stock Dividends Distributable		56,250
	Declare 5% common stock dividend.		
	*(40,000 − 2,500) × 5% × $30		
Dec. 1	Cash Dividends Payable	21,250	
	Stock Dividends Distributable	56,250	
	Cash		21,250
	Common Shares		56,250
	Pay cash dividends and distribute stock dividends.		
Dec. 31	Retained Earnings	50,000	
	Appropriation for plant expansion		50,000
	Appropriation declared by board of directors.		

SELF-EXAMINATION QUESTIONS (ANSWERS AT END OF CHAPTER)

1. If a corporation has outstanding 1,000 $9 cumulative preferred no par shares, and dividends have been passed for the preceding three years, what is the amount of preferred dividends that must be declared in the current year before a dividend can be declared on common shares?
   A. $9,000
   B. $27,000
   C. $36,000
   D. $45,000

2. Paid-in capital for a corporation may arise from which of the following sources?
   A. Issuing cumulative preferred shares
   B. Receiving donations of real estate from a shareholder
   C. Extraordinary items
   D. A and B only

3. The Shareholders' Equity section of the balance sheet may include:
   A. Common Shares
   B. Donated Capital
   C. Preferred Shares
   D. All of the above

4. An appropriation for plant expansion would be reported on the balance sheet in the:
   A. Capital Assets section
   B. Long-Term Liabilities section
   C. Shareholders' Equity section
   D. Current Liabilities section

5. A correction of an error in last year's accounting would be reported:
   A. On the income statement
   B. As an extraordinary item
   C. As an adjustment to beginning retained earnings
   D. Ignored

DISCUSSION QUESTIONS

1. Contrast the owners' liability to creditors of (a) a partnership (partners) and (b) a corporation (shareholders).
2. Why are most large businesses organized as corporations?
3. (a) What type of expenditure is charged to the organization costs account?
   (b) Give examples of such expenditures.
   (c) In what section of the balance sheet is the balance of Organization Costs reported?
4. What are the titles of the two principal subdivisions of the Shareholders' Equity section of a corporate balance sheet?
5. Distinguish between paid-in capital and retained earnings of a corporation.
6. The retained earnings account of a corporation at the beginning of the year had a credit balance of $125,000. The only other entry in the account during the year was a debit of $170,000 transferred from the income summary account at the end of the year. (a) What is the term applied to the $170,000 debit? (b) What is the term applied to the debit balance of retained earnings at the end of the year, after all closing entries have been posted?
7. What are the four basic rights that accompany ownership of a common share?
8. a. Differentiate between common shares and preferred shares.
   b. Describe briefly (1) nonparticipating preferred shares, and (2) cumulative preferred shares.
9. A stockbroker advises a client to "buy cumulative preferred shares. . . . With that type of stock, . . .[you] will never have to worry about losing the dividends." Is the broker right?
10. What are some sources of paid-in capital other than the issuance of shares?
11. If a corporation is given land by a shareholder, (a) how should the amount of the debit to the land account be determined, and (b) what is the title of the account that should be credited for the same amount?
12. What are some of the factors that influence the market price of a corporation's shares?
13. Land with a book value of $150,000 is acquired by a corporation for 5,000 common shares, which are currently selling for $35 per share on the Toronto Stock Exchange. Prepare the entry to record the transaction.
14. A corporation reacquires 2,000 of its own common shares for $95,000. The average issue price of the shares was $40. (a) What effect does this transaction have on revenue or expense of the period? (b) What effect does it have on shareholders' equity?
15. Indicate which of the following accounts would be reported as part of paid-in capital on the balance sheet:
   a. Retained Earnings
   b. Common Shares
   c. Donated Capital
   d. Preferred Shares
   e. Cash Dividends Payable
16. a. What is a stock split?
   b. What is the primary purpose of a stock split?
17. What are the three conditions for the declaration and the payment of a cash dividend?
18. The dates in connection with the declaration of a cash dividend are April 1, May 15, and May 30. Identify the significance of each date.
19. A corporation with both cumulative preferred shares and common shares outstanding has a substantial credit balance in its retained earnings account at the beginning of the current fiscal year. Although net income for the current year is sufficient to pay the preferred dividend of $50,000 each quarter and a common dividend of $200,000 each quarter, the board of directors declares dividends only on the preferred shares. Suggest possible reasons for passing the dividends on the common shares.
20. An owner of 200 common shares of Dunston Company receives a stock dividend of four shares. (a) How does the shareholder's total equity of 204 shares compare with his or her total equity of 200 shares before the stock dividend? (b) What is the likely impact of the stock dividend on the shareholder's wealth? Explain.
21. a. Where should a declared but unpaid cash dividend be reported on the balance sheet?
   b. Where should a declared but unissued stock dividend be reported on the balance sheet?
22. What term is used to identify a distribution to shareholders from paid-in capital?

23. Appropriations of retained earnings may be (a) required by contract, or (b) made at the discretion of the board of directors. Give an illustration of each type of appropriation.

24. A credit balance in Retained Earnings does not represent cash. Explain.

25. The board of directors vote to appropriate $250,000 of retained earnings for self-insurance. What is the effect of this action on (a) cash, (b) total retained earnings, and (c) retained earnings available for dividends?

26. Why is it important to report results from discontinued operations separately from income from continuing operations? Describe two types of income or losses that might be reported with respect to discontinued operations.

27. What are the three criteria that must be met before a transaction or event is classified as extraordinary?

28. Give two examples of extraordinary items and two examples of unusual or atypical items. How are unusual items disclosed differently than extraordinary items?

29. What is a retroactive adjustment of retained earnings? How is it disclosed in the financial statements?

30. Differentiate between a change in accounting estimate and a change in accounting policy. Why is it important to account for changes in accounting policies retroactively?

31. Why is the correction of an error in prior year's accounting treated as an adjustment to the beginning balance of retained earnings?

32. a. What two financial statements are frequently combined and presented as a single statement?

    b. What is the major disadvantage of the combined statement?

EXERCISES

EXERCISE 13–1
Dividends per share
Objective 3

Meek Inc., a computer software development firm, has shares outstanding as follows: 20,000 no par $4 cumulative, nonparticipating preferred shares, and 100,000 common no par shares. During its first five years of operations, the following amounts were distributed as dividends: first year, none; second year, $20,000; third year, $80,000; fourth year, $220,000; fifth year, $240,000. Calculate the dividends per share on each class of shares for each of the five years.

EXERCISE 13–2
Entries for issuing shares
Objective 4

On June 5, Goulet Inc., a marble contractor, issued for cash 10,000 common no par shares at $24, and on August 7, it issued for cash 5,000 shares of $2 preferred stock at $14.

a. Journalize the entries for June 5 and August 7.
b. What is the total amount invested (total paid-in capital) by all shareholders as of August 7?

EXERCISE 13–3
Entries for issuing shares
Objective 4

On January 3, Rug Corp., a carpet wholesaler, issued for cash 1,000 no par common shares at $110, and on May 15, it issued 2,000 $3 preferred shares in exchange for legal services worth $22,000.

a. Journalize the entries for January 3 and May 15.
b. What is the total amount invested (total paid-in capital) by all shareholders as of May 15?

EXERCISE 13–4
Issuing shares for assets other than cash
Objective 4

On April 10, Universal Corporation, a wholesaler of hydraulic lifts, acquired land with a book value of $50,000 in exchange for 1,000 no par common shares with a current market price of $60. Journalize the entry to record the transaction.

EXERCISE 13–5
Selected shares transactions
Objective 4

Mojo Guitar Corp., an electric guitar retailer, was organized by Mike Giardinelli, Susan Mirken, and Scott Wooster. The articles on incorporation authorized 20,000 no par common shares. The following transactions affecting shareholders' equity were completed during the first year of operations:

a. Issued 1,000 shares for $10 cash each.
b. Issued 500 shares to Giardinelli for promotional services rendered in connection with the organization of the corporation, and issued 1,500 shares to Giardinelli for cash at $10 each.

c. Purchased land and a building from Mirken. The building is mortgaged for $125,000 for 22 years at 12%, and there is accrued interest of $4,000 on the mortgage note at the time of the purchase. It is agreed that the land is valued at $49,000 and the building at $130,000, and that Mirken's equity will be exchanged for shares. The corporation agreed to assume responsibility for paying the mortgage note and the accrued interest.

Journalize the entries to record the transactions.

EXERCISE 13–6
Issuing shares; reporting paid-in capital
Objectives 4, 6

Embryology Inc., with an authorization of 10,000 shares of preferred and 100,000 shares of common shares, completed several transactions involving its shares on July 1, the first day of operations. The trial balance at the close of the day follows:

Cash	550,000	
Land	110,000	
Buildings	250,000	
Preferred $5 Shares		360,000
Common Shares		550,000
	910,000	910,000

All shares within each class were sold at the same price. The preferred shares were issued in exchange for the land and buildings. The preferred had a market value of $120 each and the common a market value of $55 each.

a. Journalize the two entries to record the transactions summarized in the trial balance.
b. Prepare the Shareholders' Equity section of the balance sheet as of July 1.

EXERCISE 13–7
Corporate organization; shareholders' equity section of balance sheet
Objectives 1, 6

Progressive Products Inc., a wholesaler of office products, was organized on January 7 of the current year, with an authorization of 20,000 shares of $3 noncumulative preferred shares and 100,000 common shares.

The following selected transactions were completed during the first year of operations:

Jan. 7. Issued 15,000 common shares for cash at $20 each.
       9. Issued 100 common shares to a lawyer in payment of legal fees of $2,000 for organizing the corporation.
Feb. 4. Issued 10,000 common shares in exchange for land, buildings, and equipment with fair market prices of $80,000, $120,000, and $25,000 respectively.
Mar. 15. Issued 1,000 preferred shares at $101 for cash.

a. Journalize the transactions.
b. Prepare the Shareholders' Equity section of the balance sheet as of December 31, the end of the current year. The net income for the year amounted to $47,500.

EXERCISE 13–8
Reporting paid-in capital
Objective 6

The following accounts and their balances appear in the ledger of HWY Inc. on April 30 of the current year:

Common Shares, no par	$240,000
Contributed surplus from reacquisition of shares	3,000
Retained Earnings	215,000

Prepare the Shareholders' Equity section of the balance sheet as of June 30. Twenty-five thousand common shares are authorized, and 2,000 shares have been reacquired.

EXERCISE 13–9
Shareholders' equity section of balance sheet
Objective 6

Racorp Inc. retails racing products for BMWs, Porsches, and Ferraris. The following accounts and their balances appear in the ledger of Racorp Inc. on December 31, the end of the current year:

Common Shares, no par, 80,000 issued	$867,500
Contributed surplus from donated land	100,000
Contributed surplus from reacquisition of shares	13,875
Preferred $2 Shares, no par, 5,000 issued	537,500
Retained Earnings	617,000

Ten thousand preferred shares and 150,000 common shares are authorized.

Prepare the Shareholders' Equity section of the balance sheet as of December 31, the end of the current year.

EXERCISE 13–10
Reporting paid-in capital
Objective 6

How many errors can you find in the following Shareholders' Equity section of the balance sheet prepared as of the end of the current year?

Shareholders' Equity		
Paid-in capital:		
Preferred $2 shares, cumulative		
(2,500 shares authorized and issued)		$ 310,000
Unappropriated retained earnings		140,000
Dividends payable		135,000
Total paid-in capital		$ 585,000
Common shares (50,000 shares		
authorized, 40,000 issued)	$810,000	
Appropriated retained earnings for		
plant expansion	200,000	
Donated capital	100,000	
Organization costs	50,000	1,160,000
Total shareholders' equity		$1,745,000

EXERCISE 13–11
Effect of stock split
Objective 7

Patek Corporation wholesales ovens and ranges to restaurants throughout the West. Patek Corporation, which had 10,000 common shares outstanding, declared a five-for-one stock split (four additional shares for each share issued).

a. What will be the number of shares outstanding after the split?
b. If the common shares had a market price of $125 per share before the stock split, what would be an approximate market price per share after the split?

EXERCISE 13–12
Effect of cash dividend
Objective 8

Indicate whether the following actions would (+) increase, (–) decrease, or (0) not affect Webster Inc.'s total assets, liabilities, and shareholders' equity:

		Assets	Liabilities	Shareholders' Equity
(1)	Declaring a cash dividend	_____	_____	_____
(2)	Paying the cash dividend declared in (1)	_____	_____	_____
(3)	Declaring a stock dividend	_____	_____	_____
(4)	Issuing share certificates for the stock dividend declared in (3)	_____	_____	_____
(5)	Authorizing and issuing share certificates in a stock split	_____	_____	_____

EXERCISE 13–13
Entries for cash dividends
Objective 8

The dates of importance in connection with a cash dividend of $35,000 on a corporation's common shares are January 2, January 22, and February 1. Journalize the entries required on each date.

EXERCISE 13–14
Entries for stock dividends
Objective 8

Med-Care Inc. is a home care health agency in southern Ontario. The following account balances appear on the balance sheet of Med-Care Inc.: Common shares (50,000 no par shares authorized, 40,000 issued), $400,000; and Retained earnings, $299,500. The board of directors declared a 4% stock dividend when the market price was $15 a share. Med-Care Inc. reported no income or loss for the current year.

a. Journalize the entries to record (1) the declaration of the dividend, and (2) the issuance of the share certificates.

b. Determine the following amounts before the stock dividend was declared: (1) total paid-in capital, (2) total retained earnings, and (3) total shareholders' equity.
c. Determine the following amounts after the stock dividend was declared and closing entries were recorded at the end of the year: (1) total paid-in capital, (2) total retained earnings, and (3) total shareholders' equity.

EXERCISE 13–15
Retained earnings statement with appropriations
Objective 10

Dorite Corporation, a manufacturer of industrial pumps, reports the following results of transactions affecting net income and retained earnings for its first fiscal year of operations ended on December 31, 20—:

Appropriation for plant expansion	$ 50,000
Cash dividends declared	20,000
Net income	218,000

Prepare a retained earnings statement for the fiscal year ended December 31.

EXERCISE 13–16
Extraordinary item
Objective 9

A company received life insurance proceeds on the death of its president before the end of its fiscal year. It intends to report the amount in its income statement as an extraordinary item. Would this be in conformity with generally accepted accounting principles? Discuss.

EXERCISE 13–17
Identifying extraordinary items
Objective 9

Assume that the amount of each of the following items is material to the financial statements. Classify which items are extraordinary (E). Give reasons for why you classified each item as you did.

a. Loss on disposal of equipment considered to be obsolete because of development of new technology.
b. Uninsured loss on building due to hurricane damage. The firm was organized in 1920 and had not previously incurred hurricane damage.
c. Loss on sale of capital assets.
d. Interest income on notes receivable.
e. Uninsured flood loss. (Flood insurance is unavailable because of periodic flooding in the area.)
f. Salaries of corporate officers.
g. Gain on sale of land expropriated for public use.
h. Uncollectible accounts expense.

EXERCISE 13–18
Income statement
Objectives 9, 10

Nautical Inc. produces and distributes equipment for sailboats. On the basis of the following data for the current fiscal year ended June 30, prepare a multiple-step income statement for Nautical Inc., including earnings per share (10,000 common shares outstanding).

Administrative expenses	$ 36,250
Cost of goods sold	722,500
Cumulative effect on prior years of changing to a different inventory method (decrease in income)	50,000
Gain on expropriation of land (extraordinary item)	37,750
Income tax reduction on prior years' income applicable to change in inventory method	20,000
Income tax applicable to gain on expropriation of land	6,750
Income tax reduction applicable to loss from discontinued operations	45,500
Income tax applicable to ordinary income	107,200
Loss on discontinued operations	114,500
Sales	1,092,500
Selling expenses	65,750

EXERCISE 13–19
Correction of prior period error
Objective 10

Orthotics Company sells supplies to dentists in British Columbia. It reported the following results of transactions affecting retained earnings for the current year ended December 31, 2000:

Net income	$132,500
Dividends	40,000
Error correction for understatement of inventory on December 31, 1999, net of applicable income tax of $12,000	18,000

Assuming that the retained earnings balance reported on the retained earnings statement as of December 31, 1999, was $292,500, prepare a retained earnings statement for the year ended December 31, 2000.

EXERCISE 13–20
Income statement
Objectives 9, 10

Collegium Sound Inc. sells automotive and home stereo equipment. It has 25,000 common shares and 10,000 $2 cumulative preferred shares outstanding as of December 31, 2000. How many errors can you find in the following income statement for the year ended December 31, 2000?

Collegium Sound Inc.
Income Statement
For the Year Ended December 31, 2000

Net sales		$7,650,000
Cost of goods sold		6,100,000
Gross profit		$1,550,000
Operating expenses:		
Selling expenses	$720,000	
Administrative expenses	280,000	1,000,000
Income from continuing operations before income tax		$ 550,000
Income tax		220,000
Income from continuing operations		$ 230,000
Cumulative effect on prior years' income (decrease) of changing to a different inventory method (net of applicable income tax of $36,000)		(92,000)
Correction of error (understatement) in December 31, 1999 physical inventory (net of applicable income tax of $20,000)		30,000
Income before expropriation of land and discontinued operations		$ 168,000
Extraordinary item:		
Gain on expropriation of land, net of applicable income tax of $65,000		150,000
Loss on discontinued operations (net of applicable income tax of $64,000)		(96,000)
Net income		$ 222,000

EXERCISE 13–21
Combined income and retained earnings statement
Objective 11

Rozier Inc. is a wholesaler of surgical equipment to hospitals. Summary operating data for Rozier Inc. during the current year ended August 31, 2000, are as follows: administrative expenses, $125,000; cost of goods sold, $750,000; income tax, $55,000; interest expense, $25,000; net sales, $1,500,000; and selling expenses, $350,000. Assume that the balance of Retained Earnings was $715,000 on September 1, 1999, and that $90,000 of dividends were paid during the year.

a. Prepare a combined income and retained earnings statement for Rozier Inc. (Use the single-step form for the income statement portion.)
b. Prepare the entries to close the income summary account and dividends account to retained earnings.

EXERCISE 13–22
Summary of shareholders' equity changes
Objective 12

The shareholders' equity accounts of Reese Corporation for the current fiscal year ended December 31 are as follows.

COMMON SHARES, NO PAR

Date		Item	Debit	Credit	Balance	
					Debit	Credit
20—						
Jan.	1	Balance 100,000 shares				500,000
May	20	Issued 50,000 shares		210,000		710,000

APPROPRIATION FOR PLANT EXPANSION

Date		Item	Debit	Credit	Balance	
					Debit	Credit
20—						
Dec.	31	Retained earnings		400,000		400,000

RETAINED EARNINGS

Date		Item	Debit	Credit	Balance	
					Debit	Credit
20—						
Jan.	1	Balance				925,000
Dec.	31	Income summary		320,000		1,245,000
	31	Appropriation for plant expansion	400,000			845,000
	31	Cash dividends	15,000			830,000

CASH DIVIDENDS

Date		Item	Debit	Credit	Balance	
					Debit	Credit
20—						
Mar.	12		10,000		10,000	
June	17		5,000		15,000	
Dec.	31	Closing		15,000	—	—

Prepare a summary of changes in shareholders' equity for the fiscal year ended December 31.

PROBLEMS SERIES A

PROBLEM 13–1A
Dividends on preferred and common shares
Objective 3

Omni Inc. owns and operates movie theatres throughout the Maritimes. Omni Inc. has declared the following annual dividends over a six-year period: 1993, $26,000; 1994, $40,000; 1995, $84,000; 1996, $60,000; 1997, $72,000; and 1998, $90,000. During the entire period, the outstanding shares of the company were composed of 5,000 cumulative nonparticipating, $10 preferred no par shares, and 10,000 common no par shares.

Instructions

1. Calculate the total dividends and the per-share dividends declared on each class of shares for each of the six years. There were no dividends in arrears on January 1, 1993. Summarize the data in tabular form, using the following column headings:

Year	Total Dividends	Preferred Dividends		Common Dividends	
		Total	Per Share	Total	Per Share
1993	$26,000				
1994	40,000				
1995	84,000				
1996	60,000				
1997	72,000				
1998	90,000				

2. Calculate the average annual dividend per share for each class of shares for the six-year period.

PROBLEM 13–2A
Corporate expansion; share-holders' equity section of balance sheet
Objectives 3, 6

On January 1 of the current year, the following accounts and their balances appear in the ledger of Medallion Corp., a meat processor:

Preferred $9 Shares, no par (10,000 shares authorized, 5,000 issued)	$ 580,000
Common no par Shares (100,000 shares authorized, 75,000 issued)	1,625,000
Retained Earnings	505,000

At the annual shareholders' meeting on February 11, the board of directors presented a plan for modernizing and expanding plant operations at a cost of approximately $600,000. The plan provided (a) that the corporation borrow $175,000, (b) that 1,000 unissued preferred shares be issued through an underwriter, and (c) that a building, valued at $280,000, and the land on which it is located, valued at $50,000, be acquired in accordance with preliminary negotiations by the issuance of 15,000 common shares. The plan was approved by the shareholders and accomplished by the following transactions:

Mar. 3. Issued 15,000 common shares in exchange for land and a building, according to the plan.
    15. Issued 1,000 preferred shares, receiving $105 per share in cash from the underwriter.
    31. Borrowed $175,000 from Highland National Bank, giving a 12% mortgage note.

No other transactions occurred during March.

Instructions

1. Journalize the entries to record the foregoing transactions.
2. Prepare the Shareholders' Equity section of the balance sheet as of March 31.

PROBLEM 13–3A
Share transactions; shareholders' equity section of balance sheet
Objectives 4, 5, 6, 8, 10, 12

The following selected accounts appear in the ledger of Commack Environmental Corporation on July 1, 1998, the beginning of the current fiscal year:

Preferred $2 Shares, no par (10,000 shares authorized, 7,000 issued)	$378,000
Common no par Shares (50,000 shares authorized, 25,000 issued)	590,000
Retained Earnings	537,000

During the year, the corporation completed a number of transactions affecting the shareholders' equity. They are summarized as follows:

a. Reacquired 2,000 of the company's own common shares for $55,000.
b. Issued 5,000 common shares at $30, receiving cash.
c. Sold 1,000 preferred shares at $52.50.
d. Declared cash dividends of $2 per share on preferred shares and $1 per share on common shares.
e. Paid the cash dividends.

Instructions

1. Journalize the entries to record the transactions. Identify each entry by letter.
2. Prepare a note on shareholders' equity changes for the year ended June 30, 1999, the end of the current fiscal year. The net income for the year was $165,000.
3. Prepare the Shareholders' Equity section of the balance sheet as of June 30, 1999.

PROBLEM 13–4A
Entries for selected corporate transactions
Objectives 4, 5, 6, 8, 10

Schulman Enterprises Inc. manufactures bathroom fixtures. The shareholders' equity accounts of Schulman Enterprises Inc., with balances on January 1 of the current fiscal year, are as follows:

Common Shares, no par (100,000 shares authorized, 50,000 issued)	$1,500,000
Appropriation for Plant Expansion	150,000
Retained Earnings	725,000

The following selected transactions occurred during the year:

Jan. 20. Received land from a shareholder as a donation. The land had an estimated fair market value of $100,000.

Jan. 29. Paid cash dividends of $1 per share on the common shares. The dividend had been properly recorded when declared on December 30 of the preceding fiscal year for $47,500.

Apr. 1. Issued 6,000 common shares for $240,000.

July 1. Declared a 2% stock dividend on common shares when the market price of the stock was $40 a share.

Aug. 11. Issued the certificates for the dividend declared on July 1.

Nov. 20. Reacquired 2000 of the company's own common shares for $72,000.

Dec. 21. The board of directors authorized an increase of the appropriation for plant expansion by $50,000.

    21. Declared a $0.50-per-share dividend on common shares.

    31. Closed the credit balance of the income summary account, $169,400.

    31. Closed the two dividends accounts to Retained Earnings.

Instructions

1. Enter the January 1 balances in T accounts for the shareholders' equity accounts listed.
2. Journalize the entries to record the transactions, and post to T accounts.
3. Prepare the Shareholders' Equity section of the balance sheet as of December 31 of the current fiscal year.

PROBLEM 13–5A
Entries for selected corporate transactions
Objectives 5, 7, 8

Selected transactions completed by Chempar Boating Supply Corporation during the current fiscal year are as follows:

Jan. 9. Split the common shares four-for-one. After the split, there were 100,000 common shares outstanding. Before the split, the total share capital for common shares was $4,000,000.

Feb. 10. Purchased 5,000 shares of the corporation's own common shares at $42.

May 1. Declared semi-annual dividends of $3 on 5,000 preferred shares and $1 on the common shares to shareholders of record on May 20, payable on July 15.

July 15. Paid the cash dividends.

Nov. 30. Declared semi-annual dividends of $3 on the preferred shares and $0.80 on the common shares. In addition, a 2% common stock dividend was declared on the common shares outstanding. The fair market value of the common shares is $51.

Dec. 30. Paid the cash dividends and issued the certificates for the common stock dividend.

Instructions

Journalize the transactions.

PROBLEM 13–6A
Retained earnings statement
Objective 11

For the current fiscal year ended December 31, the retained earnings accounts of Dermo Corporation, a pharmaceutical company specializing in skin ointments, are as follows:

APPROPRIATION FOR PLANT EXPANSION

Date		Item	Debit	Credit	Balance	
					Debit	Credit
20—						
Jan.	1	Balance				250,000
Dec.	31	Retained earnings		75,000		325,000

RETAINED EARNINGS

Date		Item	Debit	Credit	Balance	
					Debit	Credit
20—						
Jan.	1	Balance				715,000
Dec.	31	Income summary		185,000		900,000
	31	Appropriation for plant expansion	75,000			825,000
	31	Cash dividends	100,000			725,000
	31	Stock dividends	150,000			575,000

CASH DIVIDENDS

Date		Item	Debit	Credit	Balance	
					Debit	Credit
20—						
July	27		100,000		100,000	
Dec.	31	Retained earnings		100,000	—	—

STOCK DIVIDENDS

Date		Item	Debit	Credit	Balance	
					Debit	Credit
20—						
July	27		150,000		150,000	
Dec.	31	Retained earnings		150,000	—	—

Instructions
Prepare a retained earnings statement for the fiscal year ended December 31.

PROBLEMS SERIES B

PROBLEM 13–1B
Dividends on preferred and common shares
Objective 3

Banyon Corp. manufactures mountain bikes and distributes them through retail outlets in Canada. Banyon Corp. has declared the following annual dividends over a six-year period: 1993, $30,000; 1994, $15,000; 1995, $10,000; 1996, $4,000; 1997, $50,000; and 1998, $75,000. During the entire period, the outstanding no par shares of the company were composed of 10,000 cumulative, nonparticipating, $2 preferred no par shares, and 25,000 common no par shares.

Instructions

1. Calculate the total dividends and the per-share dividends declared on each class of shares for each of the six years. There were $20,000 dividends in arrears on January 1, 1993. Summarize the data in tabular form, using the following column headings:

Year	Total Dividends	Preferred Dividends		Common Dividends	
		Total	Per Share	Total	Per Share
1993	$30,000				
1994	15,000				
1995	10,000				
1996	4,000				
1997	50,000				
1998	75,000				

2. Calculate the average annual dividend per share for each class of shares for the six-year period.
3. Assuming that the preferred shares were sold for $500,000 and common shares were sold at $15 at the beginning of the six-year period, calculate the percentage dividend return on initial shareholders' investment, based on the average annual dividend per share (a) for preferred and (b) for common.

PROBLEM 13–2B
Corporate expansion; shareholders' equity section of balance sheet
Objectives 3, 6

Sangean Corp. produces medical lasers for use in hospitals. The following accounts and their balances appear in the ledger of Sangean Corp. on April 30 of the current year:

Preferred $9 no par Shares (10,000 shares authorized, 8,000 issued)	$ 886,000
Common Shares, no par (100,000 shares authorized, 75,000 issued)	1,710,000
Retained Earnings	715,000

At the annual shareholders' meeting on May 12, the board of directors presented a plan for modernizing and expanding plant operations at a cost of approximately $750,000. The plan provided (a) that the corporation borrow $200,000, (b) that 1,000 unissued preferred shares be issued through an underwriter, and (c) that a building, valued at $355,000, and the land on which it is located, valued at $100,000, be acquired in accordance with preliminary negotiations by the issuance of 18,000 common shares. The plan was approved by the shareholders and accomplished by the following transactions:

June 2. Issued 18,000 common shares in exchange for land and a building, according to the plan.
    10. Issued 1,000 preferred shares, receiving $105 per share in cash from the underwriter.
    30. Borrowed $200,000 from Palmer National Bank, giving a 14% mortgage note.

No other transactions occurred during June.

Instructions

1. Journalize the entries to record the foregoing transactions.
2. Prepare the Shareholders' Equity section of the balance sheet as of June 30.

PROBLEM 13–3B
Share transactions; shareholders' equity section of balance sheet
Objectives 4, 5, 6, 8, 10, 11

Cardinal Corporation sells and services pipe welding equipment in Ontario. The following selected accounts appear in the ledger of Cardinal Corporation on January 1, 2000, the beginning of the current fiscal year:

Preferred $3 no par Shares (20,000 shares authorized, 12,500 issued)	$1,362,500
Common no par Shares (600,000 shares authorized, 400,000 issued)	4,500,000
Contributed surplus from previous reacquisition of shares	10,000
Retained Earnings	1,450,000

During the year, the corporation completed a number of transactions affecting the shareholders' equity. They are summarized as follows:

a. Reacquired 15,000 of the company's own common shares for $180,000.
b. Sold 2,000 preferred $3 shares at $105.
c. Issued 50,000 common shares at $15, receiving cash.
d. Declared cash dividends of $3 per share on preferred shares and $0.25 per share on common shares.
e. Paid the cash dividends.

Instructions

1. Journalize the entries to record the transactions. Identify each entry by letter.
2. Prepare a note on changes in shareholders' equity (share accounts) for the year ended December 31, 2000. The net income for the year was $750,000.
3. Prepare the Shareholders' Equity section of the balance sheet as of December 31, 2000.

PROBLEM 13–4B
Entries for selected corporate transactions
Objectives 4, 5, 6, 8, 10, 12

Kahn Enterprises Inc. produces aeronautical navigation equipment. The shareholders' equity accounts of Khan Enterprises Inc., with balances on January 1 of the current fiscal year, are as follows:

Common no par Shares (100,000 shares authorized, 80,000 issued)	$910,000
Appropriation for Plant Expansion	175,000
Retained Earnings	497,750

The following selected transactions occurred during the year:

Jan. 31. Paid cash dividends of $1 per common share. The dividend had been properly recorded when declared on December 28 of the preceding fiscal year for $76,000.
May 5. Issued 10,000 common shares for $155,000.
June 11. Received a grant for land from the Olinville City Council as a donation. The land had an estimated fair market value of $150,000.
July 30. Declared a 4% stock dividend on common shares, when the market price was $16 a share.
Aug. 27. Issued the certificates for the dividend declared on July 30.
Oct. 8. Purchased 2,500 shares of the corporation's own common shares for $42,500.

Dec. 20. Declared an $0.80-per-share dividend on common shares.

     20. The board of directors authorized an increase of the appropriation for plant expansion by $75,000.

     31. Closed the credit balance of the income summary account, $182,500.

     31. Closed the two dividends accounts to Retained Earnings.

Instructions

1. Enter the January 1 balances in T accounts for the shareholders' equity accounts listed.
2. Journalize the entries to record the transactions, and post to T accounts.
3. Prepare the Shareholders' Equity section of the balance sheet as of December 31 of the current fiscal year.

PROBLEM 13–5B
Entries for selected corporate transactions
Objectives 5, 7, 8, 10

Malibu Corporation manufactures and distributes leisure clothing. Selected transactions completed by Malibu Corporation during the current fiscal year are as follows:

Jan.   2. Split the common shares five for one when total share capital for common was $200,000 and the market value was $14 per share. After the split, there were 75,000 common shares outstanding.

Mar. 3. Declared semi-annual dividends of $3 on 10,000 preferred shares and $0.40 on the 75,000 common shares to shareholders of record on March 28, payable on April 15.

Apr. 15. Paid the cash dividends.

    30. Purchased 8,000 shares of the corporation's own common shares at $2.50.

July 23. Declared semi-annual dividends of $3 on the preferred shares and $0.40 on the common shares. In addition, a 2% common stock dividend was declared on the common shares outstanding, to be capitalized at the fair market value of $2.70 per share.

Aug. 25. Paid the cash dividends and issued the certificates for the common shares dividend.

Instructions
Journalize the transactions.

PROBLEM 13–6B
Retained earnings statement
Objective 11

Nederland Corporation produces and sells playground equipment. The retained earnings accounts of Nederland Corporation for the current fiscal year ended December 31 are as follows:

APPROPRIATION FOR REPAYMENT OF LONG-TERM DEBT

Date		Item	Debit	Credit	Balance	
					Debit	Credit
20—						
Jan.	1	Balance				200,000
Dec.	31	Retained earnings	200,000			

RETAINED EARNINGS

Date		Item	Debit	Credit	Balance	
					Debit	Credit
20—						
Jan.	1	Balance				515,000
June	1	Correction for prior period error in recording ending inventory (net of tax effect of $20,000)	25,000			490,000
Dec.	31	Income summary		215,000		705,000
	31	Appropriation for repayment of long-term debt		200,000		905,000
	31	Cash dividends	50,000			855,000
	31	Stock dividends	120,000			735,000

CASH DIVIDENDS

Date		Item	Debit	Credit	Balance	
					Debit	Credit
20—						
Apr.	10		25,000		25,000	
Oct.	13		25,000		50,000	
Dec.	31	Retained earnings		50,000	—	—

STOCK DIVIDENDS

Date		Item	Debit	Credit	Balance	
					Debit	Credit
20—						
Oct.	13		120,000		120,000	
Dec.	31	Retained earnings		120,000	—	—

Instructions

Prepare a retained earnings statement for the fiscal year ended December 31.

CHALLENGE PROBLEMS

PROBLEM CP13–1

Abco Limited has the following balances in its Shareholders' Equity accounts at the end of December of the current year:

Common Shares, no par, 95,000 authorized, 52,500 issued	$4,747,500
Preferred Shares, no par, $5 dividend, 20,000 authorized and issued	2,000,000
Appropriated Retained Earnings	600,000
Unappropriated Retained Earnings	1,250,000
Contributed Surplus	35,000

A review of the records indicates that the following transactions took place during the year.

1. Issued 5,000 preferred shares in January for $100 each.
2. Reacquired 5,000 common shares in February at $88.20 each. The average book value at the time was $90.20.
3. Declared dividends for the current year on preferred shares June 30.
4. Declared a $3 cash dividend on common shares June 30.
5. Issued a 5% stock dividend on common shares Oct. 31 when the market price was $95.
6. Transferred $400,000 to retained earnings appropriated for bond retirement.
7. Made a $15,000 adjustment (net of applicable taxes) to correct an overstatement of inventory at the end of the prior year.
8. Reported an extraordinary loss of $75,000 (after applicable taxes).
9. Reported net income of $800,000 for the current year.

All transactions were properly accounted for during the year.

Instructions

Reconstruct the balances in each of the shareholders' equity accounts at the beginning of the year.

PROBLEM CP13–2

A review of the records of Zedco indicates that the new bookkeeper made the following entries during the current year:

1. Over the past five years, Zedco established an Appropriation for Plant Expansion, which had a balance of $150,000 at the beginning of the current year. A $100,000 addition to a building made halfway through the current year was recorded by debiting Appropriation for Plant Expansion and crediting Cash. The addition had an expected life of 10 years.

2. During the year Zedco repurchased for $100 per share 10,000 of its own common shares that had originally been issued for $104.45 per share. The bookkeeper recorded a gain of $44,500 as Other Income.

3. Upon discovering that the previous year's amortization expense had been understated by $30,000 due to an addition error, the bookkeeper corrected the error by increasing the current year's charge to amortization by $30,000.

4. During the year a shareholder donated to Zedco a piece of land that had a book value of $20,000 and a fair market value of $50,000. The bookkeeper recorded the transaction by debiting Land for $20,000 and crediting Other Income for $20,000.

5. Common share dividends declared and paid in the amount of $122,000 were recorded by a debit to Other Expense and a credit to Cash.

6. A 10% stock dividend was accounted for as a stock split. When the dividend was declared, 61,000 common shares were outstanding with a book value of $6.00 and a market price of $6.50 per share.

Instructions

Indicate the effect of each of the above entries made by the bookkeeper on the following totals that would appear in Zedco's year end financial statements. Indicate whether the bookkeeper's entry would cause the item to be understated (U), overstated (O) and by what amount, or if the entry would not cause the item to be in error in the year end financial statements (NE).

	Assets	Paid-in Capital	Retained Earnings	Net Income
1.				
2.				
3.				
4.				
5.				
6.				

CASES

CASE 13–1
Mines Unlimited Ltd.
Value of shares

Ignacio Maglie and Don Tomlin are organizing Mines Unlimited Ltd. to undertake a high-risk gold-mining venture in Mexico. Ignacio and Don tentatively plan to request authorization for 100,000,000 common shares to be sold to the general public.

Ignacio and Don have decided to establish par of $0.10 per share in order to appeal to a wide variety of potential investors. Ignacio and Don feel that investors would be more willing to invest in the company if they received a large quantity of shares for what might appear to be a "bargain" price.

➤ Discuss whether Ignacio and Don are behaving in an ethical manner.

CASE 13–2
Protection-Plus Ltd.
Issuing shares

Protection-Plus Ltd. began operations on January 3, 1999, with the issuance of 25,000 common shares. The sole shareholders of Protection-Plus Ltd. are Judi Barnett and Dr. Herman Elfand, who orga-

nized Protection-Plus Ltd. with the objective of developing a new flu vaccine. Dr. Elfand claims that the flu vaccine, which is nearing the final development stage, will protect individuals against 99% of the flu types that have been medically identified. To complete the project, Protection-Plus Ltd. needs

$1,500,000 of additional funds. The local banks have been unwilling to loan the funds because of the lack of sufficient collateral and the riskiness of the business.

The following is a conversation between Judi Barnett, the chief executive officer of Protection-Plus Ltd., and Dr. Herman Elfand, the leading researcher.

Barnett: What are we going to do? The banks won't loan us any more money, and we've got to have $1.5 million to complete the project. We are so close! It would be a disaster to quit now. The only thing I can think of is to issue additional shares. Do you have any suggestions?

Elfand: I guess you're right. But if the banks won't loan us any more money, how do you think we can find any investors to buy shares?

Barnett: I've been thinking about that. What if we promise the investors that we will pay them 2% of net sales until they have received an amount equal to what they paid for the shares?

Elfand: What happens when we pay back the $1.5 million? Do the investors get to keep the shares? If they do, it'll dilute our ownership.

Barnett: How about, if after we pay back the $1.5 million, we make them turn in their shares for $200 per share? That's twice what they paid for it, plus they would have already gotten all their money back. That's a $200 profit per share for the investors.

Elfand: It could work. We get our money, but don't have to pay any interest, dividends, or the $200 until we start generating net sales. At the same time, the investors could get their money back plus $200 per share.

Barnett: We'll need current financial statements for the new investors. I'll get our accountant working on them and contact our lawyer to draw up a legally binding contract for the new investors. Yes, this could work.

In late 1999, the lawyer and the various regulatory authorities approved the new share offering, and 15,000 common shares were privately sold to new investors at $100 per share.

In preparing financial statements for 1999, Judi Barnett and Ed Thaxton, the controller for Protection-Plus Ltd., have the following conversation.

Thaxton: Judi, I've got a problem.
Barnett: What's that, Ed?
Thaxton: Issuing common shares to raise that additional $1.5 million was a great idea. But. . .
Barnett: But what?
Thaxton: I've got to prepare the 1999 annual financial statements, and I am not sure how to classify the common shares.
Barnett: What do you mean? It's common shares.
Thaxton: I'm not so sure. I called the auditor and explained how we are contractually obligated to pay the new shareholders 2% of net sales until $100 per share is paid. Then, we may be obligated to pay them $200 per share.
Barnett: So. . .
Thaxton: So the auditor thinks that we should classify the additional issuance of $1.5 million as debt, not equity! And, if we put the $1.5 million on the balance sheet as debt, we will violate our other loan agreements with the banks. And, if these agreements are violated, the banks may call in all our debt immediately. If they do that, we are in deep trouble. We'll probably have to file for bankruptcy. We just don't have the cash to pay off the banks.

1. ◖▬▬➤ Discuss the arguments for and against classifying the issuance of the $1.5 million of shares as debt.
2. ◖▬▬➤ What do you think might be a practical solution to this classification problem?

CASE 13–3
Sears Canada Inc.
Financial analysis

 Two profitability measures included in the stock quotations that appear daily in *The Globe and Mail* and similar publications are the price-earnings ratio and the dividend yield per common share. The price-earnings (P/E) ratio is an indication of a firm's future earnings prospects and is computed as follows:

$$\frac{\text{Price-Earnings}}{\text{Ratio}} = \frac{\text{Market Price per Common Share}}{\text{Earnings per Common Share}}$$

The market price per common share is the price at a specific date, and the earnings are the annual earnings per common share. A high P/E ratio indicates that investors expect the company's earnings to be above average for comparable companies.

The dividend yield is a profitability measure that shows the rate of return to common shareholders in terms of cash dividends. It is computed as follows:

$$\frac{\text{Dividend}}{\text{Yield}} = \frac{\text{Dividends per Common Share}}{\text{Market Price per Common Share}}$$

The dividends per common share are the annual dividends per share, and the market price per common share is the price at a specific date. Dividend yield is of special interest to investors who look for a current return (dividend) from their investment.

a. Determine Sears Canada Inc.'s price-earnings ratio on December 31 of the current and preceding years. The common share price was $19.80 and $10.10 respectively.
b. Determine Sears's dividend yield as of December 31 of the current and preceding years.
c. ◖▬▬➤ What conclusions can you reach from an analysis of these data?

CASE 13–4
Digital Corp.
Dividends

Digital Corp. has paid quarterly cash dividends since 1987. These dividends have steadily increased from $0.20 per share to the latest dividend declaration of $0.50 per share. The board of directors would like to continue this trend and is hesitant to suspend or decrease the amount of quarterly dividends. Unfortunately, sales dropped sharply in the fourth quarter of 1999 because of worsening economic conditions and increased competition. As a result, the board is uncertain as to whether it should declare a dividend for the last quarter of 1999.

On November 1, 1999, Digital Corp. borrowed $500,000 from The Royal Bank to use in modernizing its retail stores and to expand its product line in reaction to its competition. The terms of the 10-year, 12% loan require Digital Corp. to:

a. Pay monthly interest on last day of month.
b. Pay $50,000 of the principal each November 1, beginning in 2000.
c. Maintain a current ratio (current assets ÷ current liabilities) of 2:1.
d. Appropriate $500,000 of retained earnings until the loan is fully paid.
e. Maintain a minimum balance (a compensating balance) of $25,000 in its Royal Bank account.

On December 31, 1999, 25% of the $500,000 loan had been disbursed in modernization of the retail stores and in expansion of the product line, and the remainder is temporarily invested in Term Deposits. Digital Corp.'s balance sheet as of December 31, 1999, is as follows:

Digital Corp.
Balance Sheet
December 31, 1999

Assets

Current assets:			
Cash			$ 44,500
Marketable securities			375,000
Accounts receivable		$ 91,500	
Less allowance for doubtful accounts		6,500	85,000
Inventory			120,500
Prepaid expenses			4,500
Total current assets			$ 629,500
Capital assets:			
Land			150,000
Buildings		950,000	
Less accumulated amortization		215,000	735,000
Equipment		460,000	
Less accumulated amortization		110,000	350,000
Total capital assets			1,235,000
Total assets			$1,864,500

Liabilities

Current liabilities:			
Accounts payable		$ 71,800	
Notes payable (Royal Bank)		50,000	
Salaries payable		3,200	
Total current liabilities			$125,000
Long-term liabilities:			
12% Notes payable (Royal Bank)			450,000
Total liabilities			$ 575,000

Shareholders' Equity

Paid-in capital:			
Common no par shares (50,000 shares authorized, 25,000 issued)			540,000
Retained earnings:			
Appropriated for provision of Royal Bank loan		500,000	
Unappropriated		249,500	
Total retained earnings			749,500
Total shareholders' equity			1,289,500
Total liabilities and shareholders' equity			$1,864,500

The board of directors is scheduled to meet January 10, 2000, to discuss the results of operations for 1999 and to consider the declaration of dividends for the fourth quarter of 1999. The chairman of the board has asked for your advice on the declaration of dividends.

1. ◖▬▬▶ What factors should the board consider in deciding whether to declare a cash dividend?

2. ◖▬▬▶ The board is considering the declaration of a stock dividend instead of a cash dividend. Discuss the issuance of a stock dividend from the point of view of (a) a shareholder and (b) the board of directors.

ANSWERS TO SELF-EXAMINATION QUESTIONS

1. **C** If a corporation has cumulative preferred shares outstanding, dividends that have been passed for prior years plus the dividend for the current year must be paid before dividends may be declared on common shares. In this case, dividends of $27,000 ($9,000 × 3) have been passed for the preceding three years, and the current year's dividends are $9,000, making a total of $36,000 (answer C) that must be paid to preferred shareholders before dividends can be declared on common shares.

2. **D** Paid-in capital is one of the two major subdivisions of the shareholders' equity of a corporation. It may result from many sources, including the issuance of cumulative preferred shares (answer A), and the receipt of donated real estate (answer B). Hence, answer D is correct. Extraordinary items (answer C) are included in net income, which is closed to retained earnings. Retained earnings are reported in Shareholders' Equity separately from paid-in capital.

3. **D** The Shareholders' Equity section of corporate balance sheets is divided into two principal subsections: (1) investments contributed by the shareholders and others and (2) net income retained in the business. Included as part of the investments by shareholders and others is common shares (answer A), donated capital (answer B), and the preferred shares (answer C).

4. **C** An appropriation for plant expansion is a portion of total retained earnings and would be reported in the Shareholders' Equity section of the balance sheet (answer C).

5. **C** A correction of a prior period accounting error is reported as an adjustment to the beginning retained earnings balance (answer C).

14 Bonds and Other Long-Term Liabilities

YOU AND ACCOUNTING

You have just inherited $50,000 from a distant relative, and you are considering some options for investing the money. Some of your friends have suggested that you invest it in long-term bonds. As a result, you have contacted a broker who has presented you with a listing of bonds being currently traded in the Canadian bond market. You've identified the following two listings as possible bond investments, both of which mature in the year 2003:

Ontario Hydro 13½% Bonds
Thomson Corporation 7.7% Bonds

The Ontario Hydro bonds are selling for 123, while the Thomson bonds are selling for 109½. Does this mean that the Thomson Corporation bonds are a better buy? Does the 13½% mean that if you buy the Ontario Hydro bonds you can actually earn 13½% interest?

In this chapter, we will answer each of these questions. We first discuss the advantages and disadvantages of financing a corporation's operations by issuing debt rather than equity. We then discuss the accounting principles related to long-term debt from both the issuer's and the investor's perspective. Finally, we discuss accounting for other long-term liabilities such as notes payable, lease obligations, pension liabilities, and future income tax liabilities.

Financing Corporations

Objective 1
Compute the potential impact of long-term borrowing on the earnings per share of a corporation.

Corporations often finance their operations by issuing long-term notes or bonds. We have discussed notes receivable and short-term notes payable in earlier chapters. A bond is similar to a long-term note payable. Like a note, a bond requires repayment of its principal at its maturity date and usually requires periodic interest payments. As we discussed in Chapter 11, some notes are non-interest bearing. Similarly, some bonds are issued with a "zero" stated interest rate and require no periodic interest payments. Typically, a business will issue a note payable to a single creditor, such as a bank or supplier. However, a bond issuance will usually involve the sale of a large number of bonds (in denominations such as $1,000) to a number of different investors (or bondholders). A company will usually employ an underwriter to sell its bonds. The underwriter is a securities firm that either sells the bonds for a commission or purchases the entire bond issue and sells it to its clients. The bondholders are creditors of the issuing corporation, and their claims on the assets of the business rank ahead of the company's shareholders.

Several factors will influence a company's decision as to whether it should issue debt or equity (shares) in order to raise capital. One advantage of issuing bonds is that interest paid to bondholders is deductible in computing the taxable income of the corporation, whereas dividends paid to shareholders are not tax deductible. Another advantage is that the issuance of bonds does not dilute the ownership interest of the current shareholders. For example, suppose that you own 1,000 of the 20,000 shares outstanding in Brix Company, which needs to raise $1,000,000 for a new plant expansion. Brix has two choices for raising the funds: (1) issue 1,000 bonds of $1,000 denomination or (2) issue 10,000 new shares at $100 each. If Brix chooses option (1), your ownership of the business remains unchanged at 5% (1,000 ÷ 20,000 shares). However, under option (2) your ownership interest will decline to 3.3% (1,000 ÷ 30,000 shares) unless you buy 5% of the new shares issued—an additional investment of $50,000 (5% × 10,000 shares × $100).

Both the tax deductibility of interest and the impact on ownership interest must be taken into account in analysing the impact on earnings per share of the decision to issue debt or equity. To illustrate the possible effects, assume that a corporation's board of directors is considering three alternative plans for financing a $4,000,000 company. In each case, the company will issue the securities at their par or face amount. The corporation is expecting to earn $800,000 annually, before deducting interest on the bonds and estimates income tax at 40% of pretax income. Exhibit 1 shows the effect of the three plans on the income of the corporation and its common shareholders.

Under Plan 1, all the financing is from issuing common shares. In this case, the earnings per share is $1.20. Under Plan 2, one-half of the financing is from issuing 20,000 $9 preferred shares, and one-half is from issuing common shares. In this case, earnings per share are $1.50. Under Plan 3, one-half of the financing is from issuing 12% $2,000,000 bonds, and the remaining one-half is equally split between issuing 10,000 $9 preferred shares and common shares. In this case, earnings per share are $2.46.

In Exhibit 1, Plan 3 is the most attractive for common shareholders. Using debt to make investments that increase returns to common shareholders is known as "trading on the equity." If the estimated earnings are more than $800,000, the difference between the earnings per share under Plan 1 and Plan 3 is even greater. However, if smaller earnings occur, Plans 2 and 3 become less attractive. Exhibit 2 shows the effect of earnings of $440,000 rather than $800,000.

Exhibit 1

Effect of Alternative Financing Plans—$800,000 Earnings

	Plan 1	Plan 2	Plan 3
12% bonds	—	—	$2,000,000
Preferred $9 shares	—	$2,000,000	1,000,000
Common shares	$4,000,000	2,000,000	1,000,000
Total	$4,000,000	$4,000,000	$4,000,000
Earnings before interest and income tax	$ 800,000	$ 800,000	$ 800,000
Deduct interest on bonds	—	—	240,000
Income before income tax (40%)	$ 800,000	$ 800,000	$ 560,000
Deduct income tax	320,000	320,000	224,000
Net income	$ 480,000	$ 480,000	$ 336,000
Dividends on preferred shares	—	180,000	90,000
Available for dividends on common shares	$ 480,000	$ 300,000	$ 246,000
Common shares outstanding	400,000	200,000	100,000
Earnings per common share	$1.20	$1.50	$2.46

Exhibit 2

Effect of Alternative Financing Plans—$440,000 Earnings

	Plan 1	Plan 2	Plan 3
12% bonds	—	—	$2,000,000
Preferred $9 shares	—	$2,000,000	1,000,000
Common shares	$4,000,000	2,000,000	1,000,000
Total	$4,000,000	$4,000,000	$4,000,000
Earnings before interest and income tax	$ 440,000	$ 440,000	$ 440,000
Deduct interest on bonds	—	—	240,000
Income before income tax	$ 440,000	$ 440,000	$ 200,000
Deduct income tax	176,000	176,000	80,000
Net income	$ 264,000	$ 264,000	$ 120,000
Dividends on preferred shares	—	180,000	90,000
Available for dividends on common shares	$ 264,000	$ 84,000	$ 30,000
Common shares outstanding	400,000	200,000	100,000
Earnings per common share	$0.66	$0.42	$0.30

In addition to the effect on earnings per share, the board should consider other factors in deciding whether to issue debt or equity. For example, once bonds are issued, periodic interest payments and repayment of principal are beyond the control of the corporation. That is, if the company fails to make these payments, the bondholders could seek court action and potentially force the company into bankruptcy. In contrast, a corporation is not legally obligated to pay dividends. This is one disadvantage of issuing bonds. Increased debt increases the riskiness of the firm, whereas raising capital by issuing equity will reduce the likelihood of the company becoming insolvent in the future.

When interest rates are low, corporations are more likely to finance their operations with debt. For example, as interest rates fell in the early 1990s, corporations rushed to issue new debt.

Characteristics of Bonds Payable

Objective 2
Describe the characteristics of bonds.

A corporation that issues bonds enters into a contract, called a bond indenture or trust indenture, with the bondholders. A bond issue is normally divided into a number of individual bonds, which may be of varying denominations. Usually the principal of each bond (also called the face value, maturity value, or par value) is $1,000 or a multiple of $1,000. The bonds may pay interest annually, semi-annually,

USING ACCOUNTING TO UNDERSTAND BUSINESS

Some of the same factors that influence a corporation's decision on financing are also considered when a company refinances, or changes the structure of its debt and shareholders' equity. These concerns are described in the following excerpt from an article in *USA TODAY*.

When a major company like Allegis Corp. announces that it is "recapitalizing" [refinancing], many shareholders may be baffled. . . . Recapitalization plans aren't as complicated as they seem, however. . . .

How companies balance equity and debt is up to them. At IBM Corp., only 11% of total capital is debt. Sears, Roebuck and Co. has 46% debt. The level of debt a company keeps depends on the risk its managers are willing to assume.

What does risk have to do with it?

It's no different for a company than for an individual. The more debt you have, the greater the risk. Reason: Any profit you earn first must go to meet interest payments. If earnings aren't sufficient to cover the interest owed, you'll have to deplete your savings—or sell something—to raise the needed cash.

What happens in a recapitalization?

A company decides to borrow heavily to raise cash for a large, one-time cash . . . payment to shareholders. . . . [In addition,] . . . shareholders also receive new shares to replace their old shares in the company. . . . [In] the process, the company generally [reduces its equity]. It's replaced with debt.

How can the company afford the debt load?

The company is forced to operate more efficiently than ever. It will have to slash expenses to keep earnings up in the face of higher interest expenses. Owens-Corning Fiberglas Corp., for example, pared its research costs significantly after its recapitalization last year. . . .

Is there any advantage in being so heavily in debt?

Debt does have a good side. By borrowing, you gain "leverage"—the ability to control more assets by using someone else's money. That can magnify the return to shareholders, if business is good and the firm operates efficiently. . . .

Source: Neil Budde, "How Company Recapitalization Plans Work," *USA TODAY*, June 8, 1987.

or quarterly. Most bonds pay interest semi-annually. The interest payments are computed by multiplying the face value by the rate shown on the bond certificate. This is the contract rate of interest, also called the stated, nominal, or coupon rate.

Bonds may have various different characteristics. They may be either registered in the name of the bondholder or unregistered (also called bearer bonds). For registered bonds the issuing company must keep up-to-date records of who owns each bond, and will make payments of interest and principal only to the registered owners. Bearer bonds are payable to whoever is holding the bonds.

The prices of bonds are quoted on bond exchanges as a percentage of the bonds' face value. Thus, investors could purchase or sell BC Tel bonds quoted at 110½ for $1,105. Likewise, bonds quoted at 99 could be purchased or sold for $990.

When all bonds of an issue mature at the same time, they are called term bonds. If the maturities are spread over several dates, they are called serial bonds. For example, one-tenth of an issue of $1,000,000 bonds, or $100,000, may mature 16 years from the issuance date, another $100,000 in the 17th year, and so on until the final $100,000 matures in the 25th year.

Bonds may be either secured by specific assets of the issuing company or unsecured. If the issuer fails to make a payment on secured bonds, the bondholder can claim the specific assets pledged as collateral and apply any proceeds from their sale towards repayment of the debt. A company that issues unsecured bonds, also called debentures, is relying on investor confidence in the firm's reputation as a good credit risk.

Convertible bonds are those that allow the investor to exchange the debt for other securities (usually common shares) according to conditions specified in the bond indenture. For example, the agreement may allow the bondholder to convert a $1,000 bond to 10 common shares five years after the issuance date of the bond. Whether or not the conversion takes place is *at the option of the bondholder.* In this example, suppose that the bond's market value is equal to its face value. If the common shares are trading at only $95, the conversion will not take place since the $1,000 bond is worth more than the total market value of 10 common shares (10 × $95 = $950). However, if the market price of the common shares increases to $120, the bondholder should convert the bond for 10 common shares worth a total of $1,200 (10 × $120). The conversion feature allows the bondholder to benefit from increases in the market value of the common shares. Thus, investors will be willing to pay a higher price for a convertible bond than for an otherwise identical bond that is nonconvertible.

Callable bonds are those that may be redeemed before maturity *at the option of the issuer.* The bond indenture will state the date(s) and price at which the bonds can be recalled. A corporation often issues callable bonds to protect itself against significant declines in future interest rates. If rates fall substantially, the company can then recall the old bonds and issue new ones at the lower rate. However, callable bonds are more risky for bondholders, who will not likely be able to replace the called bonds with similar investments paying as high a return. Thus, investors will prefer noncallable bonds and will not be willing to pay as high a price for an otherwise identical callable bond.

The Present-Value Concept and Bonds Payable

Objective 3
Compute the present value of bonds payable.

The concept of present value plays an important role in many accounting analyses and business decisions. For example, accounting analyses based on the present-value concept are useful for evaluating proposals for long-term investments in plant and equipment. In this chapter, we discuss the concept of present value as it relates to long-term debt.

The concept of present value is based on the time value of money. What is the time value of money? An amount of cash to be received at some date in the future is not the equivalent of the same amount of cash held at an earlier date. In other words, a sum of cash to be received in the future is not as valuable as the same sum on hand today.

Why would you prefer receiving $100 today to receiving $100 a year from now? One reason is that you could use the cash on hand to buy something you want and enjoy it immediately. If you have to wait a year for the money, you will have to postpone your enjoyment of it. Moreover, if you receive the $100 today, you know for certain that you have it. Waiting to receive it in the future always involves some risk that you will never get it.

You should note that, when we refer to the time value of money, we are not talking about inflation. As we discussed in an earlier chapter, inflation involves a decline in the purchasing power of the dollar. While inflation will make a dollar received in the future worth less than a dollar received today, this effect is *in addition to* the time value of money. Even if there were no inflation, investors would still demand interest as a reward for delaying consumption and incurring the risk involved in postponing their receipt of cash to the future. If investors also expect inflation, they will require an even higher interest rate of return to compensate for this effect also.

Thus, you can invest cash on hand today to earn income. If you invest your $100 cash when the market rate of interest is 10% per year, the $100 will accumulate to $110 ($100 plus $10 earnings) in one year. The $100 on hand today is the present-value amount that is equivalent to $110 to be received a year from today.

A related concept to present value is future value. In the preceding illustration, the $110 to be received a year from today is the future value of $100 today, assuming an interest rate of 10%.

Suppose that you invest $100 for two years, and that interest is compounded annually. Compounding means that interest is computed each period on the total amount invested plus the interest accumulated to the beginning of the period. Here the interest for year two is $11, computed as 10% of the total balance of $110 accumulated at the end of year one. Therefore, the future value at the end of year two is $121 ($110 + $11). Conversely, the present value of $121 received at the end of year two is $100, computed as:

$121 valued back to the beginning of year one ($121 ÷ 1.10) = $110
$110 valued back to the beginning of year two ($110 ÷ 1.10) = $100

When a corporation issues bonds, the price that a buyer is willing to pay for the bonds is the sum of the present values of the following amounts:

1. The principal (face amount) of the bonds to be received at the maturity date.
2. Interest payments to be received at periodic intervals over the life of the bond.

PRESENT VALUE OF THE FACE AMOUNT OF BONDS

The present value of the face amount of bonds is the value today of the amount to be received at the maturity date. For example, assume you are to receive $1,000 in one year and that the market rate of interest is 12%. The present value of the $1,000 is $892.86 ($1,000 ÷ 1.12). If you are to receive the $1,000 one year later (two years in all), with the interest compounded at the end of the first year, the present value is $797.20 ($892.86 ÷ 1.12).[1]

You can determine the present value of a cash sum to be received in the future by a series of divisions as illustrated above. Alternatively, you may employ a table

[1] Note that the future value of $797.20 in two years, at an interest rate of 12% compounded annually, is $1,000.

of present values for this purpose. You can use the present value of $1 table to find the present-value factor for $1 to be received for the appropriate number of periods in the future. You then multiply the amount of the future cash sum by this factor to determine its present value. Exhibit 3 is a partial table of the present value of $1.[2]

Exhibit 3

Present Value of $1 at Compound Interest

Periods	5%	5½%	6%	6½%	7%	10%	11%	12%	13%	14%
1	0.9524	0.9479	0.9434	0.9390	0.9346	0.9091	0.9009	0.8929	0.8850	0.8772
2	0.9070	0.8985	0.8900	0.8817	0.8734	0.8264	0.8116	0.7972	0.7832	0.7695
3	0.8638	0.8516	0.8396	0.8278	0.8163	0.7513	0.7312	0.7118	0.6931	0.6750
4	0.8227	0.8072	0.7921	0.7773	0.7629	0.6830	0.6587	0.6355	0.6133	0.5921
5	0.7835	0.7651	0.7473	0.7299	0.7130	0.6209	0.5935	0.5674	0.5428	0.5194
6	0.7462	0.7252	0.7050	0.6853	0.6663	0.5645	0.5346	0.5066	0.4803	0.4556
7	0.7107	0.6874	0.6651	0.6435	0.6228	0.5132	0.4817	0.4523	0.4251	0.3996
8	0.6768	0.6516	0.6274	0.6042	0.5820	0.4665	0.4339	0.4039	0.3762	0.3506
9	0.6446	0.6176	0.5919	0.5674	0.5439	0.4241	0.3909	0.3606	0.3329	0.3075
10	0.6139	0.5854	0.5584	0.5327	0.5083	0.3855	0.3522	0.3220	0.2946	0.2697

For the preceding example, Exhibit 3 indicates that the present value of $1 to be received in two years with interest of 12% a year is 0.7972. Multiplying $1,000 by 0.7972 yields $797.20. This is the same amount that we determined previously by two consecutive divisions. In Exhibit 3, the Periods column represents the number of compounding periods and the Percentage columns represent the compound interest rate per period. For example, 12% for two years compounded annually, as in the preceding example, is 12% for two periods. Likewise, 12% for two years compounded semi-annually would be 6% (12% per year ÷ 2 semi-annual periods) for four periods (2 years × 2 semi-annual periods). Similarly, 12% for three years compounded semi-annually would be 6% (12% ÷ 2) for six periods (3 years × 2 semi-annual periods). Whenever interest is compounded more than once (*n* times) per year: (1) determine the interest rate per period by dividing the annual market rate by *n*, and (2) determine the number of periods by multiplying *n* times the number of years to maturity. Also, note that the interest is described as an annual rate. Thus, 12% compounded semi-annually is actually 6% every six months.

PRESENT VALUE OF THE PERIODIC BOND INTEREST PAYMENTS

The present value of the periodic bond interest payments is the value today of the amount of interest to be received at the end of each interest period. Such a series of equal payments at fixed intervals is called an annuity.

To illustrate the concept of an annuity, suppose that you made a purchase on an installment plan that called for equal annual payments over a period of three years. For simplicity, assume that you are required to make a single payment of $1,000 at the end of each year for three years. If the market rate of interest is 10%, you could use the table in Exhibit 3 to calculate the present value of each of your payments, as follows:

---

[2] To simplify the illustrations and homework assignments, the tables presented in this chapter are limited to 10 periods for a small number of interest rates, and the amounts are carried to only four decimal places. Computer programs are available for determining present value factors for any number of interest rates, decimal places, or periods. Appendix B at the end of the text presents more complete interest tables, including future value tables.

Present value of $1,000 paid at the end of one year ($1,000 × 0.9091)	$ 909.10
Present value of $1,000 paid at the end of two years ($1,000 × 0.8264)	826.40
Present value of $1,000 paid at the end of three years ($1,000 x 0.7513)	751.30
Total	$2,486.80

Rather than calculating the present value of each payment individually, you can use an interest table designed to calculate the present value of an annuity.

Exhibit 4 is a partial table of the present value of an annuity of $1 using compound interest. Exhibit 4 indicates the present value of $1 to be received at the end of each period for various compound rates of interest. For example, the present value of $1,000 to be received at the end of each of the next three periods at 10% compound interest per period is $2,486.90 ($1,000 × 2.4869).

Exhibit 4
Present Value of Annuity of $1 at Compound Interest

Periods	5%	5½%	6%	6½%	7%	10%	11%	12%	13%	14%
1	0.9524	0.9479	0.9434	0.9390	0.9346	0.9091	0.9009	0.8929	0.8850	0.8772
2	1.8594	1.8463	1.8334	1.8206	1.8080	1.7355	1.7125	1.6901	1.6681	1.6467
3	2.7232	2.6979	2.6730	2.6485	2.6243	2.4869	2.4437	2.4018	2.3612	2.3216
4	3.5460	3.5052	3.4651	3.4258	3.3872	3.1699	3.1024	3.0373	2.9745	2.9137
5	4.3295	4.2703	4.2124	4.1557	4.1002	3.7908	3.6959	3.6048	3.5172	3.4331
6	5.0757	4.9955	4.9173	4.8410	4.7665	4.3553	4.2305	4.1114	3.9976	3.8887
7	5.7864	5.6830	5.5824	5.4845	5.3893	4.8684	4.7122	4.5638	4.4226	4.2883
8	6.4632	6.3346	6.2098	6.0888	5.9713	5.3349	5.1461	4.9676	4.7988	4.6389
9	7.1078	6.9522	6.8017	6.6561	6.5152	5.7590	5.5370	5.3283	5.1317	4.9464
10	7.7217	7.5376	7.3601	7.1888	7.0236	6.1446	5.8892	5.6502	5.4262	5.2161

Accounting for Bonds Payable

Objective 4
Journalize entries for bonds payable.

The interest rate specified in the bond indenture is the contract rate (also called the stated, nominal, or coupon rate). This rate may differ from the market rate of interest (also called the effective or yield rate) at the time the bonds are issued. The contract rate determines the interest payments made each period. The market rate is the rate used by investors in computing the present value of the bond. If the market rate is higher than the contract rate, the bonds will sell at a discount, or less than their face amount. Why is this the case? Buyers are not willing to pay the face amount for bonds whose contract rate is lower than the return that they could earn on similar investments that are available in the current market (the market rate). The discount, in effect, represents the amount necessary to make up for the difference in the market and the contract interest rates. In contrast, if the market rate is lower than the contract rate, the bonds will sell at a premium, or more than their face amount. In this case, buyers are willing to pay more than the face amount for bonds whose contract rate is higher than the market rate. Exhibit 5 summarizes the

Exhibit 5
Relationship of Market Rate and Contract Rate to Discounts and Premiums

Market rate = Contract rate → Bonds sell at face value
Market rate > Contract rate → Bonds sell at discount
Market rate < Contract rate → Bonds sell at premium

relationship between the contract and market rates of interest and issuing bonds at face value, a discount, or a premium.

BONDS ISSUED AT FACE AMOUNT

To illustrate the journal entries for issuing bonds, assume that on January 1 a corporation issues for cash $100,000 of 12%, five-year bonds, with interest of $6,000 payable semi-annually. The market rate of interest at the time the bonds are issued is 12%. Since the contract rate and the market rate of interest are the same, the bonds will sell at their face amount. This amount is the sum of (1) the present value of the face amount of $100,000 to be repaid in five years and (2) the present value of ten semi-annual interest payments of $6,000 each. We compute the present value of the bonds using the market rate of 12%, as shown below.[3]

Present value of face amount of $100,000 due in five years, at 12% compounded semi-annually: $100,000 × 0.5584 (present value of $1 for 10 periods at 6%)	$ 55,840
Present value of 10 semi-annual interest payments of $6,000, at 12% compounded semi-annually: $6,000 × 7.3601 (present value of annuity of $1 for 10 periods at 6%)	44,160
Total present value of bonds	$100,000

We obtained the basic data for computing the above amounts from the present-value tables in Exhibits 3 and 4. The first of the two amounts, $55,840, is the present value of the $100,000 that is to be repaid in five years. To determine the $55,840:

1. In Exhibit 3, locate the present value of $1 for 10 periods (five years of semi-annual payments) at 6% semi-annually (12% annual rate).
2. Multiply the present-value factor in (1) by $100,000.

If the bond indenture provided that no interest would be paid during the entire five-year period, the bonds would be worth only $55,840 at the time of their issuance. In other words, if $55,840 were invested today, with interest at 12% compounded semi-annually, the sum accumulated at the end of 10 semi-annual periods would be $100,000.

The second of the two amounts, $44,160, is the present value of the series of 10 $6,000 interest payments. To determine the $44,160:

1. In Exhibit 4, locate the present value of an annuity of $1 for 10 periods (five years of semi-annual payments) at 6% semi-annually (12% annual rate).
2. Multiply the present-value factor in (1) by $6,000.

You can also view the present value of $44,160 as the amount that must be deposited today at an interest rate of 12% compounded semi-annually to provide 10 semi-annual withdrawals of $6,000 each. At the end of the tenth withdrawal, the original deposit will be reduced to zero.

The entry to record the issuing of the $100,000 bonds at their face amount is shown below.

Jan.	1	Cash	100,000	
		Bonds Payable		100,000
		Record issuance of bonds payable.		

At six-month intervals following the issuing of the 12% bonds, the company will make interest payments of $6,000.

---

[3] Because the present-value tables are rounded to four decimal places, minor rounding differences may appear in the illustrations.

The issuer records each interest payment as follows:

Interest Expense	6,000	
Cash		6,000
Payment of bond interest.		

At maturity, the company records the payment of the principal and removes the bonds from its books:

Bonds Payable	100,000	
Cash		100,000
Redeem bonds at maturity.		

BONDS ISSUED AT A DISCOUNT

What if the market rate of interest is higher than the contract rate of interest? If the market rate of interest is 13% and the contract rate is 12%, for example, the bonds will sell at a discount. We compute the present value of the five-year, $100,000 bonds using the market rate of 13% as follows:

Present value of face amount of $100,000 due in five years, at 13% compounded semi-annually: $100,000 × 0.5327 (present value of $1 for 10 periods at 6½%)	$53,270
Present value of 10 semi-annual interest payments of $6,000, at 13% compounded semi-annually: $6,000 × 7.1888 (present value of an annuity of $1 for 10 periods at 6½%)	43,133
Total present value of bonds	$96,403

The two present values that make up the total are both less than the comparable amounts in the preceding example. This is because the market rate of interest was 12% in the first example, while the market rate of interest was 13% in the above example. The present value of a future amount becomes less and less as the interest rate used to compute the present value increases. Stated in another way, the amount that has to be invested today to equal a future amount declines as the interest rate earned on the investment increases.

The company records the issuing of the preceding 12% bonds as follows:

Jan.	1	Cash	96,403	
		Discount on Bonds Payable	3,597	
		Bonds Payable		100,000
		Issue bonds at a discount.		

When bonds payable are issued at a discount, we record the face value of the bonds in Bonds Payable and record the amount of the discount in a separate contra account. If the company prepared a balance sheet on January 1, it would report under long-term liabilities:

12% Bonds payable due in five years	$100,000
Less discount on bonds payable	3,597
	$ 96,403

The $3,597 discount is the amount needed to entice investors to accept a contract rate of interest that is below the market rate. In other words, the discount is the market's way of adjusting a bond's effective rate of interest to the higher market rate. In this sense, the discount represents an additional interest expense beyond the amounts paid as periodic interest based on the contract rate. The discount is paid to the bondholders at the maturity date. That is, in the above example, the issuer must pay the bondholders $100,000 at maturity, even though it initially received only $96,403 when it issued the bonds. Because of this, generally accepted accounting principles require the amortization of discounts to reflect the increased interest expense over the life of a bond issue.

AMORTIZATION OF A BOND DISCOUNT

There are two methods of amortizing discount to interest expense over the life of a bond issue: (1) the straight-line method and (2) the effective interest rate method, often called the **interest method.** Both methods amortize the same total amount of discount over the life of the bonds. The interest method is required by generally accepted accounting principles. However, the straight-line method is acceptable if the results obtained do not materially differ from the results that would be obtained by using the interest method. We will illustrate amortization of bond discounts and premiums first by the straight-line method and later by the effective interest method.

The straight-line method amortizes an equal amount of bond discount each period. Applying this method to the preceding example yields amortization of $\frac{1}{10}$ of $3,597, or $359.70, each half year. The amount of the interest expense on the bonds for each half year is constant at $6,000 plus $359.70, or $6,359.70. The entry to record the first interest payment and the amortization of the related amount of discount is shown below.

June 30	Interest Expense	6,359.70	
	Discount on Bonds Payable		359.70
	Cash		6,000.00
	Interest payment and amortization of bond discount.		

Every time the company records interest expense, it must at the same time amortize the appropriate amount of bond discount.

BONDS ISSUED AT A PREMIUM

If the market rate of interest is 11% and the contract rate is 12% on the five-year, $100,000 bonds, the bonds will sell at a premium. We compute the present value of these bonds as follows:

Present value of face amount of $100,000 due in five years, at 11% compounded semi-annually: $100,000 × 0.5854 (present value of $1 for 10 periods at 5½%)	$ 58,540
Present value of 10 semi-annual interest payments of $6,000, at 11% compounded semi-annually: $6,000 × 7.5376 (present value of an annuity of $1 for 10 periods at 5½%)	45,226
Total present value of bonds	$103,766

The company records the issuing of the bonds as follows:

Jan.	1	Cash	103,766	
		Bonds Payable		100,000
		Premium on Bonds Payable		3,766
		Issue bonds at a premium.		

If the company prepared a balance sheet on January 1, it would report under long-term liabilities:

12% Bonds payable due in five years	$100,000	
Premium on bonds payable	3,766	
	$103,766	

AMORTIZATION OF A BOND PREMIUM

The amortization of bond premiums is similar to that for bond discounts, except that it decreases interest expense. In the above example, the straight-line method yields amortization of $\frac{1}{10}$ of $3,766, or $376.60, each half year. The entry to record the first interest payment and the amortization of the related premium is as follows:

June 30	Interest Expense	5,623.40	
	Premium on Bonds Payable	376.60	
	Cash		6,000.00

AMORTIZATION OF DISCOUNT BY THE EFFECTIVE INTEREST METHOD

Whereas the straight-line amortization method provides for a *constant amount* of interest expense each period, the effective interest rate method provides for a constant *interest rate* applied to the carrying amount of the bonds at the beginning of the period. The carrying value of bonds payable is the balance of the bonds payable account (face value) less any unamortized discount or plus any unamortized premium. The effective method computes interest expense by multiplying the carrying value of the bonds times the market rate in effect when the bonds were issued (also called the *historical market rate*).

Using the previous example of the five-year, 12% $100,000 bonds issued for $96,403 when the market rate was 13% (semi-annual compounding), we compute interest for the first two periods as follows under the effective rate method:

Carrying value Jan. 1	$96,403
Interest expense at effective rate (6½% × 96,403)	+6,266
Less interest payment at contract rate	−6,000
Carrying value June 30	96,669
Interest expense at effective rate (6½% × 96,669)	+6,284
Less interest payment at contract rate	−6,000
Carrying value Dec. 31	$96,953

The discount amortized each period is the difference between the interest expense and the interest payment for the period. Exhibit 6 illustrates the entries to record the interest payment at June 30 and December 31, as well as the carrying value of the bonds that would be reported in the balance sheet, under both the effective interest and straight-line methods.

Exhibit 6

Amortizing Discount on Bonds Payable: Effective Interest Rate and Straight-line Methods

	Effective Interest Rate		Straight-line Method	
	June 30	Dec. 31	June 30	Dec. 31
Interest Expense	6,266	6,284	6,360	6,360
Discount on Bonds Payable	266	284	360	360
Cash	6,000	6,000	6,000	6,000
Balance Sheet:				
Long-term Liabilities				
12% Bonds Payable	100,000	100,000	100,000	100,000
Less Discount on Bonds Payable	3,331	3,047	3,237	2,977
	96,669	96,953	96,763	97,123

In comparing the effective interest and straight-line methods, we note the following:

1. While the straight-line method reports the same amount of interest expense each period, the effective method reports a different amount of expense each period. As we amortize the discount, the carrying amount of the bonds (face value minus unamortized discount) increases. This causes interest expense (carrying amount times market rate) to increase each period under the effective interest method when bonds have been issued at a discount.

2. The order in which we calculate (i) amortization and (ii) interest expense is reversed under the straight-line and effective rate methods. With the straight-line method, *first* we calculate the amount of discount amortized and then we compute interest expense (interest payment plus the discount). With the effective rate method, *first* we calculate interest expense each period and then we compute the discount amortized (interest expense minus the interest payment).

The effective interest rate method is considered conceptually superior to the straight-line method. By showing a constant *amount* of interest expense each period, even though the carrying value of the bonds is increasing, the straight-line method falsely implies that the *rate* of interest (interest expense ÷ carrying value) is changing each period. The straight-line method is often used due to its simplicity, but is only permitted if the results reported are not materially different from the effective interest method.

You can see that the carrying value of the bonds shown under the effective interest method ($96,669 on June 30; $96,953 on December 31) always agrees with the carrying value shown on our interest schedule. Under the effective rate method, you can compute the carrying amount of the bonds at any point in time by calculating the present value of the future cash flows (principal and interest) remaining to be paid on the bond, using the historical market rate. For example, you can use the historical market rate to compute the present value of the bonds at the end of the first year (when there are four years left to maturity) as follows:

Present value of face amount of $100,000 due in eight periods
   at 13% compounded semi-annually: $100,000 × 0.6042
   (present value of $1 for eight periods at 6½%) $60,420
Present value of eight semi-annual interest payments of $6,000
   at 13% compounded semi-annually: $6,000 × 6.0888
   (present value of $1 for eight periods at 6½%)   36,533
Total present value of bonds at end of year one $96,953

The $96,953 is the carrying value of the bonds at the end of year one reported under the effective interest method and shown in the schedule used for computing interest expense.

In the example shown above we used a simplified schedule to illustrate the computation of interest expense under the effective interest method. Exhibit 7 provides a more sophisticated amortization table covering the entire life of the bond. You should note the following items in this table:

1. The interest paid (Column A) remains constant at 6% of $100,000, the face amount of the bonds.

2. The interest expense (Column B) is computed at 6½% of the bond carrying value at the beginning of each period. This results in an increasing interest expense each period.

3. The excess of the interest expense over the interest payment of $6,000 is the amount of discount to be amortized (Column C).

4. The unamortized discount (Column D) decreases from the initial balance, $3,597, to a zero balance at the maturity date of the bonds.

5. The carrying value (Column E) increases from $96,403, the amount received for the bonds, to $100,000 at maturity.

Exhibit 7

Amortization of Discount on Bonds Payable

Interest Payment	A Interest Paid (6% of Face Amount)	B Interest Expense (6½% of Bond Carrying Value)	C Discount Amortization (B – A)	D Unamortized Discount (D – C)	E Bond Carrying Value ($100,000 – D)
				$3,597	$ 96,403
1	$6,000	$6,266 (6½% of $96,403)	$266	3,331	96,669
2	6,000	6,284 (6½% of $96,669)	284	3,047	96,953
3	6,000	6,302 (6½% of $96,953)	302	2,745	97,255
4	6,000	6,322 (6½% of $97,255)	322	2,423	97,577
5	6,000	6,343 (6½% of $97,577)	343	2,080	97,920
6	6,000	6,365 (6½% of $97,920)	365	1,715	98,285
7	6,000	6,389 (6½% of $98,285)	389	1,326	98,674
8	6,000	6,415 (6½% of $98,674)	415	911	99,089
9	6,000	6,441 (6½% of $99,089)	441	470	99,530
10	6,000	6,470 (6½% of $99,530)	470	—	100,000

AMORTIZATION OF PREMIUM BY THE EFFECTIVE INTEREST METHOD

We illustrate the effective interest method for amortizing bond premium with the example used earlier to illustrate the straight-line method. Assuming five-year, 12% $100,000 bonds issued for $103,766 when the market rate was 11% (semi-annual compounding), we compute interest for the first two periods under the effective rate method as follows:

Carrying value Jan. 1	$103,766
Interest expense at effective rate (5½% × 103,766)	+5,707
Less interest payment at contract rate	−6,000
Carrying value June 30	103,473
Interest expense at effective rate (5½% × 103,473)	+5,691
Less interest payment at contract rate	−6,000
Carrying value Dec. 31	$103,164

The premium amortized each period is the difference between the interest expense and the interest payment for the period. Exhibit 8 illustrates the entries to record the interest payment at June 30 and December 31, as well as the carrying value of the bonds that would be reported in the balance sheet, under both the effective interest and straight-line methods.

Exhibit 8

Amortizing Premium on Bond Payable: Effective Interest Rate and Straight-line Method

	Effective Interest Rate		Straight-line Method	
	June 30	Dec. 31	June 30	Dec. 31
Interest Expense	5,707	5,691	5,623	5,623
Premium on Bonds Payable	293	309	377	377
Cash	6,000	6,000	6,000	6,000
Balance Sheet: Long-term Liabilities				
12% Bonds Payable	100,000	100,000	100,000	100,000
Add Premium on Bonds Payable	3,473	3,164	3,389	3,012
	103,473	103,164	103,389	103,012

While the straight-line method reports the same interest expense each period, the effective method reports a decreasing amount of expense each period. As we amortize the premium, the carrying amount of the bonds (face value plus unamortized premium) decreases. This causes interest expense (carrying amount times market rate) to decrease each period under the effective interest method when bonds have been issued at a premium. Under the effective interest method, the carrying value of the bonds on the balance sheet equals the carrying value shown on the interest schedule. Exhibit 9 provides a complete premium amortization table covering the life of the bond.

Exhibit 9
*Amortization of Premium
on Bonds Payable*

Interest Payment	A Interest Paid (6% of Face Amount)	B Interest Expense (5½% of Bond Carrying Value)	C Premium Amortization (A – B)	D Unamortized Premium (D – C)	E Bond Carrying Value ($100,000 + D)
				$3,766	$103,766
1	$6,000	$5,707 (5½% of $103,766)	$293	3,473	103,473
2	6,000	5,691 (5½% of $103,473)	309	3,164	103,164
3	6,000	5,674 (5½% of $103,164)	326	2,838	102,838
4	6,000	5,657 (5½% of $102,838)	343	2,495	102,495
5	6,000	5,638 (5½% of $102,495)	362	2,133	102,133
6	6,000	5,618 (5½% of $102,133)	382	1,751	101,751
7	6,000	5,597 (5½% of $101,751)	403	1,348	101,348
8	6,000	5,575 (5½% of $101,348)	425	923	100,923
9	6,000	5,551 (5½% of $100,923)	449	474	100,474
10	6,000	5,526 (5½% of $100,474)	474	—	100,000

Some corporations, such as Whirlpool, sell zero-coupon bonds at a large discount because these bonds do not pay periodic interest payments.

You should note the following items in this table:

1. The interest paid (Column A) remains constant at 6% of $100,000, the face amount of the bonds.
2. The interest expense (Column B) is computed at 5½% of the bond carrying value at the beginning of each period. This results in a decreasing interest expense each period.
3. The excess of the periodic interest payment of $6,000 over the interest expense is the amount of premium to be amortized (Column C).
4. The unamortized premium (Column D) decreases from the initial balance, $3,766, to a zero balance at the maturity date of the bonds.
5. The carrying value (Column E) decreases from $103,766, the amount received for the bonds, to $100,000 at maturity.

ZERO-COUPON BONDS

Some corporations issue bonds that do not provide for interest payments. Such bonds are called zero-coupon bonds.

Zero-coupon bonds provide for only the payment of the face amount of the bonds at the maturity date. Because the bonds do not provide for interest payments, they sell at a large discount. In Canada, zero-coupon bonds have been created by detaching the interest coupons from a coupon bond and selling the coupons and stripped bonds as separate investments.

To further illustrate, if the market rate of interest for five-year bonds that pay interest semi-annually is 13%, the present value of $100,000 zero-coupon, five-year bonds is as follows:

The bonds issued by companies are rated as to their riskiness as investments by such independent financial reporting services as *Moody's* and *Standard and Poor's*. These services rely heavily upon financial statements and the terms of the bond indenture (for example, whether the bonds are secured) in setting the credit rating. These credit ratings, in turn, influence how much the bonds will sell for in the marketplace.

Present value of $100,000 due in five years, at 13% compounded
   semi-annually: $100,000 × 0.5327 (present value of $1 for
   10 periods at 6½%) $53,270

The accounting for zero-coupon bonds is similar to that for interest-bearing bonds that have been sold at a discount. The company amortizes the discount as interest expense over the life of the bonds and records the issuing of the bonds as follows:

Cash	53,270	
Discount on Bonds Payable	46,730	
Bonds Payable		100,000
Issue bonds at a discount.		

BONDS ISSUED BETWEEN INTEREST DATES

In the previous illustrations we assumed that the company sold all of its bonds on their issuance date. What happens if the bonds are sold after this date? For example, suppose that the company sells five-year 12%, $100,000 bonds with an issuance date of January 1 on March 1. In this case the sale occurs between the semi-annual interest dates of January 1 and June 30.

Since the bond indenture specifies the future cash payments of principal and interest to be made to the bondholder, these remain the same regardless of when the bonds are actually sold. Thus, the investor will receive the $6,000 semi-annual interest payment on June 30 whether the bonds are sold on January 1 or March 1. However, the issuing company only incurs interest expense for the period during which it has actually borrowed money from the bondholders. Since the company did not receive any funds until March 1, it will not record interest expense for January and February. Conversely, the investor who purchases the bonds on March 1 has only actually "earned" four months of interest income by June 30. Accordingly, when the bonds are sold on March 1, the issuer will charge the investor for the two months of interest accrued since January 1.

If the market rate is 12% when the bonds are sold on March 1, the issuer will receive cash proceeds of $102,000, equal to the face value ($100,000) plus two months' accrued interest ($100,000 × 6% × 2/6 months). The following entry records the cash proceeds, bonds payable, and interest accrued on the bonds at the date of sale:

Mar. 1	Cash	102,000	
	Bonds Payable		100,000
	Interest Payable		2,000[4]
	Issuance of bonds with interest accrued since January 1.		

On the date of the first interest payment the issuer would record the $6,000 cash payment, reverse the Interest Payable and record Interest Expense of $4,000 for the four months (March 1 through June 30) that the bonds were outstanding:

June 30	Interest Expense	4,000	
	Interest Payable	2,000	
	Cash		6,000
	Interest expense from Mar. 1 to June 30.		

Suppose that the market rate on March 1 was 13%. In this case the bonds will sell at a discount, because the market rate is greater than the contract rate. However, the investor will still have to pay for the interest accrued to March 1. In this case the bonds sell for $96,492 plus $2,000 for accrued interest for total proceeds of $98,492. At the date of sale the issuer records:

Mar. 1	Cash	98,492	
	Discount on Bonds Payable	3,508	
	Interest Payable		2,000
	Bonds Payable		100,000
	Issuance of bonds at a discount with interest accrued since January 1.		

When bonds are sold at a discount or premium between interest dates, the company must amortize the discount or premium *over the period between the date of sale and the maturity date*. We will not illustrate these entries, which are included in more advanced accounting texts.

BOND INTEREST DATE DIFFERS FROM ISSUER'S ACCOUNTING PERIOD

If the issuer's accounting period does not coincide with the date on which the bonds pay interest, the company must accrue interest payable up to the end of its accounting period. As we noted previously, every time the company records interest expense, it must also amortize any discount or premium associated with the bonds.

We illustrate the interest accrual using the earlier example of the five-year, 12% $100,000 bonds issued January 1 with semi-annual interest paid every June 30 and December 31. Assume that the issuer's fiscal year end is May 31. If the bonds are issued at par on January 1, the company will have to accrue five months' interest on May 31, as follows:

May 31	Interest Expense (6% × $100,000 × $\frac{5}{6}$)	5,000	
	Interest Payable		5,000
	Accrue interest on bonds payable Jan. 1 to May 31.		

[4] Alternatively, the issuer could credit the $2,000 to Interest Expense on March 1. When the company pays the interest on June 30, it would debit Interest Expense for $6,000 and credit Cash for $6,000. This would leave a net balance of $4,000 ($6,000 debit minus $2,000 credit) recorded for Interest Expense for the period from March 1 to June 30.

On June 30 the company will record the Interest Expense for one month, reverse the Interest Payable, and record the semi-annual payment of Cash:

June 1	Interest Expense (6% × $100,000 × ⅙)	1,000	
	Interest Payable	5,000	
	Cash		6,000
	Interest payment on bonds.		

If the market rate were 13% on January 1, we illustrated earlier that the bonds would have sold at a discount for $96,403. We also calculated interest expense for the first six months as $6,266 under the effective interest method and $6,360 under the straight-line method. If the company's year end is May 31, it will record five months ($\frac{5}{6}$) of this interest expense on May 31 and one month ($\frac{1}{6}$) on June 30, as shown in Exhibit 10.

Exhibit 10

Amortization of Discount on Bonds Payable: Interest Date Different from Accounting Period

	Effective Interest Method			Straight-line Method		
May 31:						
Interest Expense	(6,266 × ⅚)	5,222		(6,360 × ⅚)	5,300	
Discount on Bonds Payable			222			300
Interest Payable			5,000			5,000
June 30:						
Interest Expense	(6,266 × ⅙)	1,044		(6,360 × ⅙)	1,060	
Interest Payable		5,000			5,000	
Discount on Bonds Payable			44			60
Cash			6,000			6,000

Note that the amounts recorded for Cash and Interest Payable at any one date are the same regardless of whether the bonds were issued at par or at a discount (or a premium), and regardless of whether the discount (or premium) is amortized using the effective interest or straight-line method. This is because the cash payments for interest (and the accruals of these payments) are fixed by the bond indenture and do not change, no matter what the selling price of the bonds or the amortization method used.

CONVERTIBLE BONDS

Convertible bonds have characteristics associated with both debt and equity. Like other bonds, they provide the security of guaranteed interest payments and repayment of principal at a specified maturity date. Like equity, they offer investors the opportunity to benefit from increases in the market value of the company's shares. Thus, a convertible bond is a **compound financial instrument,** a single security that is part liability and part equity.[5]

As we mentioned earlier, investors are willing to pay a higher price for convertible bonds than for otherwise identical nonconvertible bonds. The difference is the amount that the bondholder is willing to pay for the opportunity to convert the investment into shares in the future. When a company issues convertible bonds, it should classify the liability and equity elements separately.[6] This means that the company should record the amount paid for the conversion privilege as equity, rather than debt.

To illustrate, assume that on January 1, 2000 a company issues five-year, 12% $100,000 bonds for $103,000. The bonds pay semi-annual interest every January 1

---

[5] *CICA Handbook,* Section 3860, paragraph 26.
[6] *Ibid.,* paragraph 24.

and June 30, and are convertible into no par value common shares (10 shares for every $1,000 bond) any time after January 1, 2003. The underwriter estimates that the bonds would have sold for par if they had not been convertible. In this case, the company should record the issuance of the security by classifying $100,000 as debt and $3,000 as equity:

Jan.	1	Cash	103,000	
		Bonds Payable		100,000
		Conversion Rights		3,000
		Issuance of convertible bonds.		

Conversion Rights are included in Contributed Surplus as part of Shareholders' Equity in the balance sheet.

Suppose that one-half of the bonds were converted to common shares on January 1, 2004. The company should record the conversion by transferring one-half of the carrying value of the Bonds Payable and the Conversion Rights to Common Shares, as follows:

Jan.	1	Bonds Payable	50,000	
		Conversion Rights	1,500	
		Common Shares		51,500
		Conversion of one-half of convertible bonds into no par common shares.		

Bond Sinking Funds

Objective 5
Describe bond sinking funds.

A bond indenture may restrict dividend payments by a corporation as a means of increasing the assurance that the bonds will be paid at maturity.[7] In addition to or instead of this restriction, the bond indenture may require that funds for the payment of the face value of the bonds at maturity be set aside over the life of the bond issue. The amounts set aside are kept separate from other assets in a special fund called a sinking fund.

A bond indenture will often require the issuing company to make the deposits with a trustee who will manage the sinking fund for the company. The trustee will invest the deposits and use the accumulated funds towards retiring the bonds at maturity. Suppose the issuing company deposits $100,000 with the trustee. It will record the deposit in the Sinking Fund account as follows:

Bond Sinking Fund	100,000	
Cash		100,000
Deposit cash into bond sinking fund.		

If the trustee later reports that the fund has earned investment income of $10,000, the company records the increase in the value of the Sinking Fund:

Bond Sinking Fund	10,000	
Sinking Fund Revenue		10,000
Revenue earned on bond sinking fund.		

The company reports the Bond Sinking Fund as a long-term asset, since its use is restricted and it is not available to meet current obligations. It will report the Sinking Fund Revenue as Other Income on the income statement. If a Bond Sinking

[7] As discussed in Chapter 13, retained earnings may also be appropriated to restrict payment of dividends.

Fund that has accumulated to $500,000 is used to retire bonds of this amount at maturity, the company will record:

Bonds Payable	500,000	
Bond Sinking Fund		500,000
Payment of bonds at maturity from bond sinking fund.		

A 1996 survey of the annual reports of 200 large Canadian public companies indicates that, of 110 firms that disclosed marketable long-term debt (liabilities such as bonds that are traded on a market), 28 disclosed a sinking fund related to this debt.[8]

Bond Redemption

Objective 6
Journalize entries for bond redemptions.

A corporation may call or redeem its bonds before they mature. This is often done if the market rate of interest declines significantly before the bonds' maturity date. In this situation, the corporation may sell new bonds at a lower interest rate and use the funds to redeem the original bond issue. The corporation can thus save on future interest expense.

A corporation often issues callable bonds to protect itself against significant declines in future interest rates. The issuing corporation can redeem the callable bonds within the period of time and at the price stated in the bond indenture. Normally, the call price is above the face value. A corporation may also redeem its bonds by purchasing them on the open market.

A corporation usually redeems its bonds at a price different from that of the carrying value (or book value) of the bonds. If the company redeems the bonds for a price below their carrying value, it records the difference in these two amounts as a gain. If the redemption price is above the carrying amount, it records a loss. The company reports gains and losses on redemption of bonds on the income statement.

To illustrate, assume that on June 30 a corporation has a bond issue of $100,000 outstanding, on which there is an unamortized premium of $4,000. Assuming that the corporation purchases one-fourth ($25,000) of the bonds for $24,000 on June 30, it records the redemption as follows:

June 30	Bonds Payable	25,000	
	Premium on Bonds Payable	1,000	
	Cash		24,000
	Gain on Redemption of Bonds		2,000

In the preceding entry, only the portion of the premium relating to the redeemed bonds is written off. The difference between the carrying value of the bonds purchased, $26,000 ($25,000 + $1,000), and the price paid for the redemption, $24,000, is recorded as a gain.

If the corporation had called the entire bond issue for $105,000 on June 30, the entry to record the redemption is as follows:

June 30	Bonds Payable	100,000	
	Premium on Bonds Payable	4,000	
	Loss on Redemption of Bonds	1,000	
	Cash		105,000

[8] C. Byrd and I. Chen, *Financial Reporting in Canada,* 22nd edition, CICA, Toronto, 1997, p. 236.

If the bonds are retired between interest dates, the issuer will have to pay the bond-holder for any interest accrued since the last interest payment. Therefore, before recording the cash payment, the issuer should accrue interest and amortize any premium or discount up to the date of the retirement.

Investments in Bonds

Objective 7
Journalize entries for the purchase, interest, discount and premium amortization, and sale of bond investments.

Throughout this chapter, we have discussed bonds and the related transactions of the issuing corporation (the debtor). However, these transactions also affect investors. In this section, we discuss the accounting for bonds from the point of view of investors.

ACCOUNTING FOR BOND INVESTMENTS—PURCHASE, INTEREST, AND AMORTIZATION

Investors may purchase bonds either directly from the issuing corporation or in the bond market. Newspapers such as The Globe and Mail publish daily bond quotations. These quotations normally include the bond interest rate, maturity date, volume of sales, and the prices for bonds traded during the day. Prices for bonds are sometimes quoted as a percentage of the face amount. Thus, the price of a $1,000 bond quoted at 99½ would be $995, while the price of a bond quoted at 104¼ would be $1,042.50.

As with other assets, the cost of a bond investment includes all costs related to the purchase. For example, for bonds purchased on the bond market, the investor would include the amount paid as a broker's commission as part of the cost of the investment.

As we noted earlier, for bonds purchased between interest dates, the buyer pays for the interest accrued from the last interest payment date to the date of purchase. The investor can debit the amount of the interest paid to Interest Receivable (or to Interest Income), since it is offset against the amount that will be received at the next interest date.

To illustrate, assume that an investor purchases a $1,000 bond at 102 plus a brokerage fee of $5.30 and accrued interest of $10.20. The investor records the transaction as follows:

Apr.	2	Investment in Lewis Co. Bonds	1,025.30	
		Interest Receivable	10.20	
		Cash		1,035.50

The investor records the cost of the bond in a single investment account. The face amount of the bond and the premium (or discount) are normally not kept in separate accounts. This is different from the accounting for bonds payable. Investors do not usually maintain separate premium and discount accounts, since bond investments are often not held until their maturity dates.

When an investor purchases bonds as long-term investments at a price other than the face amount, the premium or discount should be amortized over the remaining life of the bonds. The amortization of premium decreases the amount of the investment in bonds account and interest income. The amortization of discount increases the amount of the investment in bonds account and interest income. The amortization of the premium or discount can be determined using either the straight-line or interest methods.

The bondholder records interest received by a debit to Cash and a credit to Interest Income, and accrues interest at the end of a period by a debit to Interest Receivable and a credit to Interest Income.

To illustrate, assume that on July 1, Crenshaw Inc. purchases $50,000 of 8% bonds of Deitz Corporation, due in 8¾ years. Interest on the bonds is paid semi-annually on April 1 and October 1. Crenshaw Inc. purchases the bonds directly from Deitz Corporation to yield an effective interest rate of 11%. The purchase price is $41,706 plus interest of $1,000 ($50,000 × 4% × ⅙) accrued from April 1, the date of the last semi-annual interest payment. Crenshaw uses the straight-line method for amortizing bond discounts. Entries in the accounts of Crenshaw Inc. at the time of purchase and for the remainder of the fiscal period ending December 31 are as follows:

July	1	Investment in Deitz Corp. Bonds	41,706	
		Interest Receivable	1,000	
		Cash		42,706
		Payment for investment in bonds and accrued interest.		

Cost of $50,000 of Deitz Corp. bonds	$41,706	
Interest accrued ($50,000 × 4% × ⅙)	1,000	
Total	$42,706	

Oct.	1	Cash	2,000	
		Investment in Deitz Corp. Bonds	237	
		Interest Receivable		1,000
		Interest Income		1,237
		Receipt of semi-annual interest ($50,000 × 4%) and amortization of discount from July 1 to October 1 (3 months × $79*)		

*Face value of bonds	$50,000	
Cost of bond investment	41,706	
Discount on bond investment	$ 8,294	
Number of months to maturity (8¾ years × 12)	÷ 105 months	
Discount amortization per month	= $79 per month	

Dec.	31	Interest Receivable	1,000	
		Investment in Deitz Corp. Bonds	237	
		Interest Income		1,237
		Accrue interest from October 1 to December 31 ($50,000 × 4% × ⅙) and amortize discount from October 1 to December 31 (3 months × $79*)		

ACCOUNTING FOR BOND INVESTMENTS—SALE

When long-term investments in bonds are sold before their maturity date, the seller receives the sales price (less commissions and other selling costs) plus any accrued interest since the last interest payment date. Before recording the cash proceeds, the seller should record interest income and amortize any discount or premium for the current period up to the date of sale. Any gain or loss on the sale can then be recorded when the cash proceeds are recorded. The investor normally reports such gains and losses in the Other Income section of the income statement.

To illustrate, assume that Crenshaw sells the Deitz Corporation bonds in the above example for $47,350 plus accrued interest on June 30, seven years after their purchase. The carrying *amount* of the bonds (cost plus amortized discount) as of

January 1 of the year of sale (78 months after their purchase) is $47,868 [$41,706 + ($79 per mo. × 78 months)]. The entries to amortize the discount for the current year and to record the sale of the bonds are as follows:

June 30	Interest Receivable	1,000	
	Investment in Deitz Corp. Bonds	474	
	Interest Income		1,474
	Accrual of interest ($50,000 × 4% × ⅜) and amortization of discount for current year ($79 × 6 months).		
June 30	Cash	48,350	
	Loss on Sale of Investments	992	
	Interest Receivable		1,000
	Investment in Deitz Corp. Bonds		48,342
	Receipt of interest and proceeds from sale of bonds and recognition of loss on sale of bonds.		

Carrying value of bonds on January 1	$47,868
Discount amortized, Jan. 1–June 30	474
Carrying value of bonds on June 30	$48,342
Proceeds of sale	47,350
Loss on sale	$ 992

Other Long-Term Liabilities

LONG-TERM NOTES PAYABLE

Objective 8
Review accounting for other long-term liabilities, including notes payable, leases, pensions, and income taxes.

A long-term note payable is similar to a bond payable, except that it is usually due to a single creditor, such as a bank or supplier. The proceeds that a company receives in exchange for a long-term note payable are determined in the same way in which we computed the amount received when a bond is issued. In other words, the proceeds will equal the present value of the future cash flows associated with the note, calculated using the market rate of interest at the issuance date.

To illustrate, assume that the market rate is 12%. If a business issues a five-year, $10,000 note payable that pays 12% interest annually, the note will be issued for its face value (because the contract rate equals the market rate). If the five-year, $10,000 note is non-interest bearing, it will be issued at a discount because the contract rate (0%) is less than the market rate. The proceeds will be $6,209 (present value of face amount of $10,000 due in five years at 12%: $10,000 × 0.6209).

For a note payable issued at a discount, the issuer may either (1) record the net proceeds in the Note Payable account or (2) record the face amount in the Note Payable account and keep the Discount on Note Payable in a separate account. In either case, the company must amortize the discount over the life of the note using either the straight-line or effective interest method. As with bonds, the discount should be amortized each time interest is recorded.

Suppose that a company issues a note payable for cash on January 1, 2000 when the market rate is 12%. The note will be repaid in installments of $2,000 on December 31 of each of the next five years, beginning December 31, 2000. In this case, the proceeds from issuing the note will equal $7,210 (the present value of an annuity of $2,000 for five years at 12%: $2,000 × 3.6048). If the company uses the effective interest method of amortization, we can compute interest expense and carrying value of the note for the first two years using the following simplified schedule:

Carrying value Jan. 1, 2000	$7,210
Interest expense (12% × 7,210)	+865
Less installment payment	−2,000
Carrying value Dec. 31, 2000	6,075
Interest expense (12% × 6,075)	+729
Less installment payment	−2,000
Carrying value Dec. 31, 2001	$4,804

The change in the carrying value of the note payable each year is the difference between the annual interest expense and the $2,000 annual cash payment. The entries for the first two years are as follows:

Jan. 1 2000	Cash	7,210	
	Note Payable		7,210
	Issuance of five-year installment note payable.		
Dec. 31 2000	Interest Expense	865	
	Note Payable	1,135	
	Cash		2,000
	Interest expense and cash payment on note payable.		
Dec. 31 2001	Interest Expense	729	
	Note Payable	1,271	
	Cash		2,000
	Interest expense and cash payment on note payable.		

When reporting long-term notes payable in the balance sheet, the company must show any principal to be repaid within the next 12 months as a current liability. As indicated on the above schedule, the carrying value of the note is $6,075 on December 31, 2000 and $4,804 on December 31, 2001 (a decrease of $1,271). Therefore, on December 31, 2000 the issuing company would report the note payable in its balance sheet as follows:

Current Liabilities:
  Current portion of 12% installment note payable $1,271

Long-term Liabilities
  12% installment note payable ($2,000 payment due at
    December 31 of each of the next four years) $6,075
  Less current portion reported above   1,271
                                        $4,804

Note that the amount reported under current liabilities is *not* the entire $2,000 installment due next year (which includes both principal and interest), but only the portion of that payment that will reduce the carrying value of the note.

LEASE OBLIGATIONS

In Chapter 10 we discussed accounting for capital assets acquired under long-term leases. There we defined a capital lease as one that transfers the benefits and risks of ownership from the legal owner of the property (lessor) to the party granted the rights to use the asset (lessee). We account for obligations under capital leases in the same manner as for an installment note payable.

For example, suppose that a company signed an agreement on January 1, 2000 to lease a machine for five years. Assume that the lease meets the criteria for classification as a capital lease and calls for payments of $2,000 to be made on December

31 of each year, beginning in the year 2000. The interest rate to be used for present valuing the lease payments is 12%.

Here we have a situation that is almost identical to the installment note payable illustrated above. As we computed above for the installment note payable, the present value of the lease payments is $7,210 (the present value of an annuity of $2,000 for five years at 12%: $2,000 × 3.6048). At the beginning of the lease we record the leased asset and the lease obligation at this amount:

Jan. 1, 2000	Leased machine	7,210	
	Lease liability		7,210
	Record machine acquired under a capital lease.		

The remaining journal entries on the liability for the first two years are virtually the same as those shown above for the installment note payable, with the same amount of interest expense, cash payment, and reduction in the carrying value of the liability recorded on December 31 of each year. The amounts reported under current liabilities and under long-term liabilities would also be the same as those illustrated for the installment note payable. The effective interest method is always used for computing the interest expense on lease obligations. As discussed in Chapter 10, the lessee will also make an entry to amortize the leased machine each year.

A 1996 survey of 200 large Canadian public companies indicates that 75 reported capital leases in their annual financial statements, of which 68 provided separate disclosure of their capital lease liabilities.[9] The 1996 annual report of Transat A.T. Inc. included the following note disclosures pertaining to capital lease obligations:[10]

Note 2 Significant Accounting Policies (In Part)

Capital Leases

Capital leases which transfer substantially all the benefits and inherent risks related to the ownership of the property leased to the Corporation are capitalized by recording as assets and liabilities the present value of the payments under the leases. The property leased and recorded in this way is amortized over its estimated useful life. Rental payments are recorded partly against the amount of the obligation and partly as interest.

Note 9 Obligations Under Capital Leases

	1996	1995
	$	$
Obligations totalling US$24,821,000 (US$31,440,000 in 1995) related to aircraft, maturing at various dates until 2003	33,218	42,286
Other obligations maturing at various dates until 1998	502	266
	33,720	42,552
Less current portion	4,857	4,383
	28,863	38,169

Obligations under capital leases related to aircraft were determined based on interest rates ranging between 9.5% and 11.9% (between 9.5% and 13% in 1995), and those related to other obligations were determined based on rates averaging 12% (13% in 1995).

Minimum installments payable under these leases amount to approximately $44,333,000, $10,613,000 of which is interest, payable as follows for the next five years: 1997–$8,007,000, 1998–$7,943,000, 1999–$7,841,000, 2000–$7,742,000 and 2001–$6,651,000.

---

[9] C. Byrd and I. Chen, *Financial Reporting in Canada,* 22nd edition, CICA, Toronto, 1997, p. 218.
[10]*Ibid.,* p. 221.

PENSIONS

A **pension** represents a cash payment to retired employees. Employees earn rights to pension payments during their working years, based on the pension plan established by their employers. In accordance with the **matching** principle, the employer should record pension expense during the years in which the worker renders service to the company, rather than during the retirement period when the benefits are actually paid to the employee. Pension plans fall into one of two categories: defined contribution plans and defined benefit plans.

Defined Contribution Plan

A defined contribution plan requires the employer to contribute a fixed amount to the employee's pension plan during the employee's working life. The employer will usually pay these amounts to a trustee, such as a trust company, who will manage the plan. The trustee will invest the contributions and make payments to retired employees. While the plan specifies the employer's annual contribution, it does not guarantee the pension benefits that the employee will receive during retirement. These will depend on the return earned on the pension fund contributions. Thus, the employee bears the investment risk in a defined contribution plan.

To illustrate, assume that the pension plan of Flossmoor Industries requires a contribution to the pension fund trustee, Canada Trustco, equal to 10% of employee annual salaries. If Flossmoor makes its annual contribution based on an annual payroll of $500,000, it will record:

Pension Expense	50,000	
Cash		50,000
Pension contribution and expense for the current year.		

After Flossmoor makes its required contribution to the pension plan trustee, it has fulfilled its obligation. The employee's final pension will depend on the investment return earned by Canada Trustco on the contributed balances.

Defined Benefit Plan

A defined benefit plan specifies either the benefits to be received by retired employees or the formula by which those benefits will be determined. For example, the plan might promise a pension calculated as follows: 1.5% × years of service × average salary for the most recent three years before retirement. Under a defined benefit plan, the employer bears the investment risk, as the employer must ensure that sufficient funds are available to pay the specified benefits during the employee's retirement.

The accounting for defined benefit plans is very complex due to the uncertainties of projecting future benefit obligations. These obligations depend on factors such as life expectancies, employee turnover, expected future compensation levels, and investment income on pension contributions. These estimates are prepared for the company by expert professionals known as *actuaries.*

CICA Handbook, Section 3460 sets out complex rules for determining annual pension expense under a defined benefit plan. The amount recorded for pension expense is not necessarily equal to the firm's cash contribution to the pension fund in any particular year. Depending on its financial circumstances, a company may choose to make a cash contribution that is greater or smaller than the amount that it must record for pension expense. To illustrate, assume that Hinkle Co. adopts a defined pension plan during its first year of operations. Its pension expense for the year is $80,000. If Hinkle pays only $60,000 to the fund trustee, the company must record a liability for the unfunded amount:

Pension Expense	80,000	
Cash		60,000
Unfunded Pension Liability		20,000
Contribution to pension fund and pension expense for the current year.		

On the other hand, if Hinkle Co. decides to contribute $100,000 to the pension, it should record an asset for the amount paid in excess of its pension expense:

Pension Expense	80,000	
Prepaid Pension Costs	20,000	
Cash		100,000
Contribution to pension fund and pension expense for the current year.		

Unfunded pension liabilities are usually reported under long-term liabilities, as they generally will not require payment within one year. Prepaid pension costs are usually reported as noncurrent assets, since these amounts are not available for settling current obligations.

A defined benefit plan specifies an employer's obligation to pay future pension benefits rather than stipulating its contributions to the pension plan. Thus, even though the employer may be making cash contributions to the pension fund each year, it continues to have a legal obligation to its employees for all pension benefits earned to date that have not yet been paid out of the pension fund. Therefore, for a defined benefit plan, the company must disclose separately in the notes to its financial statement both (1) the present value of its projected obligation for future pension benefits earned to date and (2) the value of its pension fund assets accumulated to date.[11]

The 1997 edition of *Financial Reporting in Canada* indicates that 163 out of 200 public companies surveyed reported some type of pension plan in 1996.[12] Of these, 148 disclosed both the projected pension benefit obligation and the value of pension fund assets in their statements. The amounts of these items is often very significant. For example, CO-STEEL INC. disclosed its pension benefit obligation to be almost $174 million in 1996, with plan assets of over $249 million.[13]

INCOME TAXES

Most corporations are required to pay federal and provincial income taxes. A corporation determines its taxable income according to the *Income Tax Act*. Taxable income is often different from pretax accounting income, which is determined in accordance with generally accepted accounting principles. The **matching** principle requires that a business calculate *income tax expense* based on accounting income before taxes. Since *taxes payable* are based on taxable income, rather than accounting income, tax expense may differ from the taxes actually payable for the period.

Why might taxable income differ from pre-tax accounting income in a period? Often this is due to temporary differences that arise because some items are recognized in one period for tax purposes and in another period for income statement purposes. Over the life of a business, temporary differences will not change the total amount of tax paid. However, they do affect the timing of when taxes are paid. Often, managers use tax-planning techniques so that temporary differences will delay or defer the payment of taxes to later years. In these cases, at the end of each year, the company will record the amount of the current tax liability and any future tax liability related to this year's accounting income that has been postponed for tax purposes. On the other hand, some temporary differences may cause taxes to be

[11]*CICA Handbook*, Section 3460, paragraph 60.
[12]C. Byrd and I. Chen, *Financial Reporting in Canada*, 22nd edition, CICA, Toronto, 1997, p. 294.
[13]*Ibid.*, p. 307.

paid in an earlier period than a business recognizes the tax expense. In these cases, the company will record a future tax asset[14] in the year in which taxable income exceeds pretax accounting income.

For illustration purposes, in the following paragraphs we discuss two types of temporary differences that may arise between accounting income and taxable income. Accounting for income taxes is a complex topic, and you will find a more comprehensive discussion of such differences in more advanced textbooks.

One type of temporary difference arises when a company claims a deduction from taxable income in an earlier period than it records the amount as an accounting expense. For example, a business will frequently claim the maximum allowable rate in calculating Capital Cost Allowance (CCA, the amortization on capital assets allowed as a deduction in computing taxable income), even though it uses a lower rate for computing amortization expense on its income statement.

To illustrate, assume that the tax rate is 50% and Ridley Company reports pretax accounting income of $800,000 in the year 2000. To match current expenses to current revenues, Ridley records tax expense of $400,000 ($800,000 × 50%) based on this period's accounting income. However, on its tax return the company claims CCA that is higher than the amount recorded for amortization expense on its income statement, so that its taxable income for the year is $700,000. Thus, current taxes payable for the year are $350,000 ($700,000 × 50%), and the company has a future tax liability of $50,000 ($400,000 − $350,000) related to this year's accounting income. *CICA Handbook,* Section 3465 requires that Ridley should record its tax expense for the year as follows:

Income Tax Expense	400,000	
Income Tax Payable		350,000
Future Income Tax Liability		50,000
Record tax expense and taxes payable for the current year.		

This temporary difference will reverse in future years when amortization expense recorded for accounting exceeds CCA for the year. For example, assume that in 2001 Ridley records pretax accounting income of $850,000 and taxable income of $900,000 due to claiming less CCA on its tax return than it records as amortization expense on its income statement. Ridley would record its tax expense for 2001 as follows:

Income Tax Expense ($850,000 × 50%)	425,000	
Future Income Tax Liability	25,000	
Income Tax Payable ($900,000 × 50%)		450,000
Record tax expense and taxes payable for the current year.		

Another type of temporary difference occurs when a company recognizes an accounting expense in an earlier period than it is allowed to claim the amount as a tax deduction. For example, in Chapter 11 we suggested that, in order to comply with the matching principle, a business should record warranty expense in the same period as it records the related sale, even though it may not actually incur the expenditures for the warranty work until a later period. However, for tax purposes the company may not be able to claim a deduction for the expense until later when it actually performs the warranty work.

To illustrate, assume that the tax rate is 50% and Gable Company reports pretax accounting income of $800,000. Gable records tax expense of $400,000 ($800,000 ×

[14]Prior to *CICA Handbook,* Section 3465, which was issued in 1998 and affects fiscal periods beginning on or after January 1, 2000, "deferred taxes" was the term used to describe amounts arising from temporary differences between pretax accounting income and taxable income. If you encounter this terminology, you may interpret deferred taxes as future tax assets or future tax liabilities, depending on where they appear on a company's balance sheet.

50%) based on this period's accounting income. However, the company is not allowed to claim $100,000 of warranty expense recorded on its income statement in computing the current year's taxable income, since this will not be tax deductible until the warranty work is actually performed in the future. Thus, Gable's taxable income for the year is $900,000 and current taxes payable for the year are $450,000 ($900,000 × 50%). Because an item on this year's income statement (warranty expense) is associated with a deduction that will be used to reduce future taxes payable, the company has a future tax asset of $50,000 ($450,000 – $400,000) related to this year's accounting income. *CICA Handbook,* Section 3465 requires that Gable record its tax expense for the year as follows:

Income Tax Expense	400,000	
Future Tax Asset	50,000	
Income Tax Payable		450,000
Record tax expense and taxes payable for the current year.		

The future tax asset will reverse in future years when warranty expenditures claimed as a deduction on the tax return exceed warranty expense reported on the year's income statement.

How should a business disclose assets and liabilities related to income taxes on the balance sheet? The company must present income tax liabilities and income tax assets separately from other liabilities and assets, and must separate taxes payable (or taxes refund receivable) from future tax liabilities (future tax assets).[15] Income tax payable (receivable) is a current liability (asset), due in the short term. Future tax liabilities and future tax assets are classified as current or noncurrent depending on the balance sheet classification of the assets or liabilities with which they are associated.[16] In the above illustrations: (1) Ridley Company should report its future tax liability as noncurrent, since it is associated with capital assets, which are classified as noncurrent; (2) Gable Company should report its future tax asset as current, since it is associated with warranty liabilities, which are classified as current liabilities.

Corporation Balance Sheet

Objective 9
Prepare a corporation balance sheet.

In previous chapters, we illustrated the income statement and retained earnings statement for a corporation. The balance sheet in Exhibit 8 illustrates the presentation of many of the items discussed in this and preceding chapters. These items include bond sinking funds, investments in bonds, goodwill, bonds payable and unamortized discount, capital leases, future tax liability, and appropriation of retained earnings.

BALANCE SHEET PRESENTATION OF BONDS PAYABLE

In Exhibit 11, Escoe Corporation's bonds payable are reported as long-term liabilities. If there were two or more bond issues, the company would report the details of each on the balance sheet or in a supporting schedule or note. A business normally maintains separate accounts for each bond issue.

When the balance sheet date is within one year of the maturity date of the bonds, the bonds may require classification as a current liability. This would be the case if the firm intends to pay the bonds out of current assets. If the bonds are to be paid from a sinking fund or if the company has made contractual arrangements to

[15]*CICA Handbook,* Section 3465, paragraph 86.
[16]*Ibid.,* paragraph 87.

Exhibit 11   *Balance Sheet of a Corporation*

Escoe Corporation
Balance Sheet
December 31, 2000

Assets

Current assets:

Cash		$ 255,000	
Short-term investments in shares (at market, cost $160,000)		152,500	
Accounts and notes receivable	$ 722,000		
Less allowance for doubtful receivables	37,000	685,000	
Inventories, at lower of cost (first-in, first-out) or market		917,500	
Prepaid expenses		70,000	
Total current assets			$2,080,000

Long-term investments:

Bond sinking fund (market value, $473,000)		$ 422,500	
Investment in bonds of			
Dalton Company (market value, $231,000)		240,000	
Total investments			662,500

	Cost	Accumulated Amortization	Net Book Value	
Capital assets (amortized by the straight-line method):				
Land	$ 250,000	—	$ 250,000	
Buildings	920,000	$ 379,955	540,045	
Machinery	2,564,400	746,200	1,818,200	
Leased equipment	200,000	20,000	180,000	
Total capital assets	$3,934,400	$1,146,155		2,788,245

Intangible assets:

Goodwill		$ 300,000	
Organization costs		50,000	
Total intangible assets			350,000
Total assets			$5,880,745

Liabilities

Current liabilities:

Accounts payable	$ 508,810	
Income tax payable	120,500	
Dividends payable	94,000	
Accrued liabilities	81,400	
Current portion of lease liability	10,000	
Total current liabilities		$ 814,710

Long-term liabilities:

Debenture 8% bonds payable, due December 31, 2010			
(market value, $950,000)	$1,000,000		
Less unamortized discount	60,000	$ 940,000	
Lease liability	125,000	115,000	
Less current portion	10,000		
Total long-term liabilities			1,055,000
Future tax liability			85,500
Total liabilities			$1,955,210

Shareholders' Equity

Paid-in capital:

Common shares (250,000 shares authorized, 100,000 issued)	$2,000,000	
$5 preferred shares (50,000 authorized, 20,000 outstanding)	320,000	
Total paid-in capital		$2,320,000

Retained earnings:

Appropriated for bonded indebtedness	$ 250,000	
Unappropriated	1,355,535	
Total retained earnings		1,605,535
Total shareholders' equity		3,925,535
Total liabilities and shareholders' equity		$5,880,745

refinance them with another bond issue, they should remain in the noncurrent category. In this case, the business would normally disclose the details of the arrangements to retire the bonds in a note to the financial statements.

The statements show the balance in Escoe's discount on bonds payable account as a deduction from the bonds payable. Conversely, the balance in a bond premium account would be reported as an addition to the related bonds payable. Either on the face of the balance sheet or in accompanying notes, the company must disclose a description of the bonds (terms, due date, and effective interest rate). In addition, the maturities and sinking fund requirements should be disclosed for each of the next five years.[17] Finally, the company should also disclose the market (fair) value of financial liabilities such as bonds payable.[18]

BALANCE SHEET PRESENTATION OF BOND INVESTMENTS

Investments in bonds or other debt securities that management intends to hold to their maturity are classified as long-term investments. The balance sheet reports these investments at their cost less any amortized premium or plus any amortized discount. In addition, the company should disclose the market (fair) value of financial assets such as bond investments, either on the face of the balance sheet or in an accompanying note.[19]

KEY POINTS

Objective 1. Compute the potential impact of long-term borrowing on the earnings per share of a corporation.
Exhibits 1 and 2 illustrate three alternative plans for financing a corporation by issuing common shares, preferred shares, or bonds. The effects of alternative financing on the earnings per share vary significantly, depending upon the level of earnings.

Objective 2. Describe the characteristics of bonds.
The characteristics of bonds depend upon the type of bonds issued by a corporation. Bonds that may be issued include term bonds, serial bonds, registered bonds, bearer bonds, secured bonds, debentures, convertible bonds, and callable bonds.

Objective 3. Compute the present value of bonds payable.
The concept of present value is based on the time value of money. That is, an amount of cash to be received at some date in the future is not the equivalent of the same amount of cash held at an earlier date. For example, if $100 cash today can be invested to earn 10% per year, the $100 today is referred to as the present value amount that is equivalent to $110 to be received a year from today.

A price that a buyer is willing to pay for a bond is the sum of (1) the present value of the face amount of the bonds at the maturity date and (2) the present value of the periodic interest payments.

Objective 4. Journalize entries for bonds payable.
The journal entry for issuing bonds payable debits Cash for the proceeds received and credits Bonds Payable for the face value of the bonds. Any difference between the face value of the bonds and the proceeds is debited to Discount on Bonds Payable or credited to Premium on Bonds Payable.

A discount or premium on bonds payable is amortized to interest expense over the life of the bonds using either the straight-line method or effective interest rate method. The entry to amortize a discount debits Interest Expense and credits Discount on Bonds Payable. The entry to amortize a premium debits Premium on Bonds Payable and credits Interest Expense.

When bonds are issued between interest dates, the buyer must pay for interest accrued to the date of sale. If the issuer's accounting period does not coincide with an interest payment date, the issuer must accrue interest payable at the end of the accounting period.

Convertible bonds are compound financial instruments, part liability and part equity. The issuer should record the amount paid for the conversion privilege as equity.

Objective 5. Describe bond sinking funds.
A bond indenture may require that funds for the payment of the bonds at maturity be set aside over the life of the bonds. The amounts set aside are kept separate from other assets in a

---

[17]*CICA Handbook*, Section 3210, paragraphs 02 and 03.
[18]*Ibid.*, Section 3860, paragraph 78.
[19]*Ibid.*

special fund called a sinking fund, which is usually administered by a trustee. The issuer reports a sinking fund as a Long-term Investment on the balance sheet. Income from a sinking fund is reported as Other Income on the income statement.

Objective 6. Journalize entries for bond redemptions.
When a corporation redeems bonds, it debits Bonds Payable for the face value of the bonds, debits the premium on bonds account (credits the discount account) for the balance related to the bonds redeemed, credits Cash, and records any gain or loss on the redemption.

Objective 7. Journalize entries for the purchase, interest, discount and premium amortization, and sale of bond investments.
An investor records a long-term investment in bonds by debiting Investment in Bonds for the acquisition cost. When bonds are purchased between interest dates, the investor should debit the amount of the interest paid to Interest Receivable. Any discount or premium on bond investments should be amortized, using the straight-line or effective interest rate methods. The investor records the amortization of a discount by debiting Investment in Bonds and crediting Interest Income. The investor records the amortization of a premium by debiting Interest Income and crediting Investment in Bonds.

When an investor sells bonds held as long-term investments, any discount or premium for the current period should first be amortized. The investor then debits Cash for the proceeds of the sale, credits Investment in Bonds, and records any gain or loss.

Objective 8. Review accounting for other long-term liabilities, including notes payable, leases, pensions, and income taxes.
The proceeds received when a long-term note payable is issued equal the present value of the future cash flows associated with the note, calculated using the market rate of interest. The issuer must record interest expense and amortize any premium or discount over the life of the note using the straight-line or effective interest method.

When a lessee acquires an asset under a capital lease, the lessee debits the Leased Asset and credits the Lease Liability for the present value of the lease payments. The lessee records interest expense using the effective interest rate method.

An employer should record pension expense during the employee's working life. Under a defined contribution pension plan, the employer has met its obligation once it has made the cash contribution required for the period. Under a defined benefit plan, the employer must record a liability for any pension expense not yet funded. If the employer has made a cash contribution in excess of pension expense, it records an asset called Prepaid Pension Costs.

A corporation's taxable income may differ from its pretax accounting income due to temporary differences that arise from recognizing items in one period for tax purposes and another period for accounting purposes. When temporary differences cause income tax expense to exceed taxes payable, the firm will record a future tax liability. When temporary differences cause taxes payable to exceed income tax expense, the firm will record a future tax asset.

Objective 9. Prepare a corporation balance sheet.
Exhibit 8 illustrates a corporation's balance sheet including bond sinking funds, investments in bonds, goodwill, bonds payable, unamortized discount, capital leases, future tax liability, and appropriation of retained earnings.

Bonds payable are usually reported as long-term liabilities. A discount on bonds should be reported as a deduction from the related bonds payable. A premium on bonds should be reported as an addition to the related bonds payable. Long-term investments in bonds are reported as Investments at cost less any amortized premium or plus any amortized discount.

GLOSSARY OF KEY TERMS

Annuity. A series of equal cash flows at fixed intervals. *Objective 3*

Bearer bond. Bond that is unregistered and payable to whoever is holding the bond. *Objective 2*

Bond. A form of note employed by corporations to borrow on a long-term basis. *Objective 1*

Bond indenture. The contract between a corporation issuing bonds and the bondholders. *Objective 2*

Callable bond. Bond that may be redeemed before maturity at the option of the issuer in accordance with the conditions specified in the bond indenture. *Objective 2*

Carrying value. The amount at which a long-term investment or a long-term liability is reported on the balance sheet (face value less any unamortized discount or plus any unamortized premium); also called book value. *Objective 6*

Contract rate. The interest rate specified on a bond that determines the interest payments each period; also called the coupon rate, stated rate, or nominal rate. *Objective 4*

Convertible bond. Bond that can be exchanged for shares at the option of the investor in accordance with the conditions specified in the bond indenture. *Objective 2*

Debenture. Unsecured bond backed only by the general creditworthiness of the issuing company. *Objective 2*

Defined benefit pension plan. Pension plan that specifies either the benefits to be received by retired employees or the formula for determining those benefits. *Objective 8*

Defined contribution pension plan. Pension plan that specifies the amount that an employer must contribute to the pension plan during the employee's working life, but does not specify pension benefits to be paid during the employee's retirement. *Objective 8*

Discount. The excess of the face amount of bonds over their issue price. *Objective 4*

Effective interest rate method. Method that calculates interest each period by multiplying the historical market rate times the carrying value of the long-term liability or long-term investment. *Objective 4*

Future tax asset. Future income tax deduction, arising from temporary differences that caused an excess of taxable income over pretax accounting income in an earlier period. *Objective 8*

Future tax liability. Future income taxes that will have to be paid, arising from temporary differences that caused an excess of pretax accounting income over taxable income in an earlier period. *Objective 8*

Market rate. The rate of interest that investors use to compute the present value of an investment such as a bond or note; also called the effective or yield rate. *Objective 4*

Premium. The excess of the issue price of bonds over the face amount. *Objective 4*

Present value. The estimated present worth of an amount of cash to be received (or paid) in the future. *Objective 3*

Present value of an annuity. The sum of the present values of a series of equal cash flows to be received at fixed intervals. *Objective 3*

Registered bond. Bond whose owner is recorded in a registry kept by the issuing company, so that the issuer makes payments of interest and principal only to that party. *Objective 2*

Secured bond. Bond backed by specific assets pledged as collateral by the issuing company. *Objective 2*

Serial bonds. An issue of bonds whose maturities are spread over several dates. *Objective 2*

Sinking fund. Assets set aside in a special fund to be used for a specific purpose. *Objective 5*

Straight-line method of amortization. Method that amortizes an equal amount of premium or discount on a long-term liability or long-term investment every interest period. *Objective 4*

Taxable income. Income calculated in accordance with the rules of the Income Tax Act and used as the basis for computing taxes payable. *Objective 8*

Temporary differences. Differences between taxable income and pretax accounting income because some items of revenue and/or expense are recognized in a different period for computing taxable income than they are recognized in the income statement. *Objective 8*

Term bonds. An issue of bonds that all mature at the same date. *Objective 2*

Underwriter. Securities firm that sells bonds on behalf on an issuing company. *Objective 1*

ILLUSTRATIVE PROBLEM

On January 1, 2000 Koi Co. issued $500,000 of 10-year, 10% callable bonds when the market rate was 11%. Interest is payable on the bonds every June 30 and December 31. The entire issue was purchased by a single institutional investor, Investment Co. Both Koi and Investment Co. have fiscal years ended December 31 and use the effective interest method to amortize any bond premium or discount. On January 1, 2008 Koi recalled one-half of the bonds at the call price of 105. The remainder of the bonds were redeemed at maturity.

Instructions

1. Calculate the issuance price of the bonds on January 1, 2000.
2. Journalize the entries for both Koi Co. and Investment Co. through to the end of December 31, 2000.
3. Prepare the balance sheet presentation for bonds payable Koi Co. on December 31, 2000.
4. **Without** preparing an interest table for seven years, prove that on January 1, 2008 the carrying value of the bonds (face value less unamortized discount) on the books of both the issuer and the bondholder was $491,239.
5. Journalize the entry to record the recall of the bonds on January 1, 2008 on the books of both the issuer and the investor.

Solution

1. Present value of face amount of $500,000 due in 10 years at 11% compounded semi-annually: $500,000 × 0.34273 (present value of $1 for 20 semi-annual periods at 5½%) $171,365

    Present value of 20 semi-annual interest payments of $25,000 at 11% compounded semi-annually: $25,000 × 11.95038 (present value of an annuity of $1 for 20 periods at 5½%)   298,760

    Total present value (and issuance price) of bonds $470,125

2.   Calculations for effective interest rate method from January 1 to December 31, 2000:

Carrying value Jan. 1	$470,125
Interest expense at effective rate (5½% × 470,125)	+25,857
Less interest payment at contract rate	−25,000
Carrying value June 30	470,982
Interest expense at effective rate (5½% × 470,982)	+25,904
Less interest payment at contract rate	−25,000
Carrying value Dec. 31	$471,886

	Koi Co. (Issuer)			Investment Co. (Bondholder)		
Jan. 1, 2000	Cash	470,125		Investment in bonds	470,125	
	Discount on bonds payable	29,875		Cash		470,125
	Bonds Payable		500,000	Purchase 10% $50,000 bond		
	Issue 10% bonds payable.			investment.		
June 30, 2000	Interest expense	25,857		Cash	25,000	
	Discount on bonds payable		857	Investment in bonds	857	
	Cash		25,000	Interest revenue		25,857
	Interest payment and			Interest received and		
	discount amortization.			discount amortization.		
Dec. 31, 2000	Interest expense	25,904		Cash	25,000	
	Discount on bonds payable		904	Investment in bonds	904	
	Cash		25,000	Interest revenue		25,904
	Interest payment and			Interest received and		
	discount amortization.			discount amortization.		

3.   Koi Co. December 31, 2000

Long-term Liabilities:

10% $500,000 callable bonds payable due December 31, 2009	$500,000
Less discount on bonds payable	28,114
	$471,886

4.   The value of the bond on January 1, 2008 is the present value of the future cash flows remaining on the bond until it matures on December 31, 2009 (four more semi-annual interest payments plus the face value at maturity).

Present value of face amount of $500,000 due in 2 years at 11% compounded semi-annually: $500,000 × 0.80722 (present value of $1 for four semi-annual periods at 5½%)	$403,610
Present value of four semi-annual interest payments of $25,000 at 11% compounded semi-annually: $25,000 × 3.50515 (present value of an annuity of $1 for four periods at 5½%)	87,629
Total present value of bonds	$491,239

	Koi Co.			Investment Co.		
Jan. 1, 2008	Bonds payable (500,000 ÷ 2)	250,000		Cash	262,500	
	Loss on bond recall	16,881		Investment in bonds		
	Discount on bonds		4,381	(491,239 ÷ 2)		245,619
	[(500,000 − 491,239) ÷ 2]			Gain on bond recall		16,881
	Cash ($500,000 × ½ × 1.05)		262,500	Bond investment recalled at 105.		
	Recall $250,000 bonds at 105.					

SELF-EXAMINATION QUESTIONS (ANSWERS AT END OF CHAPTER)

1. If a corporation plans to issue $1,000,000 of 7% bonds at a time when the market rate for similar bonds is 5%, the bonds can be expected to sell at:
   A. their face amount.
   B. a premium.
   C. a discount.
   D. a price below their face amount.

2. If the bonds payable account has a balance of $500,000 and the discount on bonds payable account has a balance of $40,000, what is the carrying value of the bonds?
   A. $460,000
   B. $500,000
   C. $540,000
   D. $580,000

3. The cash and the securities that make up the sinking fund established for the payment of bonds at maturity are classified on the balance sheet as:
   A. current assets.
   B. investments.
   C. long-term liabilities.
   D. current liabilities.

4. If a firm purchases $100,000 of bonds of X Company at 101 plus accrued interest of $2,000 and pays broker's commissions of $50, the amount debited to Investment in X Company Bonds would be:
   A. $100,000
   B. $101,050
   C. $103,000
   D. $103,050

5. The balance in the discount on bonds payable account would usually be reported in the balance sheet in the:
   A. Current Assets section.
   B. Current Liabilities section.
   C. Long-Term Liabilities section.
   D. Investments section.

DISCUSSION QUESTIONS

1. Describe the two distinct obligations incurred by a corporation when issuing bonds.
2. Explain the meaning of each of the following terms as they relate to a bond issue: (a) convertible, (b) callable, and (c) debenture.
3. What is meant by the "time value of money?"
4. Which has the higher present value: (a) $2,000 to be received at the end of two years, or (b) $1,000 to be received at the end of each of the next two years?
5. If you asked your broker to purchase for you a 9% bond when the market interest rate for such bonds was 10%, would you expect to pay more or less than the face value for the bond? Explain.
6. A corporation issues $5,000,000 of 10% coupon bonds to yield interest at the rate of 9%. (a) Was the amount of cash received from the sale of the bonds greater or less than $5,000,000? (b) Identify the following terms related to the bond issue: (1) face amount, (2) market or effective rate of interest, (3) contract or coupon rate of interest, and (4) maturity amount.
7. If bonds issued by a corporation are sold at a premium, is the market rate of interest greater or less than the coupon rate?
8. The following data are related to a $900,000, 9% bond issue for a selected semi-annual interest period:

Bond carrying amount at beginning of period	$925,000
Interest paid at end of period	40,500
Interest expense allocable to the period	36,500

   (a) Were the bonds issued at a discount or at a premium? (b) What is the unamortized amount of the discount or premium account at the beginning of the period? (c) What account was debited to amortize the discount or premium?
9. Would a zero-coupon bond ever sell for its face value? Explain.
10. A company is planning to issue 9%, 25-year bonds.
    a. Will the bonds sell for a higher or lower price if interest is paid annually rather than semi-annually? Explain why.
    b. Will the bonds sell for a higher or lower price if the bonds may be converted into common shares after 10 years? Explain why.

11. What is the purpose of a bond sinking fund?
12. How are earnings from investments in a sinking fund reported on the income statement?
13. How is a sinking fund classified on the balance sheet?
14. Assume that two 20-year, 10% bond issues are identical, except that one bond issue is callable at its face value at the end of 10 years. Which of the two bond issues do you think will sell for a higher value?
15. Bonds Payable has a balance of $750,000, and Premium on Bonds Payable has a balance of $10,000. If the issuing corporation redeems the bonds at 105, is there a gain or loss on the bond redemption?
16. How are gains or losses on bond redemptions reported on the issuing company's income statement?
17. Assume that a company purchases bonds between interest dates. What accounts would normally be debited?
18. Indicate how the following accounts should be reported on the balance sheet: (a) Premium on Bonds Payable and (b) Discount on Bonds Payable.
19. A company issues $1,000,000 bonds for $1,050,000. During the first year that the bonds are outstanding, will the company record the same amount of interest expense whether it uses the straight-line or effective interest rate amortization method? If not, which method would report the higher interest expense? Explain.
20. Why is a convertible bond described as a compound financial instrument? How does a company account differently for the issuance of a convertible bond than for a nonconvertible bond?
21. All other things being equal, why will an investor pay more for a bond issued between interest dates than for a bond issued on its interest date?
22. At what amount are long-term investments in bonds reported on the balance sheet?
23. In order to determine the proceeds from issuing a long-term note payable, what information do you need besides knowing the repayment terms?
24. What is an obligation under a capital lease? How should this be presented in the financial statements?
25. Distinguish between a defined contribution pension plan and a defined benefit pension plan.
26. What might cause accounting income before income tax to differ from taxable income as computed under the Income Tax Act?
27. What is the nature of a future tax liability? Of a future tax asset?
28. How do you determine whether a future tax liability (asset) should be classified as current or long term?

EXERCISES

EXERCISE 14–1
Effect of financing on earnings per share
Objective 1

Harvey Co., which produces and sells skiing equipment, is financed as follows:

Bonds payable, 10% (issued at face value)	$4,000,000
Preferred $9 shares (nonparticipating), no par (40,000 shares outstanding)	4,000,000
Common shares, no par (200,000 shares outstanding)	4,000,000

Income tax is estimated at 40% of income.

Determine the earnings per share, assuming that the income before bond interest and income tax is (a) $1,200,000, (b) $2,000,000, and (c) $5,000,000, and that the full preferred dividend is declared during the year.

EXERCISE 14–2
Evaluating alternative financing plans
Objective 1

Based upon the data in Exercise 14–1, discuss factors other than earnings per share that should be considered in evaluating such financing plans.

EXERCISE 14–3
Present value of amounts due
Objective 3

Determine the present value of $5,000 to be received in three years, using an interest rate of 11%, compounded annually.

EXERCISE 14–4
Present value of annuity
Objective 3

Determine the present value of $10,000 to be received at the end of each of four years, using an interest rate of 7%, compounded annually.

EXERCISE 14–5
Present value of an annuity
Objective 3

On January 1, 2000, you win $1,000,000 in a lottery. The $1,000,000 prize will be paid in equal installments of $40,000 over 25 years. The payments will be made on December 31 of each year, beginning on December 31, 2000. If the current interest rate is 5%, determine the present value of your winnings. Use the present value tables in Appendix B.

EXERCISE 14–6
Present value of an annuity
Objective 3

Assume the same data as in Exercise 14–5, except that the current interest rate is 10%.
Will the present value of your winnings using an interest rate of 10% be one-half the present value of your winnings using an interest rate of 5%? Why or why not?

EXERCISE 14–7
Issue price of bonds payable; discount
Objective 3

Safire Co. produces and sells bottle capping equipment for soft drink and spring water bottlers. To finance its operations, Safire Co. issued $20,000,000 of five-year, 7% bonds with interest payable semi-annually at an effective interest rate of 10%. Determine the issue price of the bonds payable.

EXERCISE 14–8
Issue price of bonds payable; premium
Objective 3

Artex Automotive Alarms Co. issued $10,000,000 of five-year, 12% bonds with interest payable semi-annually, at an effective interest rate of 11%. Determine the issue price of the bonds payable.

EXERCISE 14–9
Bond price
Objective 4

Thomson Corporation 6½% bonds due in 2007 were reported in *The Globe and Mail* as selling for 104.618 on March 25, 1998.
Were the bonds selling at a premium or at a discount on March 25, 1998? Explain.

EXERCISE 14–10
Entries for issuing bonds
Objective 4

Mildred Co. produces and distributes fibre-optic cable for use by telecommunications companies. Mildred Co. issued $15,000,000 of 20-year, 8% bonds on April 1 of the current year, with interest payable on April 1 and October 1. The fiscal year of the company is the calendar year. Journalize the entries to record the following selected transactions for the current year:

Apr. 1. Issued the bonds for cash at their face amount.
Oct. 1. Paid the interest on the bonds.
Dec. 31. Recorded accrued interest for three months.

EXERCISE 14–11
Issuing bonds between interest dates
Objective 4

Assume the same data as in Exercise 14–10, except that the bonds are sold on June 1 instead of April 1. Journalize the entries to record the following selected transactions for the current year:

June 1 Issued the bonds for cash at par plus accrued interest.
Oct. 1 Paid interest on the bonds.

EXERCISE 14–12
Entries for issuing bonds and amortizing discount by straight-line method
Objective 4

On the first day of its fiscal year, Sanger Company issued $10,000,000 of five-year, 10% bonds to finance its operations of producing and selling home electronics equipment. Interest is payable semi-annually. The bonds were issued at an effective interest rate of 12%, resulting in Sanger Company receiving cash of $9,264,050. The company uses the straight-line method of discount amortization.

Journalize the entries to record the following:
1. Sale of the bonds.
2. First semi-annual interest payment.
3. Second semi-annual interest payment.

EXERCISE 14–13

Entries for issuing bonds and amortizing discount by the effective interest rate method

Objective 4

Redo the journal entries in Exercise 14–12 assuming that the company uses the effective interest rate method of discount amortization.

EXERCISE 14–14

Computing bond proceeds, entries for bond issuing and amortizing premium by straight-line method

Objectives 3, 4

Lido Corporation wholesales oil and grease products to equipment manufacturers. On March 1, 1999, Lido Corporation issued $1,000,000 of five-year, 12% bonds at an effective interest rate of 10%. Interest is payable semi-annually on March 1 and September 1. The company uses the straight-line method of premium amortization. Lido's fiscal year end is March 1. Journalize the entries to record the following:

a. Sale of bonds on March 1, 1999. (You must determine the bond proceeds.)
b. First interest payment on September 1, 1999.
c. Second interest payment on March 1, 2000.

EXERCISE 14–15

Entries for issuing bonds and amortizing premium by the effective interest rate method.

Objective 4

Redo the journal entries in Exercise 14–14 assuming that the company uses the effective interest rate method for premium amortization.

EXERCISE 14–16

Computing bond proceeds, amortizing discount by the straight-line method, accruing interest at year end.

Objectives 3, 4

ProMix Co. produces and sells concrete mixing equipment. On September 1, 1999 ProMix Co. issued $8,000,000 of five-year, 7% bonds at an effective rate of 8%, with interest payable semi-annually on September 1 and March 1. ProMix Co. has a December 31 fiscal year end and uses the straight-line method for discount amortization.

Journalize the entries to record the following:
1. Sale of bonds.
2. Interest accrual on December 31, 1999.
3. Interest payment on March 1, 2000.

EXERCISE 14–17

Amortizing discount by the effective interest rate method, accruing interest at year end.

Objective 4

Redo the journal entries in Exercise 14–16 assuming that the company uses the effective interest rate method for discount amortization

EXERCISE 14–18

Computing bond proceeds, amortizing premium by the effective interest rate method, accruing interest at year end.

Objectives 3, 4

CSX Co. produces and sells spray painting equipment for construction contractors. On August 1, 1999 CSX Co. issued $20,000,000 of 10-year, 9% bonds at an effective rate of 8%, with interest payable semi-annually on August 1 and February 1. CSX Co. has a December 31 fiscal year end and uses the effective interest rate method for premium amortization.

Journalize the entries to record the following:
1. Sale of bonds.
2. Interest accrual on December 31, 1999.
3. Interest payment on February 1, 2000.

EXERCISE 14–19

Amortizing premium by the straight-line method, accruing interest at year end.

Objective 4

Redo the journal entries in Exercise 14-18 assuming that the company uses the straight-line method for premium amortization.

EXERCISE 14–20

Entries for issuing and calling bonds; loss

Objectives 4, 6

Cavalier Corp., a wholesaler of office furniture, issued $10,000,000 of 30-year, 10% callable bonds on March 1, 2000, with interest payable on March 1 and September 1. The fiscal year of the company is the calendar year. Journalize the entries to record the following selected transactions:

2000

Mar. 1. Issued the bonds for cash at their face amount.

Sep. 1. Paid the interest on the bonds.

2004

Sep. 1. Called one-half the bond issue at 105, the call price specified in the bond indenture. (Omit entry for payment of interest.)

EXERCISE 14–21
Entries for issuing and calling bonds; gain
Objectives 4, 6

Buckle Corp. produces and sells automotive and aircraft safety belts. To finance its operations, Buckle Corp. issued $6,000,000 of 20-year, 7% callable bonds on June 1, 1996, with interest payable on June 1 and December 1. The fiscal year of the company is the calendar year. The company uses the straight-line method for amortizing bond premium. Journalize the entries to record the following selected transactions:

1996

June 1. Issued the bonds for cash of $6,100,000.

Dec. 1. Paid the interest on the bonds.

2002

June 1. Called the bond issue at 101, the call price specified in the bond indenture. (Omit entry for payment of interest.)

EXERCISE 14–22
Reporting bonds
Objectives 5, 6, 8

At the beginning of the current year, a company had two bond issues (C and D) outstanding. During the year, the company redeemed bond issue C and reported a loss on the redemption of bonds as an extraordinary loss on the income statement. At the end of the year, it reported bond issue D as a current liability because its maturity date was early in the following year. It reported a sinking fund of cash and securities sufficient to pay the series D bonds in the balance sheet as a long-term investment.

Can you find any flaws in the reporting practices related to the two bond issues?

EXERCISE 14–23
Amortizing discount on bond investment
Objective 7

A company purchased a $1,000, 20-year zero-coupon bond for $189 to yield 8.5% to maturity. How is the interest income computed?

Source: "Technical Hotline," *Journal of Accountancy*, January 1989, p. 100.

EXERCISE 14–24
Entries for purchase and sale of investment in bonds; loss
Objective 7

Synoptic Co. sells optical supplies to opticians and ophthalmologists. Journalize the entries to record the following selected transactions of Synoptic Co.:

a. Purchased as a long-term investment $150,000 Blue Co. 8% bonds at 101 plus accrued interest of $2,000.

b. Received first semi-annual interest and amortized $100 on the investment.

c. Sold the bonds at 98 plus accrued interest of $3,500. The bonds were carried at $150,750 at the time of the sale.

EXERCISE 14–25
Entries for purchase and sale of investment in bonds; gain
Objective 7

Grafix Company develops and sells graphics software for use by architects. Journalize the entries to record the following selected transactions of Grafix Company:

a. Purchased as a long-term investment $300,000 Bly Co. 6% bonds at 98 plus accrued interest of $3,000.

b. Received first semi-annual interest and amortized $267 on the investment.

c. Sold the bonds at 99 plus accrued interest of $4,500. The bonds were carried at $296,000 at the time of the sale.

EXERCISE 14–26
Convertible bonds
Objective 4

Santex Ltd. issues convertible bonds on October 1, 2000 for $5,300,000. The bonds mature in 10 years, have a face value of $5,000,000 and pay 8% interest semi-annually on October 1 and April 1. They are convertible at the rate of five common shares for each $1000 bond. The underwriter estimates that similar non-convertible bonds would have sold for $5,120,000. Journalize the entry to record the issuance of the bonds.

EXERCISE 14–27
Long-term Notes payable
Objective 8

On January 1, 2001 when the market rate of interest was 6%, Abrahams Inc. purchased land in exchange for a note payable with a face value of $200,000 due in three years. The company has a December 31 year end.

a. Journalize entries to record the following transactions, assuming that the stated rate on the note is 6% and that interest payments must be made at the end of each year:
   1. Purchase of the land in exchange for the note payable.
   2. Interest on December 31, 2001
b. Redo the above journal entries assuming that the note is non-interest bearing.

EXERCISE 14–28
Lease obligation
Objective 8

The S. Topp Company Limited acquired a new machine by signing a capital lease requiring payments of $10,000 at the end of each of the next five years. At the date the company signed the lease the market rate of interest was 10%. Journalize the entries to record:

1. Acquisition of the machine.
2. Payment of the first lease payment 12 months after acquiring the machine.

EXERCISE 14–29
Income taxes
Objective 8

Apex Corp. Ltd. records show the following amounts related to income and capital assets:

	Year 1	Year 2	Year 3
Accounting income before tax	$100,000	$110,000	$120,000
Amortization of capital assets	20,000	20,000	20,000
Capital cost allowance	30,000	18,000	10,000

The amortization has been deducted to arrive at accounting income before tax. Assume a tax rate of 40%.

a. Journalize the entries to record income tax expense and income tax payable for each year.
b. Determine the balance in the future tax liability (asset) at the end of each year.

EXERCISE 14–30
Pension plans
Objective 8

Holdco Ltd. receives from its pension consultant the following information for the current year regarding its defined benefit pension plan.

Pension expense (current year)	$70,000
Cash paid to pension fund trustee during the year	30,000

a. Journalize the entries related to the pension plan for the current year assuming that all events were properly recorded in the previous year.
b. Indicate the balance, if any, that Holdco should report on the balance sheet at the end of the year with respect to pensions, and where such balance would be disclosed.

PROBLEMS SERIES A

PROBLEM 14–1A
Effect of financing on earnings per share
Objective 1

Three different plans for financing a $15,000,000 corporation are under consideration by its organizers. Under each of the following plans, the company estimates that the preferred will sell for $50 per share and the common for $30. The income tax rate is 40% of income.

	Plan 1	Plan 2	Plan 3
12% bonds			$ 6,250,000
Preferred $4 shares		$ 7,500,000	5,000,000
Common shares	$15,000,000	7,500,000	3,750,000
Total	$15,000,000	$15,000,000	$15,000,000

Instructions

1. Determine for each plan the earnings per common share, assuming that the income before bond interest and income tax is $2,500,000.

2. Determine for each plan the earnings per common share, assuming that the income before bond interest and income tax is $1,500,000.
3. ◖▬▬▬► Discuss the advantages and disadvantages of each plan.

PROBLEM 14–2A
Present value; bond premium; entries for bonds payable transactions; statement presentation
Objectives 3, 4

Icot Inc. produces and sells voltage regulators. On July 1, 2000, Icot Inc. issued $8,000,000 of 10-year, 6½% bonds at an effective interest rate of 6%. Interest on the bonds is payable semi-annually on December 31 and June 30. The fiscal year of the company is the calendar year.

Instructions

1. Compute the amount of the cash proceeds from the sale of the bonds and record the issuance of the bonds.
2. Journalize all entries required with respect to the bonds through to July 1, 2001, assuming the company amortizes premium using:
    a. the straight-line method,
    b. the effective interest rate method.
3. Show Icot's balance sheet disclosure for bonds payable on December 31, 2000 under both (a) and (b) above.
4. ◖▬▬▬► Will the bond proceeds always be greater than the face value of the bonds when the coupon rate is greater than the market rate of interest? Explain.

PROBLEM 14–3A
Present value; bond discount; entries for bonds payable transactions
Objectives 3, 4

On July 1, 1999, Tricon Communications Equipment Inc. issued $12,000,000 of 10-year, 7% bonds at an effective interest rate of 8%. Interest on the bonds is payable semi-annually on December 31 and June 30. The fiscal year of the company is the calendar year.

Instructions

1. Compute the amount of the cash proceeds from the sale of the bonds and record the issuance of the bonds.
2. Journalize all entries required with respect to the bond through to July 1, 2000, assuming the company amortizes discount using:
    a. the straight-line method,
    b. the effective interest rate method.
3. Determine the carrying value of the bonds payable at July 1, 2000 under (a) and (b) above.
4. The total interest expense Tricon will record over the life of the bond will be the same under both (a) and (b) above. Explain.

PROBLEM 14–4A
Entries for bonds payable transactions; straight-line method
Objectives 4, 6

Adtex Co. produces and sells synthetic string for tennis rackets. The following transactions were completed by Adtex Co., whose fiscal year is the calendar year:

1999
May 1. Issued $20,000,000 of 10-year, 9% callable bonds dated May 1, 1996, at an effective rate of 8%, receiving cash of $21,359,100. Interest is payable semi-annually on November 1 and May 1.
Nov. 1. Paid the semi-annual interest on the bonds.
Dec. 31. Accrued interest on bonds payable.
2000
May 1. Paid the semi-annual interest on the bonds.
Nov. 1. Paid the semi-annual interest on the bonds.
Dec. 31. Accrued interest on bonds payable.
2005
May 1. Recorded the redemption of one-half of the bonds, which were called at 101 after the payment of interest and amortization of premium have been recorded. (Record the redemption only.) *Hint:* Before recording the redemption, you must compute the balance in the premium account on July 1, 2005.

Instructions

1. Journalize the entries to record the foregoing transactions assuming the straight-line amortization method.

2. Calculate the amount of the interest expense in (a) 1999 and (b) 2000.
3. Determine the carrying value of the bonds as of December 31, 2000.

PROBLEM 14–5A
Entries for bonds payable transactions, convertibles, and sinking funds
Objectives 4, 5

The following selected transactions were completed by Dionne Inc.:

1999
April 1. Issued 7%, 10-year $1,000,000 nonconvertible bonds for face value plus accrued interest. The bonds pay semi-annual interest every August 1 and February 1.
Aug. 1. Paid interest on the 7% bonds.
Dec. 1. Issued 6%, 10-year $2,000,000 convertible bonds for $2,100,000. The bonds pay interest every June 1 and December 1. After five years the bonds may be converted to common shares at the rate of four shares for every $1,000 bond. The underwriter estimates that a similar issue of nonconvertible bonds would have sold for $1,850,000.

2001
Feb. 1. As required by its bond indenture, Dionne deposited $50,000 with a trustee to set up a sinking fund for repayment of its 7% bonds.
Dec. 31. The trustee reported that the sinking fund had earned income of $3,000 for the year.
2004
Dec. 1. All of the 6% bonds were converted to common shares.

Instructions

1. Journalize the entries to record the foregoing transactions. Assume that the company uses the straight-line method for amortization of bond premium or discount.
2. As a bondholder, would you prefer that the issuing company agree to: (a) make an annual appropriation of $70,000 retained earnings for future retirement of the bond issue or (b) make an annual deposit of $50,000 into a sinking fund administered by a trustee for future retirement of the bond issue? Explain.
3. Why do you think that the bondholders converted the 6% bonds in 2004?

PROBLEM 14–6A
Entries for bond investments
Objective 7

The following selected transactions relate to certain securities acquired by J-Spec Blueprints Inc., whose fiscal year ends on December 31:

1999
July 1. Purchased $500,000 of Schnell Company 20-year, 9% bonds dated July 1, 1999, directly from the issuing company, for $482,150.
Dec. 31. Received the semi-annual interest on the Schnell Company bonds.

(Assume that all intervening transactions and adjustments have been properly recorded and that the number of bonds owned has not changed from December 31, 1999, to December 31, 2003.)

2004
June 30. Received the semi-annual interest on the Schnell Company bonds.
Oct. 31. Sold one-half of the Schnell Company bonds at 97 plus accrued interest. The broker deducted $1,350 for commission, remitting the balance. The company recorded the interest accrued on the bonds to October 31 before recording disposal of the bonds.
Dec. 31. Received the semi-annual interest on the Schnell Company bonds.

Instructions
Journalize the entries to record the foregoing transactions assuming the bondholder uses the straight-line method for discount amortization.

PROBLEM 14–7A
Notes, leases, pensions, and income taxes
Objective 9

Brezeki Inc. incurred the following selected transactions during its first year of operations ended December 31, 2000.

Jan. 1. Purchased heavy machinery under a capital lease that called for installment payments of $40,000 to be made at the end of each of the next four years, with the first payment beginning December 31, 2000. The rate to be used for computing the present value of the lease is 8%.

July   1. Issued a non-interest-bearing note payable for $10,000 due in three years in exchange for office furniture. The market rate at the time was 8%.

Dec. 31. Recorded the lease payment and interest on the lease liability and record amortization on the leased asset.

Dec. 31. Accrued interest on the note payable.

Dec. 31. Recorded annual pension expense for the company's defined benefit pension plan of $30,000 and made a cash contribution to the pension fund of $25,000.

Dec. 31. Income tax expense for the year is $500,000. Income tax payable is $460,000. The difference is due to a temporary difference caused by an excess of capital cost allowance claimed in computing taxable income over amortization expense recorded for accounting purposes.

Instructions

1. Journalize the entries required to record all of the foregoing transactions.
2. Show how all liabilities arising from the above transactions would be recorded on the December 31, 2000 balance sheet. For each item, indicate the balance sheet classification (current or long-term).

PROBLEM 14–8A
Accounting concepts review

Indicate the generally accepted accounting principles or concepts that best justify each of the following accounting practices:

1. Income tax expense reported for a period is higher than the income tax payable for that period.
2. A bond sinking fund is not reported as a current asset.
3. In preparing the journal entry to record the issuance of bonds payable between interest dates, the accountant includes a credit to the Interest Payable account.
4. When a company issues a non-interest-bearing note payable in exchange for land, it records the land at less than the face amount of the note.
5. A company with a defined benefit pension plan records pension expense at an amount that is less than its contribution to the pension plan for the period.

PROBLEMS SERIES B

PROBLEM 14–1B
Effect of financing on earnings per share
Objective 1

Three different plans for financing a $20,000,000 corporation are under consideration by its organizers. Under each of the following plans, the company estimates that the preferred will sell for $100 per share and the common for $20. The income tax rate is 40% of income.

	Plan 1	Plan 2	Plan 3
12% bonds			$10,000,000
Preferred $8 shares		$10,000,000	5,000,000
Common shares	$20,000,000	10,000,000	5,000,000
Total	$20,000,000	$20,000,000	$20,000,000

Instructions

1. Determine for each plan the earnings per common share, assuming that the income before bond interest and income tax is $4,000,000.
2. Determine for each plan the earnings per common share, assuming that the income before bond interest and income tax is $2,000,000.
3. ◖▬▬► Discuss the advantages and disadvantages of each plan.

PROBLEM 14–2B
Present value; bond premium; entries for bonds payable transactions
Objectives 3, 4

Risotto Corporation produces and sells burial vaults. On July 1, 2000, Risotto Corporation issued $10,000,000 of 10-year, 9% bonds at an effective interest rate of 8%. Interest on the bonds is payable semi-annually on December 31 and June 30. The fiscal year of the company is the calendar year.

Instructions

1. Compute the amount of the cash proceeds from the sale of the bonds and record the issuance of the bonds.
2. Journalize all entries required with respect to the bonds through to July 1, 2001, assuming the company amortizes premium using:
   a. the straight-line method,
   b. the effective interest rate method.
3. Determine the carrying value of the bonds payable at July 1, 2001 under (a) and (b) above.
4. ◖▬▬► The total interest expense Risotto will record over the life of the bond will be the same under both (a) and (b) above. Explain.

PROBLEM 14–3B
Present value; bond discount; entries for bonds payable transactions; statement presentation
Objectives 3, 4

On July 1, 1999, Primo Corporation, a wholesaler of used robotic equipment, issued $15,000,000 of 10-year, 5% bonds at an effective interest rate of 6%. Interest on the bonds is payable semi-annually on December 31 and June 30. The fiscal year of the company is the calendar year.

Instructions

1. Compute the cash proceeds from the sale of the bonds and record the issuance of the bonds.
2. Journalize all entries required with respect to the bonds through to July 1, 2000, assuming the company amortizes discount using:
   a. the straight-line method,
   b. the effective interest rate method.
3. Show Primo's balance sheet disclosure for bonds payable on July 1, 2000 under both (a) and (b) above.
4. ◖▬▬► Will the bond proceeds always be less than the face value of the bonds when the coupon rate is less than the market rate of interest? Explain.

PROBLEM 14–4B
Entries for bonds payable transactions, effective interest rate method
Objectives 4, 6

The following transactions were completed by Lovin-Oven Appliances Inc., whose fiscal year is the calendar year:

2001
June 1. Issued $10,000,000 of 10-year, 9% callable bonds dated June 1, 2011, at an effective rate of 10%, receiving cash of $9,376,884. Interest is payable semi-annually on December 1 and June 1.
Dec. 1. Paid the semi-annual interest on the bonds.
Dec. 31. Accrued interest on bonds payable.
2002
June 1. Paid the semi-annual interest on the bonds.
Dec. 1. Paid the semi-annual interest on the bonds.
Dec. 31. Accrued interest on bonds payable.
2009
June 1. Recorded the redemption of the bonds, which were called at 102. The balance in the bond discount account is $126,423 after payment of interest and amortization of discount have been recorded. (Record the redemption only.)

Instructions

1. Journalize the entries to record the foregoing transactions assuming the effective interest rate method.
2. Indicate the amount of the interest expense in (a) 2001 and (b) 2002.
3. Determine the carrying value of the bonds as of December 31, 2002.

PROBLEM 14–5B
Entries for bonds payable transactions, convertibles, and sinking funds
Objectives 4, 5

The following selected transactions were completed by Vanderlaan Inc., which has a December 31 fiscal year end and which amortizes any premium or discount using the straight-line method.

2000

Mar. 1. Issued 7%, 15-year $1,000,000 convertible bonds for $1,130,000. The bonds pay interest every September 1 and March 1. After five years the bonds may be converted to common shares at the rate of five shares for every $1,000 bond. The underwriter estimated that a similar issue of nonconvertible bonds would have sold for $1,045,000. Vanderlaan uses the straight-line method for premium amortization.

Aug. 1. Issued 6½%, 10-year $800,000 nonconvertible bonds for face value plus accrued interest. The bonds pay semi-annual interest every June 30 and December 31.

Sept. 1. Paid interest on the 7% bonds.

Dec. 31. Paid interest on the 6½% bonds and accrued interest on the 7% bonds.

2001

June 1. As required by its bond indenture, Vanderlaan deposited $40,000 with a trustee to set up a sinking fund for repayment of its nonconvertible bonds.

Dec. 31. The trustee reported that the sinking fund had earned income of $1,500 for the year.

2010

June 30. The 6½% bonds matured and were retired using the $760,000 accumulated in the sinking fund plus additional cash from the company.

Instructions

1. Journalize the entries to record the foregoing transactions.
2. a. Why would a company want to issue convertible bonds?
   b. Why would an investor choose to buy convertible bonds?
   c. Some convertible bonds are held to maturity and never converted. Why?

PROBLEM 14–6B

Entries for bonds payable and bond investments

Objectives 4, 6, 7

Data Track Inc. develops and leases databases of publicly available information. The following selected transactions relate to certain securities acquired as a long-term investment by Data Track Inc., whose fiscal year ends on December 31:

2000

July 1. Purchased $600,000 of Marvel Company 10-year, 10% recallable bonds dated July 1, 2010, directly from the issuing company, for $617,700.

Dec. 31. Received the semi-annual interest on the Marvel Company bonds.

(Assume that all intervening transactions and adjustments have been properly recorded and that the number of bonds owned has not changed from December 31, 2000, to December 31, 2005.)

2006

June 30. Received the semi-annual interest on the Marvel Company bonds.

July 31. Marvel Company recalled one-half of the bonds at 102 plus accrued interest.

Dec. 31. Received the semi-annual interest on the Marvel Company bonds.

Instructions

Journalize the entries to record the foregoing transactions on the books of (a) Marvel Company and (b) Data Track Inc., assuming both companies use the straight-line amortization method. When preparing the July 31 journal entry, first prepare an entry to accrue interest and amortize any premium or discount to the date of the recall.

PROBLEM 14–7B

Notes, leases, pensions, and income taxes

Objective 9

Lin Inc. had the following selected transactions during its first year of operations ended December 31, 2001.

Jan. 1. Purchased equipment under a capital lease that called for a downpayment of $10,000 and installment payments of $25,000 to be made at the end of each of the next five years, with the first payment beginning December 31, 2001. The rate to be used for computing the present value of the lease is 6%. The equipment has a useful life of five years with no residual value.

Sept. 1. Issued a 6%, $20,000 note payable for cash. The note is due in four years and required annual interest payments to be made on August 31 of each year.

Dec. 31. Recorded the lease payment and interest on the lease liability. Recorded amortization on the leased equipment.

Dec. 31. Accrued interest on the note payable.

Dec. 31. Recorded annual pension expense for the company's defined benefit pension plan of $20,000 and made a cash contribution to the pension fund of $30,000.

Dec. 31. Income tax expense for the year was $300,000. Income tax payable was $310,000. The difference was due to a temporary difference between warranty expense deductible for tax purposes and warranty expense recorded on the company's income statement.

Instructions

1. Journalize the entries required to record all of the foregoing transactions.
2. Show how all assets and liabilities arising from the above transactions would be recorded on the December 31, 2001 balance sheet. For each item, indicate the balance sheet classification (current or long-term).

PROBLEM 14–8B
Accounting concepts review

Indicate which generally accepted accounting principles or concepts are violated by each of the practices described below. Do *not* prepare journal entries to correct any errors that you find.

1. Lion's Furniture advertises that customers can buy furniture with no payments and no interest for two years from the date of purchase. When Jerry Jones set up his dental practice, he made a purchase of office furniture from Lion, signing a $10,000 non-interest bearing note payable due in two years. Jones recorded the transaction as follows:

Office Furniture	10,000	
Note Payable		10,000

2. The bookkeeper at Isobel Co. prepared a preliminary balance sheet that showed "Discount on Bonds Payable" listed under Current Assets.
3. During the current year Wren Inc. reported accounting income before taxes of $800,000. Due to a temporary difference between warranty costs deducted on the company's tax return and warranty expense recorded on its income statement, taxable income was $820,000. Based on a 50% tax rate, Wren recorded income tax expense of $410,000 for the year.
4. Sloe Lee, a director of Chen Co., wants to report "Bond Sinking Fund" as a deduction from Retained Earnings. Lee argues that this presentation will clearly indicate that this amount of retained earnings is restricted and not available for distribution as dividends.
5. Retched Inc., which has a September 30 fiscal year end, issued 6%, $500,000 bonds payable for par on January 1, 2000. The bonds pay semi-annual interest every June 30 and December 31. For its fiscal year ended September 30, 2000 Retched recorded interest expense of $15,000.

CHALLENGE PROBLEMS

PROBLEM CP14–1

During your first year working as an auditor, you encounter the following **independent** situations:

1. On January 1, 2000 Turjid Co.'s books showed the following balances:

9% callable Bonds Payable, due December 31, 2009	$2,000,000
Discount on Bonds	100,000

The company immediately called one-half the bonds at the call price of 102. The accountant recorded the bond recall as follows:

Bonds Payable	1,020,000	
Cash		1,020,000

2. On April 1 Overdid Co. purchased 8% bonds with a face value of $500,000 for total cash proceeds of $510,000. The bonds pay semi-annual interest every June 30 and December 31. Overdid recorded its purchase on April 1 as follows:

Investment in Bonds	510,000	
Cash		510,000

On June 30, Overdid recorded the receipt of the semi-annual interest payment as follows:

Cash	20,000	
Interest Income		20,000

3. On August 1, when the market rate was 8%, Derlick Co. issued a three-year non-interest-bearing note payable with a face value of $90,000 in exchange for land and recorded the transaction as follows:

Land	90,000	
Note Payable		90,000

4. Dowdful Inc. reported accounting income before taxes as $900,000. Because the deduction for Capital Cost Allowance was in excess of the amount recorded for amortization expense, taxable income was $820,000. Dowdful is subject to a tax rate of 40% and recorded its income tax expense as follows:

Income tax expense	328,000	
Income tax payable		328,000

Instructions

For each of the above situations:

a. Explain the error that has been made.
b. Prepare a journal entry to correct the original entry that has already been made.

PROBLEM CP14–2

In March 2001 a flood destroyed most of the financial records of Micro Inc. You have managed to piece together a few fragmentary bits of information that show the following:

	Jan. 1, 2000	Dec. 31, 2000
Bonds Payable (issued Jan. 1, 2000)	$1,000,000	$1,000,000
Discount on bonds payable	74,383	68,764

You know that the bonds pay interest every June 30 and December 31, but you can only make out the following entry for bonds made in the journal. Other entries are too damaged to read.

June 30 Bond Interest Expense	27,768	
Discount on bonds payable		2,768
Cash		25,000
Record semi-annual interest on bonds.		

Instructions

From the information provided above, answer each of the following questions. Give reasons to justify your conclusions.

a. What is the contract rate on the bonds payable?
b. Reconstruct the journal entry for interest made on December 31. (Hint: consider the December 31 carrying value of the bonds).
c. Is the straight-line or effective interest rate method being used to amortize the bond discount?
d. What was the market rate at the date that the bonds were issued?
e. Were the bonds issued between interest dates? How can you tell?
f. Prepare the entry that was made when the bonds were issued on January 1, 2000.
g. Prepare the journal entry that will be made on June 30, 2001.

COMPREHENSIVE PROBLEM 4

Selected transactions completed by Petro Petroleum Products Inc. during the fiscal year ending July 31, 2000, were as follows:

a. Issued 10,000 no par common shares at $42, receiving cash.
b. Issued 7,500 $8 no par preferred shares at $115, receiving cash.
c. Issued $1,000,000 of 10-year, 8½% bonds at an effective interest rate of 8%, with interest payable semi-annually.
d. Declared a dividend of $0.40 per common share and $2 per preferred share. On the date of record, 100,000 common shares and 15,000 preferred shares were outstanding.
e. Paid the cash dividends declared in (d).
f. Redeemed $600,000 of eight-year, 12% bonds at 101. The balance in the bond premium account is $7,900 after the payment of interest and amortization of discount have been recorded. (Record only the redemption of the bonds payable.)
g. Transferred $600,000 of the appropriation for bonded indebtedness back to retained earnings for the bonds redeemed in (f).
h. Acquired 3,000 of its own common shares at $40 per share and retired the shares. The original issuance price of the shares was $42.
i. Declared a 5% stock dividend on common shares and a $2 cash dividend per preferred share. On the date of declaration, the market value of the common shares was $41 per share. On the date of record, 97,000 common shares and 15,000 preferred shares were outstanding.
j. Issued the share certificates for the stock dividends declared in (i) and paid the cash dividends to the preferred shareholders.
k. Purchased $50,000 of Auxiliary Inc. 10-year, 6% bonds, directly from the issuing company, for $48,500 plus accrued interest of $750.
l. Recorded the payment of semi-annual interest on the bonds issued in (c) and the amortization of the premium for six months. The amortization was determined using the straight-line method. (Round the amortization to the nearest dollar.)
m. Appropriated $100,000 of retained earnings for bonded indebtedness.
n. Appropriated $40,000 of retained earnings for plant expansion.
o. Accrued interest for four months on the Auxiliary Inc. bonds purchased in (k). Also recorded amortization of $50.

Instructions

1. Journalize the selected transactions.
2. After all of the transactions for the year ended July 31, 2000, had been posted (including the transactions recorded in (1) and all adjusting entries), the following data were selected from the records of Petro Petroleum Products Inc.:

Income statement data:

Advertising expense	$ 75,000
Cost of goods sold	3,850,000
Delivery expense	17,000
Amortization expense—office equipment	13,100
Amortization expense—store equipment	45,000
Gain on redemption of bonds	1,900
Income tax:	
Applicable to continuing operations	244,775
Credit applicable to loss from discontinued	
segment of the business	21,100
Applicable to gain on expropriation of property	10,500
Interest expense	48,500
Interest income	1,837
Loss from discontinued segment:	
From operations	15,500
From disposal	65,000

Miscellaneous administrative expenses	1,600
Miscellaneous selling expenses	6,300
Office rent expense	25,000
Office salaries expense	85,000
Office supplies expense	5,300
Sales	5,072,000
Sales commissions	95,000
Sales salaries expense	180,000
Store supplies expense	9,500
Gain on government expropriation of property	28,000

Retained earnings and balance sheet data:

Accounts payable	$ 149,500
Accounts receivable	280,500
Accumulated amortization—office equipment	835,250
Accumulated amortization—store equipment	2,214,750
Allowance for doubtful accounts	21,500
Bonds payable, 8½%, due 2007	1,000,000
Cash	146,345
Common shares, no par (400,000 shares authorized;	
104,850 shares outstanding)	2,916,250
Future tax liability (current)	4,700
Future tax liability (noncurrent)	21,000
Dividends:	
Cash dividends for common shares	120,000
Cash dividends for preferred shares	105,000
Stock dividends for common shares	198,850
Dividends payable	30,000
Income tax payable	55,900
Interest receivable	2,500
Investment in Auxiliary Inc. bonds (long-term)	48,550
Inventory (July 31, 2000), at lower of cost (FIFO) or market	425,000
Notes receivable	77,500
Office equipment	2,410,100
Organization costs	55,000
Contributed surplus—gain on reacquisition of	
common shares	6,000
Preferred $8 shares, no par (30,000 shares authorized;	
15,000 shares issued)	1,740,000
Premium on bonds payable	32,280
Prepaid expenses	15,900
Retained earnings:	
Appropriated for bonded indebtedness (August 1, 1999)	600,000
Appropriated for bonded indebtedness (July 31, 2000)	100,000
Appropriated for plant expansion (August 1, 1999)	—
Appropriated for plant expansion (July 31, 2000)	40,000
Unappropriated, August 1, 1999 (before closing)	2,529,303
Store equipment	8,603,950

a. Prepare a multiple-step income statement for the year ended July 31, 2000, concluding with earnings per share. In computing earnings per share, assume that the average number of common shares outstanding was 100,000 and preferred dividends were $105,000. Round to nearest cent.

b. Prepare a retained earnings statement for the year ended July 31, 2000.

c. Prepare a balance sheet in report form as of July 31, 2000.

CASES

CASE 14–1
Rapidwater Co.
Bond sinking funds

Rapidwater Co. produces and sells water slides for theme parks. Rapidwater Co. has outstanding a $40,000,000, 25-year, 10% debenture bond issue dated July 1, 1988. The bond issue is due June 30, 2013. The bond indenture requires a sinking fund, which has a balance of $14,000,000 as of July 1, 1999. Rapidwater Co. is currently experiencing a shortage of funds due to a recent plant expansion. Yonah Jones, treasurer of Rapidwater Co., has suggested using the sinking fund cash to temporarily relieve the shortage of funds. Jones' brother-in-law, who is trustee of the sinking fund, is willing to loan Rapidwater Co. the necessary funds from the sinking fund.

➤ Discuss whether Yonah Jones is behaving in an ethical manner.

CASE 14–2
Rotan Distributors Inc.
Present values

Rotan Distributors Inc. is a wholesaler of oriental rugs. The following is a luncheon conversation between Jennifer Dobbs, the assistant controller, and Clancy Byrne, an assistant financial analyst for Rotan.

Clancy: Jenny, do you mind if I spoil your lunch and ask you an accounting question?

Jennifer: No, go ahead. This chicken salad sandwich is pretty bad. It smells like it's three days old, and I've already picked three bones out of it.

Clancy: Well, as you know, in finance we use present values for capital budgeting analysis, assessing financing alternatives, etc. It's probably the most important concept that I learned in school that I actually use.

Jennifer: So . . . ?

Clancy: I was just wondering why accountants don't use present values more.

Jennifer: What do you mean?

Clancy: Well, it seems to me that you ought to value all the balance sheet liabilities at their present values.

➤ How would you respond if you were Jennifer?

CASE 14–3
Regis Sheats Inc.
Preferred shares vs. bonds

Regis Sheats Inc. has decided to expand its operations to owning and operating theme parks. The following is an excerpt from a conversation between the chief executive officer, JoAnn Eaves, and the vice-president of finance, Pat Seawright.

JoAnn: Pat, have you given any thought to how we're going to finance the acquisition of WaterWave Corporation?

Pat: Well, the two basic options, as I see it, are to issue either preferred shares or bonds. The equity market is a little depressed right now due to the recent volatility in some foreign stock exchanges.

JoAnn: Yes, I've heard the rumour. The problem is that we can't wait around to see what's going to happen. We'll have to move on this next week if we want any chance to complete the acquisition of WaterWave.

Pat: Well, the bond market is strong right now. Maybe we should issue debt this time around.

JoAnn: That's what I would have guessed as well. WaterWave's financial statements look pretty good, except for the volatility of their income and cash flows. But that's characteristic of their industry.

➤ Discuss the advantages and disadvantages of issuing preferred shares versus bonds.

CASE 14–4
Sears Canada Inc.
Financial analysis

A financial measure that focuses on the relative risk of the debtholders is the number of times the interest charges are earned during the year. The higher the ratio, the lower the risk that interest payments to the debtholders will not be made if earnings decrease. In other words, the higher the ratio, the greater the assurance that interest payments will be made on a continuing basis. This measure also indicates the general financial strength of the business.

The amount available to meet interest charges is not affected by taxes on income. This is because interest is deductible in determining taxable income. Thus, the number of times interest charges are earned is computed as shown below:

$$\text{Number of times interest charges earned} = \frac{\text{Income before income tax + Interest expense}}{\text{Interest expense}}$$

1. For Sears Canada Inc., determine the number of times interest charges were earned for the current and preceding years.
2. What conclusions can be drawn from the data concerning the risk of the debtholders for the interest payments and the general financial strength of Sears?

CASE 14–5
Summit Bottling Co.
Financing business expansion

You hold 25% of the common shares in a family-owned business, a soft drink bottling distributorship. Your sister, who is the manager, has proposed an expansion of plant facilities at an expected cost of $1,500,000. Two alternative plans have been suggested as methods of financing the expansion. Each plan is briefly described as follows:

Plan 1. Issue $1,500,000 of 20-year, 8% notes at face amount.
Plan 2. Issue an additional 10,000 common shares at $25 per share, and $1,250,000 of 20-year, 8% notes at face amount.

The balance sheet as of the end of the previous fiscal year is as follows:

Summit Bottling Co.
Balance Sheet
December 31, 20—

Assets	
Current assets	$2,350,000
Capital assets (net)	5,150,000
Total assets	$7,500,000

Liabilities and Shareholders' Equity	
Liabilities	$2,000,000
Common shares (80,000 authorized, 40,000 outstanding)	880,000
Retained earnings	4,620,000
Total liabilities and shareholders' equity	$7,500,000

Net income has remained relatively constant over the past several years. The expansion program is expected to increase yearly income before bond interest and income tax from $500,000 in the previous year to $600,000 for this year. Your sister has asked you, as the company treasurer, to prepare an analysis of each financing plan.

1. Prepare a table indicating the expected earnings per common share under each plan. Assume an income tax rate of 40%.
2. a. ▬▬► Discuss the factors that should be considered in evaluating the two plans.
   b. ▬▬► Which plan offers the greater benefit to the present shareholders? Give reasons for your opinion.

CASE 14–6
Platinum Co.
Secured long-term liabilities

The following is an excerpt from a telephone conversation between Stella Regis, a new commercial loan officer for Royal Bank, and Jeffrey Jarvis, the controller for Platinum Co. Platinum Co. has a $500,000 loan from Royal Bank that requires it to submit audited financial statements to the bank each year.

Stella: Jeff, thanks for returning my call.
Jeffrey: Sure, what can I help you with?
Stella: Well, I was reviewing your financial statements for this past year and I have a question concerning the value of your building and equipment.
Jeffrey: What's the question?
Stella: As you know, the building and equipment are collateral for your loan, and I can't find the market value of

these assets anywhere in the financial statements. All I can find is a note that indicates that the assets are pledged as collateral on the loan.
Jeffrey: That's right. Generally accepted accounting principles require that capital assets be reported at their cost, not at their market values. We had an appraisal on the building and equipment three years ago when we negotiated the loan. At that time, the market value was approximately $800,000—well in excess of the face value of the loan.
Stella: I'm sure the appraised value has changed. We'd like you to get a new appraisal for our files.
Jeffrey: I don't know. I'll have to discuss this with our president, Joan Golden. I'll get back to you some time tomorrow.

a. ⬤▬▬▶ Discuss the accounting principles that justify recording capital assets at their historical cost rather than at their market values.
b. What is the primary risk to Royal Bank concerning the loan of $500,000?
c. Assume that although Platinum Co. reported only a small net loss for the past year, Platinum is suffering financial distress and is likely to file for bankruptcy within a year. Should the financial statements of Platinum disclose this possibility?
d. Does Platinum Co. have to comply with Stella's request for a new appraisal on the building and equipment?

ANSWERS TO SELF-EXAMINATION QUESTIONS

1. **B** Since the contract rate on the bonds is higher than the prevailing market rate, a rational investor would be willing to pay more than the face amount, or a premium (answer B), for the bonds. If the contract rate and the market rate were equal, the bonds could be expected to sell at their face amount (answer A). Likewise, if the market rate is higher than the contract rate, the bonds would sell at a price below their face amount (answer D) or at a discount (answer C).

2. **A** The bond carrying amount, sometimes called the book value, is the face amount plus unamortized premium or less unamortized discount. For this question, the carrying amount is $500,000 less $40,000, or $460,000 (answer A).

3. **B** Although the sinking fund may consist of cash as well as securities, the fund is listed on the balance sheet as an investment (answer B) because it is to be used to pay the long-term liability at maturity.

4. **B** The amount debited to the investment account is the cost of the bonds, which includes the amount paid to the seller for the bonds (101% × $100,000) plus broker's commissions ($50), or $101,050 (answer B). The $2,000 of accrued interest that is paid to the seller should be debited to Interest Receivable, since it is an offset against the amount that will be received as interest at the next interest date.

5. **C** The balance of Discount on Bonds Payable is usually reported as a deduction from Bonds Payable in the Long-Term Liabilities section (answer C) of the balance sheet. Likewise, a balance in a premium on bonds payable account would usually be reported as an addition to Bonds Payable in the Long-Term Liabilities section of the balance sheet.

15   Statement of Cash Flows

YOU AND ACCOUNTING

How much cash do you have in the bank or in your wallet? How much cash did you have at the beginning of the month? The difference between these two amounts is the net change in your cash during the month. Knowing the reasons for the change in cash may be useful in evaluating where your money is coming from, where it is going to, whether your financial position has improved, and whether you will be able to pay your bills in the future.

For example, assume that you had $200 at the beginning of the month and $550 at the end of the month. The net change in cash is $350. Based on this net change, it appears that your financial position has improved. However, this conclusion may or may not be valid, depending upon how the change of $350 was created. If you *borrowed* $1,000 during the month and spent $650 on living expenses, your cash would have increased by $350. On the other hand, if you *earned* $1,000 and spent $650 on living expenses, your cash would have also increased by $350, but your financial position is improved compared to the first scenario.

In previous chapters, we have used the income statement, balance sheet, retained earnings statement, and other information to analyze the effects of management decisions on a business's revenues and costs. In this chapter, we present the basic preparation and use of the statement of cash flows.

After studying this chapter, you should be able to:

Objective 1
Explain why the statement of cash flows is one of the basic financial statements and define cash flows.

Objective 2
Summarize the types of cash flow activities reported in the statement of cash flows.

Objective 3
Prepare a statement of cash flows, using the indirect method.

Objective 4
Prepare a statement of cash flows, using the direct method.

Purpose of the Statement of Cash Flows

Objective 1
Explain why the statement of cash flows is one of the basic financial statements and define cash flows.

The statement of cash flows reports a firm's major cash inflows and outflows for a period. It provides useful information about a firm's ability to generate cash from operations, maintain and expand its operating capacity, meet its financial obligations, and pay dividends.

The statement of cash flows is one of the basic financial statements. The recently updated *CICA Handbook* recommendations in this area[1] require all public enterprises to include this statement as an integral part of their financial statements.[2] It highlights changes in net assets and in the financial structure of the firm. Managers use it in evaluating past operations and in planning future investing and financing activities. Creditors, investors, and others use it in assessing the ability of the enterprise to generate cash in order to adapt to changing circumstances and opportunities. It helps users to predict and compare the future cash flows of different

FOCUS ON CASH FLOW

In the past, investors and creditors have relied heavily on a company's earnings information in judging the company's performance. A 1991 survey reported a change in shareholder attitudes over the last two decades, with today's investors placing less emphasis on the income statement and exhibiting an increasing interest in cash flow information.

Between 1970 and 1973 the now bankrupt W.T. Grant Company was reporting net income above $40 million per year. At the same time, the cash flow provided by operations was decreasing at an alarming rate—by 1973 net cash outflow was more than $90 million. This story is a classic piece of evidence of the usefulness of cash flow information as a tool for predicting future firm performance.

With the aid of 20/20 hindsight, it is clear that the deteriorating cash position should have provided an early warning signal to investors and other interested parties. For many investors, however, when the news of W.T. Grant's impending bankruptcy finally reached the market, it was too late. They had accepted the reported earnings per share figures with blind faith and neglected to examine cash flows ....

Investors are more sophisticated than they were in 1973.... More aware of the reporting choices available under generally accepted accounting principles, investors are suspicious of the net income figure as a measure of firm performance. The cash flow, in contrast, is not affected by accounting rules. Cash flow provides a more "tangible" yardstick by which to measure a firm's performance.... The trend is to focus more attention on cash flow than ever before.

Source: M.J. Epstein and M.L. Pava, "How Useful is the Statement of Cash Flows?", *Management Accounting,* July 1992, pp. 52–55.

[1] The latest version of the *CICA Handbook*, Section 1540, "Cash Flow Statements," issued in June, 1998, applies to financial statements for fiscal year ends beginning on or after August 1, 1998.
[2] *CICA Handbook*, Section 1540.03.

enterprises. The statement of cash flows enhances our ability to compare the operating performance of various businesses by eliminating the effects caused by the use of different accounting methods across firms.

Cash flows are defined as inflows and outflows of **cash and cash equivalents**. Cash consists of cash on hand and demand deposits in the bank. Cash equivalents are short-term, highly liquid investments that are readily convertible to known amounts of cash and subject to an insignificant risk of changes in value.[3] To be classified as a cash equivalent, an investment would normally mature within three months from the date of acquisition and could not be an equity investment.[4] If the bank balance is often in an overdraft position, the bank overdraft may be included as a negative component of cash and cash equivalents.[5]

Reporting Cash Flows

Objective 2
Summarize the types of cash flow activities reported in the statement of cash flows.

The statement of cash flows reports cash flows associated with three types of activities:[6]

1. **Cash flows from operating activities** are cash flows primarily derived from the principal revenue-generating activities of the firm, generally resulting from transactions that affect net income.[7] Examples of such transactions include the purchase and sale of merchandise by a retailer.
2. **Cash flows from investing activities** are cash flows from transactions that affect noncurrent assets. Examples of such transactions include the sale and purchase of capital assets, such as equipment and buildings.
3. **Cash flows from financing activities** are cash flows from transactions that affect the equity and debt of the entity. Examples of such transactions include the issuing or retiring of shares and long-term debt.

The cash flows from operating activities are normally presented first, followed by the cash flows from investing activities and financing activities. The total of the net cash flow from these activities is the net increase or decrease in cash for the period. The cash balance at the beginning of the period is added to the net increase or decrease in cash, to arrive at the cash balance at the end of the period. The ending cash balance on the statement of cash flows equals the cash reported on the balance sheet.

Exhibit 1 shows common cash flow transactions reported in each of the three sections of the statement of cash flows. Reporting cash flows by operating, investing, and financing activities highlights significant relationships within and among the activities. For example, the user can more easily relate the cash receipts from issuing bonds to repayments of borrowings when both appear as financing activities. Also, the user can easily identify the impact of each of the three activities (operating, investing, and financing) on cash flows. This allows investors and creditors to evaluate the effects of cash flows on a firm's profits and ability to pay debt.

CASH FLOWS FROM OPERATING ACTIVITIES

The most frequent and often the most important cash flows of a business relate to operating activities. There are two alternative methods for reporting cash flows from operating activities in the statement of cash flows. These methods are (1) the direct method and (2) the indirect method.

[3] *Ibid.*, 1540.06.
[4] *Ibid.*, 1540.08.
[5] *Ibid.*, 1540.09.
[6] *Ibid.*, 1540.12.
[7] *Ibid.*, 1540.16.

Exhibit 1
Cash Flows

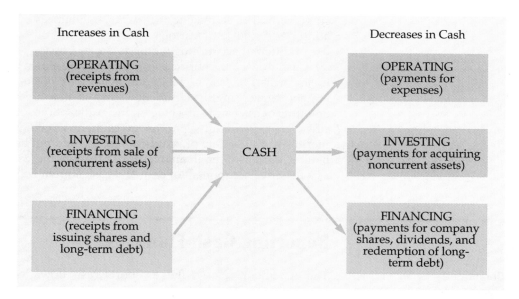

The **direct method** reports the sources of operating cash and the uses of operating cash. The major source of operating cash is cash received from customers. The major uses of operating cash include cash paid to suppliers for merchandise and services and cash paid to employees for wages. If operating cash receipts exceed cash payments, the difference between these is the **net cash flow from operating activities.**

The primary advantage of the direct method is that it reports the sources and uses of cash in the statement of cash flows. Its primary disadvantage is that the necessary data may not be readily available and may be costly to gather.

The **indirect method** reports the operating cash flows by beginning with net income and adjusting it for revenues and expenses that do not involve the receipt or payment of cash. (We adjust accrual net income to determine the net amount of cash flows from operating activities.)

A major advantage of the indirect method is that it focuses on the differences between net income and cash flows from operations. In this sense, it shows the relationship between the income statement, the balance sheet, and the statement of cash flows. Its primary disadvantage is that the sources and uses of operating cash flows are not itemized.

While both the direct and indirect methods are generally acceptable, accounting standard setters encourage the use of the direct method.[8] However, due to the historical evolution of the report, the majority of Canadian companies use the indirect method. *Financial Reporting in Canada (1997)* reports that only two out of 200 firms surveyed used the direct method for reporting cash flows from operating activities.[9]

CASH FLOWS FROM INVESTING ACTIVITIES

Cash inflows from investing activities normally arise from selling capital assets, long-term investments, and intangible assets. Cash outflows normally include payments to acquire capital assets, long-term investments, and intangible assets.

We report cash flows from investing activities on the statement of cash flows by first listing the cash inflows followed by the cash outflows. If the inflows are greater than the outflows, we report the **net cash flow provided by investing activities.**

---

[8] *Ibid.*, 1540.20–21.
[9] C. Byrd and I. Chen, *Financial Reporting in Canada,* 22nd edition, CICA, Toronto, 1997, p. 87.

If the cash inflows are less than the cash outflows, we report the **net cash flow used for investing activities.**

CASH FLOWS FROM FINANCING ACTIVITIES

Cash inflows from financing activities normally arise from issuing long-term debt or equity securities. Examples of such inflows include issuing bonds, long-term notes payable, and preferred and common shares. Cash outflows from financing activities include paying cash dividends, repaying debt, and reacquiring the company's own shares.

We report cash flows from financing activities on the statement of cash flows by first listing the cash inflows followed by the cash outflows. If the inflows are greater than the outflows, we report the **net cash flow provided by financing activities.** If the cash inflows are less than the cash outflows, we report the **net cash flow used for financing activities.**

ILLUSTRATIONS OF THE STATEMENT OF CASH FLOWS

Exhibit 2 presents two illustrations of the statement of cash flows. Both statements are for the same accounting period for Computer King, which was used in illustrations in the early chapters of this text. The first statement reports cash flows from operating activities by the direct method. The second statement reports cash flows from operating activities by the indirect method. The same amount of net cash flow from operating activities is reported, regardless of the method. The statement has been prepared using a convention of reporting cash outflows in brackets and inflows without brackets. This method eliminates the use of words like paid and received, and makes distinguishing inflows and outflows easier. As well, it becomes easier to prepare a comparative statement using two columns only (a common practice). We will illustrate both methods in detail later in this chapter.

An enterprise must disclose the components of cash and cash equivalents and present a reconciliation of the amounts in the cash flow statement with the equivalent items reported in the balance sheet.[10] It can report this information at the bottom of the statement or in a note to the financial statements. No additional disclosure is required in the Computer King example shown below, since cash and

Exhibit 2
Statements of Cash Flows

Computer King Statement of Cash Flows—Direct Method For the Month Ended November 30, 1999		
Cash flows from operating activities:		
Cash received from customers	$ 7,500	
Cash payments for expenses and payment		
to creditors	(4,600)	
Net cash flow from operating activities		$ 2,900
Cash flows from investing activities:		
Acquisition of land		(10,000)
Cash flows from financing activities:		
Owner's investment	15,000	
Withdrawals by owner	(2,000)	
Net cash flow from financing activities		13,000
Increase in cash		5,900
Cash at the beginning of the month		—
Cash at the end of the month		$ 5,900

[10]*CICA Handbook,* 1540.48.

Exhibit 2 (concluded)

Computer King
Statement of Cash Flows—Indirect Method
For the Month Ended November 30, 1999

Cash flows from operating activities:		
Net income, per income statement	$ 3,050	
Add increase in accounts payable	400	
	3,450	
Deduct increase in supplies	(550)	
Net cash flow from operating activities		$ 2,900
Cash flows from investing activities:		
Acquisition of land		(10,000)
Cash flows from financing activities:		
Owner's investment	15,000	
Withdrawals by owner	(2,000)	
Net cash flow from financing activities		13,000
Increase in cash		5,900
Cash at the beginning of the month		–
Cash at the end of the month		$ 5,900

cash equivalents consist only of the cash balance in the bank. In more complex businesses, cash and cash equivalents could be made up of cash in the bank plus short-term deposits, minus bank overdrafts, and demand loans.

NONCASH ACTIVITIES

A business may enter into investing and financing activities that do not directly involve cash and cash equivalents. We exclude such transactions from the cash flow statement and disclose them elsewhere in the financial statements in a way that provides all of the relevant information,[11] usually in the notes to the financial statements. Examples of noncash investing and financing activities include items such as:

a. the acquisition of noncash assets by assuming liabilities;
b. the acquisition of assets through a capital lease;
c. the issuance of shares to acquire an enterprise;
d. the conversion of debt to equity.[12]

In addition, the statement of cash flows also excludes other types of noncash transactions, such as stock splits, stock dividends, and appropriations of retained earnings. These transactions, which do not change the firm's assets, liabilities, or total shareholders' equity, are neither investing nor financing transactions. As discussed in Chapter 13, the corporation must disclose such changes in shareholders' equity either in the statements or in notes to the statements.

CASH FLOW PER SHARE

Several Canadian companies report *cash flow per share* in their financial statements. Users need to interpret such a number carefully, since it is not a measure of profitability (as is earnings per share), nor does it indicate the cash available for payments to shareholders. If a company chooses to disclose this information, it should report it either on the statement of cash flows or in notes cross-referenced to the statement. Cash flow per share should not appear on the income statement.[13]

[11] *Ibid.*, 1540.46.
[12] *Ibid.*, 1540.47
[13] *CICA Handbook*, Emerging Issues Committee Abstract 34, "Presentation of Cash Flow Per Share Information."

Statement of Cash Flows—The Indirect Method

Objective 3

Prepare a statement of cash flows, using the indirect method.

Because it is used in the majority of annual reports, we will discuss the indirect method of preparing the statement of cash flows first.

To collect the data for the statement of cash flows, we could analyze all the cash receipts and cash payments for a period and then report them by purpose (operating, investing, or financing). However, this procedure is expensive and time-consuming. A more efficient approach is to analyze the changes in the noncash balance sheet accounts. The logic of this approach is that a change in any balance sheet account (including cash) can be analyzed in terms of changes in the other balance sheet accounts. To illustrate, we can rewrite the accounting equation to focus on the cash account as follows:

$$\text{Assets} = \text{Liabilities} + \text{Shareholders' Equity}$$
$$\text{Cash} + \text{Noncash Assets} = \text{Liabilities} + \text{Shareholders' Equity}$$
$$\text{Cash} = \text{Liabilities} + \text{Shareholders' Equity} - \text{Noncash Assets}$$

Any change in the cash account results in a change in one or more noncash balance sheet accounts. That is, if the cash account changes, then a liability, shareholders' equity, or noncash asset account must also change. In other words, if the following two equations balance, then the third equation must be true.

If Cash = Liabilities + Shareholders' Equity − Noncash Assets,
at the beginning of the year

and

If Cash = Liabilities + Shareholders' Equity − Noncash Assets,
at the end of the year

then

Change in Cash = Change in Liabilities + Change Shareholders' Equity − Change in Noncash Assets
during the year

We can also obtain additional explanatory data by analyzing the income statement accounts and supporting records. For example, since the net income or net loss for the period is closed to Retained Earnings, a change in the retained earnings account can be partially explained by the net income or net loss reported on the income statement.

There is no order in which one must analyze the noncash balance sheet accounts. However, it is usually more efficient to analyze the accounts in the reverse order in which they appear on the balance sheet. Thus, the analysis of retained earnings provides the starting point for determining the cash flows from operating activities, which is the first section of the statement of cash flows.

We will use the comparative balance sheet for Rundell Ltd. on December 31, 1999 and 1998 to illustrate the indirect method. This balance sheet is shown in Exhibit 3. Selected ledger accounts and other data are presented as needed.[14]

RETAINED EARNINGS

The comparative balance sheet for Rundell Ltd. shows that retained earnings increased $60,500 during the year. Analyzing the entries posted to the retained

---

[14]We present an appendix that discusses using a work sheet as an aid in assembling data for the statement of cash flows at the end of this chapter. This appendix illustrates a work sheet that can be used with the indirect method and a work sheet that can be used with the direct method of reporting cash flows from operating activities.

Exhibit 3
Comparative Balance Sheet

Rundell Ltd. Comparative Balance Sheet December 31, 1999 and 1998			
	1999	1998	*Increase Decrease**
Assets			
Cash	$ 49,000	$ 26,000	$ 23,000
Trade receivables (net)	74,000	65,000	9,000
Inventories	172,000	180,000	8,000*
Prepaid expenses	4,000	3,000	1,000
Investments (long-term)	—	45,000	45,000*
Land	90,000	40,000	50,000
Building	200,000	200,000	—
Accumulated amortization—building	(36,000)	(30,000)	(6,000)
Equipment	290,000	142,000	148,000
Accumulated amortization—equipment	(43,000)	(40,000)	(3,000)
Total assets	$800,000	$631,000	$169,000
Liabilities			
Accounts payable (merchandise creditors)	$ 45,000	$ 28,200	$ 16,800
Accrued expenses (operating expenses)	5,000	3,800	1,200
Income tax payable	2,500	4,000	1,500*
Dividends payable	15,000	8,000	7,000
Bonds payable	120,000	245,000	125,000*
Total liabilities	187,500	289,000	101,500*
Shareholders' Equity			
Preferred shares	$160,000	—	$160,000
Common shares	280,000	$230,000	50,000
Retained earnings	172,500	112,000	60,500
Total shareholders' equity	$612,500	$342,000	$270,500
Total liabilities and shareholders' equity	$800,000	$631,000	$169,000

earnings account indicates how this change occurred. The retained earnings account for Rundell Ltd. is shown below.

ACCOUNT RETAINED EARNINGS   ACCOUNT NO.

Date		Item	Debit	Credit	Balance Debit	Balance Credit
1999						
Jan.	1	Balance				112,000
Dec.	31	Net income		90,500		202,500
	31	Cash dividends	30,000			172,500

The retained earnings account must be carefully analyzed because some of the entries to retained earnings may not affect cash. For example, a decrease in retained earnings resulting from issuing a stock dividend does not affect cash. Likewise, an appropriation of retained earnings does not affect cash. Such transactions are not reported on the statement of cash flows.

For Rundell Ltd., the retained earnings account indicates that the $60,500 change resulted from net income of $90,500 and cash dividends declared of $30,000. We discuss the effect of each of these items on cash flows next.

Cash Flows from Operating Activities

The net income of $90,500 reported by Rundell Ltd. normally is not equal to the amount of cash generated from operations during the period. This is because net income is determined using the accrual method of accounting.

Under the accrual method of accounting, the period in which a business records revenues and expenses often differs from when it receives or pays cash. For example, the company may sell inventory on account and receive the cash at a later date.

Likewise, insurance expense represents the amount of insurance expired during the period even though the company may have paid the premiums for the insurance in a prior period. Thus, we have to adjust the net income reported on the income statement to determine cash flows from operating activities. Exhibit 4 summarizes the typical adjustments to net income.

Exhibit 4

Adjustments to Net Income—Indirect Method

Net income, per income statement		$XX
Add: Amortization of physical capital assets	$XX	
Amortization of intangible capital assets	XX	
Decreases in current assets (receivables, inventories, prepaid expenses)	XX	
Increases in current liabilities (accounts and notes payable, accrued liabilities)	XX	
Losses on disposal of noncurrent assets and retirement of debt	XX	XX
Deduct: Increases in current assets (receivables, inventories, prepaid expenses)	$XX	
Decreases in current liabilities (accounts and notes payable, accrued liabilities)	XX	
Gains on disposal of noncurrent assets and retirement of debt	XX	XX
Net cash flow from operating activities		$XX

Some of the adjustment items in Exhibit 4 are for expenses that affect noncurrent accounts but not cash. For example, amortization of physical capital assets and amortization of intangible capital assets decrease income but do not affect cash.

Some of the adjustment items in Exhibit 4 are for revenues and expenses that affect current assets and current liabilities but not cash flows. For example, a sale of $10,000 on account increases accounts receivable by $10,000. However, cash is not affected. Thus, the increase in accounts receivable of $10,000 between two balance sheet dates is deducted from net income to arrive at cash flows from operating activities.

Cash flows from operating activities should not include investing or financing transactions. For example, assume that a business sold land costing $50,000 for $90,000 (a gain of $40,000). We should report the sale as an investing activity: "Proceeds from the sale of land, $90,000." However, the $40,000 gain on the sale of the land is included in net income on the income statement. Thus, we must *deduct* the $40,000 gain *from* net income in determining cash flows from operations in order to avoid "double counting" the cash flow from the gain. Similarly, we must *add* losses from the sale of capital assets *to* net income in determining cash flows from operations.

Suppose that a company recalled bonds payable with a carrying value of $100,000 for a call price of $105,000. We should report as a financing activity:

"Cash used to retire bonds payable, $105,000." However, a $5,000 loss on bond retirement was deducted in computing net income. Therefore, to avoid double counting, we add losses on the retirement of long-term debt to net income to determine cash flows from operating activities. Similarly, we must deduct gains on retirement of long-term debt from net income in determining cash flows from operating activities.

The effect of dividends payable on cash flows from operating activities is omitted from Exhibit 4. Dividends payable is omitted because dividends are charged directly to retained earnings and do not affect net income. Section 3860 of the *CICA Handbook* requires that certain types of complex financial instruments, which have the appearance of shares but the characteristics of debt, be classified as liabilities. A corporation must report dividends declared on these securities on the income statement. Section 1540.34 of the *CICA Handbook* requires that the company include cash flows for such dividends under operating activities on the statement of cash flows. We leave the illustration of these types of dividends to more advanced accounting texts. In all of the examples included in this chapter, we assume that dividends declared relate to common or preferred shares that are classified as shareholders' equity. Such dividends are always charged directly to retained earnings and never appear on the income statement. Cash payments for these dividends are reported under financing activities on the statement of cash flows. Later in the chapter, we discuss the reporting of such dividends in the statement of cash flows.

In the following paragraphs, we discuss the adjustment of Rundell Ltd.'s net income to "Cash flows from operating activities."

Amortization of Capital Assets

The comparative balance sheet in Exhibit 3 indicates that Accumulated Amortization—Equipment increased by $3,000 and Accumulated Amortization—Building by $6,000. As shown below, these two accounts indicate that amortization for the year was $12,000 for the equipment and $6,000 for the building, or a total of $18,000.

ACCOUNT ACCUMULATED AMORTIZATION—EQUIPMENT   ACCOUNT NO.

Date		Item	Debit	Credit	Balance Debit	Balance Credit
1999						
Jan.	1	Balance				40,000
May	9	Discarded, no salvage	9,000			31,000
Dec.	31	Amortization for year		12,000		43,000

ACCOUNT ACCUMULATED AMORTIZATION—BUILDING   ACCOUNT NO.

Date		Item	Debit	Credit	Balance Debit	Balance Credit
1999						
Jan.	1	Balance				30,000
Dec.	31	Amortization for year		6,000		36,000

The $18,000 of amortization expense reduced net income but did not require an outflow of cash. Thus, we must add back the $18,000 to net income in determining cash flows from operating activities, as follows:

Cash flows from operating activities:
  Net income $90,500
  Add: Amortization   18,000 $108,500

Current Assets and Current Liabilities

As shown in Exhibit 4, we add decreases in noncash current assets and increases in current liabilities to net income to arrive at cash from operating activities. In contrast, we deduct increases in noncash current assets and decreases in current liabilities from net income. The current asset and current liability accounts of Rundell Ltd. are as follows:

	December 31		Increase Decrease*
Accounts	1999	1998	
Accounts receivable (net)	$ 74,000	$ 65,000	$ 9,000
Inventories	172,000	180,000	8,000*
Prepaid expenses	4,000	3,000	1,000
Accounts payable (merchandise creditors)	45,000	28,200	16,800
Accrued expenses (operating expenses)	5,000	3,800	1,200
Income taxes payable	2,500	4,000	1,500*

Using the indirect method of reporting cash flows, Rundell Ltd. added the $8,000 decrease in inventories to net income to determine the cash flows from operating income.

The $9,000 increase in **accounts receivable** indicates that the sales on account during the year are $9,000 more than collections from customers on account. The amount reported as sales on the income statement therefore includes $9,000 that did not result in a cash inflow during the year. Thus, we must deduct $9,000 from net income in determining cash from operating activities.

The $8,000 decrease in **inventories** indicates that the merchandise sold exceeds the cost of the merchandise purchased by $8,000. The amount deducted as cost of goods sold on the income statement therefore includes $8,000 that did not require a cash outflow during the year. Thus, we add $8,000 to net income. The $1,000 increase in prepaid expenses indicates that the cash payments for prepaid expenses exceed the amount deducted as an expense during the year by $1,000. Thus, $1,000 is deducted from net income.

The $16,800 increase in **accounts payable** indicates that the amount recorded during the year for merchandise purchased on account exceeds the cash payments made on account by $16,800. The amount reported on the income statement for cost of goods sold therefore includes $16,800 that did not require a cash outflow during the year. Thus, we add $16,800 to net income.

The $1,200 increase in **accrued expenses** indicates that the amount recorded during the year for operating expenses exceeds the cash payments by $1,200. The amount reported on the income statement for operating expenses therefore includes $1,200 that did not require a cash outflow during the year. Thus, we add $1,200 to net income.

The $1,500 decrease in **income taxes payable** indicates that the amount paid for taxes exceeds the amount expensed during the year by $1,500. The amount reported on the income statement for income tax therefore is less than the amount paid by $1,500. Thus, we deduct $1,500 from net income.

The preceding adjustments to net income are summarized below.

Cash flows from operating activities:			
Net income			$ 90,500
Add: Amortization	$18,000		
Decrease in inventories	8,000		
Increase in accounts payable	16,800		
Increase in accrued expenses	1,200	44,000	
		134,500	
Deduct: Increase in trade receivables	(9,000)		
Increase in prepaid expenses	(1,000)		
Decrease in income taxes payable	(1,500)	(11,500)	$123,000

Gain on Sale of Investments

The ledger or income statement of Rundell Ltd. indicates that the sale of long-term investments resulted in a gain of $30,000. As we discussed previously, we include the sale proceeds (which equal the gain plus the carrying value of the investments) in cash flows from investing activities.[15] The gain is also included in net income. Thus, to avoid double reporting, we deduct the gain of $30,000 from net income in determining cash flows from operating activities, as shown below.

Cash flows from operating activities:	
Net income	$90,500
Deduct: Gain on sale of investments	(30,000)

Reporting Cash Flows from Operating Activities

We have now presented all the necessary adjustments to convert the net income to cash flows from operating activities for Rundell Ltd. Exhibit 5 summarizes these adjustments in a format suitable for the statement of cash flows.

Exhibit 5

Cash Flows from Operating Activities—Indirect Method

Cash flows from operating activities:			
Net income, per income statement			$ 90,500
Add: Amortization	$18,000		
Decrease in inventories	8,000		
Increase in accounts payable	16,800		
Increase in accrued expenses	1,200	44,000	
		134,500	
Deduct: Increase in accounts receivable	(9,000)		
Increase in prepaid expenses	(1,000)		
Decrease in income taxes payable	(1,500)		
Gain on sale of investments	(30,000)	(41,500)	
Net cash flow from operating activities			$93,000

USING ACCOUNTING TO UNDERSTAND BUSINESS

The Chief Financial Officer (CFO) of Honeywell Corporation put all managers through a financial training course in order to help them think about the cash implications of their decisions. The CFO wanted his managers to understand how cash can be tied up in current assets, such as receivables and inventory, and that growth can be achieved without significant working capital requirements. As a result, Honeywell generated cash by reducing its working capital needs from $2.2 billion to $1.6 billion, while still growing the business.

---

[15]The reporting of the proceeds (cash flows) from the sale of long-term investments as part of investing activities is discussed later in this chapter.

Cash Flows Used for Payment of Dividends

According to the retained earnings account of Rundell Ltd., shown earlier in the chapter, the corporation declared cash dividends of $30,000 during the year. However, the account, shown below, indicates that dividends of only $23,000 were paid during the year.

ACCOUNT DIVIDENDS PAYABLE   ACCOUNT NO.

Date		Item	Debit	Credit	Balance Debit	Balance Credit
1999						
Jan.	1	Balance				8,000
	10	Cash paid	8,000		—	—
June	20	Dividend declared		15,000		15,000
July	10	Cash paid	15,000		—	—
Dec.	20	Dividend declared		15,000		15,000

The $23,000 of dividend payments represent a cash outflow that is reported as a deduction from cash inflows in the financing activities section as follows:

Cash flows from financing activities:
  Less: Cash paid for dividends   ($23,000)

COMMON SHARES

The common shares account increased by $50,000, as shown below. This increase results from issuing shares in exchange for land valued at $50,000.

ACCOUNT COMMON SHARES, NO PAR   ACCOUNT NO.

Date		Item	Debit	Credit	Balance Debit	Balance Credit
1999						
Jan.	1	Balance				230,000
Dec.	28	Issued in exchange for land		50,000		280,000

Although no inflow or outflow of cash occurred, the transaction represents a significant investing and financing activity. As discussed previously, we do not report these transactions on the statement of cash flows, but disclose them in a separate note or schedule accompanying the financial statements. We could report the transaction as follows:

Note _____

Noncash investing and financing activities:
  Acquisition of land by issuance of common shares $50,000

PREFERRED SHARES

The preferred shares account increased by $160,000 as shown below. This increase resulted from issuing preferred shares for $160,000.

ACCOUNT PREFERRED SHARES, NO PAR   ACCOUNT NO.

Date		Item	Debit	Credit	Balance Debit	Balance Credit
1999 Nov.	1	30,000 shares issued for cash		160,000		160,000

This cash inflow is reported in the financing activities section as follows:

Cash flows from financing activities:
   Issuance of preferred shares $160,000

BONDS PAYABLE

The bonds payable account decreased by $125,000, as shown below. This decrease results from retiring the bonds by a cash payment for their face value.

ACCOUNT BONDS PAYABLE   ACCOUNT NO.

Date		Item	Debit	Credit	Balance Debit	Balance Credit
1999 Jan.	1	Balance				245,000
June	30	Retired by payment of cash at face amount	125,000			120,000

    We report this cash outflow as a deduction from cash inflows in the financing activities section as follows:

Cash flows from financing activities:
   Retirement of bonds payable   ($125,000)

When bonds are issued, the issuer reports as a cash inflow from financing activities the *total proceeds* received (excluding any accrued interest). On the other side, the investor reports as a cash outflow in investing activities the *total amount* paid for the bonds (excluding any accrued interest). This same treatment applies whether the bonds are issued at par or at a premium or discount. However, after issuance, the reporting on the cash flow statement of bond premium or discount amortization, early redemption, or payment at maturity for bonds issued at a premium or discount is somewhat complicated. We leave the coverage of these items to more advanced accounting texts. For simplicity, we will illustrate only bonds issued at par value throughout this chapter.

EQUIPMENT

The equipment account increased by $148,000, and the accumulated amortization—equipment account increased by $3,000, as shown below.

ACCOUNT EQUIPMENT   ACCOUNT NO.

Date		Item	Debit	Credit	Balance Debit	Balance Credit
1999 Jan.	1	Balance			142,000	
May	9	Discarded, no salvage		9,000	133,000	
Dec.	7	Purchased for cash	157,000		290,000	

ACCOUNT ACCUMULATED AMORTIZATION—EQUIPMENT   ACCOUNT NO.

Date		Item	Debit	Credit	Balance Debit	Balance Credit
1999						
Jan.	1	Balance				40,000
May	9	Discarded, no salvage	9,000			31,000
Dec.	7	Amortization for the year		12,000		43,000

The $148,000 increase in the equipment account resulted from two separate transactions. The first transaction is the discarding of equipment with a cost of $9,000. The credit of $9,000 in the equipment account and the debit of $9,000 in the accumulated amortization—equipment account indicate that the discarded equipment was fully amortized. In addition, the memorandum entry in the accounts indicates that no salvage was realized from the disposal of the equipment. Thus, the first transaction of discarding the equipment did not affect cash and does not appear on the statement of cash flows.

The second transaction is the purchase of equipment for cash of $157,000. This transaction appears as a deduction from cash inflows in the investing activities section, as follows:

Cash flows from investing activities:
  Purchase of equipment   ($157,000)

The credit of $12,000 in the accumulated amortization account represents amortization expense for the year. We already considered this amortization expense of $12,000 on the equipment as an addition to net income in determining cash flows from operating activities, as reported in Exhibit 5.

Often the proceeds received on disposal of a capital asset will be greater or less than the carrying value of the asset (cost less accumulated amortization), resulting in a gain or loss being reported in net income. Presentation of the cash flow impact of such transactions is similar to that illustrated below for the sale of a long-term investment. We show the proceeds from the sale of a capital asset as an inflow of cash from investing activities. Also, to avoid double counting, we deduct any gain on the sale from net income (or add any loss back to net income) in determining cash flows from operating activities. The illustrative problem at the end of this chapter includes an example of such a transaction.

BUILDING

The comparative balance sheet in Exhibit 3 indicates no change in buildings during the year. Also, the ledger indicates no entries to the building account during the year. For this reason, the account is not shown.

The credit in the accumulated amortization—building account, shown earlier, represents amortization expense for the year. We already considered this amortization expense of $6,000 on the building as an addition to net income in determining cash flows from operating activities, as reported in Exhibit 5.

LAND

The land account increased by $50,000, as shown below. This increase results from acquiring the land by issuing common shares.

ACCOUNT LAND   ACCOUNT NO.

Date		Item	Debit	Credit	Balance Debit	Balance Credit
1999						
Jan.	1	Balance			40,000	
Dec.	28	Acquired by issuing common shares	50,000		90,000	

Although no inflow or outflow of cash occurred, the transaction represents a significant investing and financing activity. We do not report these transactions on the statement of cash flows, but disclose them in a separate note or schedule accompanying the financial statements. In this schedule, we could report the transaction as follows:

Note _____

Noncash investing and financing activities:
   Acquisition of land by issuing common shares $50,000

LONG-TERM INVESTMENTS

The investments account decreased by $45,000, as shown below. This decrease results from selling the investments for $75,000 in cash.

ACCOUNT INVESTMENTS   ACCOUNT NO.

Date		Item	Debit	Credit	Balance Debit	Balance Credit
1999						
Jan.	1	Balance			45,000	
June	8	Sold for $75,000 cash		45,000	—	—

We report the $75,000 proceeds received from the sale of the investments in the investing activities section, as follows:

Cash flows from investing activities:
   Proceeds from sale of investments $75,000

The proceeds of $75,000 include the $30,000 gain on the sale of investments and the $45,000 carrying value of the investments. As shown in Exhibit 5, we deduct the $30,000 gain from net income in the cash flows from operating activities section. This is necessary so that the $30,000 cash inflow related to the gain is not included twice as a cash inflow.

PREPARING THE STATEMENT OF CASH FLOWS

After we have analyzed all of the changes in the noncash accounts, we can prepare the statement of cash flows for Rundell Ltd., as shown in Exhibit 6, from the data assembled and analyzed above, using the indirect method. The statement indicates that the cash position increased by $23,000 during the year. The most significant

Exhibit 6

Statement of Cash Flows—
Indirect Method

Rundell Ltd. Statement of Cash Flows For the Year Ended December 31, 1999			
Cash flows from operating activities:			
Net income, per income statement			$ 90,500
Add: Amortization	$ 18,000		
Decrease in inventories	8,000		
Increase in accounts payable	16,800		
Increase in accrued expenses	1,200	44,000	
		134,500	
Deduct: Increase in trade receivables	(9,000)		
Increase in prepaid expenses	(1,000)		
Decrease in income taxes payable	(1,500)		
Gain on sale of investments	(30,000)	(41,500)	
Net cash flow from operating activities			$93,000
Cash flows from investing activities:			
Proceeds from sale of investments		75,000	
Purchase of equipment		(157,000)	
Net cash flow from investing activities			(82,000)
Cash flows from financing activities:			
Issuance of preferred shares		160,000	
Dividends	(23,000)		
Retirement of bonds payable	(125,000)	(148,000)	
Net cash flow from financing activities			12,000
Increase in cash			23,000
Cash at the beginning of the year			26,000
Cash at the end of the year			$49,000

increase in net cash flows, $93,000, was from operating activities. The most signifi-
cant use of cash, $82,000, was for investing activities.

Statement of Cash Flows—The Direct Method

Objective 4
Prepare the statement of
cash flows, using the direct
method.

The direct method and the indirect method will report the same amount of cash
flows from operating activities. In addition, the manner of reporting cash flows
from investing and financing activities is the same under both methods. The
methods differ in how we obtain, analyze, and report the cash flows from operating
activities.

To illustrate the direct method, we will use the comparative balance sheet and
the income statement for Rundell Ltd. In this way, we can compare the statement of
cash flows under the direct method and the indirect method.

Exhibit 7 shows the changes in the current asset and liability account balances
for Rundell Ltd. The income statement in Exhibit 7 shows additional data for
Rundell Ltd.

The direct method reports cash flows from operating activities by major classes
of operating cash receipts and operating cash payments. In the following paragraphs, we describe and illustrate these classes. The difference between these major
classes of operating cash receipts and operating cash payments is the net cash flow
from operating activities.

Exhibit 7
Balance Sheet and Income Statement Data for Direct Method

| | December 31 | | |
| | | | Increase |
Accounts	1999	1998	Decrease*
Cash	$ 49,000	$ 26,000	$23,000
Accounts receivable (net)	74,000	65,000	9,000
Inventories	172,000	180,000	8,000*
Prepaid expenses	4,000	3,000	1,000
Accounts payable (merchandise creditors)	45,000	28,200	16,800
Accrued expenses (operating expenses)	5,000	3,800	1,200
Income taxes payable	2,500	4,000	1,500*

Rundell Ltd.
Income Statement
For the Year Ended December 31, 1999

Sales		$960,000
Cost of goods sold		580,000
Gross profit		380,000
Operating expenses:		
Amortization expense	$ 18,000	
Other operating expenses	260,000	
Total operating expenses		278,000
Income from operations		102,000
Other income:		
Gain on sale of investments	30,000	
Other expense:		
Interest expense	14,000	16,000
Income before income tax		118,000
Income tax		27,500
Net income		$ 90,500

CASH RECEIVED FROM CUSTOMERS

The $960,000 of sales for Rundell Ltd. is reported using the accrual method. To determine the cash received from sales made to customers, we must adjust the $960,000. The adjustment necessary to convert the sales reported on the income statement to the cash received from customers is summarized below.

Sales (reported on the income statement) { + Decrease in accounts receivable   or   − Increase in accounts receivable } = Cash received from customers

Rundell Ltd. received $951,000 cash from customers as shown below.

Sales	$960,000
Deduct increase in accounts receivable	(9,000)
Cash received from customers	$951,000

The additions to **accounts receivable** for sales on account during the year were $9,000 more than the amounts collected from customers on account. Sales reported on the income statement therefore included $9,000 that did not result in a cash inflow during the year. In other words, the increase of $9,000 in trade receivables during 1999 indicates that sales on account exceeded cash received from customers by $9,000. Thus, we deduct $9,000 from sales to determine the cash received from customers and report the $951,000 cash received as a cash inflow from operating activities in the cash flow statement.

CASH PAYMENTS FOR MERCHANDISE

The $580,000 of cost of goods sold is reported on the income statement for Rundell Ltd., using the accrual method. We summarize below the adjustments necessary to convert the cost of goods sold to cash payments for merchandise made during 1999.

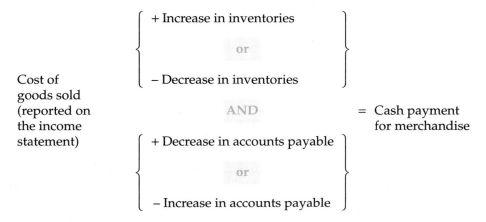

Rundell Ltd. paid $555,200 cash for merchandise as determined below.

Cost of goods sold		$580,000
Deduct: Decrease in inventories	$ (8,000)	
Increase in accounts payable	(16,800)	24,800
Cash payments for merchandise		$555,200

The $8,000 decrease in **inventories** indicates that the merchandise sold exceeded the cost of the merchandise purchased by $8,000. The amount reported on the income statement for cost of goods sold therefore includes $8,000 that did not require a cash outflow during the year. Thus, we deduct $8,000 from the cost of goods sold in determining the cash paid for merchandise.

The $16,800 increase in **accounts payable** (merchandise creditors) indicates that merchandise purchases include $16,800 for which there was no cash outflow (payment) during the year. In other words, the increase in accounts payable indicates that cash payments for merchandise were $16,800 less than the purchases on account during 1999. Thus, we deduct $16,800 from the cost of goods sold in determining the cash paid for merchandise.

CASH PAYMENTS FOR OPERATING EXPENSES

The $18,000 of amortization expense reported on the income statement did not require a cash outflow. Thus, under the direct method, we do not report it on the statement of cash flows. We adjust the $260,000 reported for other operating expenses to reflect the cash payments for operating expenses, as summarized on the next page.

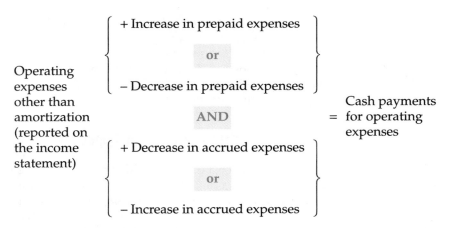

Rundell Ltd. paid $259,800 cash for operating expenses, determined as follows:

Operating expenses other than amortization	$260,000
Add increase in prepaid expenses	1,000
	$261,000
Deduct increase in accrued expenses	(1,200)
Cash payments for operating expenses	$259,800

The cash outflow for **prepaid expenses** exceeded the amount deducted as an expense by $1,000 during the year. Hence, we add $1,000 to the amount of operating expenses (other than amortization) reported on the income statement in determining the cash paid for operating expenses.

The increase in **accrued expenses** (operating expenses) indicates that operating expenses include $1,200 for which there was no cash outflow (payment) during the year. In other words, the increase in accrued expenses indicates that the cash payments for operating expenses were $1,200 less than the amount reported as an expense during the year. Thus, we deduct $1,200 from the operating expenses on the income statement in determining the cash paid for operating expenses.

GAIN ON SALE OF INVESTMENTS

The income statement for Rundell Ltd. in Exhibit 7 reports a gain of $30,000 on the sale of long-term investments. As we discussed previously, we report the total proceeds from the sale of investments as a cash inflow from investing activities. Since the direct method does not include the gain on sale in determining cash flows from operating activities, we do not need to make an adjustment to this section of the statement (as we do under the indirect method).

INTEREST EXPENSE

The income statement for Rundell Ltd. in Exhibit 7 reports interest expense of $14,000. The interest expense is related to the bonds payable that were outstanding during the year. We assume that interest on the bonds is paid on June 30 and December 31. Thus, we report $14,000 cash outflow for interest expense on the statement of cash flows as an operating activity.

If interest payable had existed at the end of the year, we would adjust the interest expense for any increase or decrease in interest payable from the beginning to the end of the year. That is, we would add a decrease in interest payable or subtract an increase in interest payable from interest expense. This is similar to the adjustment for changes in income taxes payable, which we will illustrate in the following paragraphs.

CASH PAYMENTS FOR INCOME TAXES

The adjustment to convert the income tax reported on the income statement to the cash basis is summarized below.

$$\text{Income tax (reported on income statement)} \left\{ \begin{array}{c} + \text{Decrease in income taxes payable} \\ \textit{or} \\ - \text{Increase in income taxes payable} \end{array} \right\} = \text{Cash payments for income tax}$$

Rundell Ltd. paid $29,000 cash for income tax, determined as follows:

Income tax	$27,500
Add decrease in income taxes payable	1,500
Cash payments for income tax	$29,000

The cash outflow for **income taxes** exceeded the income tax deducted as an expense during the period by $1,500. Thus, we add $1,500 to the amount of income tax reported on the income statement in determining the cash payments for income tax.

REPORTING CASH FLOWS FROM OPERATING ACTIVITIES—DIRECT METHOD

Exhibit 8 is a complete statement of cash flows for Rundell Ltd. using the direct method for reporting cash flows from operating activities. The portions of this statement that differ from the indirect method are highlighted in colour.

Exhibit 8
Statement of Cash Flows—Direct Method

Rundell Ltd.
Statement of Cash Flows
For the Year Ended December 31, 1999

Cash flows from operating activities:			
Received from customers		$951,000	
Payments for merchandise	($555,200)		
Payments for operating expenses	(259,800)		
Payments for interest	(14,000)		
Payments for income tax	(29,000)	(858,000)	
Net cash flow from operating activities			$ 93,000
Cash flows from investing activities:			
Proceeds from sale of investments		75,000	
Purchase of equipment		(157,000)	
Net cash flow from investing activities			(82,000)
Cash flows from financing activities:			
Issuance of preferred shares		160,000	
Dividends	(23,000)		
Retirement of bonds payable	(125,000)	(148,000)	
Net cash flow from financing activities			12,000
Increase in cash			23,000
Cash at the beginning of the year			26,000
Cash at the end of the year			$ 49,000

Appendix: Work Sheet for Statement of Cash Flows

Some accountants prefer to use a work sheet to assist them in assembling data for the statement of cash flows. Although a work sheet is not essential, it may be useful when you have a large number of transactions to analyze. Whether or not you use a work sheet, the concepts of cash flow and the statements of cash flows presented in this chapter remain the same.

In this appendix, we will describe and illustrate the use of work sheets in preparing the statement of cash flows for both the indirect method and the direct method.

WORK SHEET—INDIRECT METHOD

We will use the data for Rundell Ltd., presented in Exhibit 3, as a basis for illustrating the work sheet for the indirect method. The procedures used in preparing this work sheet, shown in Exhibit 9, are as follows:

1. List the title of each balance sheet account in the Accounts column. For each account, enter its balance as of December 31, 1998 in the first column and its balance as of December 31, 1999 in the last column. Place the credit balances in parentheses. The column totals should equal zero, since the total of the debits in a column should equal the total of the credits in a column.
2. Analyze the change during the year in each account to determine the net increase (decrease) in cash and the cash flows from operating activities, investing activities, financing activities, and the noncash activities. Show the effect of the change on cash flows by making analysis entries in the Analysis columns.

Analyzing Accounts

As we discussed in this chapter, an efficient method of analyzing cash flows is to determine the type of cash flow activity that led to changes in balance sheet accounts during the period. As we analyze each noncash account, we make entries on the work sheet for specific types of cash flow activities related to the noncash accounts. After we have analyzed all the noncash accounts, we make an entry for the increase (decrease) in cash during the period. *These analysis entries, however, are not posted to the ledger.* They only aid in assembling the data on the work sheet for use in preparing the statement of cash flows.

The order in which the accounts are analyzed is unimportant. However, it is more efficient to begin with the retained earnings account and proceed upward in the account listing.

RETAINED EARNINGS. The work sheet shows a Retained Earnings balance of $112,000 at December 31, 1998, and $172,500 at December 31, 1999. Thus, Retained Earnings increased $60,500 during the year. This increase resulted from two factors: (1) net income of $90,500 and (2) declaring cash dividends of $30,000. To identify the cash flows by activity, we will make two entries on the work sheet. These entries also serve to account for or explain, in terms of cash flows, the increase of $60,500.

In closing the accounts at the end of the year, the business credited the retained earnings account for the net income of $90,500. The $90,500 is reported on the statement of cash flows as "cash flows from operating activities." We make the following entry in the Analysis columns on the work sheet. This entry (1) accounts for the credit portion of the closing entry (to Retained Earnings) and (2) identifies the cash flow in the bottom portion of the work sheet.

Exhibit 9
Work Sheet for Statement of Cash Flows—Indirect Method

Rundell Ltd.
Work Sheet for Statement of Cash Flows
For the Year Ended December 31, 1999

Accounts	Balance, Dec. 31, 1998	Analysis Debit		Analysis Credit		Balance, Dec. 31, 1999
Cash	26,000	(s)	23,000			49,000
Accounts Receivable	65,000	(r)	9,000			74,000
Inventories	180,000			(q)	8,000	172,000
Prepaid Expenses	3,000	(p)	1,000			4,000
Investments	45,000			(o)	45,000	—
Land	40,000	(n)	50,000			90,000
Building	200,000					200,000
Accumulated Amortization—Building	(30,000)			(m)	6,000	(36,000)
Equipment	142,000	(l)	157,000	(k)	9,000	290,000
Accumulated Amortization—Equipment	(40,000)	(k)	9,000	(j)	12,000	(43,000)
Accounts Payable	(28,200)			(h)	16,800	(45,000)
Accrued Expenses	(3,800)			(i)	1,200	(5,000)
Income Taxes Payable	(4,000)	(g)	1,500			(2,500)
Dividends Payable	(8,000)			(f)	7,000	(15,000)
Bonds Payable	(245,000)	(e)	125,000			(120,000)
Preferred Shares	—			(d)	160,000	(160,000)
Common Shares	(230,000)			(c)	50,000	(280,000)
Retained Earnings	(112,000)	(b)	30,000	(a)	90,500	(172,500)
Totals	0		405,500		405,500	0
Operating activities:						
Net income		(a)	90,500			
Decrease in income taxes payable				(g)	1,500	
Increase in accounts payable		(h)	16,800			
Increase in accrued expenses		(i)	1,200			
Amortization of equipment		(j)	12,000			
Amortization of building		(m)	6,000			
Gain on sale of investments				(o)	30,000	
Increase in prepaid expenses				(p)	1,000	
Decrease in inventories		(q)	8,000			
Increase in trade receivables				(r)	9,000	
Investing activities:						
Purchased equipment				(l)	157,000	
Sold investments		(o)	75,000			
Financing activities:						
Declared cash dividends				(b)	30,000	
Issued preferred shares		(d)	160,000			
Retired bonds payable				(e)	125,000	
Increase in dividends payable		(f)	7,000			
Schedule of noncash investing and financing activities:						
Acquisition of land by issuing common shares		(c)	50,000	(n)	50,000	
Net increase in cash				(s)	23,000	
Totals			426,500		426,500	

(a) Operating Activities—Net Income	90,500	
Retained Earnings		90,500

In closing the accounts at the end of the year, the company debited the retained earnings account for dividends declared of $30,000. The $30,000 is reported as a financing activity on the statement of cash flows. The following analysis entry on the work sheet (1) accounts for the debit portion of the closing entry (to Retained Earnings) and (2) identifies the cash flow in the bottom portion of the work sheet.

(b) Retained Earnings	30,000	
Financing Activities—Declared Cash Dividends		30,000

We will adjust the $30,000 of declared dividends later for the actual amount of cash dividends paid during the year.

OTHER ACCOUNTS. We discussed in this chapter the analysis of the changes in the other accounts and their effect on cash flows and therefore will not repeat that discussion in this appendix. The related analysis entries are made in the work sheet in a manner similar to entries (a) and (b). A summary of these entries is as follows:

(c) Schedule of Noncash Investing and Financing Activities—		
Acquisition of Land by Issuing Common Shares	50,000	
Common Shares		50,000
(d) Financing Activities—Issued Preferred Shares	160,000	
Preferred Shares		160,000
(e) Bonds Payable	125,000	
Financing Activities—Retired Bonds Payable		125,000
(f) Financing Activities—Increase in Dividends Payable	7,000	
Dividends Payable		7,000
(g) Income Taxes Payable	1,500	
Operating Activities—Decrease in Income Taxes Payable		1,500
(h) Operating Activities—Increase in Accounts Payable	16,800	
Accounts Payable		16,800
(i) Operating Activities—Increase in Accrued Expenses	1,200	
Accrued Expenses		1,200
(j) Operating Activities—Amortization of Equipment	12,000	
Accumulated Amortization—Equipment		12,000
(k) Accumulated Amortization—Equipment	9,000	
Equipment		9,000
(l) Equipment	157,000	
Investing Activities—Purchase of Equipment		157,000
(m) Operating Activities—Amortization of Building	6,000	
Accumulated Amortization—Building		6,000
(n) Land	50,000	
Schedule of Noncash Investing		
and Financing Activities—Acquisition of Land by Issuing		
Common Shares		50,000
(o) Investing Activities—Sale of Investments	75,000	
Operating Activities—Gain on Sale of Investments		30,000
Investments		45,000
(p) Prepaid Expenses	1,000	
Operating Activities—Increase in Prepaid Expenses		1,000
(q) Operating Activities—Decrease in Inventories	8,000	
Inventories		8,000
(r) Accounts Receivable	9,000	
Operating Activities—Increase in Accounts Receivable		9,000
(s) Cash	23,000	
Net Increase in Cash		23,000

Completing the Work Sheet

After we have analyzed all the balance sheet accounts and made the analysis entries on the work sheet, all the operating, investing, and financing activities are identified in the bottom portion of the work sheet. The accuracy of the work sheet entries is verified by the equality of the totals of the debit and credit Analysis columns.

Preparing the Statement of Cash Flows

The statement of cash flows prepared from the work sheet is identical to the statement in Exhibit 6. We obtain the data for the three sections of the statement from the bottom portion of the work sheet. Some of these data may not be reported exactly as they appear in the work sheet. For example, in reporting the cash flows from operating activities, we present the total amortization expense ($18,000) instead of the two separate amounts ($12,000 and $6,000).

In the cash flows from operating activities section, we often present the effect of amortization first, followed by the effects of increases and decreases in current assets and current liabilities. The effects of any gains and losses on operating activities are normally reported last. The cash paid for dividends appears as $23,000 instead of the amount of dividends declared ($30,000) less the increase in dividends payable ($7,000). The issuing of the common shares for land ($50,000) is a noncash financing and investing event reported in the notes or a separate schedule to the financial statements.

WORK SHEET—DIRECT METHOD

We can also use a work sheet in assembling data for preparing a statement of cash flows using the direct method for reporting operating cash flows. As a basis for illustration, we will use the balance sheet data for Rundell Ltd. in Exhibit 3 and the income statement data in Exhibit 7. The procedures used in preparing the work sheet shown in Exhibit 10 are as follows:

1. List the title of each asset account in the Accounts column. For each account, enter its balance as of December 31, 1998, in the first column and its balance as of December 31, 1999, in the last column. Place the credit balances in parentheses. The column totals should equal zero, since the total of the debits in a column should equal the total of the credits in a column.
2. List the title of each income statement account and "Net Income" on the work sheet.
3. Analyze the effect of each income statement item on cash flows from operating activities. Beginning with sales, enter the balance of each item in the proper Analysis column. Complete the entry in the Analysis columns to show the effect on cash flows.
4. Analyze the change during the year in each balance sheet account to determine the net increase (decrease) in cash and the cash flows from operating activities, investing activities, financing activities, and the noncash investing and financing activities. Show the effect of the change on cash flows by making entries in the Analysis columns.

Analyzing Accounts

Under the direct method of reporting cash flows from operating activities, analyzing accounts begins with the income statement. As we analyze each income statement account, we make analysis entries on the work sheet that show the effect on cash flows from operating activities. After we have analyzed the income statement accounts, we analyze changes in the balance sheet accounts.

The order in which the balance sheet accounts are analyzed is unimportant. However, it is more efficient to begin with the retained earnings account and pro-

Exhibit 10 *Work Sheet for Statement of Cash Flows—Direct Method*

Rundell Ltd.
Work Sheet for Statement of Cash Flows
For the Year Ended December 31, 1999

Accounts	Balance, Dec. 31, 1998	Analysis Debit		Analysis Credit		Balance, Dec. 31, 1999
Balance Sheet						
Cash	26,000	(w)	23,000			49,000
Accounts Receivable	65,000	(v)	9,000			74,000
Inventories	180,000			(u)	8,000	172,000
Prepaid Expenses	3,000	(t)	1,000			4,000
Investments	45,000			(e)	45,000	—
Land	40,000	(s)	50,000			90,000
Building	200,000					200,000
Accumulated Amortization—Building	(30,000)			(c)	6,000	(36,000)
Equipment	142,000	(r)	157,000	(q)	9,000	290,000
Accumulated Amortization—Equipment	(40,000)	(q)	9,000	(c)	12,000	(43,000)
Accounts Payable	(28,200)			(p)	16,800	(45,000)
Accrued Expenses	(3,800)			(o)	1,200	(5,000)
Income Taxes Payable	(4,000)	(n)	1,500			(2,500)
Dividends Payable	(8,000)			(m)	7,000	(15,000)
Bonds Payable	(245,000)	(l)	125,000			(120,000)
Preferred Shares	—			(k)	160,000	(160,000)
Common Shares	(230,000)			(j)	50,000	(280,000)
Retained Earnings	(112,000)	(i)	30,000	(h)	90,500	(172,500)
Totals	0					0
Income Statement						
Sales				(a)	960,000	
Cost of Goods Sold		(b)	580,000			
Amortization Expense		(c)	18,000			
Other Operating Expenses		(d)	260,000			
Gain on Sale of Investments				(e)	30,000	
Interest Expense		(f)	14,000			
Income Taxes		(g)	27,500			
Net Income		(h)	90,500			
Cash Flows						
Operating activities:						
Cash received from customers		(a)	960,000	(v)	9,000	
Cash payments:						
Merchandise		(p)	16,800	(b)	580,000	
		(u)	8,000			
Operating expenses		(o)	1,200	(d)	260,000	
				(t)	1,000	
Interest expense				(f)	14,000	
Income taxes				(g)	27,500	
				(n)	1,500	
Investing activities:						
Sold investments		(e)	75,000			
Purchased equipment				(r)	157,000	
Financing activities:						
Declared cash dividends				(i)	30,000	
Issued preferred stock		(k)	160,000			
Retired bonds payable				(l)	125,000	
Increase in dividends payable		(m)	7,000			
Schedule of noncash investing & financing activities:						
Acquired land by issuing common stock		(j)	50,000	(s)	50,000	
Net increase in cash				(w)	23,000	
Totals			2,673,500		2,673,500	

ceed upward in the account listing. As we analyze each noncash balance sheet account, we make entries on the work sheet for the related cash flow activities. After we have analyzed all the noncash accounts, we make an entry for the increase (decrease) in cash during the period.

SALES. The income statement for Rundell Ltd. shows sales of $960,000 for the year. Sales for cash provide cash when the sale is made. Sales on account provide cash when customers pay their bills. The analysis entry on the work sheet is as follows:

(a) Operating Activities—Receipts from Customers   960,000
       Sales   960,000

COST OF GOODS SOLD. The income statement for Rundell Ltd. shows cost of goods sold of $580,000 for the year. The cost of goods sold requires cash payments for cash purchases of merchandise. For purchases on account, the business pays cash when the invoices are due. The analysis entry on the work sheet is as follows:

(b) Cost of Goods Sold   580,000
       Operating Activities—Payments for Merchandise   580,000

AMORTIZATION EXPENSE. The income statement for Rundell Ltd. shows amortization expense of $18,000. Because amortization expense does not require a cash outflow, we do not report it on the statement of cash flows. The analysis entry on the work sheet to fully account for the amortization expense is as follows:

(c) Amortization Expense   18,000
       Accumulated Amortization—Building   6,000
       Accumulated Amortization—Equipment   12,000

OTHER ACCOUNTS. We discussed in this chapter the analysis of the changes in the other accounts and their effect on cash flows and therefore will not repeat that discussion in this appendix. The related analysis entries are made on the work sheet in a manner similar to entries (a), (b), and (c). A summary of these entries is as follows:

(d) Other Operating Expenses   260,000
       Operating Activities—Paid Operating Expenses   260,000
(e) Investing Activities—Sold Investments   75,000
       Investments   45,000
       Gain on Sale of Investments   30,000
(f) Interest Expense   14,000
       Operating Activities—Paid Interest   14,000
(g) Income Taxes   27,500
       Operating Activities—Paid Income Taxes   27,500
(h) Net Income   90,500
       Retained Earnings   90,500
(i) Retained Earnings   30,000
       Financing Activities—Declared Cash Dividends   30,000
(j) Schedule of Noncash Investing and Financing Activities—
       Acquired Land by Issuing Common Shares   50,000
       Common Shares   50,000
(k) Financing Activities—Issued Preferred Shares   160,000
       Preferred Shares   160,000
(l) Bonds Payable   125,000
       Financing Activities—Retired Bonds Payable   125,000
(m) Financing Activities—Increase in Dividends Payable   7,000
       Dividends Payable   7,000

(n) Income Taxes Payable	1,500	
Operating Activities—Decrease in Income Taxes Payable		1,500
(o) Operating Activities—Cash Paid for Operating Expenses	1,200	
Accrued Expenses		1,200
(p) Operating Activities—Cash Paid for Merchandise	16,800	
Accounts Payable		16,800
(q) Accumulated Amortization—Equipment	9,000	
Equipment		9,000
(r) Equipment	157,000	
Investing Activities—Purchased Equipment		157,000
(s) Land	50,000	
Schedule of Noncash Investing and Financing Activities—		
Acquired Land by Issuing Common Shares		50,000
(t) Prepaid Expenses	1,000	
Operating Activities—Cash Paid for Operating Expenses		1,000
(u) Operating Activities—Cash Paid for Merchandise	8,000	
Inventories		8,000
(v) Accounts Receivable	9,000	
Operating Activities—Cash Received from Customers		9,000
(w) Cash	23,000	
Net Increase in Cash		23,000

Completing the Work Sheet

After we have analyzed all the income statement and balance sheet accounts and have made the entries on the work sheet, all the operating, investing, and financing activities are identified in the bottom portion of the work sheet. The mathematical accuracy of the work sheet entries is verified by the equality of the totals of the debit and credit Analysis columns.

Preparing the Statement of Cash Flows

The statement of cash flows prepared from the work sheet is identical to the statement in Exhibit 8. We obtain the data for the three sections of the statement from the bottom portion of the work sheet. Some of these data may not be reported exactly as they appear on the work sheet. The cash paid for dividends appears as $23,000 instead of the amount of dividends declared ($30,000) less the increase in dividends payable ($7,000). The issuing of the common shares for land ($50,000) is a noncash financing and investing event reported in the notes or a schedule to the financial statements.

KEY POINTS

Objective 1. Explain why the statement of cash flows is one of the basic financial statements and define cash flows.

The statement of cash flows helps users to assess the firm's ability to generate cash from operations, expand operations, pay obligations, pay dividends, and adapt to changing circumstances. It highlights changes in net assets and in the financial structure of the firm, and helps users predict and compare the future cash flows of different enterprises. Cash flows are defined as inflows and outflows of cash and cash equivalents. These include cash on hand, demand deposits, and short-term highly liquid non-equity investments minus bank overdrafts.

Objective 2. Summarize the types of cash flow activities reported in the statement of cash flows.

The statement of cash flows reports cash receipts and cash payments by three types of activities: operating activities, investing activities, and financing activities.

Cash flows from operating activities are cash flows from the principal revenue-generating activities of the firm. There are two methods of reporting cash flows from operating activities: (1) the direct method and (2) the indirect method.

Cash inflows from investing activities are cash flows from the sale of long-term investments, physical capital assets, and intangible assets. Cash outflows generally include payments to acquire long-term investments and capital assets.

Cash inflows from financing activities include proceeds from issuing equity securities, such as preferred and common shares. Cash inflows also arise from issuing bonds, mortgage notes payable, and other long-term debt. Cash outflows from financing activities arise from paying cash dividends, reacquiring shares, and repaying amounts borrowed.

Investing and financing for a business may be affected by transactions that do not involve cash. The effect of such transactions should be reported in a separate note or schedule accompanying the financial statements.

If reported, cash flow per share should be disclosed on the statement of cash flows.

Objective 3. Prepare a statement of cash flows, using the indirect method.

To prepare the statement of cash flows, we analyze changes in the noncash balance sheet accounts. This logic relies on the fact that a change in any balance sheet account can be analyzed in terms of changes in the other balance sheet accounts. Thus, by analyzing the noncash balance sheet accounts, we can identify those activities that resulted in cash flows. Although we may analyze the noncash balance sheet accounts in any order, it is usually more efficient to begin with retained earnings. We obtain additional data by analyzing the income statement accounts and supporting records.

Objective 4. Prepare a statement of cash flows, using the direct method.

The direct method and the indirect method will report the same amount of cash flows from operating activities. Also, the manner of reporting cash flows from investing and financing activities is the same under both methods. The methods differ in how the cash flows from operating activities data are obtained, analyzed, and reported. The direct method reports cash flows from operating activities by major classes of operating cash receipts and cash payments. The difference between the major classes of total operating cash receipts and total operating cash payments is the net cash flow from operating activities.

We obtain the data for reporting cash flows from operating activities by the direct method by analyzing the cash flows related to the revenues and expenses reported on the income statement. We adjust the revenues and expenses from the accrual basis of accounting to the cash basis for purposes of preparing the statement of cash flows.

GLOSSARY OF KEY TERMS

Cash. Cash consists of cash on hand and demand deposits. *Objective 1*

Cash equivalents. Short-term, highly liquid non-equity investments that are readily convertible to cash and subject to an insignificant risk of changes in value. *Objective 1*

Cash flows from financing activities. The section of the statement of cash flows that reports cash flows from transactions affecting the equity and long-term debt of the entity. *Objective 2*

Cash flows from investing activities. The section of the statement of cash flows that reports cash flows from transactions affecting investments in noncurrent assets. *Objective 2*

Cash flows from operating activities. The section of the statement of cash flows that reports the cash transactions derived from the principal revenue-generating activities of the firm. *Objective 2*

Direct method. A method of reporting the cash flows from operating activities as the difference between the operating cash receipts and the operating cash payments. *Objective 2*

Indirect method. A method of reporting the cash flows from operating activities as the net income from operations adjusted for all deferrals of past cash receipts and payments and all accruals of expected future cash receipts and payments. *Objective 2*

Statement of cash flows. A summary of the major cash receipts and cash payments for a period. *Objective 1*

The comparative balance sheet of Dowling Company for December 31, 1999 and 1998, is as follows:

Dowling Company
Comparative Balance Sheet
December 31, 1999 and 1998

	1999	1998
Assets		
Cash	$ 140,350	$ 95,900
Accounts receivable (net)	95,300	102,300
Inventories	165,200	157,900
Prepaid expenses	6,240	5,860
Investments (long-term)	35,700	84,700
Land	75,000	90,000
Buildings	375,000	260,000
Accumulated amortization—buildings	(71,300)	(58,300)
Machinery and equipment	428,300	428,300
Accumulated amortization—machinery and equipment	(148,500)	(138,000)
Patents	58,000	65,000
Total assets	$1,159,290	$1,093,660
Liabilities and Shareholders' Equity		
Accounts payable (merchandise creditors)	$ 43,500	$ 46,700
Accrued expenses (operating expenses)	14,000	12,500
Income taxes payable	7,900	8,400
Dividends payable	14,000	10,000
Mortgage note payable, due 2001	40,000	0
Bonds payable	150,000	250,000
Common shares	516,250	416,250
Retained earnings	373,640	349,810
Total liabilities and shareholders' equity	$1,159,290	$1,093,660

The income statement for Dowling Company is shown below.

Dowling Company
Income Statement
For the Year Ended December 31, 1999

Sales		$1,180,000
Cost of goods sold		790,000
Gross profit		390,000
Operating expenses:		
Amortization expense (physical assets)	$ 23,500	
Amortization of patent	7,000	
Other operating expenses	201,000	
Total operating expenses		231,500
Income from operations		158,500
Other income:		
Gain on sale of investments	11,000	
Gain on sale of land	5,000	
Other expense:		
Interest expense	26,000	(10,000)
Income before income tax		148,500
Income tax		50,000
Net income		$ 98,500

An examination of the accounting records revealed the following additional information applicable to 1999:

a. Sold land costing $15,000 for $20,000.
b. Issued a mortgage note for $40,000.
c. Constructed a building costing $115,000.
d. Issued 2,500 common shares at 40 to redeem bonds payable.
e. Declared cash dividends of $74,670.

Instructions

1. Prepare a statement of cash flows, using the indirect method of reporting cash flows from operating activities, and any required notes to the financial statements.
2. Prepare a statement of cash flows, using the direct method of reporting cash flows from operating activities, and any required notes to the financial statements.

Solution

1.

Dowling Company
Statement of Cash Flows—Indirect Method
For the Year Ended December 31, 1999

Cash flows from operating activities:			
Net income, per income statement		$ 98,500	
Add: Amortization of physical assets	$ 23,500		
Amortization of patents	7,000		
Decrease in accounts receivable	7,000		
Increase in accrued expenses	1,500	39,000	
		137,500	
Deduct: Increase in inventories	(7,300)		
Increase in prepaid expenses	(380)		
Decrease in accounts payable	(3,200)		
Decrease in income taxes payable	(500)		
Gain on sale of investments	(11,000)		
Gain on sale of land	(5,000)	(27,380)	
Net cash flow from operating activities			$110,120
Cash flows from investing activities:			
Proceeds from sale of investments	60,000		
Proceeds from sale of land	20,000	80,000	
Construction of building		(115,000)	
Net cash flow from investing activities			(35,000)
Cash flows from financing activities:			
Issuing mortgage note payable		40,000	
Dividend paid		(70,670)	
Net cash flow provided by financing activities			(30,670)
Increase in cash			44,450
Cash at the beginning of the year			95,900
Cash at the end of the year			$140,350

Note to Financial Statements: Noncash Financing Activity:
2,500 common shares were issued to redeem
bonds with a book value of $100,000.

2.

Dowling Company
Statement of Cash Flows—Direct Method
For the Year Ended December 31, 1999

Cash flows from operating activities:
    Cash received from customers[1] $1,187,000
    Cash paid for merchandise[2]   ($800,500)
    Cash paid for operating expenses[3]   (199,880)
    Cash paid for interest expense   (26,000)
    Cash paid for income tax[4]   (50,500)   (1,076,880)
    Net cash flow from operating activities $110,120
Cash flows from investing activities:
    Proceeds from sale of investments   60,000
    Proceeds from sale of land   20,000   80,000
    Construction of building   (115,000)
    Net cash flow from investing activities   (35,000)
Cash flows from financing activities:
    Issuing mortgage note payable   40,000
    Dividends[5]   (70,670)
    Net cash flow from financing activities   (30,670)
Increase in cash $ 44,450
Cash at the beginning of the year   95,900
Cash at the end of the year $140,350

Computations: [1] $1,180,000 + $7,000 = $1,187,000
                    [2] $790,000 + $3,200 + $7,300 = $800,500
                    [3] $201,000 + $380 − $1,500 = $199,880
                    [4] $50,000 + $500 = $50,500
                    [5] $74,670 + $10,000 − $14,000 = $70,670

Note to Financial Statements: Noncash Financing Activity:
                                     25,000 common shares were issued to redeem
                                       bonds with a book value of $120,000.

SELF-EXAMINATION QUESTIONS (ANSWERS AT END OF CHAPTER)

1. An example of a cash flow from an operating activity is:
   A. receipt of cash from issuing shares.
   B. receipt of cash from issuing bonds.
   C. payment of cash for dividends.
   D. receipt of cash from customers on account.

2. An example of a cash flow from an investing activity is:
   A. receipt of cash from the sale of equipment.
   B. receipt of cash from issuing shares.
   C. payment of cash for dividends.
   D. payment of cash to reacquire the company's own shares.

3. An example of a cash flow from a financing activity is:
   A. receipt of cash from customers on account.
   B. receipt of cash from the sale of equipment.
   C. payment of cash for dividends.
   D. payment of cash to acquire a patent.

4. Which of the following methods of reporting cash flows from operating activities adjusts net income for revenues and expenses not involving the receipt or payment of cash?
   A. Direct method   C. Reciprocal method
   B. Purchase method   D. Indirect method

5. The net income reported on the income statement for the year was $55,000, and amortization of capital assets for the year was $22,000. The balances of the current asset and current liability accounts at the beginning and end of the year are as follows:

	End	Beginning
Cash	$ 65,000	$ 70,000
Accounts receivable	100,000	90,000
Inventories	145,000	150,000
Prepaid expenses	7,500	8,000
Accounts payable (merchandise creditors)	51,000	58,000

The total amount reported for cash flows from operating activities in the statement of cash flows, using the indirect method, is:
   A. $33,000   C. $65,500
   B. $55,000   D. $77,000

DISCUSSION QUESTIONS

1. Which financial statement is most useful in evaluating past operations and in planning future investing and financing activities?
2. What are the three types of activities reported on the statement of cash flows?
3. Name the two alternative methods of reporting cash flows from operating activities in the statement of cash flows.
4. What is the principal advantage of the direct method of reporting cash flows from operating activities?
5. What is the major advantage of the indirect method of reporting cash flows from operating activities?
6. On the statement of cash flows, if the cash inflows from investing activities exceed the cash outflows, how do we describe the difference?
7. On the statement of cash flows, if the cash outflows from investing activities exceed the cash inflows, how do we describe the difference?
8. On the statement of cash flows, if the cash inflows from financing activities exceed the cash outflows, how do we describe the difference?
9. On the statement of cash flows, if the cash outflows from financing activities exceed the cash inflows, how do we describe the difference?
10. A corporation issued $200,000 of common shares in exchange for $200,000 of capital assets. Would we report this transaction on the statement of cash flows?
11. A corporation acquired as a long-term investment all of the shares of XL Co., valued at $5,000,000, by issuing $5,000,000 of its own common shares. Should we report the transaction on the statement of cash flows?
12. a. What is the effect on cash flows of declaring and issuing a stock dividend?
    b. Is the stock dividend reported on the statement of cash flows?
13. What is the effect on cash flows of appropriating retained earnings for bonded indebtedness? Is this transaction reported on the statement of cash flows?
14. A retail business, using the accrual method of accounting, owed merchandise creditors (accounts payable) $290,000 at the beginning of the year and $315,000 at the end of the year. How would we adjust net income in determining the amount of cash flows from operating activities by the indirect method? Explain.
15. If salaries payable were $75,000 at the beginning of the year and $65,000 at the end of the year, should you add $10,000 to or deduct $10,000 from income to determine the amount of cash flows from operating activities by the indirect method? Explain.
16. A long-term investment with a cost of $75,000 was sold for $80,000 cash. (a) What was the gain or loss on the sale? (b) What was the effect of the transaction on cash flows? (c) How should you report the transaction in the statement of cash flows if cash flows from operating activities are reported by the indirect method?
17. A corporation issued $5,000,000 of 20-year bonds for cash at par. How would you report the transaction on the statement of cash flows?
18. A company discarded fully amortized equipment costing $55,000. What was the effect of the transaction on cash flows if (a) $5,000 cash is received, (b) there is no salvage value?
19. For the current year, Accord Company decided to switch from the indirect method to the direct method for reporting cash flows from operating activities on the statement of cash flows. Will the change cause the amount of net cash flow from operating activities to be (a) larger, (b) smaller, or (c) the same as if the indirect method had been used? Explain.
20. Name five common major classes of operating cash receipts or operating cash payments presented on the statement of cash flows when a company reports the cash flows from operating activities by the direct method.
21. Why does the definition of cash flows include cash and cash equivalents? What are cash equivalents?

EXERCISES

EXERCISE 15–1
Cash and cash equivalents
Objective 1

Selected account balances from the comparative balance sheet of Novem Ltd. are as follows:

	Current Year	Last Year
Cash in bank	$ 10,000	$ —
Accounts receivable	116,500	102,800
Term deposits due in 90 days	30,000	55,000
Short-term investments in shares	98,700	60,300
Bank overdraft	—	(76,000)
Accounts payable	68,300	71,600

Using this information, prepare a schedule summarizing cash and cash equivalents at the end of each year and the change in cash and cash equivalents for the year.

EXERCISE 15–2
Cash flows from operating activities—net loss
Objective 2

On its income statement for the current year, Lafleur Company reported a net loss of $75,000 from operations. On its statement of cash flows, it reported $20,000 of cash flows from operating activities.

Explain this apparent contradiction between the loss and the positive cash flows.

EXERCISE 15–3
Effect of transactions on cash flows
Objective 2

State the effect (cash receipt or payment, and amount) of each of the following transactions, considered individually, on cash flows:

a. Sold a new issue of $100,000 of bonds at 100.
b. Sold equipment with a net book value of $42,500 for cash, recording a gain of $3,500.
c. Sold 5,000 common shares for $45 per share.
d. Purchased land for $120,000 cash.
e. Reacquired 5,000 common shares at $50 per share.
f. Paid dividends of $1.50 per share. There were 5,000 shares issued and 30,000 shares outstanding.
g. Purchased a building by paying $20,000 cash and issuing a $90,000 mortgage note payable.

EXERCISE 15–4
Classifying cash flows
Objective 2

Identify the type of cash flow activity for each of the following events (operating, investing, or financing):

a. Sold equipment.
b. Issued preferred shares.
c. Purchased patents for cash.
d. Paid cash dividends.
e. Reacquired common shares.
f. Redeemed bonds.
g. Issued bonds.
h. Net income.
i. Sold long-term investments.
j. Issued common shares.
k. Purchased buildings for cash.

EXERCISE 15–5
Cash flows from operating activities—indirect method
Objectives 2, 3

Indicate whether each of the following would be added to or deducted from net income in determining net cash flow from operating activities by the indirect method:

a. Decrease in prepaid expenses
b. Amortization of patents
c. Decrease in salaries payable
d. Loss on disposal of physical capital assets
e. Decrease in accounts receivable

f.   Increase in notes receivable due in 90 days
g.   Increase in taxes payable
h.   Increase in inventory
i.   Amortization of physical capital assets
j.   Decrease in accounts payable
k.   Increase in notes payable due in 90 days

EXERCISE 15–6
Cash flows from operating activities—indirect method
Objectives 2, 3

The net income reported on the income statement for the current year was $106,400. Amortization recorded on equipment and a building amounted to $24,500 for the year. Balances of the current asset and current liability accounts at the beginning and end of the year are as follows:

	End of Year	Beginning of Year
Cash	$ 64,250	$ 60,500
Accounts receivable	98,750	92,500
Inventories	110,000	95,000
Prepaid expenses	6,400	7,650
Accounts payable (merchandise creditors)	77,200	72,700
Salaries payable	3,250	5,750

a.   Prepare the cash flows from operating activities section of the statement of cash flows, using the indirect method.
b.   ◀━━▶ If the direct method had been used, would the net cash flow from operating activities have been the same? Explain.

EXERCISE 15–7
Cash flows from operating activities—indirect method
Objectives 2, 3

The net income reported on the income statement for the current year was $78,625. Amortization recorded on store equipment for the year amounted to $29,250. Balances of the current asset and current liability accounts at the beginning and end of the year are as follows:

	End of Year	Beginning of Year
Cash	$ 70,150	$ 66,500
Accounts receivable	79,250	83,750
Inventory	110,000	102,000
Prepaid expenses	8,000	7,500
Accounts payable (merchandise creditors)	70,200	73,200
Wages payable	6,900	5,650

Prepare the cash flows from operating activities section of a statement of cash flows, using the indirect method.

EXERCISE 15–8
Determining cash payments to shareholders
Objectives 2, 3

The board of directors declared cash dividends totalling $160,000 during the current year. The comparative balance sheet indicates dividends payable of $30,000 at the beginning of the year and $40,000 at the end of the year. What was the amount of cash payments to shareholders during the year?

EXERCISE 15–9
Reporting changes in equipment on statement of cash flows
Objectives 2, 3

An analysis of the general ledger accounts indicates that office equipment, which had cost $75,000 and on which accumulated amortization totalled $67,500 on the date of sale, was sold for $6,000 during the year. Using this information, indicate the items to be reported on the statement of cash flows.

EXERCISE 15–10
Reporting changes in equipment on statement of cash flows
Objectives 2, 3

An analysis of the general ledger accounts indicates that delivery equipment, which had cost $45,000 and on which accumulated amortization totalled $39,000 on the date of sale, was sold for $8,000 during the year. Using this information, indicate the items to be reported on the statement of cash flows.

EXERCISE 15–11
Reporting land transactions on statement of cash flows
Objectives 2, 3

On the basis of the details of the following asset account, indicate the items to be reported on the statement of cash flows:

ACCOUNT LAND   ACCOUNT NO.

Date		Item	Debit	Credit	Balance Debit	Balance Credit
20—						
Jan.	1	Balance			500,000	
Feb.	5	Purchased for cash	165,000		665,000	
Oct.	30	Sold for $70,000		50,000	615,000	

EXERCISE 15–12
Reporting shareholders' equity items on statement of cash flows
Objectives 2, 3

On the basis of the following shareholders' equity accounts, indicate the items, exclusive of net income, you would report on the statement of cash flows. There were no unpaid dividends at either the beginning or the end of the year.

ACCOUNT COMMON SHARES   ACCOUNT NO.

Date		Item	Debit	Credit	Balance Debit	Balance Credit
20—						
Jan.	1	Balance, 50,000 shares				590,000
Feb.	11	10,000 shares issued for cash		140,000		730,000
June	30	5,500-share stock dividend		75,000		805,000

ACCOUNT RETAINED EARNINGS   ACCOUNT NO.

Date		Item	Debit	Credit	Balance Debit	Balance Credit
20—						
Jan.	1	Balance				275,000
June	30	Stock dividend	75,000			200,000
Dec.	30	Cash dividend	110,000			90,000
	31	Net income		195,000		285,000

EXERCISE 15–13
Reporting land acquisition for cash and mortgage note on statement of cash flows
Objectives 2, 3

On the basis of the details of the following asset account, indicate the items you would report on the statement of cash flows:

ACCOUNT LAND   ACCOUNT NO.

Date		Item	Debit	Credit	Balance Debit	Balance Credit
20—						
Jan.	1	Balance			450,000	
Feb.	10	Purchased for cash	65,000		515,000	
Nov.	20	Purchased with long-term mortgage note	150,000		665,000	

EXERCISE 15–14
Determining net income from net cash flow from operating activities
Objectives 2, 3

Larado Inc. reported a net cash flow from operating activities of $61,250 on its statement of cash flows for the year ended December 31, 2000. The following information was reported in the cash flows from operating activities section of the statement of cash flows, using the indirect method:

Decrease in income tax payable	$ 750	Increase in accounts payable	$7,300
Decrease in inventories	4,500	Increase in prepaid expenses	500
Amortization	10,600	Increase in accounts receivable	4,700
Gain on sale of investments	11,750		

Determine the net income reported by Larado Inc. for the year ended December 31, 2000.

EXERCISE 15–15
Cash flows from operating
activities—direct method
Objectives 2, 4

The cash flows from operating activities are reported by the direct method on the statement of cash flows. Determine the following:

a. If sales for the current year were $650,000 and accounts receivable decreased by $25,000 during the year, what was the amount of cash received from customers?

b. If income tax for the current year was $80,000 and income tax payable decreased by $25,000 during the year, what was the amount of cash paid for income tax?

EXERCISE 15–16
Determining selected amounts
for cash flows from operating
activities—direct method
Objectives 2, 4

Selected data taken from the accounting records of D'George Company for the current year ended December 31 are as follows:

	Balance January 1	Balance December 31
Accrued expenses (operating expenses)	$12,000	$ 5,500
Accounts payable (merchandise creditors)	85,000	70,000
Inventories	62,500	53,500
Prepaid expenses	17,500	10,000

During the current year, the cost of goods sold was $940,000 and the operating expenses other than amortization were $265,000. The company uses the direct method for presenting the cash flows from operating activities on the statement of cash flows.

Determine the amount reported on the statement of cash flows for (a) cash paid for merchandise and (b) cash paid for operating expenses.

EXERCISE 15–17
Cash flows from operating
activities—direct method
Objectives 2, 4

The income statement of Trenton Company for the current year ended June 30 is as follows:

Sales		$995,000
Cost of goods sold		600,000
Gross profit		$395,000
Operating expenses:		
Amortization expense	$ 31,500	
Other operating expenses	248,500	
Total operating expenses		280,000
Income before income tax		$115,000
Income tax		35,000
Net income		$ 80,000

Changes in the balances of selected accounts from the beginning to the end of the current year are as follows:

	Increase Decrease*
Accounts receivable (net)	$32,000*
Inventories	8,500
Prepaid expenses	1,750*
Accounts payable (merchandise creditors)	14,100*
Accrued expenses (operating expenses)	8,700
Income tax payable	5,800*

Prepare the cash flows from operating activities section of the statement of cash flows, using the direct method.

EXERCISE 15–18
Cash flows from operating activities—direct method
Objectives 2, 4

The income statement for Crowe Company for the current year ended June 30 and balances of selected accounts at the beginning and the end of the year are as follows:

Sales		$872,500
Cost of goods sold		500,000
Gross profit		372,500
Operating expenses:		
Amortization expense	$ 32,250	
Other operating expenses	213,750	
Total operating expenses		246,000
Income before income tax		126,500
Income tax		32,500
Net income		$ 94,000

	End of Year	Beginning of Year
Accounts receivable (net)	$ 90,000	$82,000
Inventories	102,500	85,000
Prepaid expenses	6,900	8,150
Accounts payable (merchandise creditors)	74,200	71,100
Accrued expenses (operating expenses)	3,750	5,850
Income tax payable	2,225	2,225

Prepare the cash flows from operating activities section of the statement of cash flows, using the direct method.

EXERCISE 15–19
Cash flows from operating activities—direct method
Objectives 2, 4

The income statement for the current year and balances of selected accounts at the beginning and end of the current year are as follows:

Sales		$1,400,000
Cost of goods sold		820,000
Gross profit		580,000
Operating expenses:		
Amortization expense	$ 54,000	
Other operating expenses	295,500	
Total operating expenses		349,500
Operating income		230,500
Other expense:		
Interest expense		18,000
Income before income tax		212,500
Income tax		78,000
Net income		$ 134,500

	End of Year	Beginning of Year
Accounts receivable	$ 86,350	$ 92,450
Inventories	108,500	102,300
Prepaid expenses	8,900	8,300
Accounts payable (merchandise creditors)	81,250	88,300
Accrued expenses (operating expenses)	7,150	6,450
Interest payable	1,900	1,900
Income tax payable	4,400	5,400

Prepare the cash flows from operating activities section of the statement of cash flows, using the direct method.

EXERCISE 15–20
Statement of cash flows
Objectives 2, 3, 4

List the errors you find in the following statement of cash flows. The cash balance at the beginning of the year was $70,700. All other figures are correct.

Davenport Carpets
Statement of Cash Flows
For the Year Ended December 31, 20—

Cash flows from operating activities:			
Net income, per income statement		$100,500	
Add: Amortization	$ 49,000		
Increase in accounts receivable	9,500	58,500	
		159,000	
Deduct: Increase in accounts payable	4,400		
Increase in inventories	18,300		
Gain on sale of investments	5,000		
Decrease in accrued expenses	1,600	29,300	
Net cash flow from operating activities			$129,700
Cash flows from investing activities:			
Proceeds from sale of investments		85,000	
Paid for purchase of land	(90,000)		
Paid for purchase of equipment	(150,100)	(240,100)	
Net cash flow from investing activities			(155,100)
Cash flows from financing activities:			
Issuance of common shares		107,000	
Dividends		(36,800)	
Net cash flow from financing activities			143,800
Increase in cash			$118,400
Cash at the end of the year			105,300
Cash at the beginning of the year			$223,700

PROBLEMS SERIES A

PROBLEM 15–1A
Statement of cash flows—
indirect method
Objective 3

The comparative balance sheet of Emerald Inc. for June 30, 2000 and 1999, is as follows:

	June 30, 2000	June 30, 1999
Assets		
Cash	$ 75,900	$ 69,200
Accounts receivable (net)	104,800	93,500
Inventories	133,300	108,900
Investments	—	85,000
Land	112,000	—
Equipment	425,700	329,700
Accumulated amortization	(171,800)	(137,200)
	$679,900	$549,100
Liabilities and Shareholders' Equity		
Accounts payable (merchandise creditors)	$ 71,600	$ 63,000
Accrued expenses (operating expenses)	6,100	5,000
Dividends payable	14,400	12,500
Common shares	397,400	319,400
Retained earnings	190,400	149,200
	$679,900	$549,100

The following additional information was taken from the records of Emerald Inc.:

a. Equipment and land were acquired for cash.
b. There were no disposals of equipment during the year.
c. The investments were sold for $100,000 cash.
d. The common shares were issued for cash.
e. There was a $94,300 credit to Retained Earnings for net income.
f. Cash dividends were declared during the year.

Instructions

Prepare a statement of cash flows, using the indirect method of presenting cash flows from operating activities.

PROBLEM 15–2A
Statement of cash flows—
indirect method
Objective 3

The comparative balance sheet of Davis Inc. at June 30, 2000 and 1999, is as follows:

	June 30, 2000	June 30, 1999
Assets		
Cash	$ 43,300	$ 74,400
Accounts receivable (net)	116,300	134,100
Inventory	351,200	346,400
Prepaid expenses	5,200	2,900
Plant assets	444,000	396,800
Accumulated amortization—capital assets	(232,300)	(271,100)
	$727,700	$683,500
Liabilities and Shareholders' Equity		
Accounts payable (merchandise creditors)	$ 70,000	$ 65,400
Mortgage note payable	—	95,000
Common shares	339,800	304,800
Retained earnings	317,900	218,300
	$727,700	$683,500

Additional data obtained from the income statement and from an examination of the accounts in the ledger are as follows:

a. Net income, $139,600.
b. Amortization reported on the income statement, $34,100.
c. An addition to the building was constructed at a cost of $120,100, and fully amortized equipment costing $72,900 was discarded, with no salvage realized.
d. The mortgage note payable was not due until 2000, but the terms permitted earlier payment without penalty.
e. 1,000 common shares were issued for cash.
f. Cash dividends were declared and paid.

Instructions

Prepare a statement of cash flows, using the indirect method of presenting cash flows from operating activities.

PROBLEM 15–3A
Statement of cash flows—
indirect method
Objective 3

The comparative balance sheet of Olson Corporation at December 31, 2000 and 1999, is as follows:

	Dec. 31, 2000	Dec. 31, 1999
Assets		
Cash	$ 83,400	$ 76,800
Accounts receivable (net)	94,300	100,500
Inventories	196,000	178,600
Prepaid expenses	6,400	2,900
Land	75,000	75,000
Buildings	465,300	316,800
Accumulated amortization—buildings	(158,600)	(144,000)
Machinery and equipment	206,300	206,300
Accumulated amortization—machinery & equip.	(92,000)	(81,300)
Patents	32,000	37,500
	$908,100	$769,100

	Dec. 31, 2000	Dec. 31, 1999
Liabilities and Shareholders' Equity		
Accounts payable (merchandise creditors)	$ 27,200	$ 38,900
Dividends payable	18,800	15,000
Salaries payable	7,900	14,600
Mortgage note payable, due 2001	105,000	—
Bonds payable	—	80,000
Common shares	485,000	405,000
Retained earnings	264,200	215,600
	$908,100	$769,100

An examination of the income statement and the accounting records revealed the following additional information applicable to 1997:

a.   Net income, $76,100.
b.   Amortization expense reported on the income statement: buildings, $14,600; machinery and equipment, $10,700.
c.   Patent amortization was reported on the income statement. No patents were purchased or sold during the year.
d.   Purchased a building for cash.
e.   A mortgage note for $105,000 was issued for cash.
f.   4,000 common shares were issued at $20 in exchange for the bonds payable.

Instructions
Prepare a statement of cash flows, using the indirect method of presenting cash flows from operating activities, and any required note to the financial statements

PROBLEM 15–4A
Statement of cash flows—indirect method
Objective 3

The comparative balance sheet of Addams Inc. at December 31, 2000 and 1999, is as follows:

	Dec. 31, 2000	Dec. 31, 1999
Assets		
Cash	$ 220,500	$ 81,400
Accounts receivable (net)	165,000	151,700
Income tax refund receivable	9,000	—
Inventories	255,600	269,400
Prepaid expenses	9,300	11,100
Investments	70,000	250,000
Land	170,000	230,000
Buildings	950,000	450,000
Accumulated amortization—buildings	(209,000)	(193,800)
Equipment	641,400	470,400
Accumulated amortization—equipment	(234,400)	(205,700)
	$2,047,400	$1,514,500
Liabilities and Shareholders' Equity		
Accounts payable (merchandise creditors)	$ 96,000	$ 108,720
Income tax payable	—	10,880
Bonds payable	600,000	—
Common shares	711,000	672,000
Appropriation for plant expansion	280,000	230,000
Retained earnings	360,400	492,900
	$2,047,400	$1,514,500

The noncurrent asset, the noncurrent liability, and the shareholders' equity accounts for 2000 are as follows:

ACCOUNT INVESTMENTS   ACCOUNT NO.

Date		Item	Debit	Credit	Balance Debit	Balance Credit
2000						
Jan.	1	Balance			250,000	
Mar.	22	Realized $240,000 cash from sale		180,000	70,000	

ACCOUNT LAND   ACCOUNT NO.

Date		Item	Debit	Credit	Balance Debit	Balance Credit
2000						
Jan.	1	Balance			230,000	
April	20	Realized $65,000 cash from sale		60,000	170,000	

ACCOUNT BUILDINGS   ACCOUNT NO.

Date		Item	Debit	Credit	Balance Debit	Balance Credit
2000						
Jan.	1	Balance			450,000	
April	20	Acquired for cash	500,000		950,000	

ACCOUNT ACCUMULATED AMORTIZATION—BUILDINGS   ACCOUNT NO.

Date		Item	Debit	Credit	Balance Debit	Balance Credit
2000						
Jan.	1	Balance				193,800
Dec.	31	Amortization for year		15,200		209,000

ACCOUNT EQUIPMENT   ACCOUNT NO.

Date		Item	Debit	Credit	Balance Debit	Balance Credit
2000						
Jan.	1	Balance			470,400	
	26	Realized $5,000 cash from sale		35,000	435,400	
May	27	Purchased for cash	96,000		531,400	
Aug.	11	Purchased for cash	110,000		641,400	

ACCOUNT ACCUMULATED AMORTIZATION—EQUIPMENT   ACCOUNT NO.

Date		Item	Debit	Credit	Balance Debit	Balance Credit
2000						
Jan.	1	Balance				205,700
	26	Equipment sold	34,000			171,700
Dec.	31	Amortization for year		62,700		234,400

ACCOUNT BONDS PAYABLE   ACCOUNT NO.

Date		Item	Debit	Credit	Balance Debit	Balance Credit
2000						
May	1	Issued 20-year bonds		600,000		600,000

ACCOUNT COMMON SHARES   ACCOUNT NO.

Date		Item	Debit	Credit	Balance Debit	Balance Credit
2000						
Jan.	1	Balance				672,000
Dec.	7	Stock dividend		39,000		711,000

ACCOUNT APPROPRIATION FOR PLANT EXPANSION   ACCOUNT NO.

Date		Item	Debit	Credit	Balance Debit	Balance Credit
2000						
Jan.	1	Balance				230,000
Dec.	31	Appropriation		50,000		280,000

ACCOUNT RETAINED EARNINGS   ACCOUNT NO.

Date		Item	Debit	Credit	Balance Debit	Balance Credit
2000						
Jan.	1	Balance				492,900
Dec.	7	Stock dividend	39,000			453,900
	31	Net loss	11,500			442,400
	31	Cash dividends	32,000			410,400
	31	Appropriated	50,000			360,400

Instructions
Prepare a statement of cash flows, using the indirect method of presenting cash flows from operating activities.

PROBLEM 15–5A
Statement of cash flows—direct method
Objective 4

The comparative balance sheet of D. E. Frank Inc. for December 31, 2000 and 1999, is as follows:

	Dec. 31, 2000	Dec. 31, 1999
Assets		
Cash	$148,700	$ 25,500
Accounts receivable (net)	92,500	80,000
Inventories	100,200	91,400
Investments	—	75,000
Land	30,000	—
Equipment	330,000	275,000
Accumulated amortization	(156,000)	(114,000)
	$545,400	$432,900

	Dec. 31, 2000	Dec. 31, 1999
Liabilities and Shareholders' Equity		
Accounts payable (merchandise creditors)	$ 63,000	$ 57,000
Accrued expenses (operating expenses)	4,500	7,000
Dividends payable	15,000	10,000
Common shares	337,000	262,000
Retained earnings	125,900	96,900
	$545,400	$432,900

The income statement for the year ended December 31, 1999, is as follows:

Sales		$956,500
Cost of goods sold		585,500
Gross profit		$371,000
Operating expenses:		
Amortization expense	$ 42,000	
Other operating expenses	290,000	
Total operating expenses		332,000
Operating income		$ 39,000
Other income:		
Gain on sale of investments		15,000
Income before income tax		$ 54,000
Income tax		10,000
Net income		$ 44,000

The following additional information was taken from the records:

a. Equipment and land were acquired for cash.
b. There were no disposals of equipment during the year.
c. The investments were sold for cash.
d. The common shares were issued for cash.
e. There was a debit to Retained Earnings for cash dividends declared.

Instructions

Prepare a statement of cash flows, using the direct method of presenting cash flows from operating activities.

PROBLEM 15–6A
Statement of cash flows—
direct method
Objective 4

The comparative balance sheet of Diamond Inc. for June 30, 2000 and 1999, is as follows:

	June 30, 2000	June 30, 1999
Assets		
Cash	$ 111,800	$ 138,400
Accounts receivable (net)	209,600	187,000
Inventories	266,600	217,800
Investments	—	170,000
Land	224,000	—
Equipment	851,400	659,400
Accumulated amortization	(343,600)	(274,400)
	$1,319,800	$1,098,200
Liabilities and Shareholders' Equity		
Accounts payable (merchandise creditors)	$ 143,200	$126,000
Accrued expenses (operating expenses)	12,200	10,000
Dividends payable	28,800	25,000
Common shares	794,800	638,800
Retained earnings	340,800	298,400
	$1,319,800	$1,098,200

The income statement for the year ended June 30, 2000, is as follows:

Sales		$1,960,000
Cost of goods sold		1,060,000
Gross profit		$ 900,000
Operating expenses:		
Amortization expense	$ 69,200	
Other operating expenses	570,000	
Total operating expenses		639,200
Operating income		$260,800
Other income:		
Loss on sale of investments		10,000
Income before income tax		$250,800
Income tax		102,200
Net income		$148,600

The following additional information was taken from the records of Emerald Inc.:

a. Equipment and land were acquired for cash.
b. There were no disposals of equipment during the year.
c. The investments were sold for cash.
d. Common shares were issued for cash.
e. Cash dividends were declared.

Instructions

Prepare a statement of cash flows, using the direct method of presenting cash flows from operating activities.

PROBLEMS SERIES B

PROBLEM 15–1B
Statement of cash flows—
indirect method
Objective 3

The comparative balance sheet of Jasper Inc. for December 31, 2000 and 1999, is as follows:

	Dec. 31, 2000	Dec. 31, 1999
Assets		
Cash	$ 97,500	$ 51,600
Accounts receivable (net)	123,200	110,500
Inventories	146,200	128,100
Investments	—	91,000
Land	70,000	—
Equipment	874,600	724,500
Accumulated amortization—equipment	(211,800)	(159,600)
	$1,099,700	$946,100
Liabilities and Shareholders' Equity		
Accounts payable (merchandise creditors)	$ 75,000	$ 70,600
Accrued expenses (operating expenses)	4,800	7,100
Dividends payable	20,000	14,000
Common shares	473,800	366,800
Retained earnings	526,100	487,600
	$1,099,700	$946,100

The following additional information was taken from the records:

a. The investments were sold for $105,000 cash.
b. Equipment and land were acquired for cash.
c. There were no disposals of equipment during the year.
d. The common shares were issued for cash.
e. There was a $55,000 debit to Retained Earnings for cash dividends declared.

Instructions

Prepare a statement of cash flows, using the indirect method of presenting cash flows from operating activities.

PROBLEM 15–2B
Statement of cash flows—indirect method
Objective 3

The comparative balance sheet of King Corporation at December 31, 2000 and 1999, is as follows:

	Dec. 31, 2000	Dec. 31, 1999
Assets		
Cash	$ 74,700	$ 77,400
Accounts receivable (net)	69,300	76,200
Inventory	126,300	97,400
Prepaid expenses	7,660	4,960
Plant assets	472,440	425,240
Accumulated amortization—capital assets	(145,100)	(157,500)
	$605,300	$523,700
Liabilities and Shareholders' Equity		
Accounts payable (merchandise creditors)	$ 68,500	$ 53,500
Mortgage note payable	—	75,000
Common shares	334,500	281,500
Retained earnings	202,300	113,700
	$605,300	$523,700

Additional data obtained from the income statement and from an examination of the accounts in the ledger are as follows:

a. Net income, $98,600.
b. Amortization was reported on the income statement.
c. An addition to the building was constructed at a cost of $100,800, and fully amortized equipment costing $53,600 was discarded, with no salvage realized.
d. The mortgage note payable was not due until 2003, but the terms permitted earlier payment without penalty.
e. 2,000 common shares were issued at $26.50 for cash.
f. Cash dividends were declared and paid.

Instructions

Prepare a statement of cash flows, using the indirect method of presenting cash flows from operating activities.

PROBLEM 15–3B
Statement of cash flows—indirect method
Objective 3

The comparative balance sheet of Paxton Corporation at December 31, 2000 and 1999, is as follows:

	Dec. 31, 2000	Dec. 31, 1999
Assets		
Cash	$ 91,400	$ 33,400
Accounts receivable (net)	86,100	68,000
Inventories	126,600	141,700
Prepaid expenses	4,500	3,100
Land	65,000	65,000
Buildings	381,500	291,500
Accumulated amortization—buildings	(152,800)	(143,400)
Machinery and equipment	300,500	300,500
Accumulated amortization—machinery and equipment	(105,000)	(71,500)
Patents	32,500	38,500
	$830,300	$726,800

	Dec. 31, 2000	Dec. 31, 1999
Liabilities and Shareholders' Equity		
Accounts payable (merchandise creditors)	$ 58,800	$ 72,400
Dividends payable	9,400	8,250
Salaries payable	5,000	5,450
Mortgage note payable, due 2005	70,000	—
Bonds payable	—	110,000
Common shares	530,000	420,000
Retained earnings	157,100	110,700
	$830,300	$726,800

An examination of the income statement and the accounting records revealed the following additional information applicable to 2000:

a. Net income, $81,400.
b. Amortization expense was reported on the income statement for buildings and for machinery and equipment.
c. A building was constructed for $90,000.
d. Patent amortization reported on the income statement, $6,000.
e. A mortgage note for $70,000 was issued for cash.
f. 10,000 common shares were issued at 11 in exchange for the bonds payable.
g. Cash dividends were declared.

Instructions

Prepare a statement of cash flows, using the indirect method of presenting cash flows from operating activities, and any required note to the financial statements.

PROBLEM 15–4B
*Statement of cash flows—
indirect method*
Objective 3

The comparative balance sheet of Jenkins Inc. at December 31, 2000 and 1999, is as follows:

	Dec. 31, 2000	Dec. 31, 1999
Assets		
Cash	$ 34,100	$ 38,800
Accounts receivable (net)	63,400	54,100
Inventories	134,250	121,000
Prepaid expenses	3,850	4,100
Investments	—	45,000
Land	28,500	28,500
Buildings	201,000	126,000
Accumulated amortization—buildings	(47,400)	(41,400)
Equipment	296,200	239,500
Accumulated amortization—equipment	(72,800)	(77,400)
	$641,100	$538,200
Liabilities and Shareholders' Equity		
Accounts payable (merchandise creditors)	$ 39,500	$ 48,300
Income tax payable	3,600	2,800
Bonds payable	70,000	—
Common shares	355,200	333,000
Appropriation for plant expansion	50,000	30,000
Retained earnings	122,800	124,100
	$641,100	$538,200

The noncurrent asset, the noncurrent liability, and the stockholders' equity accounts for 2000 are as follows:

ACCOUNT INVESTMENTS   ACCOUNT NO.

Date		Item	Debit	Credit	Balance Debit	Balance Credit
2000						
Jan.	1	Balance			45,000	
Mar.	5	Realized $38,000 cash from sale		45,000	—	—

ACCOUNT LAND   ACCOUNT NO.

Date		Item	Debit	Credit	Balance Debit	Balance Credit
2000						
Jan.	1	Balance			28,500	

ACCOUNT BUILDINGS   ACCOUNT NO.

Date		Item	Debit	Credit	Balance Debit	Balance Credit
2000						
Jan.	1	Balance			126,000	
July	1	Acquired for cash	75,000		201,000	

ACCOUNT ACCUMULATED AMORTIZATION—BUILDINGS   ACCOUNT NO.

Date		Item	Debit	Credit	Balance Debit	Balance Credit
2000						
Jan.	1	Balance				41,400
Dec.	31	Amortization for year		6,000		47,400

ACCOUNT EQUIPMENT   ACCOUNT NO.

Date		Item	Debit	Credit	Balance Debit	Balance Credit
2000						
Jan.	1	Balance			239,500	
Mar.	1	Discarded, no salvage		21,000	218,500	
	5	Purchased for cash	50,000		268,500	
Dec.	1	Purchased for cash	27,700		296,200	

ACCOUNT ACCUMULATED AMORTIZATION—EQUIPMENT   ACCOUNT NO.

Date		Item	Debit	Credit	Balance Debit	Balance Credit
2000						
Jan.	1	Balance				77,400
Mar.	1	Equipment discarded	21,000			56,400
Dec.	31	Amortization for year		16,400		72,800

ACCOUNT BONDS PAYABLE   ACCOUNT NO.

Date		Item	Debit	Credit	Balance Debit	Balance Credit
2000						
May	1	Issued 20-year bonds		70,000		70,000

ACCOUNT COMMON SHARES   ACCOUNT NO.

Date		Item	Debit	Credit	Balance Debit	Balance Credit
2000						
Jan.	1	Balance				333,000
June	29	Stock dividend		22,200		355,200

ACCOUNT APPROPRIATION FOR PLANT EXPANSION   ACCOUNT NO.

Date		Item	Debit	Credit	Balance Debit	Balance Credit
2000						
Jan.	1	Balance				30,000
Dec.	31	Appropriation		20,000		50,000

ACCOUNT RETAINED EARNINGS   ACCOUNT NO.

Date		Item	Debit	Credit	Balance Debit	Balance Credit
2000						
Jan.	1	Balance				124,100
June	29	Stock dividend	22,200			101,900
Dec.	31	Net income		65,900		167,800
	31	Cash dividends	25,000			142,800
	31	Appropriated	20,000			122,800

Instructions

Prepare a statement of cash flows, using the indirect method of presenting cash flows from operating activities.

PROBLEM 15–5B
*Statement of cash flows—
direct method*
Objective 4

The comparative balance sheet of D. Jacobs Co. for December 31, 2000 and 1999, is as follows:

	Dec. 31, 2000	Dec. 31, 1999
Assets		
Cash	$ 42,900	$ 74,900
Accounts receivable (net)	94,500	80,000
Inventories	100,100	90,500
Investments	—	45,000
Land	75,000	—
Equipment	382,400	282,400
Accumulated amortization	(144,000)	(119,000)
	$550,900	$453,800
Liabilities and Shareholders' Equity		
Accounts payable (merchandise creditors)	$ 58,400	$ 55,000
Accrued expenses (operating expenses)	5,000	4,000
Dividends payable	12,000	10,000
Common shares	322,000	262,000
Retained earnings	153,500	122,800
	$550,900	$453,800

The income statement for the year ended December 31, 2000, is as follows:

Sales		$940,000
Cost of goods sold		520,000
Gross profit		$420,000
Operating expenses:		
Amortization expense	$ 25,000	
Other operating expenses	310,000	
Total operating expenses		335,000
Operating income		$ 85,000
Other income:		
Gain on sale of investments		10,000
Income before income tax		$ 95,000
Income tax		35,800
Net income		$ 59,200

The following additional information was taken from the records:

a. Equipment and land were acquired for cash.
b. There were no disposals of equipment during the year.
c. The investments were sold for cash.
d. The common shares were issued for cash.
e. Cash dividends were declared.

Instructions

Prepare a statement of cash flows, using the direct method of presenting cash flows from operating activities.

PROBLEM 15–6B
*Statement of cash flows—
direct method*
Objective 4

The comparative balance sheet of Banff Inc. for December 31, 2000 and 1999, is as follows:

Banff Inc.
Comparative Balance Sheet
December 31, 2000 and 1999

	Dec. 31, 2000	Dec. 31, 1999
Assets		
Cash	$ 185,000	$ 98,200
30-day term deposits	10,000	5,000
Accounts receivable (net)	246,400	221,000
Inventories	290,400	250,200
Prepaid Expense	2,000	6,000
Investments	—	182,000
Land	140,000	—
Equipment	1,749,200	1,449,000
Accumulated amortization	(423,600)	(319,200)
	$2,199,400	$1,892,200
Liabilities and Shareholders' Equity		
Accounts payable (merchandise creditors)	$ 150,000	$ 141,200
Accrued expenses (operating expenses)	9,600	14,200
Dividends payable	40,000	28,000
Common shares	947,600	733,600
Retained earnings – unappropriated	1,012,200	955,200
appropriated for plant expansion	40,000	20,000
	$2,199,400	$1,892,200

The income statement for the year ended December 31, 2000, is as follows:

Banff Inc.
Income Statement
For the Year Ended December 31, 2000

Sales		$2,460,000
Cost of goods sold		1,590,600
Gross profit		$ 869,400
Operating expenses:		
Amortization expense	$104,400	
Other operating expenses	510,000	
Total operating expenses		614,400
Operating income		$ 255,000
Other income:		
Gain on sale of investments		28,000
Income before income tax		$ 283,000
Income tax		96,000
Net income		$ 187,000

The following additional information was taken from the records:

a. The investments were sold for cash at the beginning of the year.
b. Equipment and land were acquired for cash.
c. There were no disposals of equipment during the year.
d. The common stock was issued for cash.

Instructions
Prepare a statement of cash flows (defined as cash and cash equivalents), using the direct method of presenting cash flows from operating activities.

CHALLENGE PROBLEMS

PROBLEM CP15–1

A comparative balance sheet and an income statement for Freehold Company are as follows:

Freehold Company
Comparative Balance Sheet
December 31, 2000 and 1999

	2000	1999
Assets		
Cash	$ 29,210	$ 53,200
60-day term deposits	20,000	10,000
Accounts receivable (net)	142,900	117,800
Inventories	209,600	190,150
Prepaid expenses	5,160	6,120
Investments	69,900	93,500
Land	104,000	75,000
Buildings	425,000	225,000
Accumulated amortization—buildings	(93,600)	(81,220)
Equipment	486,500	447,500
Accumulated amortization—equipment	(184,500)	(156,750)
Total assets	$1,214,170	$980,300

	2000	1999
Liabilities and Shareholders' Equity		
Bank overdraft	$ 3,000	$ —
Accounts payable (merchandise creditors)	55,715	51,875
Accrued expenses (operating expenses)	12,000	10,500
Interest payable	1,875	1,875
Income tax payable	4,800	8,500
Dividends payable	15,660	12,500
Mortgage note payable	195,000	—
Bonds payable	90,000	250,000
Common shares	497,250	416,250
Retained earnings	338,870	228,800
Total liabilities and shareholders' equity	$1,214,170	$980,300

Freehold Company
Income Statement
For the Year Ended December 31, 2000

Sales		$1,710,000
Cost of goods sold		1,250,000
Gross profit		$ 460,000
Operating expenses:		
Amortization expense	$ 47,130	
Other operating expenses	234,000	
Total operating expenses		281,130
Operating income		$ 178,870
Other income:		
Gain on sale of land	$ 19,000	
Gain on sale of investments	19,200	
	$ 38,200	
Other expense:		
Interest expense	28,000	
Loss on sale of equipment	1,000	9,200
Income before income tax		$ 188,070
Income tax		38,000
Net income		$ 150,070

The following additional information on cash flows during the year was obtained from an examination of the ledger:

a. Investments (long-term) were purchased for $53,100.
b. Investments (long-term) costing $76,700 were sold.
c. Equipment was purchased for $49,000.
d. A building valued at $200,000 and land valued at $100,000 were acquired by a cash payment of $300,000. Amortization on the buildings was $12,380 for the year.
e. Land that cost $71,000 was sold for cash.
f. A mortgage note payable for $195,000 was issued for cash.
g. Bonds payable of $160,000 were retired by the payment of their face amount.
h. 3,000 shares were issued for cash.

Instructions

1. Prepare a statement of cash flows (defined as cash and cash equivalents), using the direct method of presenting cash flows from operating activities.
2. Prepare a statement of cash flows (defined as cash and cash equivalents), using the indirect method of presenting cash flows from operating activities.
3. ▬▬► Which method of reporting cash flows from operating activities is more widely used? Explain.

PROBLEM CP15–2

An income statement and a comparative balance sheet for Comstock Company are as follows:

Comstock Company
Income Statement
For the Year Ended December 31, 2000

Sales		$1,350,000
Cost of goods sold		980,000
Gross profit		$ 370,000
Operating expenses:		
Amortization expense	$ 27,200	
Other operating expenses	182,000	
Total operating expenses		209,200
		$ 160,800
Other income:		
Gain on sale of land	$ 35,000	
Gain on sale of investments	22,500	
Gain on sale of equipment	1,000	
	$ 58,500	
Other expense:		
Interest expense	27,500	31,000
Income before income tax		$ 191,800
Income tax		65,000
Net income		$ 126,800

Comstock Company
Comparative Balance Sheet
December 31, 2000 and 1999

	2000	1999
Assets		
Cash	$ 131,570	$ 56,700
90-day term deposits	50,000	—
Accounts receivable (net)	128,500	116,700
Inventories	215,400	188,050
Prepaid expenses	5,160	6,120
Investments	40,600	93,500
Land	85,000	75,000
Buildings	425,000	225,000
Accumulated amortization—buildings	(92,420)	(81,220)
Equipment	485,900	447,500
Accumulated amortization—equipment	(165,750)	(155,750)
Total assets	$1,308,960	$971,600
Liabilities and Shareholders' Equity		
Bank overdraft	$ —	$ 2,300
Accounts payable (merchandise creditors)	57,200	46,000
Accrued expenses (operating expenses)	12,000	11,000
Interest payable	3,000	3,000
Income tax payable	6,250	9,750
Dividends payable	15,660	12,500
Mortgage note payable	225,000	—
Bonds payable	175,000	250,000
Common shares	497,250	416,250
Retained earnings	317,600	220,800
Total liabilities and shareholders' equity	$1,308,960	$971,600

The following additional information on cash flows during the year was obtained from an examination of the ledger:

a. Investments (long-term) were purchased for $36,600.
b. Investments (long-term) costing $89,500 were sold.
c. Equipment was purchased for $48,400.
d. Amortization on the building was $11,200 and equipment $16,000.
e. A building valued at $200,000 and land valued at $50,000 were acquired by a cash payment of $250,000.
f. Land was sold for $75,000 cash.
g. A mortgage note payable for $225,000 was issued for cash.
h. Bonds payable of $75,000 were retired by the payment of their face amount.
i. 3,000 common shares were issued for cash.

Instructions

1. Prepare a statement of cash flows (defined as cash and cash equivalents), using the direct method of presenting cash flows from operating activities.
2. Prepare a statement of cash flows (defined as cash and cash equivalents), using the indirect method of presenting cash flows from operating activities.
3. ◀▬▬▶ Which method of reporting cash flows from operating activities is more widely used? Explain.

PROBLEM CP15–3

The comparative balance sheet for Nedek Ltd. and statement of cash flows for the current year are set out below.

Nedek Ltd.
Balance Sheet
As at December 31, 2001 (with 2000 for comparison)

	Dec. 31, 2001	Dec. 31, 2000
Assets		
Cash	$ 29,000	$ 13,000
Accounts receivable (net)	40,000	38,000
Inventory	84,000	91,000
Prepaid expenses	5,000	4,000
Equipment	255,000	220,000
Accumulated amortization	(70,000)	(60,000)
Goodwill (net)	32,000	36,000
Total assets	$375,000	$342,000
Liabilities and Shareholders' Equity		
Accounts payable	$30,000	$ 24,000
Wages payable	5,000	6,000
Income tax payable	2,000	4,000
Bonds payable	—	25,000
Common shares	225,000	195,000
Retained earnings	113,000	88,000
Total liabilities and shareholders' equity	$375,000	$342,000

Nedek Ltd.
Statement of Cash Flows
For the Year Ended December 31, 2001

Cash flows from operating activities:		
Received from customers	$382,000	
Paid to suppliers (purchases 214,000)	(234,000)	
Paid to employees	(59,000)	
Paid for income taxes	(12,000)	
Net cash flow from operating activities		$77,000
Cash flows from investing activities		
Proceeds from sale of equipment (= nbv)	$ 6,000	
Purchase of equipment	(55,000)	
Net cash flow from investing activities		(49,000)
Cash flows from financing activities:		
Retirement of bonds	$(25,000)	
Issuance of common shares	30,000	
Dividends	(17,000)	
Net cash flow from financing activities		(12,000)
Increase in cash		$16,000
Cash, beginning of the year		13,000
Cash, end of the year		$29,000

Instructions

Prepare an income statement for Nedek Ltd. for the year ended December 31, 2001. The equipment was sold for its net book value.

CASES

CASE 15–1
Fashion King Inc.
Operating cash flow per share

 Ben Howard, president of Fashion King Inc., believes that reporting operating cash flow per share on the income statement would be a useful addition to the company's just completed financial statements. The following discussion took place between Ben Howard and Fashion King's controller, Kim Lang, in January, after the close of the fiscal year.

Ben: I have been reviewing our financial statements for the last year. I am disappointed that our earnings per share has dropped by 10% from last year. This is not going to look good to our shareholders. Isn't there anything we can do about this?

Kim: What do you mean? The past is the past, and the numbers are in. There isn't much that can be done about it. Our financial statements were prepared according to generally accepted accounting principles, and I don't see much leeway for significant change at this point.

Ben: No, no. I'm not suggesting that we "cook the books." But look at the cash flow from operations on the statement of cash flows. The cash flow from operations has increased by 20%. This is very good news—and, I might add, useful information. The higher cash flow from operations will give our creditors comfort.

Kim: Well, the cash flow from operations is on the statement of cash flows, so I guess users will be able to see the improved cash flow figures there.

Ben: This is true, but somehow I feel that this information should be given a much higher profile. I don't like this information being "buried" in the statement of cash flows. You know as well as I do that many users will focus on the income statement. Therefore, I think we ought to include an operating cash flow per share number on the face of the income statement—someplace under the earnings per share number. In this way users will get the complete picture of our operating performance. Yes, our earnings per share dropped this year, but our cash flow from operations improved! And all the information is in one place where users can see and compare the figures. What do you think?

Kim: I've never really thought about it like that before. I guess we could put the operating cash flow per share on the income statement under the earnings per share. Users would really benefit from this disclosure. Thanks for the idea—I'll get working on it.

Ben: Glad to be of service.

How would you interpret this situation? Is Kim following professional ethics?

CASE 15-2
DiscArt Inc.
Using the statement of cash flows

 You are considering an investment in a new start-up software company, DiscArt Inc. A review of the company's financial statements reveals a negative retained earnings. In addition, it appears as though the company has been running a negative cash flow from operations since the company's inception.

➤ How is the company staying in business under these circumstances? Could this be a good investment?

CASE 15-3
Walker Company
Analysis of cash flow from operations

The Retailing Division of Walker Company provided the following information on its cash flow from operations:

Net income	$ 450,000
Increase in accounts receivable	(340,000)
Increase in inventory	(300,000)
Decrease in accounts payable	(90,000)
Amortization	100,000
Cash flow from operations	$(180,000)

The manager of the Retailing Division provided the accompanying memo with this report:

From: Senior Vice-President, Retailing Division

I am pleased to report that we had earnings of $450,000 over the last period. This resulted in a return on invested capital of 10%, which is near our targets for this division. I have been aggressive in building the revenue volume in the division. As a result, I am happy to report that we have increased the number of new credit card customers as a result of an aggressive marketing campaign. In addition, we have found some excellent merchandise opportunities. Some of our suppliers have made some of their apparel merchandise available at a deep discount. We have purchased as much of these goods as possible in order to improve profitability. I'm also happy to report that our vendor payment problems have improved. We are nearly caught up on our overdue payables balances.

➤ Comment on the Senior Vice-President's memo in light of the cash flow information.

CASE 15-4
Shaw Communications Inc.
Analysis of statement of cash flows

The statement of cash flows on page 667 is taken from the annual report of Shaw Communications Inc. for the year ended December 31, 1997.

a. In 1997 Shaw Communications Inc. reported net income of $16,592,000. How could it show a negative cash flow when it had positive earnings for the year?
b. Why is the "Gain on sale of cable systems" subtracted in determining the 1996 cash flow from operating activities?

Why is the "Writedown of paging assets" added in determining the 1997 cash flow from operating activities?
c. The company shows a negative cash position at the end of 1997. How can cash be a negative amount?
d. Does the negative cash position reported at the end of 1997 mean that the company must be in financial difficulty? What is driving the cash flows for 1997? Is there anything positive to be said about the company's cash flows for the year?

Consolidated Statements of Cash Flows

[thousands of dollars except per share amounts]	1997	1996
Operating Activities		
Net income from continuing operations	218	80,127
Add (deduct):		
Amortization	108,842	92,169
Deferred income taxes	11,505	60,955
Amortization of non-current program rights	9,025	
Writedown of paging assets	23,094	
Equity income		(1,250)
Gain on sale of cable systems		(109,907)
Other	(937)	1,601
Cash flow from continuing operations	151,747	123,695
Net change in non-cash working capital balances related to operations	42,328	4,464
	194,075	128,159
Investing Activities		
Additions to property, plant and equipment	(227,003)	(199,778)
Business acquisitions net of amounts payable [note 4]	(71,321)	(61,861)
Proceeds on sale of assets		263,105
Investments and other assets	(72,466)	(14,214)
Additions to deferred charges	(27,498)	(5,969)
	(398,288)	(18,717)
Financing Activities		
Increase in long-term debt	497,112	223,645
Long-term debt repayments	(319,918)	(235,280)
Proceeds on issue of debenture purchase warrants	31,388	
Repurchase of preferred shares		(75,000)
Preferred shares redeemed	(2,840)	(720)
Dividends paid	(4,811)	(4,810)
	200,931	(92,165)
Net increase (decrease) in cash during the year	(3,282)	17,277
Cash position, beginning of the year	(17,594)	(34,871)
Cash position, end of the year	(20,876)	(17,594)
Cash flow from continuing operations per share	$2.17	$1.77

CASE 15–5
A. W. Hoyt Inc.
Analysis of statement of cash flows

Alan Hoyt is the president and majority shareholder of A. W. Hoyt Inc., a small retail store chain. Recently, Hoyt submitted a loan application for A. W. Hoyt Inc. to the Bank of Montreal. It called for a $200,000, 8%, 10-year loan to help finance the construction of a building and the purchase of store equipment, costing a total of $250,000 to enable A. W. Hoyt Inc. to open a store in Hamilton. Land for this purpose was acquired last year. The bank's loan officer requested a statement of cash flows in addition to the most recent income statement, balance sheet, and retained earnings statement that Hoyt had submitted with the loan application.

As a close family friend, Hoyt asked you to prepare a statement of cash flows. From the records provided, you prepared the statement shown on page 668.

After reviewing the statement, Hoyt telephoned you and commented, "Are you sure this statement is right?" Hoyt then raised the following questions:

a. "How can amortization be a cash flow?"
b. "How can the gain on sale of investments be a deduction from net income in determining the cash flow from operating activities?"
c. "Why isn't the issuance of common shares listed on the statement under financing activities?"
d. "Why does the bank need this statement anyway? They can compute the increase in cash from the balance sheets for the last two years."

After jotting down Hoyt's questions, you assured him that this statement was "right." However, to alleviate Hoyt's concern, you arranged a meeting for the following day.

A. W. Hoyt Inc.
Statement of Cash Flows
For the Year Ended December 31, 20—

Cash flows from operating activities:			
Net income, per income statement		$ 86,400	
Add: Amortization	$31,000		
Decrease in trade receivables	11,500	42,500	
		$128,900	
Deduct: Increase in inventory	$12,000		
Increase in prepaid expenses	1,500		
Decrease in accounts payable	3,000		
Gain on sale of investments	7,500	24,000	
Net cash flow from operating activities			$104,900
Cash flows from investing activities:			
Proceeds from investments sold		$ 42,500	
Purchase of store equipment		(31,000)	
Net cash flow from investing activities			11,500
Cash flows from financing activities:			
Cash paid for dividends		($ 40,000)	
Net cash flow used for financing activities			(40,000)
Increase in cash			$ 76,400
Cash at the beginning of the year			27,500
Cash at the end of the year			$103,900
Note to Financial Statements: Noncash Financing Activity:			
Issued common shares at par for land			$40,000

1. ◖▬▬▶ How would you respond to each of Hoyt's questions?

2. ◖▬▬▶ Do you think that the statement of cash flows enhances the chances of A. W. Hoyt Inc. receiving the loan? Discuss.

ANSWERS TO SELF-EXAMINATION QUESTIONS

1. **D** Cash flows from operating activities arise from the principal revenue-generating activities of the firm such as the receipt of cash from customers on account (answer D). Receipts of cash from issuing shares (answer A) and issuing bonds (answer B) and payments of cash for dividends (answer C) are cash flows from financing activities.

2. **A** Cash flows from investing activities include receipts from the sale of noncurrent assets, such as equipment (answer A), and payments to acquire noncurrent assets. Receipts of cash from issuing shares (answer B) and payments of cash for dividends (answer C) and to reacquire the company's own shares (answer D) are cash flows from financing activities.

3. **C** Payment of cash dividends (answer C) is an example of a financing activity. The receipt of cash from customers on account (answer A) is an operating activity. The receipt of cash from the sale of equipment (answer B) is an investing activity. The payment of cash to acquire a patent (answer D) is an example of an investing activity.

4. **D** The indirect method (answer D) reports cash flows from operating activities by beginning with net income and adjusting it for revenues and expenses not involving the receipt or payment of cash.

5. **C** The cash flows from operating activities section of the statement of cash flows would report net cash flow from operating activities of $65,500, determined as follows:

Net income		$55,000
Add: Amortization	$22,000	
Decrease in inventories	5,000	
Decrease in prepaid expenses	500	27,500
		$82,500
Deduct: Increase in trade receivables	$10,000	
Decrease in accounts payable	7,000	17,000
Net cash flow from operating activities		$65,500

Financial Statement Analysis and Annual Reports

YOU AND ACCOUNTING

The *Globe and Mail* (March 25, 1998) reported that the common shares of **Canadian Tire** were selling for $37 per share and **Future Shop** shares were selling at $12.25 per share. If you had funds to invest, would you invest in Canadian Tire or Future Shop shares?

Canadian Tire and Future Shop are well-known Canadian companies. However, **Steinberg's, Bramalea,** and **Pennington Stores** were also well-known Canadian companies. These latter companies share the common characteristic of having gone out of business due to financial difficulties!

Obviously, being well known is not necessarily a good basis for investing. Knowledge that a company has a good product, by itself, may also be an inadequate basis for investing in the company. Even with a good product, a company may go bankrupt for a variety of reasons, such as inadequate financing. For example, **Orion Pictures** went bankrupt, even though it produced the award-winning motion pictures *Dances With Wolves* and *Silence of the Lambs*.

How, then, does one decide on the companies in which to invest? This chapter describes and illustrates common financial data that can be analyzed to assist you in making investment decisions. In addition, we also discuss the contents of corporate annual reports.

> **After studying this chapter, you should be able to:**
>
> **Objective 1**
> List basic financial statement analytical procedures.
>
> **Objective 2**
> Apply financial statement analysis to assess the solvency of a business.
>
> **Objective 3**
> Apply financial statement analysis to assess the profitability of a business.
>
> **Objective 4**
> Summarize the uses and limitations of analytical measures.
>
> **Objective 5**
> Describe the contents of corporate annual reports.

Basic Analytical Procedures

Objective 1
List basic financial statement analytical procedures.

Basic financial statements provide much of the information users need to make economic decisions about businesses. In this chapter, we illustrate how to perform an analysis of these statements by integrating a variety of individual analytical measures.

You may use analytical procedures to compare items on a current statement with related items on earlier statements. For example, cash of $150,000 on the current balance sheet may be compared with cash of $100,000 on the balance sheet of a year earlier. The current year's cash may be expressed as 1.5 or 150% of the earlier amount or as an increase of 50% or $50,000.[1]

You may also use analytical procedures to examine relationships within a financial statement. To illustrate, assume that cash of $50,000 and inventories of $250,000 are included in the total assets of $1,000,000 on a balance sheet. In relative terms, the cash balance is 5% of the total assets, and the inventories are 25% of the total assets.

In the following discussion, we emphasize the importance of each of the various analytical measures illustrated. The measures are not ends in themselves. They are only guides in evaluating financial and operating data. When using these measures, you should also consider many other factors, such as trends in the industry, average industry measures, and general economic conditions. Industry data is available from Statistics Canada and trade associations, and other organizations such as Dunn and Bradstreet.

HORIZONTAL ANALYSIS

Horizontal analysis involves the percentage analysis of increases and decreases in related items in comparative financial statements. The amount of each item on the most recent statement is compared with the related item on one or more earlier statements. The amount of increase or decrease in the item is listed, along with the percent of increase or decrease.

Horizontal analysis may include a comparison between two statements. In this case, you use the earlier statement as the base. Horizontal analysis may also include three or more comparative statements. In this case, you may use the earliest date or period as the base for comparing all later dates or periods. Alternatively, you may compare each statement to the immediately preceding statement. Exhibit 1 is a con-

---

[1] Increases or decreases in items may be expressed in percentage terms only when the initial or base amount is positive. If the base amount is zero or a negative value, the amount of change cannot be expressed as a percentage.

Exhibit 1
Comparative Balance Sheet—
Horizontal Analysis

Laurier Company
Comparative Balance Sheet
December 31, 2000 and 1999

	2000	1999	Increase (Decrease) Amount	Percent
Assets				
Current assets	$ 550,000	$ 533,000	$ 17,000	3.2%
Long-term investments	95,000	177,500	(82,500)	(46.5%)
Capital assets (net)	444,500	470,000	(25,500)	(5.4%)
Intangible assets	50,000	50,000	—	
Total assets	$1,139,500	$1,230,500	$ (91,000)	(7.4%)
Liabilities				
Current liabilities	$ 210,000	$ 243,000	$ (33,000)	(13.6%)
Long-term liabilities	100,000	200,000	(100,000)	(50.0%)
Total liabilities	$ 310,000	$ 443,000	$(133,000)	(30.0%)
Shareholders' Equity				
Preferred $6 no par (1,500 shares outstanding)	$ 150,000	$ 150,000	—	—
Common no par (50,000 shares outstanding)	500,000	500,000	—	—
Retained earnings	179,500	137,500	$ 42,000	30.5%
Total shareholders' equity	$ 829,500	$ 787,500	$ 42,000	5.3%
Total liabilities and shareholders' equity	$1,139,500	$1,230,500	$ (91,000)	(7.4%)

densed comparative balance sheet for two years for Laurier Company, with horizontal analysis.

We cannot fully evaluate the significance of the various increases and decreases in the items shown in Exhibit 1 without additional information. Although total assets at the end of 2000 were $91,000 (7.4%) less than at the beginning of the year, liabilities were reduced by $133,000 (30%), and shareholders' equity increased $42,000 (5.3%). It appears that the reduction of $100,000 in long-term liabilities was achieved mostly through the sale of long-term investments.

The balance sheet in Exhibit 1 may be expanded to include the details of the various categories of assets and liabilities. An alternative is to present the details in separate schedules. Exhibit 2 is a supporting schedule with horizontal analysis.

The decrease in accounts receivable may be due to changes in credit terms or improved collection policies. Likewise, a decrease in inventories during a period of increased sales may indicate an improvement in the management of inventories.

Exhibit 2
Comparative Schedule of
Current Assets—Horizontal
Analysis

Laurier Company
Comparative Schedule of Current Assets
December 31, 2000 and 1999

	2000	1999	Increase (Decrease) Amount	Percent
Cash	$ 90,500	$ 64,700	$25,800	39.9%
Marketable securities	75,000	60,000	15,000	25.0%
Accounts receivable (net)	115,000	120,000	(5,000)	(4.2%)
Inventories	264,000	283,000	(19,000)	(6.7%)
Prepaid expenses	5,500	5,300	200	3.8%
Total current assets	$550,000	$533,000	$17,000	3.2%

The changes in the current assets in Exhibit 2 appear favourable. This assessment is supported by the 24.8% increase in net sales shown in Exhibit 3.

Exhibit 3
Comparative Income Statement—Horizontal Analysis

Laurier Company
Comparative Income Statement
December 31, 2000 and 1999

	2000	1999	Increase (Decrease) Amount	Percent
Sales	$1,530,500	$1,234,000	$296,500	24.0%
Sales returns and allowances	32,500	34,000	(1,500)	(4.4%)
Net sales	$1,498,000	$1,200,000	$298,000	24.8%
Cost of goods sold	1,043,000	820,000	223,000	27.2%
Gross profit	$ 455,000	$ 380,000	$ 75,000	19.7%
Selling expenses	$ 191,000	$ 147,000	$ 44,000	29.9%
Administrative expenses	104,000	97,400	6,600	6.8%
Total operating expenses	$ 295,000	$ 244,400	$ 50,600	20.7%
Operating income	$ 160,000	$ 135,600	$ 24,400	18.0%
Other income	8,500	11,000	(2,500)	(22.7%)
	$ 168,500	$ 146,600	$ 21,900	14.9%
Other expense	6,000	12,000	(6,000)	(50.0%)
Income before income tax	$ 162,500	$ 134,600	$ 27,900	20.7%
Income tax	71,500	58,100	13,400	23.1%
Net income	$ 91,000	$ 76,500	$ 14,500	19.0%

An increase in net sales may not have a favourable effect on operating performance. The percentage increase in Laurier Company's net sales is accompanied by a greater percentage increase in the cost of goods sold. This has the effect of reducing gross profit. Selling expenses increased significantly and administrative expenses increased slightly. Overall operating expenses increased by 20.7%, whereas gross profit increased by only 19.7%.

The increase in operating income and in net income is favourable. However, we need to make additional analyses and comparisons of the expenses before reaching a conclusion.

Exhibit 4 illustrates a comparative retained earnings statement with horizontal analysis. It reveals an increase of 30.5% in retained earnings for the year. The increase is due to net income of $91,000 for the year less dividends of $49,000.

Exhibit 4
Comparative Retained Earnings Statement—Horizontal Analysis

Laurier Company
Comparative Retained Earnings Statement
December 31, 2000 and 1999

	2000	1999	Increase (Decrease) Amount	Percent
Retained earnings, January 1	$137,500	$100,000	$37,500	37.5%
Net income for the year	91,000	76,500	14,500	19.0%
Total	$228,500	$176,500	$52,000	29.5%
Dividends:				
On preferred shares	$ 9,000	$ 9,000	—	—
On common shares	40,000	30,000	$10,000	33.3%
Total	$ 49,000	$ 39,000	$10,000	25.6%
Retained earnings, December 31	$179,500	$137,500	$42,000	30.5%

VERTICAL ANALYSIS

You may also use a percentage analysis to show the relationship of each component to the total within a single statement. This type of analysis is called vertical analysis. As with horizontal analysis, you may prepare the statements in either detailed or condensed form. In the latter case, you may analyze additional details of the changes in individual items in supporting schedules. In such schedules, the percentage analysis may be based on either the total of the schedule or the statement total. Although vertical analysis is limited to an individual statement, you may improve its significance by preparing comparative statements.

In vertical analysis of the balance sheet, you state each asset item as a percent of the total assets and each liability and shareholders' equity item as a percent of the total liabilities and shareholders' equity. Exhibit 5 is a condensed comparative balance sheet with vertical analysis for Laurier Company.

Exhibit 5
Comparative Balance Sheet—
Vertical Analysis

Laurier Company
Comparative Balance Sheet
December 31, 2000 and 1999

	2000		1999	
	Amount	Percent	Amount	Percent
Assets				
Current assets	$ 550,000	48.3%	$ 533,000	43.3%
Long-term investments	95,000	8.3	177,500	14.4
Capital assets (net)	444,500	39.0	470,000	38.2
Intangible assets	50,000	4.4	50,000	4.1
Total assets	$1,139,500	100.0%	$1,230,500	100.0%
Liabilities				
Current liabilities	$ 210,000	18.4%	$ 243,000	19.7%
Long-term liabilities	100,000	8.8	200,000	16.3
Total liabilities	$ 310,000	27.2%	$ 443,000	36.0%
Shareholders' Equity				
Preferred $6 no par (1,500 shares outstanding)	$ 150,000	13.2%	$ 150,000	12.2%
Common no par (50,000 shares outstanding)	500,000	43.9	500,000	40.6
Retained earnings	179,500	15.7	137,500	11.2
Total shareholders' equity	$ 829,500	72.8%	$ 787,500	64.0%
Total liabilities and shareholders' equity	$1,139,500	100.0%	$1,230,500	100.0%

The major percentage changes in Laurier Company's assets are in the current asset and long-term investment categories. In the Liabilities and Shareholders' Equity sections of the balance sheet, the greatest percentage changes are in long-term liabilities and retained earnings. Shareholders' equity increased from 64% to 72.8% of total liabilities and shareholders' equity in 2000. There is a comparable decrease in liabilities.

In a vertical analysis of the income statement, you state each item as a percent of net sales. Exhibit 6 is a condensed comparative income statement with vertical analysis for Laurier Company.

We must be careful when judging the significance of differences between percentages for the two years. For example, the decline of the gross profit rate from 31.7% in 1999 to 30.4% in 2000 is only 1.3 percentage points. In terms of dollars of potential gross profit, however, it represents a decline of approximately $19,500 (1.3% × $1,498,000).

Exhibit 6

Comparative Income Statement—Vertical Analysis

	2000		1999	
	Amount	**Percent**	**Amount**	**Percent**
Sales	$1,530,500	102.2%	$1,234,000	102.8%
Sales returns and allowances	32,500	2.2	34,000	2.8
Net sales	$1,498,000	100.0%	$1,200,000	100.0%
Cost of goods sold	1,043,000	69.6	820,000	68.3
Gross profit	$ 455,000	30.4%	$ 380,000	31.7%
Selling expenses	$ 191,000	12.8%	$ 147,000	12.3%
Administrative expenses	104,000	6.9	97,400	8.1
Total operating expenses	$ 295,000	19.7%	$ 244,400	20.4%
Operating income	$ 160,000	10.7%	$ 135,600	11.3%
Other income	8,500	0.6	11,000	0.9
	$ 168,500	11.3%	$ 146,600	12.2%
Other expense	6,000	0.4	12,000	1.0
Income before income tax	$ 162,500	10.9%	$ 134,600	11.2%
Income tax	71,500	4.8	58,100	4.8
Net income	$ 91,000	6.1%	$ 76,500	6.4%

Laurier Company
Comparative Income Sheet
December 31, 2000 and 1999

COMMON-SIZE STATEMENTS

Horizontal and vertical analyses with both dollar and percentage amounts are useful in assessing relationships and trends in financial conditions and operations of a business. Vertical analysis with both dollar and percentage amounts is also useful in comparing one company with another or with industry averages. Such comparisons are easier to make with the use of common-size statements. In a common-size statement, we express all items in percentages.

Common-size statements are useful in comparing the current period with prior periods, individual businesses, or one business with industry percentages. Industry data are often available from trade associations and financial information services. Exhibit 7 is a comparative common-size income statement for two businesses.

Exhibit 7

Common-Size Income Statement

Laurier Company and MacDonald Corporation
Condensed Common-Size Income Statement
For the Year Ended December 31, 2000

	Laurier Company	MacDonald Corporation
Sales	102.2%	102.3%
Sales returns and allowances	2.2	2.3
Net sales	100.0%	100.0%
Cost of goods sold	69.6	70.0
Gross profit	30.4%	30.0%
Selling expenses	12.8%	11.5%
Administrative expenses	6.9	4.1
Total operating expenses	19.7%	15.6%
Operating income	10.7%	14.4%
Other income	0.6	0.6
	11.3%	15.0%
Other expense	0.4	0.5
Income before income tax	10.9%	14.5%
Income tax	4.8	5.5
Net income	6.1%	9.0%

Exhibit 7 indicates that Laurier Company has a slightly higher rate of gross profit than MacDonald Corporation. However, this advantage is more than offset by Laurier Company's higher percentage of selling and administrative expenses. As a result, the operating income of Laurier Company is 10.7% of net sales, compared with 14.4% for MacDonald Corporation—an unfavourable difference of 3.7 percentage points.

OTHER ANALYTICAL MEASURES

In addition to the preceding analyses, we may express other relationships in ratios and percentages. Often, we take these items from the financial statements and thus prepare a type of vertical analysis. Comparison of these items with items from earlier periods is a type of horizontal analysis.

Solvency Analysis

Objective 2

Apply financial statement analysis to assess the solvency of a business.

Some aspects of a business's financial condition and operations are of greater importance to some users than others. However, all users are interested in the ability of a business to pay its debts as they come due and to earn income. The ability of a business to meet its financial obligations (debts) is called solvency. The ability of a business to earn income is called profitability.

The factors of solvency and profitability are interrelated. A business that cannot pay its debts on a timely basis may experience difficulty in obtaining credit. A lack of available credit may, in turn, lead to a decline in the business's profitability. Eventually, the business may be forced into bankruptcy. Likewise, a business that is less profitable than its competitors is likely to be at a disadvantage in obtaining credit or new capital from shareholders.

Analyses of historical data are useful in assessing the past performance of a business and in forecasting its future performance. The results of financial analyses may be even more useful when we compare them with those of competing businesses and with industry averages.

In the following paragraphs, we discuss various types of financial analyses that are useful in evaluating the solvency of a business. In the next section, we discuss various types of profitability analyses. The examples in both sections are based on Laurier Company's financial statements presented earlier. In some cases, we also employ data from Laurier Company's financial statements of the preceding year and from other sources.

Solvency is the ability of a business to meet its financial obligations (debts) as they are due. Solvency analysis, therefore, focuses on the ability of a business to pay or otherwise satisfy its current and noncurrent liabilities. We normally assess this ability by examining balance sheet relationships, using the following major analyses:

1. Current position analysis
2. Accounts receivable analysis
3. Inventory analysis
4. The ratio of capital assets to long-term liabilities
5. The ratio of liabilities to shareholders' equity
6. The number of times interest charges are earned

CURRENT POSITION ANALYSIS

To be useful in assessing solvency, a ratio or other financial measure must relate to a business's ability to pay or otherwise satisfy its liabilities. The use of such measures to assess the ability of a business to pay its current liabilities is called current position analysis. Such analysis is of special interest to short-term creditors.

An analysis of a firm's current position normally includes determining the working capital, the current ratio, and the acid-test ratio. The current and acid-test ratios are most useful when analyzed together and compared to previous periods and other firms in the industry.

Working Capital

Working capital is the excess of the current assets of a business over its current liabilities. *The working capital is often used in evaluating a company's ability to meet currently maturing debts.* It is especially useful in making monthly or other period-to-period comparisons for a company. However, it is difficult to assess the adequacy of amounts of working capital when comparing companies of different sizes or in comparing such amounts with industry figures. For example, working capital of $250,000 may be adequate for a small residential contractor, but it may be inadequate for a large commercial contractor.

Current Ratio

Another means of expressing the relationship between current assets and current liabilities is the current ratio (or working capital ratio). You compute the ratio by dividing the total current assets by the total current liabilities. For Laurier Company, working capital and the current ratio for 2000 and 1999 are as follows:

	2000	1999
Current assets	$550,000	$533,000
Current liabilities	210,000	243,000
Working capital	$340,000	$290,000
Current ratio	2.6:1	2.2:1

The current ratio is a more reliable indicator of solvency than is working capital. To illustrate, assume that as of December 31, 2000, the working capital of a competitor is much greater than $340,000, but its current ratio is only 1.3:1. Considering these facts alone, Laurier Company, with its current ratio of 2.6:1, is in a more favourable position to obtain short-term credit than the competitor, which has the **greater amount** of working capital.

Acid-Test Ratio

The working capital and the current ratio do not consider the makeup of the current assets. To illustrate the importance of this consideration, the current position data for Laurier Company and Bennett Corporation as of December 31, 2000, are as follows:

	Laurier Company	Bennett Corporation
Current assets:		
Cash	$ 90,500	$ 45,500
Marketable securities	75,000	25,000
Accounts receivable (net)	115,000	90,000
Inventories	264,000	380,000
Prepaid expenses	5,500	9,500
Total current assets	$550,000	$550,000
Current liabilities	210,000	210,000
Working capital	$340,000	$340,000
Current ratio	2.6:1	2.6:1

Both companies have a working capital of $340,000 and a current ratio of 2.6:1. But the ability of each company to pay its current debts is significantly different.

Bennett Corporation has more of its current assets invested in inventories. Bennett would have to sell some of these inventories and collect the receivables before it could pay its current liabilities in full. Thus, it may need a significant amount of time to convert these inventories into cash. Declines in market prices and a reduction in demand could also impair its ability to pay current liabilities. In contrast, Laurier Company has cash and other current assets (marketable securities and accounts receivable) that it can convert to cash rather quickly to meet its current liabilities.

The acid-test ratio or quick ratio is *a ratio that measures the "instant" debt-paying ability of a company.* It is the ratio of the total quick assets to the total current liabilities. Quick assets are cash and other current assets that can be quickly converted to cash. Quick assets normally include cash, marketable securities, and receivables. The acid-test ratio data for Laurier Company are as follows:

	2000	1999
Quick assets:		
Cash	$ 90,500	$ 64,700
Marketable securities	75,000	60,000
Accounts receivable (net)	115,000	120,000
Total	$280,500	$244,700
Current liabilities	$210,000	$243,000
Acid-test ratio	1.3:1	1.0:1

ACCOUNTS RECEIVABLE ANALYSIS

The size and makeup of accounts receivable change constantly during business operations. Sales on account increase accounts receivable, whereas collections from customers decrease accounts receivable. Firms that grant long credit terms usually have larger accounts receivable balances than those granting short credit terms. Increases or decreases in the volume of sales also affect the balance of accounts receivable.

It is desirable to collect receivables as promptly as possible. The cash collected from receivables improves solvency. In addition, a business may use the cash generated by prompt collections from customers in operations for such purposes as purchasing merchandise in large quantities at lower prices. It may also use the cash for payment of dividends to shareholders or for other investing or financing purposes. Prompt collection also lessens the risk of loss from uncollectible accounts. Two measures that are useful in evaluating the management of receivables are the accounts receivable turnover and the number of days' sales in receivables.

Accounts Receivable Turnover

The accounts receivable turnover ratio describes the relationship between credit sales and accounts receivable. You compute this ratio by dividing net credit sales by the average net accounts receivable. It is desirable to base the average on monthly balances, which allows for seasonal changes in sales. When such data are not available, it may be necessary to use the average of the accounts receivable balance at the beginning and the end of the year. If there are trade notes receivable as well as accounts, the two may be combined. The accounts receivable turnover data for Laurier Company are as follows. All sales were made on account.

	2000	1999
Net sales on account	$1,498,000	$1,200,000
Accounts receivable (net):		
Beginning of year	$ 120,000	$ 140,000
End of year	115,000	120,000
Total	$ 235,000	$ 260,000
Average	$ 117,500	$ 130,000
Accounts receivable turnover	12.7	9.2

The increase in the accounts receivable turnover for 2000 indicates that there has been an improvement in the collection of receivables. This may be due to a change in the granting of credit or the collecting practices or both.

Number of Days' Sales in Receivables

Another measure of the relationship between credit sales and accounts receivable is the number of days' sales in receivables. You compute this ratio by dividing the net accounts receivable at the end of the year by the average daily sales on account. You determine average daily sales on account by dividing net sales on account by 365 days. The number of days' sales in receivables for Laurier Company is as follows:

	2000	1999
Accounts receivable (net), end of year	$ 115,000	$ 120,000
Net sales on account	$1,498,000	$1,200,000
Average daily sales on account	$ 4,104	$ 3,288
Number of days' sales in receivables*	28.0	36.5

*Accounts receivable ÷ Average daily sales on account

The number of days' sales in receivables is an estimate of the length of time the accounts receivable have been outstanding. Comparing this measure with the company's credit terms provides information on the efficiency in collecting receivables. For example, assume that the number of days' sales in receivables for Grant Inc. is 40. If Grant Inc.'s credit terms are n/45, then its collection process appears to be efficient. On the other hand, if Grant Inc.'s credit terms are n/30, its collection process does not appear to be efficient. A comparison with other firms in the same industry and with prior years also provides useful information. Such comparisons may indicate the efficiency of collection procedures and trends in credit management.

INVENTORY ANALYSIS

A business should keep enough inventory on hand to meet the needs of its customers and its operations. At the same time, however, an excessive amount of inventory reduces solvency by tying up funds. Excess inventories also increase insurance expense, property taxes, storage costs, and other related expenses. These expenses further reduce funds that could be used elsewhere to improve operations. Finally, excess inventory also increases the risk of losses because of price declines or obsolescence of the inventory. Two measures that are useful for evaluating the management of inventory are the inventory turnover and the number of days' sales in inventory.

Inventory Turnover

The inventory turnover ratio describes the relationship between the volume of goods sold and inventory. You compute it by dividing the cost of goods sold by the average inventory. If monthly data are not available, you may use the average of the inventories at the beginning and the end of the year. The inventory turnover for Laurier Company is as follows:

	2000	1999
Cost of goods sold	$1,043,000	$820,000
Inventories:		
Beginning of year	$ 283,000	$311,000
End of year	264,000	283,000
Total	$ 547,000	$594,000
Average	$ 273,500	$297,000
Inventory turnover	3.8	2.8

The inventory turnover improved for Laurier Company because of an increase in the cost of goods sold and a decrease in the average inventories. Differences across inventories, companies, and industries are too great to allow a general statement on what is a good inventory turnover. For example, a firm selling food should have a higher turnover than a firm selling furniture or jewellery. Likewise, the perishable foods department of a supermarket should have a higher turnover than the soaps and cleansers department. However, for each business or each department within a business, there is a reasonable turnover rate. A turnover lower than this rate could mean that inventory is not being managed properly.

Number of Days' Sales in Inventory

Another measure of the relationship between the cost of goods sold and inventory is the number of days' sales in inventory. You compute this measure by dividing the inventory at the end of the year by the average daily cost of goods sold (cost of goods sold divided by 365). The number of days' sales in inventory for Laurier Company is as follows:

	2000	1999
Inventories, end of year	$ 264,000	$283,000
Cost of goods sold	$1,043,000	$820,000
Average daily cost of goods sold	$ 2,858	$ 2,247
Number of days' sales in inventory	92.4	125.9
(Inventories ÷ avg. daily cost of goods sold)		

The number of days' sales in inventory is a rough measure of the length of time it takes to acquire, sell, and replace the inventory. For Laurier Company, there is a major improvement in the number of days' sales in inventory during 2000. However, a comparison with earlier years and similar firms would be useful in assessing Laurier Company's overall inventory management.

RATIO OF CAPITAL ASSETS TO LONG-TERM LIABILITIES

Long-term notes and bonds are often secured by mortgages on capital assets. The ratio of total capital assets to long-term liabilities *is a solvency measure that indicates the margin of safety for the noteholders or bondholders. It also indicates the ability of the business to borrow additional funds on a long-term basis.* The ratio of capital assets to long-term liabilities for Laurier Company is as follows:

	2000	1999
Capital assets (net)	$444,500	$470,000
Long-term liabilities	$100,000	$200,000
Ratio of plant assets to long-term liabilities	4.4:1	2.4:1

The major increase in this ratio at the end of 2000 is mainly due to liquidating one-half of Laurier Company's long-term liabilities. If the company needs to borrow additional funds on a long-term basis in the future, it is in a strong position to do so.

RATIO OF LIABILITIES TO SHAREHOLDERS' EQUITY

Claims against the total assets of a business consist of two groups: (1) claims of creditors and (2) claims of owners. *The relationship between the total claims of the creditors and owners is a solvency measure that indicates the margin of safety for creditors. It also indicates the ability of the business to withstand adverse business conditions.* When the claims of creditors are large in relation to the equity of the shareholders, there are usually significant interest payments. If earnings decline to the point where the company is unable to meet its interest payments, the business may be taken over by the creditors.

The vertical analysis of the balance sheet shows the relationship between creditors' and shareholders' equity. For example, the balance sheet of Laurier Company in Exhibit 5 indicates that on December 31, 2000, liabilities represented 27.2% and shareholders' equity represented 72.8% of the total liabilities and shareholders' equity (100.0%). Instead of expressing each item as a percent of the total, we may express this relationship as a ratio of one to the other, as follows:

	2000	1999
Total liabilities	$310,000	$443,000
Total shareholders' equity	$829,500	$787,500
Ratio of liabilities to shareholders' equity	0.37:1	0.56:1

The balance sheet of Laurier Company shows that the major factor affecting the change in the ratio was the $100,000 decrease in long-term liabilities during 2000. The ratio at the end of both years shows a large margin of safety for the creditors.

NUMBER OF TIMES INTEREST CHARGES EARNED

Corporations in some industries, such as airlines, normally have high ratios of debt to shareholders' equity. For such corporations, we normally measure *the relative risk of the debtholders as the* number of times the interest charges are earned during the year. The higher the ratio, the lower the risk that the company will not make interest payments if earnings decrease. In other words, the higher the ratio, the greater the assurance that the company will make interest payments on a continuing basis. *This measure also indicates the general financial strength of the business, which is of interest to shareholders and employees as well as creditors.*

Income tax does not affect the amount available to meet interest charges. This is because interest is deductible in determining taxable income. For example, the number of times interest charges are earned for Pearson Co. is computed as shown.

	2000	1999
Income before income tax	$ 900,000	$ 800,000
Add interest expense	300,000	250,000
Amount available to meet interest charges	$1,200,000	$1,050,000
Number of times interest charges earned	4	4.2

We can also apply analysis such as this to dividends on preferred shares. In such a case, we divide net income by the amount of preferred dividends to yield the number of times preferred dividends are earned. This measure indicates the risk that dividends to preferred shareholders may not be paid.

Profitability Analysis

Objective 3
Apply financial statement analysis to assess the profitability of a business.

Profitability is the ability of an entity to earn profits. This ability to earn profits depends on the effectiveness and efficiency of operations as well as resources available to the business. Profitability analysis, therefore, focuses primarily on the relationship between operating results as reported in the income statement and resources available to the business as reported in the balance sheet. Major analyses for assessing profitability include the following:

1. Ratio of net sales to assets (also called asset turnover)

2. Rate earned on total assets
3. Rate earned on shareholders' equity
4. Rate earned on common shareholders' equity
5. Earnings per common share
6. Price-earnings ratio
7. Dividend yield

RATIO OF NET SALES TO ASSETS (ASSET TURNOVER)

The ratio of net sales to assets *is a profitability measure that shows how effectively a firm utilizes its assets.* For example, two competing businesses have equal amounts of assets. If the sales of one are twice the sales of the other, the business with the higher sales is making better use of its assets.

In computing the ratio of net sales to assets, we often exclude any long-term investments from total assets. This is because such investments are unrelated to normal operations involving the sale of goods or services. Assets may be measured as the total at the end of the year, the average at the beginning and end of the year, or the average of monthly totals. The basic data and the computation of this ratio for Laurier Company are as follows:

	2000	1999
Net sales	$1,498,000	$1,200,000
Total assets (excluding long-term investments):		
Beginning of year	$1,053,000	$1,010,000
End of year	1,044,500	1,053,000
Total	$2,097,500	$2,063,000
Average	$1,048,750	$1,031,500
Ratio of net sales to assets	1.4:1	1.2:1

There was an improvement in this ratio during 2000. This was primarily due to an increase in sales volume. A comparison with similar companies or industry averages would be helpful in assessing the effectiveness of Laurier Company's use of its assets.

RATE EARNED ON TOTAL ASSETS

The rate earned on total assets *measures the profitability of total assets, without considering how the assets are financed.* This rate is therefore not affected by whether the assets are financed primarily by creditors or shareholders.

We compute the rate earned on total assets by adding interest expense (net of tax) to net income and dividing this sum by the average total assets. The addition of interest expense (net of tax) to net income eliminates the effect of whether the assets are financed by debt or equity. The reason that we adjust interest expense for taxes when adding it back to net income is because net income is calculated after deducting income taxes. Any item added back to net income should also be a "net" amount, after deducting the item's tax effect. Since interest expense is a deduction in computing taxable income, it reduces income tax expense. Interest expense (net of tax) may be estimated as: Interest Expense $\times$ (1 – tax rate).

Assume that in Exhibit 3 "Other expense" represents "Interest expense." We can estimate the tax rate as the ratio of "Income tax" to "Income before income tax." Based on the data in Exhibit 3, the tax rate appears to be 44% ($71,500 $\div$ $162,500) in 2000 and 43.2% ($58,100 $\div$ $134,500) in 1999. We compute interest expense (net of tax) for Laurier Company for 2000 and 1999 as follows:

2000 Interest Expense (net of tax): $6,000 $\times$ (1 – 0.44) = $3,360
1999 Interest Expense (net of tax): $12,000 $\times$ (1 – 0.432) = $6,816

The rate earned by Laurier Company on total assets is then computed as follows:

	2000	1999
Net income	$ 91,000	$ 76,500
Plus interest expense (net of tax)	3,360	6,816
Total	$ 94,360	$ 83,316
Total assets:		
Beginning of year	$1,230,500	$1,187,500
End of year	1,139,500	1,230,500
Total	$2,370,000	$2,418,000
Average	$1,185,000	$1,209,000
Rate earned on total assets	8%	6.9%

The rate earned on total assets of Laurier Company during 2000 improved over that of 1999. A comparison with similar companies and industry averages would be useful in evaluating Laurier Company's profitability on total assets.

Sometimes it may be desirable to compute the rate of operating income to total assets. This is especially true if the income statement shows significant amounts of nonoperating income and expense. In this case, we should exclude any assets related to the nonoperating income and expense items from total assets in computing the rate. In addition, using operating income (which is before tax) has the advantage of eliminating the effects of any changes in the tax structure on the rate of earnings. When evaluating published data on rates earned on assets, you should be careful to determine the exact nature of the measure that is reported.

RATE EARNED ON SHAREHOLDERS' EQUITY

Another measure of profitability is the rate earned on shareholders' equity. You compute this by dividing net income by average total shareholders' equity. In contrast to the rate earned on total assets, *this measure emphasizes the rate of income earned on the amount invested by the shareholders.*

The total shareholders' equity may vary throughout a period. For example, a business may issue or retire stock, pay dividends, and earn net income. If monthly amounts are not available, you normally use the average of the shareholders' equity at the beginning and the end of the year to compute this rate. For Laurier Company, the rate earned on shareholders' equity is as follows:

	2000	1999
Net income	$ 91,000	$ 76,500
Shareholders' equity:		
Beginning of year	$ 787,500	$ 750,000
End of year	829,500	787,500
Total	$1,617,000	$1,537,500
Average	$ 808,500	$ 768,750
Rate earned on shareholders' equity	11.3%	10.0%

The rate earned by a business on the equity of its shareholders is usually higher than the rate earned on total assets. This occurs when the amount earned on assets acquired with creditors' funds is more than the interest paid to creditors. This difference in the rate on shareholders' equity and the rate on total assets is called leverage.

Laurier Company's rate earned on shareholders' equity for 2000, 11.3%, is greater than the rate of 8.2% earned on total assets. The leverage of 3.1% (11.3% – 8.2%) for 2000 compares favourably with the 2.7% (10.0% – 7.3%) leverage for 1999. Exhibit 8 shows the 2000 and 1999 leverages for Laurier Company.

Exhibit 8
Leverage

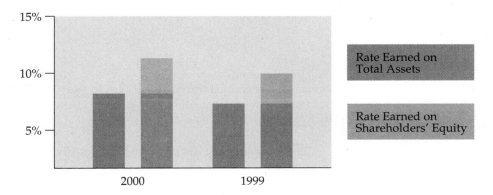

RATE EARNED ON COMMON SHAREHOLDERS' EQUITY

A corporation may have both preferred and common shares outstanding. In this case, the common shareholders have the residual claim on earnings. The rate earned on common shareholders' equity focuses only on the rate of profits earned on the amount invested by the common shareholders. You compute it by subtracting preferred dividend requirements from the net income and dividing by the average common shareholders' equity.

Laurier Company has 1,500 $6 cumulative nonparticipating preferred shares outstanding on December 31, 2000 and 1999. Thus, the annual preferred dividend requirement is $9,000 (1,500 shares × $6). The common shareholders' equity equals the total shareholders' equity, including retained earnings, less the carrying value of the preferred shares ($150,000). The basic data and the rate earned on common shareholders' equity for Laurier Company are as follows:

	2000	1999
Net income	$ 91,000	$ 76,500
Preferred dividends	9,000	9,000
Remainder—identified with common shares	$ 82,000	$ 67,500
Common shareholders' equity:		
Beginning of year	$ 637,500	$ 600,000
End of year	679,500	637,500
Total	$1,317,000	$1,237,500
Average	$ 658,500	$ 618,750
Rate earned on common shareholders' equity	12.5%	10.9%

The rate earned on common shareholders' equity differs from the rates earned by Laurier Company on total assets and total shareholders' equity. This occurs if there are borrowed funds and also preferred shares outstanding, which rank ahead of the common shares in their claim on earnings. Thus, the concept of leverage, as we discussed in the preceding section, can also be applied to the use of funds from the sale of preferred shares as well as borrowing. Funds from both sources can be used in an attempt to increase the return on common shareholders' equity.

EARNINGS PER SHARE ON COMMON STOCK

One of the profitability measures often quoted by the financial press is **earnings per share (EPS)** on common stock. As discussed in Chapter 13, the *CICA Handbook* requires most companies to report EPS in their annual income statement or in notes referenced to their income statement. If a company has issued only one class of shares, it computes EPS by dividing net income by the average number of shares outstanding. If preferred and common shares are outstanding, the net income is first reduced by the amount of preferred dividend requirements.

The data on the EPS of common stock for Laurier Company are as follows:

	2000	1999
Net income	$91,000	$76,500
Preferred dividends	9,000	9,000
Remainder—identified with common shares	$82,000	$67,500
Shares of common outstanding	50,000	50,000
Earnings per share on common	$1.64	$1.35

Since earnings are the primary basis for dividends, investors often use EPS and dividends per common share in assessing alternative stock investments. Some companies report dividends per share with EPS to indicate the relationship between dividends and earnings. A comparison of these two per-share amounts indicates the extent to which the corporation is retaining its earnings for use in operations. Exhibit 9 shows these relationships for Laurier Company.

Exhibit 9

Earnings and Dividends per Common Share

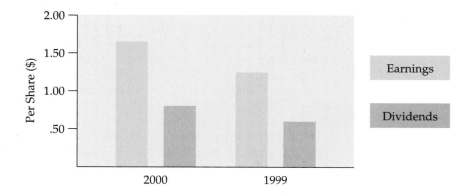

PRICE-EARNINGS RATIO

Another profitability measure commonly quoted by the financial press is the price-earnings (P/E) ratio on common shares. *The price-earnings ratio is an indicator of a firm's future earnings prospects.* You compute it by dividing the market price per share of common at a specific date by the annual earnings per share. To illustrate, assume that the market prices per common share for Laurier Company are 20½ at the end of 2000 and 13½ at the end of 1999. The price-earnings ratio on common shares is as follows:

	2000	1999
Market price per share of common	$20.50	$13.50
Earnings per share on common	÷ 1.64	÷ 1.35
Price-earnings ratio on common	12.5	10.0

The price-earnings ratio indicates that a common share of Laurier Company was selling for 10 times the amount of earnings per share at the end of 1999. At the end of 2000, the common shares were selling for 12.5 times the amount of earnings per share.

DIVIDENDS PER SHARE AND DIVIDEND YIELD

The dividend yield on common shares is a profitability measure that shows the rate of return to common shareholders in terms of cash dividends. It is of special interest to investors whose main investment objective is to receive current returns (dividends) on an investment rather than an increase in the market price of the investment. We compute the dividend yield by dividing the annual dividends paid per common share by the market price per share on a specific date. To illustrate, assume that dividends were $0.80 per common share and the market price was 20½ at the end of 2000. Dividends were $0.60 per share, and the market price was 13½ at the end of 1999. The dividend yield on Laurier Company's common shares is as follows:

	2000	1999
Dividends per share of common	$ 0.80	$ 0.60
Market price per share of common ÷	20.50 ÷	13.50
Dividend yield on common	3.9%	4.4%

Summary of Analytical Measures

Objective 4
Summarize the uses and limitations of analytical measures.

Exhibit 10 presents a summary of the analytical measures that we have discussed. These measures can be computed for most medium-size businesses. Depending on the specific business being analyzed, we might omit some measures or develop

Exhibit 10
Summary of Analytical Measures

	Method of Computation	*Use*
Solvency measures:		
Working capital	Current assets – Current liabilities	**To indicate the ability to meet currently maturing obligations**
Current ratio	$\dfrac{\text{Current assets}}{\text{Current liabilities}}$	
Acid-test ratio	$\dfrac{\text{Quick assets}}{\text{Current liabilities}}$	**To indicate instant debt-paying ability**
Accounts receivable turnover	$\dfrac{\text{Net sales on account}}{\text{Average accounts receivable}}$	**To assess the efficiency in collecting receivables and in the management of credit**
Number of days' sales in receivables	$\dfrac{\text{Accounts receivable, end of year}}{\text{Average daily sales on account}}$	
Inventory turnover	$\dfrac{\text{Cost of goods sold}}{\text{Average inventory}}$	**To assess the efficiency in the management of inventory**
Number of days' sales in inventory	$\dfrac{\text{Inventory, end of year}}{\text{Average daily cost of goods sold}}$	
Ratio of capital assets to long-term liabilities	$\dfrac{\text{Capital assets (net)}}{\text{Long-term liabilities}}$	**To indicate the margin of safety to long-term creditors**
Ratio of liabilities to shareholders' equity	$\dfrac{\text{Total liabilities}}{\text{Total shareholders' equity}}$	**To indicate the margin of safety to creditors**
Number of times interest charges earned	$\dfrac{\text{Income before income tax + Interest expense}}{\text{Interest expense}}$	**To assess the risk to debtholders in terms of number of times interest charges were earned**
Profitability measures:		
Ratio of net sales to assets (asset turnover)	$\dfrac{\text{Net sales}}{\text{Average total assets (excluding long-term investments)}}$	**To assess the effectiveness in the use of assets**
Rate earned on total assets	$\dfrac{\text{Net income + Interest expense (net of tax)}}{\text{Average total assets}}$	**To assess the profitability of the assets**

Exhibit 10 (continued)

	Method of Computation	*Use*
Profitability measures:		
Rate earned on shareholders' equity	$\dfrac{\text{Net income}}{\text{Average total shareholders' equity}}$	**To assess the profitability of the investment by shareholders**
Rate earned on common shareholders' equity	$\dfrac{\text{Net income} - \text{Preferred dividends}}{\text{Average common shareholders' equity}}$	**To assess the profitability of the investment by common shareholders**
Earnings per share on common	$\dfrac{\text{Net income} - \text{Preferred dividends}}{\text{Average number of common shares outstanding}}$	
Price-earnings ratio	$\dfrac{\text{Market price per share of common}}{\text{Earnings per share of common}}$	**To indicate future earnings prospects, based on the relationship between market value of common shares and earnings**
Dividends per share of common	$\dfrac{\text{Dividends}}{\text{Average number of common shares outstanding}}$	**To indicate the extent to which earnings are being distributed to common shareholders**
Dividend yield	$\dfrac{\text{Dividends per share of common}}{\text{Market price per share of common}}$	**To indicate the rate of return to common shareholders in terms of dividends**

additional measures. The type of industry, the capital structure, and the diversity of the business's operations usually affect the measures used. For example, analysis for an airline might include revenue per passenger mile and cost per available seat as measures. Likewise, analysis for a hotel might focus on occupancy rates.

Percentage analyses, ratios, turnovers, and other measures of financial position and operating results are useful analytical measures. They are helpful in assessing a business's past performance and predicting its future. They are not, however, a substitute for sound judgment. In selecting and interpreting analytical measures, you should consider conditions peculiar to a business or its industry, as well as the influence of the general economic and business environment.

In determining trends, you need to study carefully the interrelationship of the measures used in assessing a business and comparable indexes of earlier periods. Data from competing businesses may be useful in assessing the efficiency of operations for the firm under analysis. In making such comparisons, however, you should also consider the effects of any differences in the accounting methods used by the businesses.

Corporate Annual Reports

Objective 5
Describe the contents of corporate annual reports.

Corporations normally issue annual reports to their shareholders and other interested parties. Such reports summarize the corporation's operating activities for the past year and plans for the future. There are many variations in the order and form for presenting the major sections of annual reports. However, one section of the annual report is devoted to the financial statements. In addition, annual reports usually include the following sections:

1. Financial Highlights
2. President's Letter to the Shareholders
3. Management Report
4. Independent Auditors' Report

5. Historical Summary
6. Notes to the Financial Statements and Other Information.

In the following paragraphs, we describe these sections as well as the notes to the financial statements and other information contained in the annual report. Each section, as well as the financial statements, is illustrated in the current year's annual report for Sears Canada Inc. which accompanies this text.

FINANCIAL HIGHLIGHTS

The Financial Highlights section summarizes the operating results for the last year or two. It is sometimes called *Results in Brief.* It is usually presented on the first one or two pages of the annual report. The 1997 edition of *Financial Reporting in Canada* indicates that 94% of companies surveyed included a Financial Highlights section in their annual reports.[2]

There are many variations in the format and content of the Financial Highlights section. The section typically presents such items as sales, net income, net income per common share, cash dividends paid, cash dividends per common share, and the amount of capital expenditures. In addition to these data, information about the financial position at the end of the year may be presented.

PRESIDENT'S LETTER TO THE SHAREHOLDERS

Most annual corporate reports include a letter from the company president to the shareholders. These letters usually discuss such items as reasons for an increase or decrease in net income, changes in existing plants, purchase or construction of new plants, significant new financing commitments, social responsibility issues, and future plans.

MANAGEMENT REPORT

The *CICA Handbook* Accounting Guideline, "The Management Report," suggests that companies whose annual financial statements are widely distributed should include a management report (paragraph .03).

The management of the corporation is responsible for the corporation's accounting system and financial statements. In the Management Report section, the chief financial officer or other corporate officer normally includes the following:

1. A statement that the financial statements are management's responsibility and that they have been prepared according to generally accepted accounting principles.
2. Management's assessment of the company's internal accounting control system.
3. Comments on any other relevant matters related to the accounting system, the financial statements, and the examination by the independent auditor.

The 1997 edition of *Financial Reporting in Canada* reports that 90% of the companies surveyed included a management report in their 1996 annual reports.[3]

INDEPENDENT AUDITORS' REPORT

Before issuing annual statements, all publicly held corporations are required to have an independent audit (examination) of their financial statements. Other companies that have loans outstanding with banks or other financial institutions may

[2] C. Byrd and I. Chen, *Financial Reporting in Canada,* 22nd ed., CICA, Toronto, 1997, p. 4.
[3] C. Byrd and I. Chen, *op. cit.,* p. 19.

be required to have their financial statements audited. Still other companies may choose voluntarily to have an independent audit in order to add more credibility to their financial statements.

Such audits are conducted by independent public accountants, who use generally accepted accounting principles to assess the fairness of the company's statements. The auditor's opinion is contained in the Auditor's Report, which accompanies the financial statements. The standard audit report includes the following three paragraphs:

1. An introductory paragraph identifying the financial statements audited.
2. A scope paragraph describing the nature of the audit.
3. An opinion paragraph presenting the auditor's opinion as to the fairness of the statements.

For most companies, the auditor renders an unqualified or clean audit opinion, in a format similar to that shown in Exhibit 11 below.

Auditors may add a paragraph to the unqualified or clean opinion to call attention to an important event or fact. For example, if the auditor has "substantial doubt" about the ability of the company to continue operating as a going concern, the auditor will add a paragraph to the audit report calling the reader's attention to this possibility. Likewise, if a company changes accounting methods, the auditor will add a paragraph to the audit report, calling the reader's attention to the change.

Sometimes, an auditor who has formed a positive opinion on the company's financial statements as a whole, will issue a qualified audit opinion because the company has departed from generally accepted accounting principles or because the auditor has not been able to carry out all the tests necessary in the circumstances. A more serious reservation is an adverse audit opinion, which indicates that the financial statements are not presented fairly in accordance with generally accepted accounting principles. A denial of opinion indicates that the auditor has been unable to gather sufficient appropriate evidence to form an opinion as to whether the statements are presented fairly and in accordance with generally accepted accounting principles.

Exhibit 11
Sample of Auditor's Report

Auditor's Report

To the Shareholders of ....

I have audited the balance sheet of .... as at ...., 20...... and the statements of income, retained earnings, and changes in financial position for the year then ended. These financial statements are the responsibility of the company's management. My responsibility is to express an opinion on these financial statements based on my audit.

I conducted my audit in accordance with generally accepted auditing standards. Those standards require that I plan and perform an audit to obtain reasonable assurance whether the financial statements are free of material misstatement. An audit includes examining, on a test basis, evidence supporting the amounts, and disclosures in the financial statements. An audit also includes assessing the accounting principles used and significant estimates made by management, as well as evaluating the overall financial statement presentation.

In my opinion, these financial statements present fairly, in all material respects, the financial position of the company as at ...., 20...... and the results of its operations and the changes in its financial position for the year then ended in accordance with generally accepted accounting principles.

City   (signed) ....
Date   CHARTERED ACCOUNTANT

Source: *CICA Handbook*, Section 5400, paragraph 26.

USING ACCOUNTING TO UNDERSTAND BUSINESS

An additional source of information about a corporation is the independent auditor's report, which must accompany the financial statements of a public corporation. The purpose of this report is to provide assurance to investors that the financial statements are fairly presented in conformity with generally accepted accounting principles.

The auditor's report may raise "red flags" that indicate that profitability and solvency measures require further analysis. In such cases, an investor should read the auditor's report carefully to see if the "reliability" of these measures has been affected by one or more of the following factors:

1. Part of the audit was done by another auditor.
2. There may be substantial doubt as to the ability of the company to continue as a going concern beyond one year.
3. An unusual accounting practice is being followed.
4. The company changed accounting principles from prior years.
5. The auditor wants to call your attention to a specific matter of importance.
6. The auditor's examination of the financial statements was limited in some way.
7. The financial statements are not in conformity with generally accepted accounting principles.
8. The auditor is not independent.

The date of the auditor's report is also significant. It represents the last date that the auditor searched for events occurring subsequent to the date of the financial statements—events that might be significant to the interpretation of those statements. For example, the company may have sold a subsidiary after year-end or suffered a substantial loss as a result of some disaster. Such events should be disclosed in notes to the financial statements.

HISTORICAL SUMMARY

The *CICA Handbook* requires that companies prepare their financial statements on a comparative basis, showing figures for the corresponding preceding period, when it is meaningful.[4] In addition, a survey of large public Canadian companies indicates that approximately 80% provide additional comparative data in some form of Historical Summary.[5]

The Historical Summary section reports selected financial and operating data of past periods, usually for five or ten years. It is usually presented near the financial statements for the current year. There are wide variations in the types of data reported and the title of this section. In the annual report for Sears Canada Inc., this section is called the "Eleven-Year Summary."

NOTES TO THE FINANCIAL STATEMENTS AND OTHER INFORMATION

Some annual reports may include other financial information. For example, some reports may include forecasts that indicate financial plans and expectations for the year ahead and other supplemental data.

The notes to the financial statements are considered an integral part of the statement[6] and are covered by the auditor's report.[7] Companies may use their notes for

---

[4] *CICA Handbook,* Section 1500, paragraph .09.
[5] C. Byrd and I. Chen, *op. cit.,* p. 3.
[6] *CICA Handbook,* Section 1000, paragraph .04.
[7] *Ibid.,* Section 7500, paragraph 13.

various types of disclosures, such as providing additional details on items contained in the financial statements, explanations of accounting principles and procedures, or other information. Below we discuss some of the items most commonly found in the notes to the financial statements.

1. Disclosure of Accounting Policies

Enterprises are required to disclose the significant accounting policies that have been used in the preparation of their financial statements.[8] For example, *Financial Reporting in Canada (1997)* reports that in 1996, 99% of companies surveyed disclosed their accounting policy for valuing and amortizing capital assets. Approximately 88% of the respondents disclosed their accounting policies in the notes to the financial statements.[9]

2. Contingencies

As we discussed in Chapter 11, a contingency is an existing situation involving uncertainty as to possible gain or loss, the outcome of which will be resolved in the future. A company will record a contingent liability on its balance sheet only if the liability is probable and the amount can be estimated. The business must disclose contingent liabilities not recorded on the balance sheet in the notes to its financial statements. Common examples of contingent liabilities disclosed in the notes include potential future losses arising from litigation, loan guarantees, and discounted notes receivable. Contingencies that may give rise to possible future gains can only be disclosed in the notes, but not accrued as assets on the balance sheet. *Financial Reporting in Canada (1997)* indicates that 60% of the firms surveyed disclosed contingencies in notes to their financial statements, and 55% discussed litigation against the company in their notes.[10]

3. Financial Instruments

In the past decade there has been widespread growth in the variety and types of financial instruments issued by businesses. The *CICA Handbook* defines a **financial instrument** as "any contract that gives rise to both a financial asset of one party and a financial liability or equity instrument of another party" (Section 3860, paragraph 03). Examples of financial instruments include items such as receivables, payables, and financial derivatives such as options and futures contracts. Generally accepted accounting principles require specific disclosures related to financial instruments. These disclosures, which are usually reported in the notes, include the terms and conditions of the financial instruments, the interest rate risk and credit risk associated with these contracts, and their fair market value.[11] *Financial Reporting in Canada (1997)* indicates that 67% of the firms surveyed made note disclosures on financial instruments in their 1996 annual reports.[12]

4. Segmented Information

Many companies are involved in more than one type of business activity or market. For example, a company may operate both radio and television stations in both domestic and foreign markets. The individual segments of such companies nor-

---

[8] *Ibid.,* Section 1500, paragraph .04.
[9] C. Byrd and I. Chen, *op. cit.,* p. 56.
[10] C. Byrd and I. Chen, *op. cit.,* p. 35.
[11] *CICA Handbook,* Section 3860, paragraphs .52, .57, .67, and .78.
[12] C. Byrd and I. Chen, *op. cit.,* p. 35

mally experience differing rates of profit, degrees of risk, and growth. To help financial statement users assess operating results, Section 1700 of the *CICA Handbook* requires that publicly traded companies disclose information on their significant segments. This information, which is often presented in the notes, includes revenue, operating profit or loss, and identifiable assets related to the segment. *Financial Reporting in Canada (1997)* indicates that 73% of the firms surveyed made note disclosures of segmented information in their 1996 annual reports.[13] The example shown below is an excerpt from the notes included in the annual report of Finning International Inc. for the year ended December 31, 1996.

Note 16 Segmented Information

The Company and its subsidiaries have operated primarily in one industry during the year, that being the selling, servicing and financing of heavy equipment and related products.

Operating branches are located in the following geographic areas:
- *In Canada, including British Columbia, Alberta, the western part of the Northwest Territories and the Yukon.*
- *In Europe, including the southwest and Industrial Midlands of England, Scotland, Wales and Poland.*
- *In Chile, throughout the country.*

The reportable geographic segments are:

(dollars in thousands)			1996		
	Canada	Europe	Chile	Segment Eliminations	Consolidated
Revenue from external sources	$1,010,979	$460,174	$408,616	$ (5,060)	$1,874,709
Income before provision for income taxes	$ 71,888	$ 38,869	$ 17,746		$ 128,503
Provision for income taxes	28,621	11,698	–		40,319
Net income	$ 43,267	$ 27,171	$ 17,746		$88,184
Identifiable assets	$1,374,818	$403,640	$241,099	$(208,743)	$1,810,814

Source: C. Byrd and I. Chen, *Financial Reporting in Canada*, 22nd ed., CICA, Toronto, 1997, p. 142.

5. Related Party Transactions

A related party transaction is a transaction in which one of the parties involved has the ability to significantly influence the action of the other party. Examples of such transactions would include sales between affiliated companies or a loan from a company to its management. Such transactions may not always take place at fair market value. For example, the sale price could be inflated or the interest charged on a loan to management could be set below current market rates. In order to keep financial statement users fully informed about the economic substance of such transactions, Section 3840 of the *CICA Handbook* requires detailed disclosures about related party transactions. *Financial Reporting in Canada (1997)* reports that approximately 50% of companies surveyed included disclosures about related party transactions in the notes to their financial statements.[14] The example shown below is an excerpt from a note included in the annual report of Ivaco Inc. for the year ended December 31, 1996.

[13]*Ibid.*, p. 35.
[14]C. Byrd and I. Chen, *op. cit.*, p. 35.

Note 18 Transactions With Related Parties

Loans To Officers

Loans to officers bear interest at prime rates, are due in 1997 and are unsecured. Such loans to officers outstanding at December 31, 1996 amounted to $7.5 million (1995–$7.1 million) and were made predominantly in connection with the purchase of shares of the Company.

Loans From Officers

From time to time, the Company borrows short-term funds from senior officers of the Company and makes drawings available to them, all at rates equal to the Company's borrowing rate. At December 31, 1996, borrowings from officers amounting to $1.3 million were outstanding (1995–$0.6 million). These transactions are measured at the exchange amount, which is the amount of consideration established and agreed to by the related parties.

Source: C. Byrd and I. Chen, *Financial Reporting in Canada,* 22nd ed., CICA, Toronto, 1997, pp. 378–79.

6. Events Subsequent to the Balance Sheet Date

Events that have a significant effect on the financial statements may occur or become known after the close of the fiscal period. Such events should be disclosed in the financial statements.[15] For example, a business might suffer a loss from a fire, flood, or other natural disaster between the end of its fiscal year and the issuance of statements for that year. In such a case, the facts of the event should be disclosed, even though the event occurred after the end of the fiscal year. Likewise, the issuance of long-term debt or the purchase of another business after the close of the period should be disclosed.

    Financial Reporting in Canada (1997) indicates that over 27% of the companies surveyed included notes to their financial statements disclosing events subsequent to the balance sheet date.[16] The example shown below is taken from the annual report of Loewen Group Inc. for the year ended December 31, 1996.

Note 20 Subsequent Events

During the period from January 1, 1997 to March 3, 1997, the Company acquired 19 funeral homes and 11 cemeteries. The aggregate cost of these transactions was approximately $35,467,000.

In March 1997, the Company has committed to acquire certain funeral homes, cemeteries and related operations, subject in most instances to certain conditions including approval by the Company's Board of Directors. The aggregate cost of these transactions, if completed, will be approximately $284,254,000.

Source: C. Byrd and I. Chen, *Financial Reporting in Canada,* 22nd ed., CICA, Toronto, 1997, p. 364.

7. Other Notes

Financial Reporting in Canada (1997) indicates that companies often make note disclosures of many other items. For example, details on each of the following individual financial statement items were included in the notes by more than half of the firms surveyed: capital assets, long-term debt, commitments under long-term leases, share capital, long-term investments, receivables, income taxes, and interest expense.[17]

---

[15]*CICA Handbook,* Section 3820, paragraph 10.
[16]C. Byrd and I. Chen, *op. cit.,* p. 35.
[17]*Ibid.,* p. 35.

KEY POINTS

Objective 1. List basic financial statement analytical procedures.

The analysis of percentage increases and decreases in related items in comparative financial statements is called horizontal analysis. The analysis of percentages of component parts to the total in a single statement is called vertical analysis. Common-size statements are financial statements in which all amounts are expressed in percentages for purposes of analysis.

Objective 2. Apply financial statement analysis to assess the solvency of a business.

The primary focus of financial statement analysis is the assessment of solvency and profitability. All users are interested in the ability of a business to pay its debts as they come due (solvency) and to earn income (profitability). Solvency analysis is normally assessed by examining the following balance sheet relationships: (1) current position analysis, (2) accounts receivable analysis, (3) inventory analysis, (4) the ratio of capital assets to long-term liabilities, and (5) the number of times interest charges are earned.

Objective 3. Apply financial statement analysis to assess the profitability of a business.

Profitability analysis focuses mainly on the relationship between operating results (income statement) and resources available (balance sheet). Major analyses used in assessing profitability include (1) the ratio of net sales to assets, (2) the rate earned on total assets, (3) the rate earned on shareholders' equity, (4) the rate earned on common shareholders' equity, (5) earnings per common share, (6) the price-earnings ratio, and (7) dividend yield.

Objective 4. Summarize the uses and limitations of analytical measures.

In selecting and interpreting analytical measures, you should consider conditions peculiar to a business or its industry. For example, the type of industry, capital structure, and diversity of the business's operations affect the measures used. In addition, you should consider the influence of the general economic and business environment.

Objective 5. Describe the contents of corporate annual reports.

Corporate annual reports normally include financial statements and the following sections: Financial Highlights, President's Letter to the Shareholders, Management Report, Independent Auditors' Report, Historical Summary, and Notes to the Financial Statements.

GLOSSARY OF KEY TERMS

Accounts receivable turnover. Net credit sales divided by average accounts receivable. *Objective 2*

Acid-test (quick) ratio. Quick assets divided by current liabilities. *Objective 2*

Adverse audit opinion. Audit report indicating that the auditor believes that the financial statements are not presented fairly in accordance with generally accepted accounting principles. *Objective 5*

Common-size statement. Financial statement in which all items are expressed in percentages. *Objective 1*

Current position analysis. Analysis to assess the ability of a business to pay its current liabilities. *Objective 2*

Current (working capital) ratio. Current assets divided by current liabilities. *Objective 2*

Denial of opinion. Audit report indicating that the auditor has been unable to gather sufficient appropriate evidence to form an opinion as to whether the financial statements are presented fairly and in accordance with generally accepted accounting principles. *Objective 5*

Dividends per common share. Common dividends divided by average number of common shares outstanding during the period. *Objective 3*

Dividend yield. Dividends per share divided by market price per share. *Objective 3*

Historical summary. Section usually included in the annual report disclosing selected financial and operating data of past periods. *Objective 5*

Horizontal analysis. Percentage analysis of increases and decreases in related terms in comparative financial statements of two or more years. *Objective 1*

Inventory turnover. Cost of goods sold divided by average inventory. *Objective 2*

Leverage. Difference between the rate earned on shareholders' equity and the rate earned on total assets. *Objective 3*

Management report. Statement by management usually included in the annual report accepting responsibility for preparation of the financial statements and commenting on internal control and other related matters. *Objective 5*

Number of days' sales in inventory. Inventory divided by average daily cost of sales. *Objective 2*

Number of days' sales in receivables. Accounts receivable divided by average daily credit sales. *Objective 2*

Number of times interest charges earned. Income before tax and interest expense divided by interest expense. *Objective 2*

Price-earnings ratio. Market price per share divided by earnings per share. *Objective 3*

Profitability. Ability of a firm to earn income. *Objective 3*

Qualified audit opinion. Audit report that is qualified because the financial statements do not conform with generally acceptable accounting principles or because the auditor has been unable to carry out all the tests necessary in the circumstances. *Objective 5*

Quick assets. Cash and other current assets (such as marketable securities and receivables) that can be readily converted to cash. *Objective 2*

Rate earned on common shareholders' equity. Income available to common shareholders divided by average number of common shares outstanding during the period. *Objective 3*

Rate earned on shareholders' equity. Net income divided by average total shareholders' equity. *Objective 3*

Rate earned on total assets. Net income plus interest expense (net of tax) divided by average total assets. *Objective 3*

Ratio of capital assets to long-term liabilities. Net capital assets divided by long-term liabilities. *Objective 2*

Ratio of liabilities to shareholders' equity. Total liabilities divided by total shareholders' equity. *Objective 2*

Ratio of net sales to assets. Net sales divided by total assets excluding long-term investments. *Objective 3*

Related party transaction. Transaction in which one of the parties involved has the ability to significantly influence the action of the other party. *Objective 5*

Segmented information. Data, often presented in the notes to the financial statements, which disclose information about the operating activities and assets of various segments of a business. *Objective 5*

Solvency. Ability of a business to meet its financial obligations as they come due. *Objective 2*

Subsequent events. Events, which occur or become known after the close of the fiscal period, that could have a significant effect on the financial statements. *Objective 5*

Unqualified (clean) audit opinion. Auditor's report that concludes that financial statements are presented fairly and in accordance with generally acceptable accounting principles. *Objective 5*

Vertical analysis. Percentage analysis to show the relationship of each component to the total in a single statement. States each item on the balance sheet as a percentage of total assets and each item on the income statement as a percentage of sales. *Objective 1*

Working capital. Excess of current assets over current liabilities. *Objective 2*

ILLUSTRATIVE PROBLEM

Rainbow Paint Co.'s comparative financial statements for the years ending December 31, 2000 and 1999, are as follows. The market price of Rainbow Paint Co.'s common share was $30 on December 31, 1999, and $25 on December 31, 2000.

Rainbow Paint Co.
Comparative Income Statement
For the Years Ended December 31, 2000 and 1999

	2000	1999
Sales (all on account)	$5,125,000	$3,257,600
Sales returns and allowances	125,000	57,600
Net sales	$5,000,000	$3,200,000
Cost of goods sold	3,400,000	2,080,000
Gross profit	$1,600,000	$1,120,000
Selling expenses	$ 650,000	$ 464,000
Administrative expenses	325,000	224,000
Total operating expenses	$ 975,000	$ 688,000
Operating income	$ 625,000	$ 432,000
Other income	25,000	19,200
	$ 650,000	$ 451,200
Other expense (interest)	105,000	64,000
Income before income tax	$ 545,000	$ 387,200
Income tax expense	300,000	176,000
Net income	$ 245,000	$ 211,200

Rainbow Paint Co.
Comparative Retained Earnings Statement
For the Years Ended December 31, 2000 and 1999

	2000	1999
Retained earnings, January 1	$723,000	$581,800
Add net income for year	245,000	211,200
Total	$968,000	$793,000
Deduct dividends:		
On preferred shares	$ 40,000	$ 40,000
On common shares	45,000	30,000
Total	$ 85,000	$ 70,000
Retained earnings, December 31	$883,000	$723,000

Rainbow Paint Co.
Comparative Balance Sheet
December 31, 2000 and 1999

	2000	*1999*
Assets		
Current assets:		
Cash	$ 175,000	$ 125,000
Marketable securities	150,000	50,000
Accounts receivable (net)	425,000	325,000
Inventories	720,000	480,000
Prepaid expenses	30,000	20,000
Total current assets	$1,500,000	$1,000,000
Long-term investments	250,000	225,000
Property, plant, and equipment	2,093,000	1,948,000
Total assets	$3,843,000	$3,173,000
Liabilities		
Current liabilities	$ 750,000	$ 650,000
Long-term liabilities:		
Mortgage note payable, 10%, due 2003	$ 410,000	—
Bonds payable, 8%, due 2006	800,000	$ 800,000
Total long-term liabilities	$1,210,000	$ 800,000
Total liabilities	$1,960,000	$1,450,000
Shareholders' Equity		
Preferred $8 no par shares (5,000 shares outstanding)	$ 500,000	$ 500,000
Common no par shares (50,000 shares outstanding)	500,000	500,000
Retained earnings	883,000	723,000
Total shareholders' equity	$1,883,000	$1,723,000
Total liabilities and shareholders' equity	$3,843,000	$3,173,000

Instructions

Determine the following measures for 2000:

1. Working capital
2. Current ratio
3. Acid-test ratio
4. Accounts receivable turnover
5. Number of days' sales in receivables
6. Inventory turnover
7. Number of days' sales in inventory
8. Ratio of capital assets to long-term liabilities
9. Ratio of liabilities to shareholders' equity
10. Number of times interest charges earned
11. Number of times preferred dividends earned
12. Ratio of net sales to assets
13. Rate earned on total assets
14. Rate earned on shareholders' equity
15. Rate earned on common shareholders' equity
16. Earnings per common share
17. Price-earnings ratio
18. Dividend yield

Solution

(Ratios are rounded to the nearest single digit after the decimal point.)

1. Working capital: $750,000
   $1,500,000 − $750,000
2. Current ratio: 2.0
   $1,500,000 ÷ $750,000
3. Acid-test ratio: 1.0
   $750,000 ÷ $750,000

4. Accounts receivable turnover: 13.3
   $5,000,000 ÷ [($425,000 + $325,000) ÷ 2]
5. Number of days' sales in receivables: 31 days
   $5,000,000 ÷ 365 = $13,699
   $425,000 ÷ $13,699
6. Inventory turnover: 5.7
   $3,400,000 ÷ [($720,000 + $480,000) ÷ 2]
7. Number of days' sales in inventory: 77.3 days
   $3,400,000 ÷ 365 = $9,315
   $720,000 ÷ $9,315
8. Ratio of capital assets to long-term liabilities: 1.7
   $2,093,000 ÷ $1,210,000
9. Ratio of liabilities to shareholders' equity: 1.0
   $1,960,000 ÷ $1,883,000
10. Number of times interest charges earned: 6.2
    ($545,000 + $105,000) ÷ $105,000
11. Number of times preferred dividends earned: 6.1
    $245,000 ÷ $40,000
12. Ratio of net sales to assets: 1.5
    $5,000,000 ÷ [($3,593,000 + $2,948,000) ÷ 2]
13. Rate earned on total assets: 8.3%
    {$245,000 + [$105,000 × ($245,000 ÷ $545,000)]} ÷ [($3,843,000 + $3,173,000) ÷ 2]
14. Rate earned on shareholders' equity: 13.6%
    $245,000 ÷ [($1,883,000 + $1,723,000) ÷ 2]
15. Rate earned on common shareholders' equity: 15.7%
    ($245,000 − $40,000) ÷ [($1,383,000 + $1,223,000) ÷ 2]
16. Earnings per common share: $4.10
    ($245,000 − $40,000) ÷ 50,000
17. Price-earnings ratio: 6.1
    $25 ÷ $4.10
18. Dividend yield: 3.6%
    ($45,000 ÷ 50,000 shares)
    ─────────────────────
    $25

SELF-EXAMINATION QUESTIONS (ANSWERS AT END OF CHAPTER)

Matching
Match each of the following statements with its proper term. Some terms may not be used.

A. accounts receivable turnover
B. acid-test ratio
C. common-size statement
D. current ratio
E. dividend per share
F. dividend yield
G. earnings per share (EPS) on common stock
H. horizontal analysis
I. inventory turnover
J. leverage
K. number of days' sales in inventory
L. number of days' sales in receivables
M. number of times interest charges earned

___ 1. The percentage of increases and decreases in corresponding items in comparative financial statements.
___ 2. The sum of cash, receivables, and marketable securities.
___ 3. The relationship between the volume of sales and inventory, computed by dividing the inventory at the end of the year by the average daily cost of goods sold.
___ 4. The ability of a firm to pay its debts as they come due.
___ 5. The relationship between credit sales and accounts receivable, computed by dividing the net accounts receivable at the end of the year by the average daily sales on account.
___ 6. The relationship between credit sales and accounts receivable, computed by dividing net sales on account by the average net accounts receivable.
___ 7. The tendency of the rate earned on shareholders' equity to vary from the rate earned on total assets because the amount earned on assets acquired through the use of funds provided by creditors varies from the interest paid to these creditors.
___ 8. A financial statement in which all items are expressed only in relative terms.

N. price-earnings (P/E) ratio
O. profitability
P. quick assets
Q. rate earned on common share-
   holders' equity
R. rate earned on shareholders'
   equity
S. rate earned on total assets
T. ratio of capital assets to long-
   term liabilities
U. ratio of liabilities to share-
   holders' equity
V. ratio of net sales to assets
W. solvency
X. vertical analysis
Y. working capital

___ 9. A measure of profitability computed by dividing net income by total share-holders' equity.
___ 10. The excess of total current assets over total current liabilities at some point in time.
___ 11. The ratio of the market price per common share, at a specific date, to the annual earnings per share.
___ 12. A measure of the profitability of assets, without regard to the equity of creditors and shareholders in the assets.
___ 13. The profitability ratio of net income available to common shareholders to the number of common shares outstanding.
___ 14. The ratio of the sum of cash, receivables, and marketable securities to current liabilities.
___ 15. The percentage analysis of component parts in relation to the total of the parts in a single financial statement.
___ 16. A measure of profitability computed by dividing net income, reduced by preferred dividend requirements, by common shareholders' equity.
___ 17. The ratio of current assets to current liabilities.
___ 18. The relationship between the volume of goods sold and inventory, computed by dividing the cost of goods sold by the average inventory.
___ 19. The ability of a firm to earn income.

Multiple Choice

1. What type of analysis is indicated by the following?

	Amount	Percent
Current assets	$100,000	20%
Property, plant, and equipment	400,000	80
Total assets	$500,000	100%

A. Vertical analysis
B. Horizontal analysis
C. Profitability analysis
D. Contribution margin analysis

2. Which of the following measures is useful as an indication of the ability of a firm to pay its current liabilities?
A. Working capital
B. Current ratio
C. Acid-test ratio
D. All of the above

3. The ratio determined by dividing total current assets by total current liabilities is:
A. current ratio
B. debt ratio
C. acid-test ratio
D. all of the above

4. The ratio of the quick assets to current liabilities, which indicates the "instant" debt-paying ability of a firm, is:
A. current ratio
B. working capital ratio
C. acid-test ratio
D. debt ratio

5. A measure useful in evaluating the efficiency in the management of inventories is:
A. working capital ratio
B. acid-test ratio
C. number of days' sales in inventory
D. ratio of capital assets to long-term liabilities

DISCUSSION QUESTIONS

1. What is the difference between horizontal and vertical analysis of financial statements?
2. What is the advantage of using comparative statements for financial analysis rather than statements for a single date or period?
3. The current year's amount of net income (after income tax) is 15% larger than that of the preceding year. Does this indicate an improved operating performance? Discuss.
4. How would you respond to a horizontal analysis that showed an expense increasing by over 100%?
5. a. Name the major ratios useful in assessing solvency and profitability.
   b. Why is it important not to rely on only one ratio or measure in assessing the solvency or profitability of a business?
6. How would the current and acid-test ratios of a service business compare?
7. For Lindsay Corporation, the working capital at the end of the current year is $50,000 greater than the working capital at the end of the preceding year, reported as follows:

	Current Year	Preceding Year
Current assets:		
Cash, marketable securities, and receivables	$340,000	$300,000
Inventories	510,000	325,000
Total current assets	$850,000	$625,000
Current liabilities	425,000	250,000
Working capital	$425,000	$375,000

Has the current position improved? Explain.

8. A company that grants terms of n/30 on all sales has a yearly accounts receivable turnover, based on monthly averages, of 6. Is this a satisfactory turnover? Discuss.

9. What does an increase in the number of days' sales in receivables ordinarily indicate about the credit and collection policy of the firm?

10. a. Why is it advantageous to have a high inventory turnover?
    b. Is it possible for the inventory turnover to be too high? Discuss.
    c. Is it possible to have a high inventory turnover and a high number of days' sales in inventory? Discuss.

11. What do the following data taken from a comparative balance sheet indicate about the company's ability to borrow additional funds on a long-term basis in the current year as compared to the preceding year?

	Current Year	Preceding Year
Capital assets (net)	$1,750,000	$1,700,00
Total long-term liabilities	700,000	850,000

12. What does a decrease in the ratio of liabilities to shareholders' equity indicate about the margin of safety for a firm's creditors and the ability of the firm to withstand adverse business conditions?

13. In computing the ratio of net sales to assets, why are long-term investments excluded in determining the amount of the total assets?

14. In determining the number of times interest charges are earned, why are interest charges added to income before income tax?

15. In determining the rate earned on total assets, why is interest expense (net of tax) added to net income before dividing by total assets?

16. a. Why is the rate earned on shareholders' equity by a thriving business ordinarily higher than the rate earned on total assets?
    b. Should the rate earned on common shareholders' equity normally be higher or lower than the rate earned on total shareholders' equity? Explain.

17. The net income (after income tax) of A. L. Gibson Inc. was $25 per common share in the latest year and $40 per common share for the preceding year. At the beginning of the latest year, the number of shares outstanding was doubled by a stock split. There were no other changes in the amount of shares outstanding. What were the earnings per share in the preceding year, adjusted for comparison with the latest year?

18. The price-earnings ratio for the common stock of Essian Company was 10 at December 31, the end of the current fiscal year. What does the ratio indicate about the selling price of the common shares in relation to current earnings?

19. Why would the dividend yield differ significantly from the rate earned on common shareholders' equity?

20. Favourable business conditions may bring about certain seemingly unfavourable ratios, and unfavourable business operations may result in apparently favourable ratios. For example, Sanchez Company increased its sales and net income substantially for the current year, yet the current ratio at the end of the year is lower than at the beginning of the year. Discuss some possible causes of the apparent weakening of the current position, while sales and net income have increased substantially.

21. a. What are the major components of an annual report?
    b. Indicate the purpose of the Financial Highlights section and the President's Letter.

22. Why are companies required to disclose information in the notes to their financial state-
    ments about (a) related party transactions and (b) events subsequent to the balance sheet
    date?

EXERCISES

EXERCISE 16–1
*Vertical analysis of income
statement*
Objective 1

Revenue and expense data for Cabot Cabinet Co. are as follows:

	2000	1999
Sales	$660,000	$600,000
Cost of goods sold	389,400	384,000
Selling expenses	105,600	84,000
Administrative expenses	66,000	54,000
Income tax expense	46,200	42,000

a. Prepare an income statement in comparative form, stating each item for both 2000 and
   1999 as a percent of sales.
b. Comment on the significant changes disclosed by the comparative income statement.

EXERCISE 16–2
*Vertical analysis of income
statement*
Objective 1

The following comparative income statement (in thousands of dollars) for the years ending
February 2, 1997, and January 31, 1996, was adapted from the 1997 annual report of Dell
Computer Corporation:

	1997	1996
Revenues	$7,759,000	$5,296,000
Costs and expenses:		
Cost of sales	6,093,000	4,229,000
Gross profit	$1,666,000	$1,067,000
Selling, distribution, and administrative expenses	952,000	690,000
Operating income	$ 714,000	$ 377,000

a. Prepare a comparative income statement for 1997 and 1996 in vertical form, stating each
   item as a percent of revenues. Round your calculations to one decimal place.
b. Based upon the 1996 income statement, comment on the significant changes.

EXERCISE 16–3
*Common-size income
statement*
Objective 1

Revenue and expense data for the current calendar year for Keystone Publishing Company
and for the publishing industry are as follows. The Keystone Publishing Company data are
expressed in dollars. The publishing industry averages are expressed in percentages.

	Keystone Publishing Company	Publishing Industry Average
Sales	$7,070,000	100.5%
Sales returns and allowances	70,000	.5
Cost of goods sold	4,900,000	69.0
Selling expenses	560,000	9.0
Administrative expenses	490,000	8.2
Other income	42,000	.6
Other expense	100,000	1.4
Income tax expense	350,000	5.0

a. Prepare a common-size income statement comparing the results of operations for
   Keystone Publishing Company with the industry average.
b. As far as the data permit, comment on significant relationships revealed by the comparisons.

EXERCISE 16–4
Horizontal analysis of balance sheet
Objective 1

Balance sheet data for Fisher Fabrics Company on December 31, the end of the fiscal year, are as follows:

	2000	1999
Current assets	$280,000	$260,000
Property, plant, and equipment	480,000	400,000
Intangible assets	40,000	40,000
Current liabilities	100,000	70,000
Long-term liabilities	180,000	220,000
Common shares	250,000	200,000
Retained earnings	270,000	210,000

Prepare a comparative balance sheet with horizontal analysis, indicating the increase (decrease) for 2000 when compared with 1999.

EXERCISE 16–5
Horizontal analysis of the income statement
Objective 1

Income statement data for Neon Flashlight Company for the years ended December 31, 2000 and 1999, are as follows:

	2000	1999
Sales	$940,000	$850,000
Cost of goods sold	610,000	580,000
Gross profit	$330,000	$270,000
Selling expenses	$126,000	$137,000
Administrative expenses	44,000	53,500
Total operating expenses	$170,000	$190,500
Income before income tax	$160,000	$ 79,500
Income tax expense	60,000	22,000
Net income	$100,000	$ 57,500

a. Prepare a comparative income statement with horizontal analysis, indicating the increase (decrease) for 2000 when compared with 1999.
b. What conclusions can be drawn from the horizontal analysis?

EXERCISE 16–6
Current position analysis
Objective 2

The following data were abstracted from the balance sheet of Precision Engine Company:

	Current Year	Preceding Year
Cash	$ 89,500	$139,000
Marketable securities	110,000	98,000
Accounts and notes receivable (net)	190,500	153,000
Inventories	250,500	222,000
Prepaid expenses	19,500	38,000
Accounts and notes payable (short-term)	245,000	203,500
Accrued liabilities	55,000	56,500

a. Determine for each year (1) the working capital, (2) the current ratio, and (3) the acid-test ratio.
b. What conclusions can be drawn from these data as to the company's ability to meet its currently maturing debts?

EXERCISE 16–7
Current position analysis
Objective 2

The bond indenture for the 10-year, 9½% debenture bonds dated January 2, 1999, required working capital of $350,000, a current ratio of 1.5, and an acid-test ratio of 1 at the end of each calendar year until the bonds mature. At December 31, 2000, the three measures were computed as follows:

1. Current assets:

Cash	$295,000	
Marketable securities	148,000	
Accounts and notes receivable (net)	172,000	
Inventories	300,000	
Prepaid expenses	135,000	
Goodwill	150,000	
Total current assets		$1,200,000
Current liabilities:		
Accounts and short-term notes payable	$500,000	
Accrued liabilities	250,000	
Total current liabilities		750,000
Working capital		$ 450,000

2. Current ratio = 1.6 ($1,200,000 ÷ $750,000)
3. Acid-test ratio = 1.23 ($615,000 ÷ $500,000)
   a. Can you find any errors in the determination of the three measures of current position analysis?
   b. Is the company satisfying the terms of the bond indenture?

EXERCISE 16–8
Accounts receivable analysis
Objective 2

The following data are taken from the financial statements of North Company. Terms of all sales are 1/10, n/60.

	Current Year	Preceding Year
Accounts receivable, end of year	$ 572,000	$ 408,333
Monthly average accounts receivable (net)	476,667	350,000
Net sales on account	2,860,000	2,450,000

a. Determine for each year (1) the accounts receivable turnover and (2) the number of days' sales in receivables.
b. What conclusions can be drawn from these data concerning accounts receivable and credit policies?

EXERCISE 16–9
Inventory analysis
Objective 2

The following data were abstracted from the income statement of Cascade Instruments Inc.:

	Current Year	Preceding Year
Sales	$7,400,000	$5,200,000
Beginning inventories	642,500	607,500
Cost of goods sold	5,280,000	3,750,000
Ending inventories	677,500	642,500

a. Determine for each year (1) the inventory turnover and (2) the number of days' sales in inventory.
b. What conclusions can be drawn from these data concerning the inventories?

EXERCISE 16–10
Ratio of liabilities to share-holders' equity and number of times interest charges earned
Objective 2

The following data were taken from the financial statements of Mountain Spring Water Co. for December 31, 2000 and 1999:

	December 31, 2000	December 31, 1999
Accounts payable	$ 200,000	$ 400,000
Current maturities of serial bonds payable	400,000	400,000
Serial bonds payable, 12%, issued 1995, due 2004	1,600,000	2,000,000
Common shares (100,000 shares outstanding)	1,100,000	1,100,000
Retained earnings	2,860,000	2,400,000

The net income before income tax was $780,000 and $216,000 for the years 2000 and 1999, respectively.

a. Determine the ratio of liabilities to shareholders' equity at the end of each year.
b. Determine the number of times the interest charges are earned during the year for both years.
c. What conclusions can be drawn from these data as to the company's ability to meet its currently maturing debts?

EXERCISE 16–11
Profitability ratios
Objective 3

The following selected data were taken from the financial statements of Ontario Cement Co. for December 31, 2001, 2000, and 1999:

	December 31, 2001	December 31, 2000	December 31, 1999
Total assets	$3,200,000	$2,800,000	$2,000,000
Notes payable, 8%	500,000	500,000	500,000
Common shares	900,000	900,000	900,000
Preferred $10 shares, no par, cumulative, nonparticipating (no change during year, 3,000 shares outstanding)	300,000	300,000	300,000
Retained earnings	1,430,000	1,050,000	250,000

No dividends were declared between 1999 and 2001.

a. Determine the rate earned on total assets, the rate earned on shareholders' equity, and the rate earned on common shareholders' equity for the years 2000 and 2001.
b. What conclusions can be drawn from these data as to the company's profitability?

EXERCISE 16–12
Six measures of solvency or profitability
Objectives 2, 3

The following data were taken from the financial statements of Premium Printers Inc. for the current fiscal year:

Property, plant, and equipment (net)			$1,000,000
Liabilities:			
Current liabilities		$400,000	
Mortgage note payable, 10%, issued 1990, due 2005		800,000	
Total liabilities			$1,200,000
Shareholders' equity:			
Preferred $4 no par shares, cumulative, nonparticipating (no change during year, 8,000 shares outstanding)			$ 400,000
Common shares (no change during year, 20,000 shares outstanding)			1,200,000
Retained earnings:			
Balance, beginning of year	$650,000		
Net income	250,000	$900,000	
Preferred dividends	$ 20,000		
Common dividends	80,000	100,000	
Balance, end of year			800,000
Total shareholders' equity			$2,400,000
Net sales			$4,500,000
Interest expense			$ 80,000

Assuming that long-term investments totalled $175,000 throughout the year and that total assets were $3,000,000 at the beginning of the year, determine the following: (a) ratio of capital assets to long-term liabilities, (b) ratio of liabilities to shareholders' equity, (c) ratio of net sales to assets, (d) rate earned on total assets, (e) rate earned on shareholders' equity, and (f) rate earned on common shareholders' equity.

EXERCISE 16–13
Five measures of solvency or profitability
Objectives 2, 3

The balance sheet for Aspen Avionics Corporation at the end of the current fiscal year indicated the following:

Bonds payable, 10% (issued in 1990, due in 2010)	$4,000,000
Preferred $10 no par shares (10,000 shares outstanding)	1,000,000
Common shares (400,000 shares outstanding)	8,000,000

Income before income tax was $1,000,000 and income taxes were $300,000 for the current year. Cash dividends paid on common shares during the current year totalled $288,000. The common shares were selling for $36 per share at the end of the year. Determine each of the following: (a) number of times bond interest charges were earned, (b) number of times preferred dividends were earned, (c) earnings per share on common, (d) price-earnings ratio, and (e) dividend yield.

EXERCISE 16–14
Earnings per share, price-earnings ratio, dividend yield
Objective 3

The following information was taken from the financial statements of Cool Breeze Air Conditioners Inc. for December 31 of the current fiscal year:

Common shares, no par (no change during the year, 30,000 shares outstanding)	$ 4,500,000
Preferred $8 shares, no par, cumulative, nonparticipating (no change during year, 8,000 shares outstanding)	800,000

The net income was $574,000 and the declared dividends were $225,000 for the current year. The market price is $25.50 per share.

Determine the (a) earnings per share on common stock, (b) price-earnings ratio, and (c) dividend yield.

EXERCISE 16–15
Earnings per share
Objective 3

The net income reported on the income statement of United Fruit Co. was $4,200,000. There were 400,000 shares of no par common and 200,000 shares of $8 cumulative preferred outstanding throughout the current year. The income statement included two extraordinary items: a $1,250,000 gain from expropriation of land and a $250,000 loss arising from flood damage, both after applicable income tax. Determine the per-share figures for common for (a) income before extraordinary items and (b) net income.

PROBLEMS SERIES A

PROBLEM 16–1A
Horizontal analysis for income statement
Objective 1

For 2000, Wang Company reported its most significant decline in net income in years. At the end of the year, Hai Wang, the president, is presented with the following condensed comparative income statement:

Wang Company
Comparative Income Statement
For the Years Ended December 31, 2000 and 1999

	2000	1999
Sales	$495,000	$450,000
Sales returns and allowances	5,000	2,000
Net sales	$490,000	$448,000
Cost of goods sold	312,000	260,000
Gross profit	$178,000	$188,000
Selling expenses	$ 84,000	$ 70,000
Administrative expenses	38,500	35,000
Total operating expenses	$122,500	$105,000
Operating income	$ 55,500	$ 83,000
Other income	2,500	2,000
Income before income tax	$ 58,000	$ 85,000
Income tax expense	20,000	28,000
Net income	$ 38,000	$ 57,000

Instructions

1. Prepare a comparative income statement with horizontal analysis for the two-year period, using 1999 as the base year.
2. To the extent the data permit, comment on the significant relationships revealed by the horizontal analysis prepared in (1).

PROBLEM 16–2A
Vertical analysis for income statement
Objective 1

For 2000, Kasouski Company initiated a sales promotion campaign that included the expenditure of an additional $10,000 for advertising. At the end of the year, Leszek Kasouski, the president, is presented with the following condensed comparative income statement:

Kasouski Company
Comparative Income Statement
For the Years Ended December 31, 2000 and 1999

	2000	1999
Sales	$720,000	$650,000
Sales returns and allowances	20,000	15,000
Net sales	$700,000	$635,000
Cost of goods sold	290,000	270,000
Gross profit	$410,000	$365,000
Selling expenses	200,000	190,000
Administrative expenses	125,000	115,000
Total operating expenses	$325,000	$305,000
Operating income	$ 85,000	$ 60,000
Other income	10,000	9,000
Income before income tax	$ 95,000	$ 69,000
Income tax expense	35,000	26,000
Net income	$ 60,000	$ 43,000

Instructions

1. Prepare a comparative income statement for the two-year period, presenting an analysis of each item in relationship to net sales for each of the years.
2. To the extent the data permit, comment on the significant relationships revealed by the vertical analysis prepared in (1).

PROBLEM 16–3A
Effect of transactions on current position analysis
Objective 2

Data pertaining to the current position of Clarity Glass Company are as follows:

Cash	$256,000
Marketable securities	84,000
Accounts and notes receivable (net)	360,000
Inventories	532,000
Prepaid expenses	18,000
Accounts payable	380,000
Notes payable (short-term)	80,000
Accrued expenses	40,000

Instructions

1. Compute (a) the working capital, (b) the current ratio, and (c) the acid-test ratio.
2. List the following captions on a sheet of paper:

Transaction	Working Capital	Current Ratio	Acid-Test Ratio

Compute the working capital, the current ratio, and the acid-test ratio after each of the following transactions, and record the results in the appropriate columns. Consider each transaction separately and assume that only that transaction affects the data given above. Round to two digits after the decimal point.

a. Sold marketable securities at no gain or loss, $56,000.
b. Paid accounts payable, $40,000.
c. Purchased goods on account, $80,000.
d. Paid notes payable, $30,000.
e. Declared a cash dividend, $25,000.
f. Declared a stock dividend on common shares, $28,500.
g. Borrowed cash from bank on a long-term note, $140,000.
h. Received cash on account, $164,000.
i. Issued additional shares for cash, $200,000.
j. Paid cash for prepaid expenses, $10,000.

PROBLEM 16–4A
Eighteen measures of solvency and profitability
Objectives 2, 3

The comparative financial statements of Montreal Bagel Company are as follows. The market price of Montreal Bagel Company common shares was $36 on December 31, 2000.

Montreal Bagel Company
Comparative Income Statement
For the Years Ended December 31, 2000 and 1999

	2000	1999
Sales (all on account)	$2,450,000	$2,100,000
Sales returns and allowances	50,000	40,000
Net sales	$2,400,000	$2,060,000
Cost of goods sold	1,100,000	960,000
Gross profit	$1,300,000	$1,100,000
Selling expenses	426,000	395,000
Administrative expenses	354,000	345,000
Total operating expenses	$ 780,000	$ 740,000
Operating income	$ 520,000	$ 360,000
Other income	80,000	30,000
	$ 600,000	$ 390,000
Other expense (interest)	130,000	90,000
Income before income tax	$ 470,000	$ 300,000
Income tax expense	140,000	100,000
Net income	$ 330,000	$ 200,000

Montreal Bagel Company
Comparative Retained Earnings Statement
For the Years Ended December 31, 2000 and 1999

	Dec. 31, 2000	Dec. 31, 1999
Retained earnings, January 1	$275,000	$113,000
Add net income for year	330,000	200,000
Total	$605,000	$313,000
Deduct dividends:		
On preferred shares	$ 30,000	$ 18,000
On common shares	20,000	20,000
Total	$ 50,000	$ 38,000
Retained earnings, December 31	$555,000	$275,000

Montreal Bagel Company
Comparative Balance Sheet
December 31, 2000 and 1999

	Dec. 31, 2000	Dec. 31, 1999
Assets		
Current assets:		
Cash	$ 67,000	$ 84,000
Marketable securities	152,000	161,000
Accounts receivable (net)	261,000	295,000
Inventories	325,000	348,000
Prepaid expenses	25,000	22,000
Total current assets	$ 830,000	$ 910,000
Long-term investments	1,000,000	300,000
Property, plant, and equipment	1,675,000	1,290,000
Total assets	$3,505,000	$2,500,000
Liabilities		
Current liabilities	$ 450,000	$ 325,000
Long-term liabilities:		
Mortgage note payable, 10%, due 2005	$ 400,000	—
Bonds payable, 15%, due 2009	600,000	$ 600,000
Total long-term liabilities	$1,000,000	$ 600,000
Total liabilities	$1,450,000	$ 925,000
Shareholders' Equity		
Preferred $6 no par shares (3,000 shares outstanding Dec. 31, 1999; 5,000 shares outstanding Dec. 31, 2000)	$ 500,000	$ 300,000
Common shares, no par (100,000 shares outstanding)	1,000,000	1,000,000
Retained earnings	555,000	275,000
Total shareholders' equity	$2,055,000	$1,575,000
Total liabilities and shareholders' equity	$3,505,000	$2,500,000

Instructions

Determine the following measures for 2000, rounding to nearest single digit after the decimal point:

1. Working capital.
2. Current ratio.
3. Acid-test ratio.
4. Accounts receivable turnover.
5. Number of days' sales in receivables.
6. Inventory turnover.
7. Number of days' sales in inventory.
8. Ratio of capital assets to long-term liabilities.
9. Ratio of liabilities to shareholders' equity.
10. Number of times interest charges earned.
11. Number of times preferred dividends earned.
12. Ratio of net sales to assets.
13. Rate earned on total assets.
14. Rate earned on shareholders' equity.
15. Rate earned on common shareholders' equity.
16. Earnings per share on common.
17. Price-earnings ratio.
18. Dividend yield.

PROBLEM 16–5A
Solvency and profitability trend analysis
Objectives 2, 3

Song Shoe Company has provided the following comparative information:

	2000	1999	1998	1997	1996
Net income	$ 600,000	$ 300,000	$ 200,000	$ 100,000	$ 50,000
Interest	140,000	100,000	30,000	20,000	20,000
Average total assets	3,800,000	2,800,000	1,800,000	1,500,000	1,400,000
Average total shareholders' equity	2,400,000	1,800,000	1,500,000	1,300,000	1,200,000

You have been asked to evaluate the historical performance of the company over the last five years.

Selected industry ratios have remained relatively steady for the last five years at the following levels:

	1996–2000
Rate earned on total assets	14%
Rate earned on shareholders' equity	18%
Number of times interest charges earned	5.0
Ratio of liabilities to shareholders' equity	.6

Instructions

1. Prepare four line graphs, with the ratio on the vertical axis and the years on the horizontal axis for the following four ratios:
   a. Rate earned on total assets
   b. Rate earned on shareholders' equity
   c. Number of times interest charges earned
   d. Ratio of liabilities to shareholders' equity
   Display both the company ratio and the industry benchmark on each graph (each graph should have two lines).
2. Prepare an analysis of the graphs in (1).

PROBLEMS SERIES B

PROBLEM 16–1B
Horizontal analysis for income statement
Objective 1

For 2000, Better Biscuit Company reported its most significant increase in net income in years. At the end of the year, John Newton, the president, is presented with the following condensed comparative income statement:

Better Biscuit Company
Comparative Income Statement
For the Years Ended December 31, 2000 and 1999

	2000	1999
Sales	$840,000	$700,000
Sales returns and allowances	5,000	5,000
Net sales	$835,000	$695,000
Cost of goods sold	450,000	400,000
Gross profit	$385,000	$295,000
Selling expenses	$115,000	$100,000
Administrative expenses	49,500	45,000
Total operating expenses	$164,500	$145,000
Operating income	$220,500	$150,000
Other income	4,500	6,000
Income before income tax	$225,000	$156,000
Income tax expense	70,000	50,000
Net income	$155,000	$106,000

Instructions

1. Prepare a comparative income statement with horizontal analysis for the two-year period, using 1999 as the base year.
2. To the extent the data permit, comment on the significant relationships revealed by the horizontal analysis prepared in (1).

PROBLEM 16–2B
Vertical analysis for income statement
Objective 1

For 2000, Stainless Exhaust Systems Inc. initiated a sales promotion campaign that included the expenditure of an additional $50,000 for advertising. At the end of the year, Edmundo Gonzalez, the president, is presented with the following condensed comparative income statement:

Stainless Exhaust Systems Inc.
Comparative Income Statement
For the Years Ended December 31, 2000 and 1999

	2000	1999
Sales	$490,000	$460,000
Sales returns and allowances	10,000	10,000
Net sales	$480,000	$450,000
Cost of goods sold	215,000	200,000
Gross profit	$265,000	$250,000
Selling expenses	$150,000	$100,000
Administrative expenses	85,000	80,000
Total operating expenses	$235,000	$180,000
Operating income	$ 30,000	$ 70,000
Other income	10,000	9,000
Income before income tax	$ 40,000	$ 79,000
Income tax expense	14,000	30,000
Net income	$ 26,000	$ 49,000

Instructions

1. Prepare a comparative income statement for the two-year period, presenting an analysis of each item in relationship to net sales for each of the years.
2. To the extent the data permit, comment on the significant relationships revealed by the vertical analysis prepared in (1).

PROBLEM 16–3B
Effect of transactions on current position analysis
Objective 2

Data pertaining to the current position of Granular Aggregates Inc. are as follows:

Cash	$143,000
Marketable securities	57,000
Accounts and notes receivable (net)	250,000
Inventories	266,000
Prepaid expenses	9,000
Accounts payable	190,000
Notes payable (short-term)	40,000
Accrued expenses	20,000

Instructions

1. Compute (a) the working capital, (b) the current ratio, and (c) the acid-test ratio.
2. List the following captions on a sheet of paper:

Transaction	Working Capital	Current Ratio	Acid-Test Ratio

Compute the working capital, the current ratio, and the acid-test ratio each of the following transactions, and record the results in the appropriate columns. Consider each transaction separately and assume that only that transaction affects the data given above. Round to two digits after the decimal point.
  a. Sold marketable securities at no gain or loss, $34,000.
  b. Paid accounts payable, $60,000.
  c. Purchased goods on account, $50,000.
  d. Paid notes payable, $20,000.
  e. Declared a cash dividend, $15,000.
  f. Declared a stock dividend on common shares, $16,500.

g. Borrowed cash from bank on a long-term note, $120,000.
h. Received cash on account, $86,000.
i. Issued additional shares for cash, $160,000.
j. Paid cash for prepaid expenses, $12,000.

PROBLEM 16–4B
Eighteen measures of solvency and profitability
Objectives 2, 3

The comparative financial statements of General Grains Company are as follows. The market price of General Grains Company common was $18 on December 31, 2000.

General Grains Company
Comparative Income Statement
For the Years Ended December 31, 2000 and 1999

	2000	1999
Sales (all on account)	$5,000,000	$4,200,000
Sales returns and allowances	50,000	50,000
Net sales	$4,950,000	$4,150,000
Cost of goods sold	2,350,000	1,950,000
Gross profit	$2,600,000	$2,200,000
Selling expenses	1,000,000	950,000
Administrative expenses	700,000	650,000
Total operating expenses	$1,700,000	$1,600,000
Operating income	$ 900,000	$ 600,000
Other income	80,000	40,000
	$ 980,000	$ 640,000
Other expense (interest)	200,000	120,000
Income before income tax	$ 780,000	$ 520,000
Income tax expense	300,000	200,000
Net income	$ 480,000	$ 320,000

General Grains Company
Comparative Retained Earnings Statement
For the Years Ended December 31, 2000 and 1999

	Dec. 31, 2000	Dec. 31, 1999
Retained earnings, January 1	$350,000	$102,000
Add net income for year	480,000	320,000
Total	$830,000	$422,000
Deduct dividends:		
On preferred	$ 48,000	$ 32,000
On common	40,000	40,000
Total	$ 88,000	$ 72,000
Retained earnings, December 31	$742,000	$350,000

General Grains Company
Comparative Balance Statement
December 31, 2000 and 1999

	Dec. 31, 2000	Dec. 31, 1999
Assets		
Current assets:		
Cash	$ 264,000	$ 124,000
Marketable securities	202,000	182,000
Accounts receivable (net)	364,000	344,000
Inventories	469,000	422,000
Prepaid expenses	31,000	28,000
Total current assets	$1,330,000	$1,100,000
Long-term investments	1,200,000	400,000
Property, plant, and equipment	3,212,000	2,700,000
Total assets	$5,742,000	$4,200,000
Liabilities		
Current liabilities	$ 600,000	$ 450,000
Long-term liabilities:		
Mortgage note payable, 10%, due 2005	$ 800,000	—
Bonds payable, 12%, due 2009	1,000,000	$1,000,000
Total long-term liabilities	$1,800,000	$1,000,000
Total liabilities	$2,400,000	$1,450,000
Shareholders' Equity		
Preferred $8 no par shares (4,000 shares outstanding Dec. 31, 1999; 6,000 shares outstanding Dec. 31, 2000)	$ 600,000	$ 400,000
Common no par shares (200,000 shares outstanding)	2,000,000	2,000,000
Retained earnings	742,000	350,000
Total shareholders' equity	$3,342,000	$2,750,000
Total liabilities and shareholders' equity	$5,742,000	$4,200,000

Instructions

Determine the following measures for 2000, rounding to nearest single digit after the decimal point:

1. Working capital.
2. Current ratio.
3. Acid-test ratio.
4. Accounts receivable turnover.
5. Number of days' sales in receivables.
6. Inventory turnover.
7. Number of days' sales in inventory.
8. Ratio of capital assets to long-term liabilities.
9. Ratio of liabilities to shareholders' equity.
10. Number of times interest charges earned.
11. Number of times preferred dividends earned.
12. Ratio of net sales to assets.
13. Rate earned on total assets.
14. Rate earned on shareholders' equity.
15. Rate earned on common shareholders' equity.
16. Earnings per share on common.
17. Price-earnings ratio.
18. Dividend yield.

PROBLEM 16–5B
Solvency and profitability trend analysis
Objectives 2, 3

Asian Arts Company has provided the following comparative information:

	2000	1999	1998	1997	1996
Net income	$ 300,000	$ 500,000	$1,000,000	$ 800,000	$ 500,000
Interest	300,000	200,000	170,000	100,000	50,000
Average total assets	8,600,000	7,300,000	6,500,000	4,800,000	3,500,000
Average total shareholders' equity	5,600,000	5,300,000	4,800,000	3,800,000	3,000,000

You have been asked to evaluate the historical performance of the company over the last five years.

Selected industry ratios have remained relatively steady for the last five years at the following levels:

	1996–2000
Rate earned on total assets	12%
Rate earned on shareholders' equity	15%
Number of times interest charges earned	8.0
Ratio of liabilities to shareholders' equity	0.40

Instructions

1. Prepare four line graphs, with the ratio on the vertical axis and the years on the horizontal axis for the following four ratios:
   a. Rate earned on total assets
   b. Rate earned on shareholders' equity
   c. Number of times interest charges earned
   d. Ratio of liabilities to shareholders' equity
   Display both the company ratio and the industry benchmark on each graph (each graph should have two lines).
2. Prepare an analysis of the graphs in (1).

CHALLENGE PROBLEMS

PROBLEM CP16–1

The following ratios are available for Stanfield Company for its fiscal year ended December 31, 2001:

1. Return on sales is 5%
2. Gross profit percentage is 30%.
3. Ratio of net sales to assets is 2:1. Total assets at the beginning and end of the year are the same.
4. Rate of liabilities to shareholders' equity is 2:3.
5. Current ratio is 2:1.
6. Acid-test ratio is .9:1.
7. Accounts receivable turnover is 12. Opening accounts receivable totalled $950,000. All sales were on account.

Instructions
Complete the missing information in the following statements prepared for Stanfield Company.

Income Statement
Year Ended December 31, 2001
(In 000s)

Net Sales	$
Cost of Goods Sold	_____
Gross Profit	
Operating Expenses	_____
Operating Income	$ 960
Bond Interest Expense	_____
Income before Income Tax	
Income Tax Expense (40%)	_____
Net Income	$ 540

Balance Sheet
At December 31, 2001
(In 000s)

Assets	
Cash	$
Accounts Receivable (net)	
Inventory	
Plant Assets (net)	_____
Total Assets	_____

Liabilities and Shareholders' Equity	
Current Liabilities	
6% Bonds Payable	
Common Shares	
Retained Earnings	840
Total Liabilities and Shareholders' Equity	$ _____

PROBLEM CP16–2

For each of the **independent** cases listed in the following table, what is the effect of the transaction described on the ratio listed? Use a letter to indicate whether the transaction would increase (I), decrease (D), or have no effect (NE) on the ratio. The first case is shown as an example.

Ratio	Transaction	Effect
1. Ratio of capital assets to long-term liabilities	Record amortization expense on plant assets.	D
2. Current ratio	Write off an account receivable that has proven uncollectible. The company uses the allowance method for recording bad debt expense.	
3. Inventory turnover	Switch from FIFO to average cost method in a period when prices and quantities of inventory held are rising.	
4. Ratio of liabilities to shareholders' equity	Acquire equipment under a capital lease.	
5. Price-earnings ratio	Declare a 2 for 1 stock split.	
6. Acid-test ratio	Purchase inventory on account.	
7. Rate earned on common shareholders' equity	Declare 5% stock dividend on common shares.	

CASES

CASE 16–1
Taylor Equipment Co.
Ethics and professional conduct in business

Lee Taylor, president of Taylor Equipment Co., prepared a draft of the President's Letter to be included with Taylor Equipment Co.'s 2000 annual report. The letter mentions a 10% increase in sales and a recent expansion of plant facilities, but fails to mention the net loss of $175,000 for the year. You have been asked to review the letter for inclusion in the annual report.

How would you respond to the omission of the net loss of $175,000? Specifically, is such an action ethical?

CASE 16–2
Cascade Brewery
Analysis of financing corporate growth

Assume that the president of Cascade Brewery made the following statement in the President's Letter to Shareholders:

"The founding family, and majority shareholders, of the company do not believe in using debt to finance future growth. The founding family learned from hard experience during Prohibition and the Great Depression that debt can cause loss of flexibility and eventual loss of corporate control. The company will not place itself at such risk. As such, all future growth will be financed either by sales of shares to the public or by internally generated resources."

As a public shareholder of this company, how would you respond to this policy?

CASE 16–3
Pinnacle Computer Company
Receivables and inventory turnover

Pinnacle Computer Company has completed its fiscal year on December 31, 2000. The auditor, Carol Blake, has approached the CFO, Chase Williams, regarding the year-end receivables and inventory levels of Pinnacle. The following conversation takes place:

Carol: We are beginning our audit of Pinnacle and have prepared ratio analyses to determine if there have been significant changes in operations or financial position. This helps us guide the audit process. This analysis indicates that the inventory turnover has decreased from 5 to 2.8, while the accounts receivable turnover has decreased from 12 to 8. I was wondering if you could explain this change in operations.

Chase: There is little need for concern. The inventory represents computers that we were unable to sell during the holiday buying season. We are confident, however, that we will be able to sell these computers as we move into the next fiscal year.

Carol: What gives you this confidence?

Chase: We will increase our advertising and provide some very attractive price concessions to move these machines. We have no choice. Newer technology is already out there, and we have to unload this inventory.

Carol: ...and the receivables?

Chase: As you may be aware, the company is under tremendous pressure to expand sales and profits. As a result, we lowered our credit standards to our commercial customers, so that we would be able to sell products to a broader customer base. As a result of this policy change, we have been able to expand sales by 35%.

Carol: Your responses have not been reassuring to me.

Chase: I'm a little confused. Assets are good, right? Why don't you look at our current ratio? It has improved, hasn't it? I would think that you would view that very favourably.

Why is Carol concerned about the inventory and accounts receivable turnover ratios, and Chase's responses to them? What action may Carol need to take? How would your respond to Chase's last comment?

CASE 16–4
Apple Computer and Dell Computer
Vertical analysis

The condensed income statements for Apple Computer Co. and Dell Computer Co. are reproduced below for recent fiscal years:

Prepare comparative vertical analyses. Interpret the analyses.

	Dell Computer Co. For the Year Ended February 2, 1997	Apple Computer Co. For the Year Ended September 27, 1996
Sales (net)	$7,759	$ 9,833
Cost of sales	6,093	8,865
Gross profit	$1,666	$ 968
Selling, general, and administrative expense	826	1,568
Research and development	126	604
Operating income	$ 714	$(1,204)
Other income and expenses	33	(91)
Income before taxes	$ 747	$(1,295)
Income tax (benefit)	216	(479)
Income before extraordinary items	$ 531	$ (816)

CASE 16–5
Sears Canada Inc.
Financial statement analysis

The financial statements for Sears Canada Inc. accompany this textbook.

Assume that all revenue represents credit sales.

Instructions

1. Determine the following measures for the current year:
   a. Working capital
   b. Current ratio
   c. Acid-test ratio
   d. Accounts receivable turnover
   e. Number of days' sales in receivables
   f. Ratio of capital assets to long-term liabilities
   g. Ratio of liabilities to shareholders' equity
   h. Number of times interest charges earned
   i. Ratio of net sales to average total assets
   j. Rate earned on average total assets
   k. Rate earned on average common shareholders' equity
   l. Percentage relationship of net income and net sales
   m. Amount of change and percent of change in (1) total revenue and (2) cost of goods sold, operating, administrative, and selling expense
   n. Amount of change and percent of change in net income for the current year

2. a. Identify the accounting methods used by Sears Canada
        Inc. in:
        1. valuing inventories
        2. amortizing capital assets

    b. What segments are used by Sears in reporting seg-
        ment information?

ANSWERS TO SELF-EXAMINATION QUESTIONS

Matching

1. **G**	5. **L**	9. **R**	13. **G**	17. **D**
2. **P**	6. **A**	10. **Y**	14. **B**	18. **I**
3. **K**	7. **J**	11. **N**	15. **X**	19. **O**
4. **W**	8. **C**	12. **S**	16. **Q**	

APPENDICES

Appendix A: Accounting Concepts

A. CONCEPTUAL FRAMEWORK

Overview

The Accounting Standards Board (AcSB) of the Canadian Institute of Chartered Accountants is responsible for setting accounting standards in Canada. The standards are contained in the *CICA Handbook* and form the basis for Generally Accepted Accounting Principles (GAAP). The conceptual framework of financial accounting embodies the financial statement concepts that guide the AcSB in development of generally accepted accounting principles.

Section 1000 of the *CICA Handbook* outlines the basic components of the financial statement concepts:

1. objectives of financial statements;
2. qualitative characteristics;
3. elements of financial statements;
4. criteria for recognition and measurement; and
5. generally accepted accounting principles.

The notes that follow are a summary of the conceptual framework as set out in Section 1000 of the *CICA Handbook*. These notes were prepared by the Society of Management Accountants of Ontario for a Professional Examination Orientation review manual. We thank the Society for permitting us to reproduce that material here.

1. Objectives of Financial Statements

The objective of financial statements is to communicate information that is useful to investors, members, contributors, creditors, and other users in making their **resource allocation decisions and/or assessing management stewardship.**

Consequently, financial statements provide information about:

a. an entity's economic resources, obligations, and equity/new assets;
b. changes in an entity's economic resources, obligations, and equity/net assets; and
c. the economic performance of the entity.

(Section 1000.15)

2. Qualitative Characteristics

The financial statements identify and define the qualities of accounting information. These qualities are illustrated in Exhibit 1.

A. UNDERSTANDABILITY For the information provided in financial statements to be useful, it must be capable of being understood by users. Users are assumed to have a reasonable understanding of business and economic activities and accounting, together with a willingness to study the information with reasonable diligence. (Section 1000.19)

B. RELEVANCE For the information provided in financial statements to be useful, it must be relevant to the decisions made by users. Information is relevant by its nature when it can influence the decisions of users by helping them evaluate the financial impact of past, present, or future transactions and events or confirm, or correct, previous evaluations. Relevance is achieved through information that has predictive value or feedback value and by its timeliness.

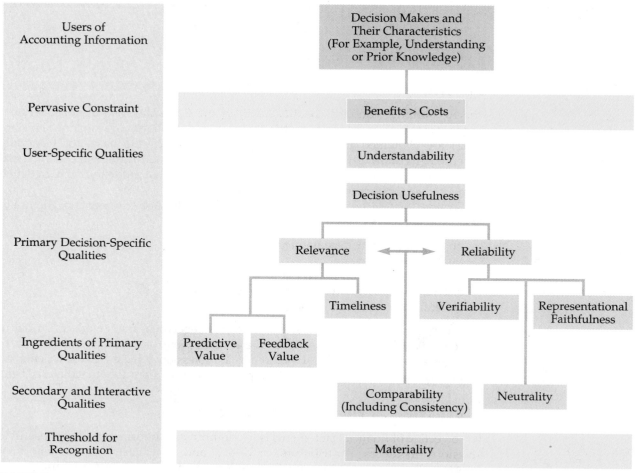

Users of Accounting Information	Decision Makers and Their Characteristics (For Example, Understanding or Prior Knowledge)
Pervasive Constraint	Benefits > Costs
User-Specific Qualities	Understandability
	Decision Usefulness
Primary Decision-Specific Qualities	Relevance ↔ Reliability
	Timeliness / Verifiability / Representational Faithfulness
Ingredients of Primary Qualities	Predictive Value / Feedback Value
Secondary and Interactive Qualities	Comparability (Including Consistency) / Neutrality
Threshold for Recognition	Materiality

Exhibit 1
A Hierarchy of Accounting Qualities

i. Predictive value and feedback value Information that helps users to predict an entity's future income and cash flows has predictive value. Although information provided in the financial statements will not normally be a prediction in itself, it may be useful in making predictions. The predictive value of the income statement, for example, is enhanced if abnormal items are disclosed separately. Information that confirms or corrects previous prediction has feedback value. Information often has both predictive value and feedback value.

ii. Timeliness For information to be useful for decision making, it must be received by the decision maker before it loses its capacity to influence decisions. The usefulness of information for decision making declines as time elapses. (Section 1000.20)

C. RELIABILITY For the information provided in financial statements to be useful, it must be reliable. Information is reliable when it is in agreement with the actual underlying transactions and events, the agreement is capable of independent verification, and the information is reasonably free from error and bias. Reliability is achieved through representational faithfulness, verifiability, and neutrality. Neutrality is affected by the use of conservatism in making judgments under conditions of uncertainty.

i. Representational faithfulness Representational faithfulness is achieved when transactions and events affecting the entity are presented in financial statements in a manner that is in agreement with the actual underlying transactions or events.

Thus, transactions and events are accounted for and presented in a manner that conveys their substance rather than necessarily their legal or other form.

The substance of transactions and events may not always be consistent with that apparent from their legal or other form. To determine the substance of a transaction or event it may be necessary to consider a group of related transitions and events as a whole. The determination of the substance of a transaction or event will be a matter of professional judgment in the circumstances.

ii. Verifiability The financial statement presentation of a transaction or event is verifiable if knowledgeable and independent observers would concur that it is in agreement with the actual underlying transactions or event with a reasonable degree of precision. Verifiability focuses on the correct application of a basis of measurement rather than its appropriateness.

iii. Neutrality Information is neutral when it is free from bias that would lead users towards making decisions that are influenced by the way the information is measured or presented. Bias in measurement occurs when a measure tends to consistently overstate or understate the items being measured. In the selection of accounting principles, bias may occur when the selection is made with the interests of particular users or with particular economic or political objectives in mind.

Financial statements that do not include everything necessary for faithful representation of transactions and events affecting the entity would be incomplete and, therefore, potentially biased.

iv. Conservatism Use of conservatism in making judgments under conditions of uncertainty affects the neutrality of financial statements in an acceptable manner. When uncertainty exists, estimates of a conservative nature attempt to ensure that assets, revenues, and gain are not overstated and, conversely, that liabilities, expenses, and losses are not understated. However, conservatism does not encompass the deliberate understatement of assets, revenues, and gains or the deliberate overstatement of liabilities, expenses, and losses. (Section 1000.21)

D. COMPARABILITY Comparability is a characteristic of the relationship between two pieces of information rather than of a particular piece of information by itself. It enables users to identify similarities in and differences between the information provided by two sets of financial statements. Comparability is important when comparing the financial statements of two different entities and when comparing the financial statements of the same entity over two periods or at two different points in time. (Section 1000.22)

Comparability in the financial statements of an entity is enhanced when the same accounting policies are used consistently from period to period. Consistency helps prevent misconceptions that might result from the application of different accounting policies in different periods. When a change in accounting policy is deemed to be appropriate, disclosure of the effects of the change may be necessary to maintain comparability. (Section 1000.23)

E. CONSTRAINTS

i. Benefit Versus Cost Constraint The benefits expected to arise from providing information in financial statements should exceed the cost of doing so. This constraint applies to the development of accounting standards by the Committee. It is also a consideration in the preparation of financial statements in accordance with those standards, for example, in considering disclosure of information beyond that required by the standards. The Committee recognizes that the benefits and costs may accrue to different parties and that the evaluation of the nature and amount of benefits and costs is substantially a judgmental process. (Section 1000.16)

It is recognized that costs are incurred whenever a new accounting standard is introduced. These costs may be tangible–collection and presentation of information;

Trade-off: Relevance versus Reliability

In practice, a trade-off between qualitative characteristics is often necessary, particularly between relevance and reliability. For example, there is often a trade-off between the timeliness of producing financial statements and the reliability of the information reported in the statements. Generally, the aim is to achieve an appropriate balance among the characteristics in order to meet the objective of financial statements. The relative importance of the characteristics in different cases is a matter of professional judgment. (Section 1000.24)

---

or intangible–disclosure. The benefits of introducing a new standard are mainly intangible–the availability of the information to users of the financial statements. A careful balancing is required whenever a new standard is considered, to ensure the costs of introducing such a standard do not outweigh the benefits.

ii. Materiality Users are interested in information that may affect their decision making. Materiality is the term used to describe the significance of financial statement information to decision makers. An item of information, or an aggregate of items, is material if it is probable that its omission or misstatement would influence or change a decision. Materiality is a matter of professional judgment in the particular circumstances. (Section 1000.17)

The threshold for recognition is materiality. An item that is not material need not be reported.

iii. Industry Practice In order for accounting information to be useful, any selective exceptions to GAAP regularly followed by industry participants would be permitted provided there is clear precedent in the industry. Often differences result from differing legal requirements.

3. Elements of Financial Statements

The *CICA Handbook* also contains some definitions of the various elements of financial statements.

A. ASSETS Assets are economic resources controlled by an entity as a result of past transactions or events and from which future economic benefits may be obtained. (Section 1000.29)

Assets have three essential characteristics:

i.   they embody a future benefit that involves a capacity, singly or in combination with other assets, in the case of profit-oriented enterprises, to contribute directly or indirectly to future net cash flows, and, in the case of not-for-profit organizations, to provide services;
ii. the entity can control access to the benefits; and
iii. the transaction or event giving rise to the entity's right to, or control of, the benefit has already occurred.

It is not essential for control of access to the benefit to be legally enforceable for a resource to be an asset, provided the entity can control its use by other means. (Section 1000.31)

B. LIABILITIES Liabilities are obligations of an entity arising from past transactions or events, the settlement of which may result in the transfer or use of assets, provision of services, or other yielding of economic benefits in the future. (Section 1000.32)

Liabilities have three essential characteristics:

i.   they embody a duty or responsibility to others that entails settlement by future transfer of use of assets, provision of services, or other yielding of economic benefits, at a specified or determinable date, on occurrence of a specified event, or on demand;

ii. the duty or responsibility obligates the entity, leaving it little or no discretion to avoid it; and

iii. the transaction or event obligating the entity has already occurred. (Section 1000.33)

Liabilities do not have to be legally enforceable provided that they otherwise meet the definition of liabilities; they can be based on equitable or constructive obligations. An equitable obligation is a duty based on ethical or moral considerations. A constructive obligation is one that can be inferred from the facts in a particular situation as opposed to a contractually based obligation. (Section 1000.34)

C. EQUITY/NET ASSETS Equity is the ownership interest in the assets of a profit-oriented enterprise after deducting its liabilities. While equity of a profit-oriented enterprise in total is residual, it includes specific categories of items, for example, types of share capital, contributed surplus, and retained earnings. (Section 1000.35)

In the case of a not-for-profit organization, net assets, sometimes referred to as equity or fund balances, is the residual interest in its assets after deducting its liabilities. Net assets may include specific categories of items that may be either restricted or unrestricted as their use. (Section 1000.36)

D. REVENUES Revenues are increases in economic resources, either by way of inflows or enhancements of assets or reductions of liabilities, resulting from the ordinary activities of an entity. Revenues of entities normally arise from the sale of goods, the rendering of services, or the use by others of entity resources yielding rent, interest, royalties, or dividends. In addition, many not-for-profit organizations receive a significant proportion of their revenues from donation, government grants, and other contributions. (Section 1000.37)

E. EXPENSES Expenses are decreases in economic resources, either by way of outflows or reductions of assets or incurrences of liabilities, resulting from an entity's ordinary revenue generating or service delivery activities. (Section 1000.38)

F. GAINS Gains are increases in equity/net assets from peripheral or incidental transactions and events affecting an entity and from all other transactions, events, and circumstances affecting the entity except those that result from expenses or distributions of equity/net assets. (Section 1000.39)

G. LOSSES Losses are decreases in equity/net assets from peripheral or incidental transactions, events, and circumstances affecting the entity except those that result from expenses or distributions of equity/net assets. (Section 1000.40)

4. Recognition and Measurement Criteria

A. RECOGNITION CRITERIA Recognition is the process of including an item in the financial statements of an entity. Recognition consists of the addition of the amount involved into statement totals together with a narrative description of the item (e.g., "inventory," "sales," or "donations") in a statement. Similar items may be grouped together in the financial statements for the purpose of presentation. (Section 1000.41)

Recognition means inclusion of an item within one or more individual statements and does not mean disclosure in the notes of the financial statements. Notes either provide further details about items recognized in the financial statements, or provide information about items that do not meet the criteria for recognition and thus are not recognized in the financial statements. (Section 1000.42)

The recognition criteria below provide general guidance on when an item is recognized in the financial statements. Whether any particular item is recognized or not will require the application of professional judgment in considering whether the specific circumstances meet the recognition criteria. (Section 1000.43)

The recognition criteria are as follows:

i.   the item has an appropriate basis of measurement and a reasonable estimate can be made of the amount involved: and
ii. for items involving obtaining or giving up future economic benefits, it is probable that such benefits will be obtained or given up. (Section 1000.44)

It is possible that an item will meet the definition of an element but still not be recognized in the financial statements because it is not probable that future economic benefits will be obtained or given up or because a reasonable estimate cannot be made of the amount involved. It may be appropriate to provide information about items that do not meet the recognition criteria in the notes to the financial statements. (Section 1000.45)

B. BASES OF MEASUREMENT Measurement is the process of determining the amount at which an item is recognized in the financial statements. There are a number of bases on which an amount can be measured. However, financial statements are prepared primarily using the historical cost basis of measurement whereby transactions and events are recognized in financial statements at the amount of cash equivalents paid or received or the fair value ascribed to them when they took place. (Section 1000.53)

Other bases of measurement are also used but only in limited circumstances. They include:

i.   **Replacement cost**—the amount that would be needed currently to acquire an equivalent asset. This may be used, for example, when inventories are valued at the lower of historical cost and replacement cost.
ii. **Realizable value**—the amount that would be received by selling an asset. This may be used, for example, to value temporary and portfolio investments. Market value may be used to estimate realizable value when a market for an asset exists.
iii. **Present value**—the discounted amount of future cash flows expected to be received from an asset or required to settle a liability. This is used, for example, to estimate the cost of pension benefits. (Section 1000.54)

C. REVENUE RECOGNITION Items recognized in the financial statements are accounted for in accordance with the accrual basis of accounting. The accrual basis of accounting recognizes the effect of transactions and events in the period in which the transactions and events occur, regardless of whether there has been a receipt of payment of cash or its equivalent. Accrual accounting encompasses deferrals that occur when a cash receipt or payment occurs prior to the criteria for recognition of revenue or expense being satisfied. (Section 1000.46)

Revenues are generally recognized when performance is achieved and reasonable assurance regarding measurement and collectibility of the consideration exists. (Section 1000.47)

Unrestricted contributions to not-for-profit organizations do not normally arise from the sale of goods or the rendering of services and consequently performance achievement is generally not relevant to the recognition of unrestricted contributions; such revenues, since they are not linked with specific expenses, are generally recognized when received or receivable. Other contributions are recognized based on the nature of the related restriction. (Section 1000.48)

Gains are generally recognized when realized. (Section 1000.49)

D. MATCHING Expenses and losses are generally recognized when an expenditure or previously recognized asset does not have future economic benefit. Expenses that are not linked with specific revenues are related to a period on the basis of transactions or events occurring in that period or by allocation. The cost of assets that benefit more than one period is normally allocated over the periods benefited. (Section 1000.50)

Expenses that are linked to revenue generating activities in a cause-and-effect relationship are normally matched with the revenue in the accounting period in which the revenue is recognized. (Section 1000.52)

Expenses incurred by not-for-profit organizations for service delivery activities, as opposed to revenue generating activities, would normally be recognized when the service is delivered. (Section 1000.52)

E. FULL DISCLOSURE All relevant accounting information should be disclosed in either the body of the financial statements, the notes thereto, or supplementary schedules.

A clear and concise description of the significant accounting policies of an enterprise should be included as an integral part of the financial statements. (Section 1505.04)

F. ECONOMIC ENTITY For accounting purposes, accounting information is accumulated from the viewpoint of a single entity. For example, a corporation, a partnership, or a sole proprietorship would constitute a separate accounting unit apart from its owners or other entities. The identifiable business entity need not be a separate legal entity.

G. GOING CONCERN ASSUMPTION Financial statements are prepared on the assumption that the entity is a going concern, meaning it will continue in operation for the foreseeable future and will be able to realize assets and discharge liabilities in the normal course of operations. Different bases of measurement may be appropriate when the entity is not expected to continue in operation for the foreseeable future. (Section 1000.58)

H. MONETARY UNIT Financial statements are prepared with capital maintenance measured in financial terms and with no adjustment being made for the effect on capital of a change in the general purchasing power of the currency during the period. (Section 1000.55)

The concept of capital maintenance used by profit-oriented enterprises in preparing financial statements affects measurement because income in an economic sense exists only after the capital of an enterprise has been maintained. Thus, income is the increase or decrease in the amount of capital at the end of the period over the amount at the beginning of the period, excluding the effects of capital contributions and distributions. (Section 1000.56)

I. PERIODICITY Accounting information is reported on a periodic basis recognizing that decision makers need timely financial information and that accruals and deferrals are a necessary part of preparing the information.

5. Generally Accepted Accounting Principles (GAAP)

Generally accepted accounting principles is the term used to describe the basis on which financial statements are normally prepared. There are special circumstances where a different basis of accounting may be appropriate, for example, in financial statements prepared in accordance with regulator legislation or contractual requirements. (Section 1000.59)

The term generally accepted accounting principles encompasses not only specific rules, practices, and procedures relating to particular circumstances but also broad principles and conventions of general application, including the underlying concepts described in this Section. Specifically, generally accepted accounting principles comprise the Accounting Recommendations in the Handbook and, when a matter is not covered by a Recommendation, other accounting principles that either:

a. are generally accepted by virtue of their use in similar circumstances by a significant number of entities in Canada; or

b. are consistent with the Recommendations in the Handbook and are developed through the exercise of professional judgment, including consultation with other informed accountants where appropriate, and the application of the concepts described in this Section.

In exercising professional judgment, established principles for analogous situations dealt with in the Handbook would be taken into account and reference would be made to:

i.   other relevant matters dealt within the Handbook;
ii.   practice in similar circumstances;
iii. Accounting Guidelines;
iv.   Abstracts of Issues Discussed by the CICA Emerging Issues Committee;
v.   International Accounting Standards published by the International Accounting Standards committee;
vi.   standards published by bodies authorized to establish financial accounting standards in other jurisdictions;
vii. CICA research studies; and
viii. other sources of accounting literature such as textbooks and journals.

The relative importance of these various sources is a matter of professional judgment in the circumstances. (Section 1000.60)

Appendix B: Interest Tables

Future Amount of $1 at Compound Interest Due in n Periods: $a_{\overline{n}|i} = (1 + i)^n$						
$n \setminus i$	3%	4%	5%	5.5%	6%	6.5%
1	1.0300	1.0400	1.0500	1.0550	1.0600	1.0650
2	1.0609	1.0816	1.1025	1.1130	1.1236	1.1342
3	1.0927	1.1249	1.1576	1.1742	1.1910	1.2079
4	1.1255	1.1699	1.2155	1.2388	1.2625	1.2865
5	1.1593	1.2167	1.2763	1.3070	1.3382	1.3701
6	1.1941	1.2653	1.3401	1.3788	1.4185	1.4591
7	1.2299	1.3159	1.4071	1.4547	1.5036	1.5540
8	1.2668	1.3686	1.4775	1.5347	1.5938	1.6550
9	1.3048	1.4233	1.5513	1.6191	1.6895	1.7626
10	1.3439	1.4802	1.6289	1.7081	1.7908	1.8771
11	1.3842	1.5395	1.7103	1.8021	1.8983	1.9992
12	1.4258	1.6010	1.7959	1.9012	2.0122	2.1291
13	1.4685	1.6651	1.8856	2.0058	2.1329	2.2675
14	1.5126	1.7317	1.9799	2.1161	2.2609	2.4149
15	1.5580	1.8009	2.0789	2.2325	2.3966	2.5718
16	1.6047	1.8730	2.1829	2.3553	2.5404	2.7390
17	1.6528	1.9479	2.2920	2.4848	2.6928	2.9170
18	1.7024	2.0258	2.4066	2.6215	2.8543	3.1067
19	1.7535	2.1068	2.5270	2.7656	3.0256	3.3086
20	1.8061	2.1911	2.6533	2.9178	3.2071	3.5236
21	1.8603	2.2788	2.7860	3.0782	3.3996	3.7527
22	1.9161	2.3699	2.9253	3.2475	3.6035	3.9966
23	1.9736	2.4647	3.0715	3.4262	3.8197	4.2564
24	2.0328	2.5633	3.2251	3.6146	4.0489	4.5331
25	2.0938	2.6658	3.3864	3.8134	4.2919	4.8277
26	2.1566	2.7725	3.5557	4.0231	4.5494	5.1415
27	2.2213	2.8834	3.7335	4.2444	4.8223	5.4757
28	2.2879	2.9987	3.9201	4.4778	5.1117	5.8316
29	2.3566	3.1187	4.1161	4.7241	5.4184	6.2107
30	2.4273	3.2434	4.3219	4.9840	5.7435	6.6144
31	2.5001	3.3731	4.5380	5.2581	6.0881	7.0443
32	2.5751	3.5081	4.7649	5.5473	6.4534	7.5022
33	2.6523	3.6484	5.0032	5.8524	6.8406	7.9898
34	2.7319	3.7943	5.2533	6.1742	7.2510	8.5092
35	2.8139	3.9461	5.5160	6.5138	7.6861	9.0623
40	3.2620	4.8010	7.0400	8.5133	10.2857	12.4161
45	3.7816	5.8412	8.9850	11.1266	13.7646	17.0111
50	4.3839	7.1067	11.4674	14.5420	18.4202	23.3067

Future Amount of $1 at Compound Interest Due in n Periods: $a_{\overline{n}|i} = (1 + i)^n$

n \ i	7%	8%	9%	10%	11%	12%
1	1.0700	1.0800	1.0900	1.1000	1.1100	1.1200
2	1.1449	1.1664	1.1881	1.2100	1.2321	1.2544
3	1.2250	1.2597	1.2950	1.3310	1.3676	1.4049
4	1.3108	1.3605	1.4116	1.4641	1.5181	1.5735
5	1.4026	1.4693	1.5386	1.6105	1.6851	1.7623
6	1.5007	1.5869	1.6771	1.7716	1.8704	1.9738
7	1.6058	1.7138	1.8280	1.9487	2.0762	2.2107
8	1.7182	1.8509	1.9926	2.1436	2.3045	2.4760
9	1.8385	1.9990	2.1719	2.3579	2.5580	2.7731
10	1.9672	2.1589	2.3674	2.5937	2.8394	3.1058
11	2.1049	2.3316	2.5804	2.8531	3.1518	3.4785
12	2.2522	2.5182	2.8127	3.1384	3.4985	3.8960
13	2.4098	2.7196	3.0658	3.4523	3.8833	4.3635
14	2.5785	2.9372	3.3417	3.7975	4.3104	4.8871
15	2.7590	3.1722	3.6425	4.1772	4.7846	5.4736
16	2.9522	3.4259	3.9703	4.5950	5.3109	6.1304
17	3.1588	3.7000	4.3276	5.0545	5.8951	6.8660
18	3.3799	3.9960	4.7171	5.5599	6.5436	7.6900
19	3.6165	4.3157	5.1417	6.1159	7.2633	8.6128
20	3.8697	4.6610	5.6044	6.7275	8.0623	9.6463
21	4.1406	5.0338	6.1088	7.4002	8.9492	10.8038
22	4.4304	5.4365	6.6586	8.1403	9.9336	12.1003
23	4.7405	5.8715	7.2579	8.9543	11.0263	13.5523
24	5.0724	6.3412	7.9111	9.8497	12.2392	15.1786
25	5.4274	6.8485	8.6231	10.8347	13.5855	17.0001
26	5.8074	7.3964	9.3992	11.9182	15.0799	19.0401
27	6.2139	7.9881	10.2451	13.1100	16.7386	21.3249
28	6.6488	8.6271	11.1671	14.4210	18.5799	23.8839
29	7.1143	9.3173	12.1722	15.8631	20.6237	26.7499
30	7.6123	10.0627	13.2677	17.4494	22.8923	29.9599
31	8.1451	10.8677	14.4618	19.1943	25.4104	33.5551
32	8.7153	11.7371	15.7633	21.1138	28.2056	37.5817
33	9.3253	12.6760	17.1820	23.2252	31.3082	42.0915
34	9.9781	13.6901	18.7284	25.5477	34.7521	47.1425
35	10.6766	14.7853	20.4140	28.1024	38.5749	52.7996
40	14.9745	21.7245	31.4094	45.2593	65.0009	93.0510
45	21.0025	31.9204	48.3273	72.8905	109.5302	163.9876
50	29.4570	46.9016	74.3575	117.3909	184.5648	289.0022

Future Amount of Ordinary Annuity of \$1 per Period: $A_{\overline{n}|i} = \dfrac{(1 + i)^n - 1}{i}$

$n \backslash i$	3%	4%	5%	5.5%	6%	6.5%
1	1.0000	1.0000	1.0000	1.0000	1.0000	1.0000
2	2.0300	2.0400	2.0500	2.0550	2.0600	2.0650
3	3.0909	3.1216	3.1525	3.1680	3.1836	3.1992
4	4.1836	4.2465	4.3101	4.3423	4.3746	4.4072
5	5.3091	5.4163	5.5256	5.5811	5.6371	5.6936
6	6.4684	6.6330	6.8019	6.8881	6.9753	7.0637
7	7.6625	7.8983	8.1420	8.2669	8.3938	8.5229
8	8.8923	9.2142	9.5491	9.7216	9.8975	10.0769
9	10.1591	10.5828	11.0266	11.2563	11.4913	11.7319
10	11.4639	12.0061	12.5779	12.8754	13.1808	13.4944
11	12.8078	13.4864	14.2068	14.5835	14.9716	15.3716
12	14.1920	15.0258	15.9171	16.3856	16.8699	17.3707
13	15.6178	16.6268	17.7130	18.2868	18.8821	19.4998
14	17.0863	18.2919	19.5986	20.2926	21.0151	21.7673
15	18.5989	20.0236	21.5786	22.4087	23.2760	24.1822
16	20.1569	21.8245	23.6575	24.6411	25.6725	26.7540
17	21.7616	23.6975	25.8404	26.9964	28.2129	29.4930
18	23.4144	25.6454	28.1324	29.4812	30.9057	32.4101
19	25.1169	27.6712	30.5390	32.1027	33.7600	35.5167
20	26.8704	29.7781	33.0660	34.8683	36.7856	38.8253
21	28.6765	31.9692	35.7193	37.7861	39.9927	42.3490
22	30.5368	34.2480	38.5052	40.8643	43.3923	46.1016
23	32.4529	36.6179	41.4305	44.1118	46.9958	50.0982
24	34.4265	39.0826	44.5020	47.5380	50.8156	54.3546
25	36.4593	41.6459	47.7271	51.1526	54.8645	58.8877
26	38.5530	44.3117	51.1135	54.9660	59.1564	63.7154
27	40.7096	47.0842	54.6691	58.9891	63.7058	68.8569
28	42.9309	49.9676	58.4026	63.2335	68.5281	74.3326
29	45.2189	52.9663	62.3227	67.7114	73.6398	80.1642
30	47.5754	56.0849	66.4388	72.4355	79.0582	86.3749
31	50.0027	59.3283	70.7608	77.4194	84.8017	92.9892
32	52.5028	62.7015	75.2988	82.6775	90.8898	100.0335
33	55.0778	66.2095	80.0638	88.2248	97.3432	107.5357
34	57.7302	69.8579	85.0670	94.0771	104.1838	115.5255
35	60.4621	73.6522	90.3203	100.2514	111.4348	124.0347
40	75.4013	95.0255	120.7998	136.6056	154.7620	175.6319
45	92.7199	121.0294	159.7002	184.1192	212.7435	246.3246
50	112.7969	152.6671	209.3480	246.2175	290.3359	343.1797

Future Amount of Ordinary Annuity of $1 per Period: $A_{\overline{n}|i} = \dfrac{(1 + i)^n - 1}{i}$

$n \setminus i$	7%	8%	9%	10%	11%	12%
1	1.0000	1.0000	1.0000	1.0000	1.0000	1.0000
2	2.0700	2.0800	2.0900	2.1000	2.1100	2.1200
3	3.2149	3.2464	3.2781	3.3100	3.3421	3.3744
4	4.4399	4.5061	4.5731	4.6410	4.7097	4.7793
5	5.7507	5.8666	5.9847	6.1051	6.2278	6.3528
6	7.1533	7.3359	7.5233	7.7156	7.9129	8.1152
7	8.6540	8.9228	9.2004	9.4872	9.7833	10.0890
8	10.2598	10.6366	11.0285	11.4359	11.8594	12.2997
9	11.9780	12.4876	13.0210	13.5795	14.1640	14.7757
10	13.8164	14.4866	15.1929	15.9374	16.7220	17.5487
11	15.7836	16.6455	17.5603	18.5312	19.5614	20.6546
12	17.8885	18.9771	20.1407	21.3843	22.7132	24.1331
13	20.1406	21.4953	22.9534	24.5227	26.2116	28.0291
14	22.5505	24.2149	26.0192	27.9750	30.0949	32.3926
15	25.1290	27.1521	29.3609	31.7725	34.4054	37.2797
16	27.8881	30.3243	33.0034	35.9497	39.1899	42.7533
17	30.8402	33.7502	36.9737	40.5447	44.5008	48.8837
18	33.9990	37.4502	41.3013	45.5992	50.3959	55.7497
19	37.3790	41.4463	46.0185	51.1591	56.9395	63.4397
20	40.9955	45.7620	51.1601	57.2750	64.2028	72.0524
21	44.8652	50.4229	56.7645	64.0025	72.2651	81.6987
22	49.0057	55.4568	62.8733	71.4027	81.2143	92.5026
23	53.4361	60.8933	69.5319	79.5430	91.1479	104.6029
24	58.1767	66.7648	76.7898	88.4973	102.1742	118.1552
25	63.2490	73.1059	84.7009	98.3471	114.4133	133.3339
26	68.6765	79.9544	93.3240	109.1818	127.9988	150.3339
27	74.4838	87.3508	102.7231	121.0999	143.0786	169.3740
28	80.6977	95.3388	112.9682	134.2099	159.8173	190.6989
29	87.3465	103.9659	124.1354	148.6309	178.3972	214.5828
30	94.4608	113.2832	136.3075	164.4940	199.0209	241.3327
31	102.0730	123.3459	149.5752	181.9434	221.9132	271.2926
32	110.2182	134.2135	164.0370	201.1378	247.3236	304.8477
33	118.9334	145.9506	179.8003	222.2515	275.5292	342.4294
34	128.2588	158.6267	196.9823	245.4767	306.8374	384.5210
35	138.2369	172.3168	215.7108	271.0244	341.5896	431.6635
40	199.6351	259.0565	337.8824	442.5926	581.8261	767.0914
45	285.7493	386.5056	525.8587	718.9048	986.6386	1358.2300
50	406.5289	573.7702	815.0836	1163.9085	1668.7712	2400.0182

Present Value of \$1 at Compound Interest Due in n Periods: $p_{\overline{n}|i} = \dfrac{1}{(1+i)^n}$

$n \diagdown i$	3%	4%	5%	5.5%	6%	6.5%
1	0.9709	0.9615	0.9524	0.9479	0.9434	0.9390
2	0.9426	0.9246	0.9070	0.8985	0.8900	0.8817
3	0.9151	0.8890	0.8638	0.8516	0.8396	0.8278
4	0.8885	0.8548	0.8227	0.8072	0.7921	0.7773
5	0.8626	0.8219	0.7835	0.7651	0.7473	0.7299
6	0.8375	0.7903	0.7462	0.7252	0.7050	0.6853
7	0.8131	0.7599	0.7107	0.6874	0.6651	0.6435
8	0.7894	0.7307	0.6768	0.6516	0.6274	0.6042
9	0.7664	0.7026	0.6446	0.6176	0.5919	0.5674
10	0.7441	0.6756	0.6139	0.5854	0.5584	0.5327
11	0.7224	0.6496	0.5847	0.5549	0.5268	0.5002
12	0.7014	0.6246	0.5568	0.5260	0.4970	0.4697
13	0.6810	0.6006	0.5303	0.4986	0.4688	0.4410
14	0.6611	0.5775	0.5051	0.4726	0.4423	0.4141
15	0.6419	0.5553	0.4810	0.4479	0.4173	0.3888
16	0.6232	0.5339	0.4581	0.4246	0.3936	0.3651
17	0.6050	0.5134	0.4363	0.4024	0.3714	0.3428
18	0.5874	0.4936	0.4155	0.3815	0.3503	0.3219
19	0.5703	0.4746	0.3957	0.3616	0.3305	0.3022
20	0.5537	0.4564	0.3769	0.3427	0.3118	0.2838
21	0.5375	0.4388	0.3589	0.3249	0.2942	0.2665
22	0.5219	0.4220	0.3418	0.3079	0.2775	0.2502
23	0.5067	0.4057	0.3256	0.2919	0.2618	0.2349
24	0.4919	0.3901	0.3101	0.2767	0.2470	0.2206
25	0.4776	0.3751	0.2953	0.2622	0.2330	0.2071
26	0.4637	0.3607	0.2812	0.2486	0.2198	0.1945
27	0.4502	0.3468	0.2678	0.2356	0.2074	0.1826
28	0.4371	0.3335	0.2551	0.2233	0.1956	0.1715
29	0.4243	0.3207	0.2429	0.2117	0.1846	0.1610
30	0.4120	0.3083	0.2314	0.2006	0.1741	0.1512
31	0.4000	0.2965	0.2204	0.1902	0.1643	0.1420
32	0.3883	0.2851	0.2099	0.1803	0.1550	0.1333
33	0.3770	0.2741	0.1999	0.1709	0.1462	0.1252
34	0.3660	0.2636	0.1904	0.1620	0.1379	0.1175
35	0.3554	0.2534	0.1813	0.1535	0.1301	0.1103
40	0.3066	0.2083	0.1420	0.1175	0.0972	0.0805
45	0.2644	0.1712	0.1113	0.0899	0.0727	0.0588
50	0.2281	0.1407	0.0872	0.0688	0.0543	0.0429

Present Value of $1 at Compound Interest Due in n Periods: $p_{\overline{n}|i} = \dfrac{1}{(1+i)^n}$

n \ i	7%	8%	9%	10%	11%	12%
1	0.9346	0.9259	0.9174	0.9091	0.9009	0.8929
2	0.8734	0.8573	0.8417	0.8264	0.8116	0.7972
3	0.8163	0.7938	0.7722	0.7513	0.7312	0.7118
4	0.7629	0.7350	0.7084	0.6830	0.6587	0.6355
5	0.7130	0.6806	0.6499	0.6209	0.5935	0.5674
6	0.6663	0.6302	0.5963	0.5645	0.5346	0.5066
7	0.6227	0.5835	0.5470	0.5132	0.4817	0.4523
8	0.5820	0.5403	0.5019	0.4665	0.4339	0.4039
9	0.5439	0.5002	0.4604	0.4241	0.3909	0.3606
10	0.5083	0.4632	0.4224	0.3855	0.3522	0.3220
11	0.4751	0.4289	0.3875	0.3505	0.3173	0.2875
12	0.4440	0.3971	0.3555	0.3186	0.2858	0.2567
13	0.4150	0.3677	0.3262	0.2897	0.2575	0.2292
14	0.3878	0.3405	0.2992	0.2633	0.2320	0.2046
15	0.3624	0.3152	0.2745	0.2394	0.2090	0.1827
16	0.3387	0.2919	0.2519	0.2176	0.1883	0.1631
17	0.3166	0.2703	0.2311	0.1978	0.1696	0.1456
18	0.2959	0.2502	0.2120	0.1799	0.1528	0.1300
19	0.2765	0.2317	0.1945	0.1635	0.1377	0.1161
20	0.2584	0.2145	0.1784	0.1486	0.1240	0.1037
21	0.2415	0.1987	0.1637	0.1351	0.1117	0.0926
22	0.2257	0.1839	0.1502	0.1228	0.1007	0.0826
23	0.2109	0.1703	0.1378	0.1117	0.0907	0.0738
24	0.1971	0.1577	0.1264	0.1015	0.0817	0.0659
25	0.1842	0.1460	0.1160	0.0923	0.0736	0.0588
26	0.1722	0.1352	0.1064	0.0839	0.0663	0.0525
27	0.1609	0.1252	0.0976	0.0763	0.0597	0.0469
28	0.1504	0.1159	0.0895	0.0693	0.0538	0.0419
29	0.1406	0.1073	0.0822	0.0630	0.0485	0.0374
30	0.1314	0.0994	0.0754	0.0573	0.0437	0.0334
31	0.1228	0.0920	0.0691	0.0521	0.0394	0.0298
32	0.1147	0.0852	0.0634	0.0474	0.0355	0.0266
33	0.1072	0.0789	0.0582	0.0431	0.0319	0.0238
34	0.1002	0.0730	0.0534	0.0391	0.0288	0.0212
35	0.0937	0.0676	0.0490	0.0356	0.0259	0.0189
40	0.0668	0.0460	0.0318	0.0221	0.0154	0.0107
45	0.0476	0.0313	0.0207	0.0137	0.0091	0.0061
50	0.0339	0.0213	0.0134	0.0085	0.0054	0.0035

Present Value of Ordinary Annuity of $1 per Period: $P_{\overline{n}|i} = \dfrac{1 - \dfrac{1}{(1+i)^n}}{i}$

$n \backslash i$	3%	4%	5%	5.5%	6%	6.5%
1	0.9709	0.9615	0.9524	0.9479	0.9434	0.9390
2	1.9135	1.8861	1.8594	1.8463	1.8334	1.8206
3	1.9135	1.8861	1.8594	1.8463	1.8334	1.8206
4	3.7171	3.6299	3.5460	3.5052	3.4651	3.4258
5	4.5797	4.4518	4.3295	4.2703	4.2124	4.1557
6	5.4172	5.2421	5.0757	4.9955	4.9173	4.8410
7	6.2303	6.0021	5.7864	5.6830	5.5824	5.4845
8	7.0197	6.7327	6.4632	6.3346	6.2098	6.0888
9	7.7861	7.4353	7.1078	6.9522	6.8017	6.6561
10	8.5302	8.1109	7.7217	7.5376	7.3601	7.1888
11	9.2526	8.7605	8.3064	8.0925	7.8869	7.6890
12	9.9540	9.3851	8.8633	8.6185	8.3838	8.1587
13	10.6350	9.9856	9.3936	9.1171	8.8527	8.5997
14	11.2961	10.5631	9.8986	9.5896	9.2950	9.0138
15	11.9379	11.1184	10.3797	10.0376	9.7122	9.4027
16	12.5611	11.6523	10.8378	10.4622	10.1059	9.7678
17	13.1661	12.1657	11.2741	10.8646	10.4773	10.1106
18	13.7535	12.6593	11.6896	11.2461	10.8276	10.4325
19	14.3238	13.1339	12.0853	11.6077	11.1581	10.7347
20	14.8775	13.5903	12.4622	11.9504	11.4699	11.0185
21	15.4150	14.0292	12.8212	12.2752	11.7641	11.2850
22	15.9369	14.4511	13.1630	12.5832	12.0416	11.5352
23	16.4436	14.8568	13.4886	12.8750	12.3034	11.7701
24	16.9355	15.2470	13.7986	13.1517	12.5504	11.9907
25	17.4131	15.6221	14.0939	13.4139	12.7834	12.1979
26	17.8768	15.9828	14.3752	13.6625	13.0032	12.3924
27	18.3270	16.3296	14.6430	13.8981	13.2105	12.5750
28	18.7641	16.6631	14.8981	14.1214	13.4062	12.7465
29	19.1885	16.9837	15.1411	14.3331	13.5907	12.9075
30	19.6004	17.2920	15.3725	14.5337	13.7648	13.0587
31	20.0004	17.5885	15.5928	14.7239	13.9291	13.2006
32	20.3888	17.8736	15.8027	14.9042	14.0840	13.3339
33	20.7658	18.1476	16.0025	15.0751	14.2302	13.4591
34	21.1318	18.4112	16.1929	15.2370	14.3681	13.5766
35	21.4872	18.6646	16.3742	15.3906	14.4982	13.6870
40	23.1148	19.7928	17.1591	16.0461	15.0463	14.1455
45	24.5187	20.7200	17.7741	16.5477	15.4558	14.4802
50	25.7298	21.4822	18.2559	16.9315	15.7619	14.7245

Present Value of Ordinary Annuity of $1 per Period: $P_{\overline{n}|i} = \dfrac{1 - \dfrac{1}{(1+i)^n}}{i}$

$n \diagdown i$	7%	8%	9%	10%	11%	12%
1	0.9346	0.9259	0.9174	0.9091	0.9009	0.8929
2	1.8080	1.7833	1.7591	1.7355	1.7125	1.6901
3	2.6243	2.5771	2.5313	2.4869	2.4437	2.4018
4	3.3872	3.3121	3.2397	3.1699	3.1024	3.0373
5	4.1002	3.9927	3.8897	3.7908	3.6959	3.6048
6	4.7665	4.6229	4.4859	4.3553	4.2305	4.1114
7	5.3893	5.2064	5.0330	4.8684	4.7122	4.5638
8	5.9713	5.7466	5.5348	5.3349	5.1461	4.9676
9	6.5152	6.2469	5.9952	5.7590	5.5370	5.3282
10	7.0236	6.7101	6.4177	6.1446	5.8892	5.6502
11	7.4987	7.1390	6.8052	6.4951	6.2065	5.9377
12	7.9427	7.5361	7.1607	6.8137	6.4924	6.1944
13	8.3577	7.9038	7.4869	7.1034	6.7499	6.4235
14	8.7455	8.2442	7.7862	7.3667	6.9819	6.6282
15	9.1079	8.5595	8.0607	7.6061	7.1909	6.8109
16	9.4466	8.8514	8.3126	7.8237	7.3792	6.9740
17	9.7632	9.1216	8.5436	8.0216	7.5488	7.1196
18	10.0591	9.3719	8.7556	8.2014	7.7016	7.2497
19	10.3356	9.6036	8.9501	8.3649	7.8393	7.3658
20	10.5940	9.8181	9.1285	8.5136	7.9633	7.4694
21	10.8355	10.0168	9.2922	8.6487	8.0751	7.5620
22	11.0612	10.2007	9.4424	8.7715	8.1757	7.6446
23	11.2722	10.3711	9.5802	8.8832	8.2664	7.7184
24	11.4693	10.5288	9.7066	8.9847	8.3481	7.7843
25	11.6536	10.6748	9.8226	9.0770	8.4217	7.8431
26	11.8258	10.8100	9.9290	9.1609	8.4881	7.8957
27	11.9867	10.9352	10.0266	9.2372	8.5478	7.9426
28	12.1371	11.0511	10.1161	9.3066	8.6016	7.9844
29	12.2777	11.1584	10.1983	9.3696	8.6501	8.0218
30	12.4090	11.2578	10.2737	9.4269	8.6938	8.0552
31	12.5318	11.3498	10.3428	9.4790	8.7331	8.0850
32	12.6466	11.4350	10.4062	9.5264	8.7686	8.1116
33	12.7538	11.5139	10.4644	9.5694	8.8005	8.1354
34	12.8540	11.5869	10.5178	9.6086	8.8293	8.1566
35	12.9477	11.6546	10.5668	9.6442	8.8552	8.1755
40	13.3317	11.9246	10.7574	9.7791	8.9511	8.2438
45	13.6055	12.1084	10.8812	9.8628	9.0079	8.2825
50	13.8007	12.2335	10.9617	9.9148	9.0417	8.3045

Financial Highlights

For the 53 weeks ended January 3, 1998 and the 52 weeks ended December 28, 1996	1997	1996
RESULTS FOR THE YEAR (in millions)		
Total revenues	$ **4,584**	$ 3,956
Interest expense	**86**	96
Earnings from operations		
before unusual items and income taxes	**215**	70
Unusual items expense	**-**	45
Income tax expense	**99**	16
Net earnings	**116**	9
YEAR END POSITION (in millions)		
Working capital	$ **971**	$ 741
Total assets	**3,007**	2,734
Shareholders' equity	**1,042**	949
PER SHARE OF CAPITAL STOCK (in dollars)		
Net earnings	$ **1.10**	$ 0.09
Dividends declared	**0.24**	0.24
Shareholders' equity	**9.84**	8.98

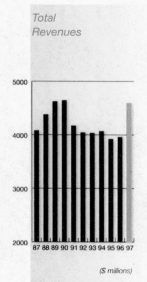

Total Revenues

($ millions)

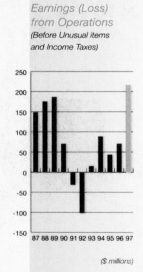

Earnings (Loss) from Operations
(Before Unusual items and Income Taxes)

($ millions)

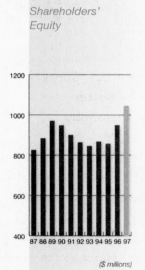

Shareholders' Equity

($ millions)

1

To our Shareholders

1997 was an outstanding year for our Company. Revenues increased 15.9% to $4.6 billion, contributing to the best performance in our 45 year history. Most importantly, earnings more than tripled and at $116.5 million also represent a new high for our Company.

These results are extremely gratifying for all of us as our customers responded to our efforts to improve their shopping experience in the numerous sales and merchandise distribution channels that make us uniquely Sears. A key measure of our success is our strong sales gain in stores open for at least a year. Sales increased 14.7% during 1997, more than double the 6.4% posted by the industry.

The dedication of our 39,000 associates from coast to coast is at the core of our success and their satisfaction with Sears as a Great Place to Work continues to improve. We are committed to creating a winning team that treats every person with dignity and challenges them to place customer satisfaction as their top priority in everything they do.

LEVERAGING OUR STRENGTHS FOR GROWTH

Delivering a superior return to our shareholders is also squarely embedded in our goals, benefiting investors and associates alike. We are especially pleased that Sears shares posted a total return of 98% in 1997.

Last year I had indicated in my message to shareholders that the growth of our business was a key focus for us over both the short and longer term. Buoyed by a much improved economic environment in Canada, our strategies to grow our Company and create value by leveraging the strengths that make us uniquely Sears are clearly working.

Without exception, all of our sales channels posted strong growth, well in excess of the market.

We are focused on the continuous improvement of our business strengths which include our reputation for trust, integrity and value, as well as our excellent store locations, our growing stable of private and national brands and our portfolio of high quality Sears Card charge account receivables.

"Our continuing challenge is to use all our resources to better serve our target customer and build a

Our continuing challenge is to use these unique resources to better serve our target customer and build a lifelong relationship with her and her family.

Our full-line store repositioning strategy, launched in the all-important Greater Toronto Area (GTA) market earlier this year, is an important example of our commitment to make the Sears proposition more attractive to her on every dimension.

These repositioned stores have performed exceptionally well both during and after their transformation, and we believe we have a compelling format with which to move forward. As a result, in 1998 we will reposition a further 14 stores in major markets across Canada including Vancouver, Edmonton, Toronto and Montreal.

Our catalogue business had an exceptional year and was solidly profitable on a stand-alone basis. Our Christmas Wish Book, the biggest ever in our history, was a huge success reflecting our commitment to expand our merchandise assortments, value and service delivery to millions of customers in some of Canada's remotest communities.

OFF-MALL STRATEGY EXTENDS OUR PRESENCE

Our dealer store format now includes 79 locations, an addition of 19 stores over last year. These stores take the best of Sears, our strength in merchandise categories like appliances and lawn and garden equipment, and combine them with our world class brands such as Craftsman and Kenmore. Our strategy here is to continue to grow our market leading share of these businesses by extending our presence further into the market by making store access easier for our customers.

In 1997 we continued the development of our successful Sears Whole Home Furniture Stores. We added 4 stores over the past year, concentrating on the Greater Toronto Area market.

In two of these locations we added our Sears Brand Central major appliance assortment and expanded the stores by 25%. Coupled with Canada's broadest furniture assortment under one roof, this represents a substantial growth opportunity for us. In the coming year our plans are to accelerate the growth of this format by tripling the number of locations. In 1998 we will open Sears Whole Home Furniture Stores featuring Sears Brand Central in British Columbia, Alberta, Ontario and Quebec.

Home services will also play an important role in the future growth of Sears. In this highly fragmented business where reputation is paramount, we are ideally positioned to serve our customer base via Sears 2,800 repair technicians and a network of home improvement and home maintenance specialists, together making more than a million home visits annually.

lifelong relationship with her and her family."

GIVING CREDIT WHERE IT IS DUE

The Sears Card is one of the most important ways we strengthen our relationship with our 8 million customer households.

Our Credit business continues to perform very well and providing credit is critical to the ability of moderate-income families to finance the purchases they require. Our portfolio of charge account receivables is of very high quality and we enjoy one of the lowest write-off rates in the industry.

While 1997 represents a year of substantial progress for our Company on all fronts, we are nevertheless well aware that we have much work ahead of us. The consumer recovery is still somewhat fragile and our year-over-year comparisons will now become more difficult.

We are extremely appreciative and proud of the support we have received from our associate team and from our supplier partners who share our commitment and vision for sustained growth in revenues and earnings.

The confidence within our organization continues to build and when combined with dedication and effort, success is usually the result. On behalf of all of our management and associates we thank our shareholders for their support of our business and rededicate ourselves to providing you with the return on your investment that you expect and deserve.

I would like to express my gratitude to Harold Corrigan for his contribution to Sears Canada during his 18 years on the Board of Directors and to extend my warmest wishes for his good health and happiness in his retirement. On a sadder note, Sears Canada would like to reflect on the passing of Michel F. Bélanger, a distinguished Director of our Company for almost 20 years.

In addition to Mr. Bélanger's significant contribution to the growth and success of Sears Canada, he also played an important role in the business community and political life of Quebec and Canada. He held various positions in the Provincial Civil Service and was one of the principal architects of the nationalization of Quebec's hydro-electric resources and the establishment of Hydro-Quebec. A former Chair of the National Bank of Canada, he became well known in the early 1990s when the late Premier Robert Bourassa recruited him to serve as Co-Chair of the Bélanger-Campeau Commission on Quebec's constitutional future. His last prominent role was as Co-Chair of the NO Committee in the 1995 Quebec Referendum Campaign. His sound advice and counsel were of constant help and guidance to the management of our Company. We will all miss him greatly.

Paul S. Walters,
Chairman & CEO

How did Sears achieve growth this year at a rate above market growth, and significantly improve shareholder return? The bottom line: in 1997, Sears became more relevant to its customers.

"To move our business into the future, our first step was to better understand who our customers were," says Paul Walters, Chairman and Chief Executive Officer. "She is a woman, 25 to 54, the CEO and CFO of the family. She is the leader who makes 80% of the family's buying decisions even in categories like automotive, electronics and appliances. Another key customer segment is the 18-25 year olds, who are making major changes in their lives, moving into new homes and entering into new relationships. In many ways, Sears is the store for every generation."

REINVENTING THE SHOPPING EXPERIENCE

Concurrently, Sears adapted a number of the successful strategies of its U.S. parent and began the process of branding Sears as the place to go for consistent quality in goods. "After all, a powerful brand is the first step to building a closer relationship with our customers," explains Rick Sorby, Executive Vice-President, Marketing. "It is what makes people come into our stores, and what makes them come back, time after time."

To achieve our **best performance ever**, Sears became more **relevant** to **customers**

Sears made a major investment in the revitalization of 9 stores in the Greater Toronto Area market resulting in a 31% sales increase in the fourth quarter of 1997 compared to the same period last year. Based on the success of this program, the Company started rolling out a number of these innovative changes to many of its stores across Canada. Major national and Toronto-focused marketing programs, created to bring to life the new Sears brand and to highlight 'The Many Sides of Sears', supported these efforts.

Growth in 1997 was also a result of Sears firmly repositioning itself as a fashion apparel retailer, as it dramatically expanded its exclusive private label program and added 50% more national brands to its apparel assortments.

The Company continued its initiative to retain the loyalty of Sears traditional market. This was accomplished by increasing its established dominance in such areas as major appliances and furniture with its Sears Brand Central concept, Sears Whole Home Furniture Stores and dealer stores. Sears also enhanced its catalogue offerings and began looking at the vast new opportunities that exist with electronic commerce. ⁂

James R. Clifford,
President and Chief Operating Officer

Sears
MD&A and
Financial
Highlights

"1997's record profit performance is a tribute to the entire Sears organization and their efforts over the last several years. During this period we repositioned the Company and each business strategically, operationally and financially. We invested in our core businesses and in new formats. We also invested in redesigning business processes and in technology designed to make Sears Canada more efficient, more responsive and more flexible. It is those strategic initiatives executed by all Sears associates that drove our improved performance in 1997."

"Although we are pleased with 1997's performance, we recognize that shareholder value is built on consistent and profitable growth. We accept this challenge and believe Sears Canada is well positioned to achieve this goal."

Financial
Information
1997

Eleven Year Summary [1]

Fiscal Year	1997	1996	1995	1994	1993	1992	1991	1990	1989	1988	1987
Results for the Year (in millions)											
Total revenues	$ 4,584	$ 3,956	$ 3,918	$ 4,066	$ 4,032	$ 4,042	$ 4,169	$ 4,642	$ 4,621	$ 4,377	$ 4,079
Depreciation	78	78	74	67	69	70	56	55	48	47	45
Earnings (loss) from operations before unusual items and income taxes	215	70	43	88	15	(101)	(31)	70	186	175	148
Unusual items gain (loss)[2]	0	(45)	(21)	(5)	(5)	(46)	(8)	(31)	0	0	27
Earnings (loss) from operations before income taxes	215	25	22	83	10	(147)	(39)	39	186	175	175
Income taxes (recovery)	99	16	10	38	6	(56)	(10)	19	83	82	73
Net earnings (loss)	116	9	12	45	4	(91)	(29)	21	106	96	107
Dividends declared	25	23	23	23	23	21	20	20	21	21	21
Capital expenditures	160	63	76	60	37	55	235	204	116	118	63
Year End Position (in millions)											
Accounts receivable	$ 1,225	$ 1,033	$ 926	$ 1,324	$ 1,101	$ 909	$ 1,090	$ 1,877	$ 1,784	$ 1,496	$ 1,272
Inventories	640	491	507	559	563	628	693	665	807	747	740
Net capital assets	825	744	763	800	813	941	997	803	665	572	504
Total assets	3,007	2,734	2,554	2,949	2,746	2,796	3,069	3,581	3,512	3,103	2,793
Working capital	971	741	661	1,016	888	885	1,112	1,486	1,451	1,177	1,172
Long-term obligations	836	634	662	1,032	947	1,063	1,245	1,362	1,185	964	944
Shareholders' equity	1,042	949	856	867	845	863	900	948	970	883	825
Per Share of Capital Stock (in dollars)											
Net earnings (loss)	$ 1.10	$ 0.09	$ 0.13	$ 0.47	$ 0.05	$ (1.04)	$ (0.34)	$ 0.25	$ 1.23	$ 1.11	$ 1.22
Dividends declared	0.24	0.24	0.24	0.24	0.24	0.24	0.24	0.24	0.24	0.24	0.24
Shareholders' equity	9.84	8.98	9.02	9.13	8.90	9.10	10.67	11.25	11.26	10.27	9.43
Financial Ratios											
Return on average shareholders' equity (%)	11.7	1.0	1.4	5.2	0.5	(10.3)	(3.1)	2.2	11.4	11.2	13.7
Current ratio	1.9	1.7	1.7	2.0	2.0	2.1	2.4	2.3	2.1	2.0	2.2
Return on total revenues (%)	2.5	0.2	0.3	1.1	0.1	(2.2)	(0.7)	0.5	2.3	2.2	2.6
Debt/Equity ratio	45/55	46/54	48/52	59/41	58/42	59/41	61/39	67/33	66/34	65/35	63/37
Pre-tax margin (%)	4.7	0.6	0.6	2.0	0.3	(3.6)	(0.9)	0.8	4.0	4.0	4.3
Number of Selling Units											
Retail stores	110	110	110	110	110	109	106	97	92	84	80
Furniture stores	8	4	1	0	0	0	0	0	0	0	0
Outlet stores	8	9	10	11	12	13	15	18	17	16	15
Dealer stores	79	60	19	4	0	0	0	0	0	0	0
Catalogue selling locations	1,752	1,746	1,623	1,542	1,483	1,579	1,701	1,701	1,708	1,726	1,719

1 Certain amounts have been restated to reflect accounting changes related to the consolidation of the Company's proportionate share of the assets, liabilities and expenses of real estate joint ventures as recommended by the Canadian Institute of Chartered Accountants. The change in policy, effective in 1995, has been applied retroactively.

2 Extraordinary items have been restated in 1987 to reflect the reclassification of items from extraordinary items to unusual items. All amounts are restated in pre-tax dollars and the income tax amounts have been adjusted accordingly.

Management's Discussion & Analysis

Sears is Canada's largest single retailer of general merchandise, with department and specialty stores as well as catalogue selling units located across Canada. The Company emphasizes quality, value, and service in appealing to a broad cross-section of Canadian consumers.

The Company's vision is to be Canada's most successful retailer by providing customers with total shopping satisfaction, associates with opportunities for career advancement and personal growth, and shareholders with superior returns on their investment.

OVERVIEW OF CONSOLIDATED RESULTS

For purposes of this discussion, "Sears" or "the Company" refers to Sears Canada Inc. and its subsidiaries together with the Company's proportionate share of the assets, liabilities, revenues and expenses of real estate joint ventures.

The 1997 fiscal year refers to the 53 week period ended January 3, 1998 and comparatively, the 1996 fiscal year refers to the 52 week period ended December 28, 1996.

The following table summarizes the Company's operating results for 1997 and 1996.

(in millions, except per share amounts)	1997	1996
Total revenues	$ 4,583.5	$ 3,955.9
Earnings from operations before interest, unusual items and income taxes	301.3	166.3
Interest expense	86.1	96.3
Earnings from operations before unusual items and income taxes	215.2	70.0
Unusual items expense[1]	-	45.0
Income taxes	98.7	16.2
Net earnings	$ 116.5	$ 8.8
Earnings per share	$ 1.10	$ 0.09

1 Refer to Financial Statement Note 10.

Total revenues increased in 1997 by $627.6 million or 15.9% over 1996 due primarily to an increase in merchandise revenues of 16.8%, with strong growth in both retail and catalogue operations. Fiscal 1997 contained 53 weeks. On a comparable 52 week basis, total revenues increased by 14.4%.

In 1997, Sears achieved significant growth in revenues, building on the initiatives implemented in recent years. The Company's strategy for growth is directed at meeting the needs of its target customer, and involves increased investment in inventories, fixed assets, and marketing. In 1997, the Company completed substantial renovations to nine stores in the Greater Toronto Area, opened four new **Sears Whole Home Furniture Stores**, and nineteen dealer stores.

The Company's earnings from operations before unusual items and income taxes were $215.2 million in 1997, just over three times 1996 earnings of $70.0 million. Operational expenses, and investments in inventory and capital assets were all effectively managed, resulting in a substantial increase in net earnings. Interest expense declined by $10.2 million primarily due to a reduction in the average amount of debt outstanding during the year. (Refer to the section entitled "Analysis of Funding Costs" on page 30).

Number of Associates

	1997	1996
Full-time associates	9,221	9,033
Part-time associates	29,324	26,263
Total associates	38,545	35,296

The total number of associates increased by 9.2% in 1997, reflecting the Company's emphasis on customer service.

SEGMENTED BUSINESS ANALYSIS

The Company's operations can be grouped into three major businesses: merchandising, credit, and real estate joint ventures.

Management's Discussion & Analysis continued

MERCHANDISING OPERATIONS

The merchandising business segment includes Sears full-line department store and catalogue operations, in addition to Sears Whole Home Furniture Stores, dealer stores and outlet stores.

(in millions)	1997	1996
Revenues	$ 4,210.6	$ 3,605.7
Earnings from operations before interest, unusual items and income taxes	$ 141.7	$ 27.0
Capital employed	$ 553.6	$ 585.8

Merchandising Operating Analysis

Merchandising revenues were $4.2 billion in 1997, an increase of 16.8% over 1996. All regions experienced increases in revenues in 1997. The Ontario region recorded the largest increase at 20.5%.

Merchandising Revenues by Region

(in millions)	1997	% of Total	% of Total Households[2]
Atlantic	$ 402.6	9.6	7.8
Quebec	876.9	20.8	26.1
Ontario	1,667.7	39.6	36.3
Prairies	754.2	17.9	16.4
BC/Yukon/NWT	509.2	12.1	13.4
Total	$ 4,210.6	100.0	100.0

2   Total Households is based on Statistics Canada, 1996 Census.

Number of Selling Units

As at January 3, 1998

	Atlantic	Que.	Ont.	Prairies	BC Yukon NWT	Total
Retail	11	25	43	19	12	110
Furniture	0	0	8	0	0	8
Outlet	1	0	5	1	1	8
Dealer	16	8	21	12	22	79
Catalogue	327	417	472	386	150	1,752

Retail Stores – 110 department stores ranging in size from 24,500 square feet to 162,000 square feet.

Furniture Stores – stores ranging in size from 35,000 square feet to 48,000 square feet featuring an expanded selection of furniture, decorator rugs and, in two stores, major appliances.

Outlet Stores – selling returned and surplus merchandise in stores ranging in size from 25,000 square feet to 104,000 square feet.

Dealer Stores – independent locally operated stores serving smaller population centres, selling home appliances and electronics, as well as lawn, garden and snow removal merchandise.

Catalogue Selling Locations – include 1,551 independent catalogue agent locations, plus catalogue pick-up locations within Sears retail stores, outlet stores and dealer stores.

During 1997, the Company opened four new Sears Whole Home Furniture Stores and 19 dealer stores.

Merchandising Gross Floor Area

(square feet – in millions)	1997	1996
Retail	13.6	13.6
Furniture	0.3	0.1
Outlet	0.6	0.7
Total	14.5	14.4
Merchandise service centres:		
Active	6.8	6.8
Subleased or dormant	1.9	2.8
Total merchandise service centres	8.7	9.6

Merchandise service centres include two catalogue order fulfillment facilities and five service centres supporting national merchandising operations.

Recent Merchandising Initiatives

• In 1997, Sears completed major renovations to nine full-line department stores in the Greater Toronto Area (GTA). Approximately $60 million was invested in major upgrades to store presentation such as fixtures and lighting. The renovated stores allow Sears to offer a broader and deeper assortment of merchandise presented in an up-to-date store environment. These stores feature an expanded assortment of fashion apparel, cosmetics, accessories and "soft" home fashions. During these renovations, Sears was able to reclaim more than 160,000 square feet of selling space by eliminating surplus stockroom and office space. The renovation of nine GTA full-line department stores completes the first phase of a three year, $300 million capital investment program to reposition Sears retail stores nationally.

• Expansion of the Sears Whole Home Furniture Store concept, launched in 1995, continued with openings in Burlington, Woodbridge, Barrie and Newmarket, Ontario in 1997. Both the Woodbridge and Barrie locations carry **Sears Brand Central** selection of major appliances in addition to the broad selection of furniture, decorator rugs and accent decor items available at all Sears Whole Home Furniture Stores. This combination of furniture and appliances offers one of Canada's widest assortments of home merchandise under one roof. The Company plans to open fourteen additional Sears Whole Home Furniture Stores in 1998. Many of these stores will also feature Sears Brand Central appliances.

• The Company continued to enhance its assortment of national brands in 1997. Sears has combined these brands with strong private label offerings in order to provide customers with a broad range of fashionable merchandise. National brands introduced this year include **First 1 Issue, Jones Studio, Calvin Klein, Point Zero, Daniel David, Private Member** and **Calvin Klein Khakis** in apparel; **Fieldcrest Royal Velvet** and **Joseph Abboud** in bed and bath; and **Pfaltzgraff** in housewares.

• In 1997, Sears invested $40.4 million to install improved fixturing in stores across the country. Fashion tables for the presentation of folded goods were installed in all apparel departments. **Levi's** shops, a unique branded shopping environment, were rolled-out to 80 retail stores in 1997 to provide a consistent and attractive presentation in men's, women's and children's apparel departments. As well, fixtures which allow for the display of approximately 50% more merchandise were installed in hardware and seasonal merchandise departments.

• Sears introduced Shop By Phone across Canada in 1997. This innovative program allows customers to purchase selected items featured in retail flyers and bearing the Shop by Phone symbol, either at a local Sears retail store, or by calling 1-888-607-3277. This initiative is designed to enhance customer convenience and service.

Management's Discussion & Analysis continued

• The dealer store program, introduced in 1994, expanded to a total of 79 stores, with 19 locations being added in 1997. The Company plans to open an additional 20 dealer stores in 1998. Dealer stores are operated under independent local ownership. These stores offer a selection of **Kenmore** and other name brand appliances, electronics, and lawn and garden furniture and equipment. Dealer stores are designed to provide the small market customer with a broad shopping selection, together with personal local service.

• 1997 marked the launch of the biggest Christmas **Wish Book** in Sears 44 year catalogue history. This year's Wish Book was larger than last year's book with 38% more pages. It featured expanded toy, fashion apparel and home electronics sections, as well as an increased national brand selection. The 1997 Sears Wish Book was distributed to almost five million Canadian households.

• Several initiatives were introduced during the year designed to improve synergies between the catalogue and retail sales channels. As part of the GTA store renovations, the presentation of catalogue shopping areas located in several Sears retail stores was updated. An inviting atmosphere was created through the use of modern fixturing, seasonal posters, and a central area in which to browse through catalogues. These catalogue shopping areas were also equipped with fitting rooms, enabling customers to try on merchandise they have ordered. In addition, the Company continued to install catalogue outposts in various areas of the store. These outposts permit customers to order merchandise via the catalogue if their particular selection is unavailable in the retail store, thereby enabling the customer to access the catalogue's expanded selection of styles and specialty sizes.

CREDIT OPERATIONS

Sears credit operations finance and manage customer charge account receivables generated from the sale of goods and services charged on the Sears Card.

(in millions)		1997		1996
Total service charge revenues	$	**364.8**	$	361.6
Less: SCRT share of revenues[3]		**(54.2)**		(69.2)
Net service charge revenues		**310.6**		292.4
Earnings before interest, unusual items and income taxes	$	**127.5**	$	109.1
Capital employed	$	**1,090.8**	$	943.6

3 Refer to the section entitled "Analysis of Funding Costs" on page 30.

Credit operations contributed $127.5 million to the Company's 1997 consolidated earnings before interest, unusual items and income taxes, compared to $109.1 million in fiscal 1996. The increase of $18.4 million in earnings reflects the increase in the Company's net revenues.

Total service charge revenues earned on customer charge account receivables increased slightly in 1997. Through its securitization program, the Company securitizes customer charge account receivables in order to obtain a more favourable cost of funding. The cost of this funding is deducted from the total service charge revenues earned on the portfolio. After adjusting for amounts securitized, net service charge revenues increased by $18.2 million or 6.2%. (Refer to the section entitled "Securitization of Charge Account Receivables" on page 29.)

Charge Account Receivables Analysis

(in millions – except average account balances)	1997	1996
Active customer accounts	3.8	3.8
Average outstanding balance of receivables per customer account at year end	$ 439	$ 424
Charge account receivables written-off during the year (net of recoveries)	$ 46.4	$ 49.9

Net write-offs as a percentage of the monthly average amounts outstanding were 3.2% in 1997 compared to 3.4% in 1996 and 2.7% in 1995. This write-off rate continues to be at the low end of industry norms.

Since October 1993, Sears has been accepting third party credit cards in addition to the Sears Card. In 1997, Sears began accepting debit cards in major centres. The chart below details the trend in method of payment.

	1997	1996	1995
Sears Card	64	66	65
Third Party Credit Cards	13	11	10
Cash	23	23	25
Total	100 %	100 %	100 %

The percentage of sales charged by customers to their Sears Card decreased to 64% of total sales from 66% in 1996. The percentage charged to third party cards increased to 13% from 11% last year. The share of cash sales remained constant at 23%.

Recent Credit Initiatives

The following initiatives have been directed at increasing usage of the Sears Card.

• A new auto club developed exclusively for Sears Card holders was launched in September 1997. **Sears AutoAssist** provides access to roadside assistance 24 hours a day, 365 days a year, anywhere in Canada or the U.S.A. Roadside services include; emergency towing, battery boosts, flat tire service, lock-out

service, emergency gasoline delivery, and up to $500 for accommodations, meals and transportation for road accidents away from home.

• In 1997, Sears enhanced the **Sears PhonePlan** program. Effective December 1, 1997 the discount offered to Sears PhonePlan members on all "time and day" billing rates for long distance calls increased from 25% to 33 1/3%. In 1997 Sears PhonePlan also introduced the **Sears Card Calling Card**. This card allows members to conveniently place long distance calls when they are away from home. All long distance calls made by members also earn Sears Club points. As at January 3, 1998, the Sears PhonePlan program had 485,640 members.

REAL ESTATE JOINT VENTURE OPERATIONS

As at January 3, 1998, the Company held joint venture interests in 19 shopping centres, 17 of which contain a Sears store. The Company has 15% to 50% interests in these joint ventures. Accordingly, the Company carries its proportionate share of the assets, liabilities, revenues and expenses of these joint ventures on its books.

(in millions)	1997	1996
Revenues[4]	$ 62.3	$ 57.8
Earnings from operations before interest, unusual items and income taxes	$ 32.1	$ 30.2
Capital employed	$ 245.7	$ 238.8

4 Excluded from revenues is the Company's proportionate share of rental revenues earned from retail stores of Sears Canada Inc. of $3.7 million ($3.6 million – 1996).

The market value of Sears interest in these properties is estimated to be approximately $400 million ($365 million – 1996). It is the Company's policy to have one-third of the properties independently appraised each year, while the appraisals of the remaining two-thirds are reviewed and updated by management. The Sears portion of the debt of these properties is $229.8 million ($223.2 million – 1996).

Management's Discussion & Analysis *continued*

OVERVIEW OF THE CONSOLIDATED STATEMENTS OF FINANCIAL POSITION

Assets

(in millions)	1997	1996
Cash	$ 68.3	$ 201.2
Accounts receivable	1,224.6	1,033.0
Inventories	640.3	491.1
Net capital assets	825.1	744.4
Other assets	249.0	264.3
Total assets	$ 3,007.3	$ 2,734.0

Total assets increased by $273.3 million or 10.0% in 1997.

In 1997, cash decreased $132.9 million. The 1996 cash balance of $201.2 million included proceeds from the issue of 10.3 million common shares in December 1996.

Accounts receivable increased by $191.6 million or 18.5% in 1997.

Accounts Receivable

(in millions)	1997	1996
Charge account receivables	$ 1,655.7	$ 1,568.5
Less amount securitized[5]	(965.6)	(961.2)
Net charge account receivables	690.1	607.3
Deferred receivables	497.4	456.1
Less amount securitized[5]	(24.4)	(97.6)
Net deferred receivables	473.0	358.5
Other receivables	61.5	67.2
Total accounts receivable	$ 1,224.6	$ 1,033.0

5 Refer to the section entitled "Securitization of Charge Account Receivables" on page 29.

Deferred receivables represent credit sales not yet billed to customers' accounts. These credit sales are billed to the customers' accounts at the end of an interest-free deferral period.

Inventories increased by $149.2 million in support of the Company's revenue growth initiatives.

Net capital assets increased by $80.7 million. Capital expenditures totaled $160.4 million in 1997, of which approximately $114 million was spent on retail store renovations and the opening of four new Sears Whole Home Furniture Stores. Depreciation expense for the year was $78.1 million.

Liabilities

(in millions)	1997	1996
Accounts payable and accrued liabilities	$ 878.6	$ 797.8
Long-term obligations due within one year	11.6	183.2
Long-term obligations	836.1	634.2
Other liabilities	238.6	170.1
Total liabilities	$ 1,964.9	$ 1,785.3

Total liabilities increased by $179.6 million or 10.1% in 1997.

Long-term obligations increased by $201.9 million due to the issuance of $125.0 million of 6.55% unsecured debentures and the refinancing of certain joint venture debts. Including amounts due within one year, long-term obligations increased by $30.3 million. (Refer to the section entitled "Analysis of Funding Costs" on page 30.)

Liquidity

As at January 3, 1998, the ratio of current assets to current liabilities increased to 1.9:1 from 1.7:1 in 1996. Working capital was $971.1 million as at January 3, 1998 compared to $741.0 million as at December 28, 1996. The increase in working capital is primarily attributable to growth in accounts receivable and merchandise inventories.

FINANCING ACTIVITIES

The Company has the flexibility to raise funds through bank borrowings, by issuing equity and corporate debt securities, and through the securitization of charge account receivables.

In 1997, the Company carried out the following significant financing activities:

• On February 26, 1997, the outstanding 9.25% unsecured debentures of Sears Canada Inc. in the amount of $100.0 million matured and were repaid.
• On November 5, 1997, Sears Canada Inc. issued $125.0 million of 6.55% unsecured debentures due November 5, 2007.
• During 1997, long-term financing for new capital projects of real estate joint ventures was obtained in the amount of $9.9 million. In addition, $81.8 million of joint venture debt matured in 1997, of which $78.5 million was refinanced.

Securitization of Charge Account Receivables

Sears Acceptance Company Inc. ("Acceptance"), a wholly owned subsidiary of Sears, purchases all Sears Card charge account receivables (including deferred receivables) generated by merchandise and service sales. Through the Company's securitization program, Acceptance sells undivided co-ownership interests in the charge account receivables (excluding deferred receivables) to Sears Canada Receivables Trust (Trust 1) and Sears Canada Receivables Trust – 1992 (Trust 2). In addition, Acceptance sells undivided co-ownership interests in its portfolio of charge account receivables (including deferred receivables) to Sears Canada Receivables Trust – 1996 (Trust 3). Trust 1, Trust 2 and Trust 3 are collectively referred to as SCRT.

As the equity units of Trust 1, Trust 2 and Trust 3 are held by independent parties, the assets and liabilities of SCRT are not reflected in the Company's consolidated financial statements. The cost to the Company of the securitization program is reflected as a reduction in the Company's share of Sears Card service charge revenues.

SCRT is an important financing vehicle which is able to obtain favourable interest rates because of its structure and the high quality of the portfolio of charge account receivables backing its debt. Securitization provides the Company with a diversified source of funds for the operation of its business.

Trust 1 – Trust 1, which was established in 1991, issues short-term commercial paper to finance the purchase of undivided co-ownership interests in charge account receivables (excluding deferred receivables).

The commercial paper of Trust 1 is rated A-1+ by CBRS Inc. (CBRS) and R-1(High) by Dominion Bond Rating Service Limited (DBRS), the highest ratings assigned by these rating agencies for commercial paper.

In order to reduce its exposure to fluctuations in short-term interest rates on Trust 1 borrowings, the Company has entered into floating-to-fixed interest rate swaps in the notional amount of $200 million with remaining terms to maturity of up to 5 years. The average amount securitized under Trust 1 in 1997 was $415.6 million, at an average rate of 4.0% ($509.0 million in 1996 at an average rate of 5.7%).

Trust 2 – Trust 2, which was established in 1993, issues long-term senior and subordinated debentures to finance the purchase of undivided co-ownership interests in charge account receivables (excluding deferred receivables).

The senior debentures of Trust 2 are rated A++ by CBRS and AAA by DBRS, the highest ratings assigned by these agencies for long-term debt. The subordinated debentures of Trust 2 are rated A by CBRS and A (High) by DBRS.

Trust 3 – Trust 3, which was established on October 22, 1996, finances the purchase of undivided co-ownership interests in Acceptance's portfolio of charge account receivables (including deferred receivables) through drawdowns under revolving senior and subordinated note facilities.

Management's Discussion & Analysis *continued*

The senior notes of Trust 3 are rated A++ by CBRS and AAA by DBRS, the highest ratings assigned by these agencies for long-term debt. The subordinated notes of Trust 3 are rated A+ by CBRS and A by DBRS.

Summary of Debt Ratings

	CBRS	DBRS
Sears Canada Inc.		
Unsecured debentures	B++ (High)	BBB
SCRT		
Commercial paper (Trust 1)	A-1+	R-1 (High)
Senior debentures (Trust 2)	A++	AAA
Subordinated debentures (Trust 2)	A	A (High)
Senior notes (Trust 3)	A++	AAA
Subordinated notes (Trust 3)	A+	A

Summary of SCRT Obligations

	1997	1996
Commercial paper	$ 374.8	$ 311.5
Senior debt:		
5.65%, due January 14, 1997[6]	–	27.9
6.50%, due December 16, 1998	150.0	150.0
8.95%, due June 1, 2004	175.0	175.0
Floating rate, due April 1, 2001	150.0	150.0
Floating rate, due June 30, 2006	43.1	139.4
	518.1	642.3
Subordinated debt:		
7.67% to 9.18%, due 1998 to 2004	7.2	7.2
Floating rate, due 1997 to 2004	13.7	18.1
Floating rate, due June 30, 2006	0.4	1.4
	21.3	26.7
Accrued liabilities	3.5	6.0
Trust units (floating rate, due 1998 to 2006)	72.3	72.3
Total SCRT obligations	$ 990.0	$ 1,058.8

6 Face value of $100.0 million debenture shown net of permitted investments as at December 28, 1996 of $72.1 million.

Analysis of Funding Costs

The following table summarizes the Company's total funding costs including the cost of the securitization program:

(in millions)	1997	1996
Interest Costs		
Total debt at end of year	$ 847.7	$ 819.5
Average debt for year	758.4	836.6
Interest on long-term debt	$ 74.5	$ 82.8
Other interest (net)[7]	11.6	13.5
Interest expense	$ 86.1	$ 96.3
Average rate of debt[8]	11.2 %	11.5 %
Securitization Costs[9]		
Amount securitized at end of year	$ 990.0	$ 1,058.8
Average amount securitized for year	1,019.6	1,103.9
Cost of funding	54.2	69.2
Average rate of securitized funding[8]	5.2 %	6.3 %
Total Funding		
Total funding at end of year	$ 1,837.7	$ 1,878.3
Total average funding for year	1,778.0	1,940.5
Total funding costs for year	140.3	165.5
Average rate of total funding[8]	7.8 %	8.5 %

7 Other interest includes $13.2 million in 1997 ($12.8 million – 1996) for payment of the interest rate differential on floating-to-fixed interest rate swaps.

8 1997 calculation based on 365 day year rather than fiscal period of 53 weeks.

9 Securitization costs for 1996 comparative figures reflect the cost of Trust 1 and Trust 2 for the fiscal year and the cost of Trust 3 for the period from November 1, 1996 to December 28, 1996.

Total funding costs for 1997 decreased by $25.2 million due primarily to lower average funding levels and lower average interest rates applicable to floating rate funding outstanding in SCRT.

SEARS CANADA

Capital Structure

The chart below highlights the improving trend in the debt to equity ratio, due primarily to the contribution of net earnings and a 1996 common share issue.

(in millions)	1997	% of Total	1996	% of Total
Current debt:				
Bank advances and short-term notes	$ 0.0	0.0	$ 2.1	0.1
Long-term debt due within one year	11.6	0.6	183.2	10.4
	11.6	0.6	185.3	10.5
Long-term debt	836.1	44.2	634.2	35.8
Total debt	847.7	44.8	819.5	46.3
Shareholders' equity	1,042.4	55.2	948.7	53.7
Total capital	$1,890.1	100.0	$1,768.2	100.0

CAPITAL EXPENDITURES

The Company expects to commit approximately $214 million for capital expenditures in 1998, compared to capital expenditures of $160.4 million in 1997. Planned expenditures for 1998 include $110.5 million for retail store enhancements and new Sears Whole Home Furniture Stores. The balance of the capital expenditures will be spent primarily on information technology, logistics and real estate operations.

ANALYSIS OF TOTAL CORPORATE TAXES

Total corporate taxes increased by $77.7 million in 1997. Income taxes increased $82.5 million, commensurate with an increase in earnings from operations before income taxes. (Refer to Financial Statement Note 11.)

(in millions)	1997	1996
Provincial capital tax	$ 6.7	$ 6.9
Property tax	45.7	54.4
Payroll taxes[10]	68.6	64.5
Total taxes expensed in cost of merchandise sold, operating, administrative and selling expense	121.0	125.8
Corporate income tax	93.9	11.2
Large corporations tax	4.8	5.0
Income taxes	98.7	16.2
Total corporate taxes	$ 219.7	$ 142.0

10 Represents contributions to the Canada and Quebec Pension Plans, Employment Insurance, health care levies and WCB premiums.

RISKS AND UNCERTAINTIES

The key elements of the Company's strategy for minimizing risk are as follows:

Interest Rates

Trust 1 has financed purchases of undivided co-ownership interests in the portfolio of charge account receivables with the issuance of $374.8 million of commercial paper as at January 3, 1998 ($311.5 million – 1996). To reduce the risk associated with fluctuating interest rates, floating-to-fixed interest rate swap transactions in the notional amount of $200 million ($250 million – 1996) have been utilized. This brings the Company's fixed-to-floating funding ratio, including securitized funding to 66/34, which is within its target ratios.

Management's Discussion & Analysis *continued*

Foreign Exchange

The Company's foreign exchange risk is limited to currency fluctuations between the Canadian and U.S. dollar. The Company's total forecasted requirement for foreign funds in 1998 is approximately U.S. $300 million. From time to time, the Company uses forward contracts to fix the exchange rate on a portion of its expected requirement for U.S. dollars. As at January 3, 1998, there were no foreign exchange contracts outstanding.

Concentration of Credit Risk

The Company's exposure to credit risk relates mainly to customer account receivables. Sears Card customers are a large and diverse group. The average balance per customer at year end was $439.

Leases

Twenty-two of Sears 110 retail stores are Company-owned and two of the eight Sears Whole Home Furniture Stores are Company-owned, with the balance held under long-term leases which include favourable renewal options. As a result, the Company's retail store rental expense is expected to remain stable.

Merchandise Sources

A major aim of the merchandise procurement process is to ensure that Sears, together with its merchandise sources, fulfills its promises and obligations to its customers. Sears will continue to work with its merchandise sources to ensure that they share this commitment.

Sears shops the world market to provide its customers with the best value for their dollar. As a result, Sears is confident in its ability to continue providing consumers with high quality merchandise at competitive prices.

Year 2000

The Year 2000 poses a significant global challenge. Date dependent systems and processes that use two digits to represent the year must be adapted in order to avoid risk of error with the turn of the century.

Sears has been preparing to meet the Year 2000 challenge for the past three years, as the Company is a significant user of current technologies. The Company has established a cross-functional team to oversee and manage the Sears Year 2000 project. The first phase of the project, which included identifying and evaluating the Company's systems and applications for Year 2000 capability, determining necessary modifications and replacements and communicating with third parties, including merchandise and non-merchandise suppliers to discuss and assess their Year 2000 readiness, was completed early in 1997.

Remedial action and testing are underway. The project is continuing to progress in accordance with the project schedule. The Company has established December 31, 1998 as the date that its critical systems will be converted, tested and Year 2000 ready. To date, approximately $7 million has been spent on personnel and contractor costs. Costs are expensed as incurred. The total estimated cost for the project is approximately $28 million for internal and external resources.

Competitive and Economic Environment

Sears believes that the general economic environment will remain positive, providing additional opportunities for growth in 1998. Although the retail market remains highly competitive, Sears is well positioned to take advantage of emerging trends in retailing, including those in the areas of specialty stores and services.

Sears is optimistic that consumer confidence will remain high in 1998, despite continuing high levels of household debt. Strong growth is forecast for the Canadian economy again this year, as labour markets are expected to further improve and inflation is forecast to remain low.

Outlook

Sears continues to position itself to capture a larger share of consumer spending through its aggressive programs of store renovations and enhanced merchandise assortment and presentation. The Company also continues to evaluate new and innovative methods of retailing. By meeting customers' needs in terms of merchandise selection, pricing, and the total shopping experience, Sears anticipates growth in revenues and profits into the future.

SEARS ▲ CANADA

Quarterly Results *Unaudited*

	First Quarter		Second Quarter		Third Quarter		Fourth Quarter	
	1997	1996	**1997**	1996	**1997**	1996	**1997**	1996
Total revenues	$ **875.1**	$ 821.7	$ **1,054.3**	$ 899.2	$ **1,065.5**	$ 928.5	$ **1,588.6**	$ 1,306.5
Earnings (loss) from operations before unusual items and income taxes	**(2.6)**	(36.1)	**42.3**	(12.2)	**37.1**	1.3	**138.4**	117.0
Net earnings (loss)	$ **(2.8)**	$ (21.8)	$ **22.8**	$ (31.9)	$ **19.4**	$ (0.5)	$ **77.1**	$ 63.0
Earnings (loss) per share	$ **(0.03)**	$ (0.23)	$ **0.22**	$ (0.34)	$ **0.18**	$ 0.00	$ **0.73**	$ 0.66

Common Share Market Information*

	First Quarter		Second Quarter		Third Quarter		Fourth Quarter	
	1997	1996	**1997**	1996	**1997**	1996	**1997**	1996
High	$ **13.95**	$ 6 5/8	$ **20.00**	$ 8.15	$ **25.20**	$ 8.15	$ **25.75**	$ 12.00
Low	$ **10.00**	$ 5 4/8	$ **12.50**	$ 6 3/8	$ **18.25**	$ 7.40	$ **19.00**	$ 7.75
Close	$ **13.35**	$ 6 6/8	$ **18.40**	$ 8.05	$ **25.00**	$ 7.75	$ **19.80**	$ 10.10
Avg. daily trading volume	**229,870**	88,198	**295,137**	84,790	**127,992**	62,142	**189,641**	202,507

* The Toronto Stock Exchange

Statement of Management Responsibility

Management is responsible for the accuracy, integrity and objectivity of the financial information contained in this Annual Report. The consolidated financial statements have been prepared in accordance with generally accepted accounting principles in Canada and include certain amounts that are based on estimates and judgements. Financial information used elsewhere in the Annual Report is consistent with that in the financial statements.

Management has developed, maintains and supports an extensive program of internal audits that provides reasonable assurance that financial records are reliable and that assets are safeguarded.

The Board of Directors, through the activities of its Audit and Corporate Governance Committee, ensures that management fulfills its responsibilities for financial reporting and internal control. The Audit and Corporate Governance Committee, the majority of whom are outside directors, meets periodically with the financial officers of the Company, the internal auditors and external auditors to discuss audit activities, internal accounting controls and financial reporting matters. The Board of Directors, on the recommendation of the Audit and Corporate Governance Committee, has approved all of the information contained in the Annual Report.

The Company's external auditors, Deloitte & Touche, have conducted audits of the financial records of the Company in accordance with generally accepted auditing standards. Their report is as follows.

President and
Chief Operating Officer

Senior Vice-President and
Chief Financial Officer

Auditors' Report to the Shareholders of Sears Canada Inc.

We have audited the consolidated statements of financial position of Sears Canada Inc. as at January 3, 1998 and December 28, 1996 and the consolidated statements of earnings, retained earnings and changes in financial position for the 53 weeks and 52 weeks then ended. These financial statements are the responsibility of the Company's management. Our responsibility is to express an opinion on these financial statements based on our audits.

We conducted our audits in accordance with generally accepted auditing standards. Those standards require that we plan and perform an audit to obtain reasonable assurance whether the financial statements are free of material misstatement. An audit includes examining, on a test basis, evidence supporting the amounts and disclosures in the financial statements. An audit also includes assessing the accounting principles used and significant estimates made by management, as well as evaluating the overall financial statement presentation.

In our opinion, these consolidated financial statements present fairly, in all material respects, the financial position of the Company as at January 3, 1998 and December 28, 1996 and the results of its operations and the changes in its financial position for the 53 weeks and 52 weeks then ended in accordance with generally accepted accounting principles.

Deloitte & Touche
Chartered Accountants

Toronto, Ontario
February 9, 1998

Consolidated Statements of Financial Position

SEARS CANADA

As at January 3, 1998 and December 28, 1996 (in millions)	1997	1996
Assets		
Current Assets		
Cash and short-term investments	$ 68.3	$ 201.2
Charge account receivables (Note 2)	690.1	607.3
Other receivables (Note 3)	534.5	425.7
Inventories	640.3	491.1
Prepaid expenses and other assets	48.9	46.5
Short-term deferred income taxes	41.9	40.0
	2,024.0	1,811.8
Investments and Other Assets (Note 4)	22.8	29.6
Net Capital Assets (Note 5)	825.1	744.4
Deferred Charges (Note 6)	135.4	148.2
	$ 3,007.3	$ 2,734.0
Liabilities		
Current Liabilities		
Bank advances and short-term notes	$ 0.0	$ 2.1
Accounts payable	560.2	472.9
Accrued liabilities	318.4	324.9
Income and other taxes payable	162.7	87.7
Principal payments on long-term obligations due within one year (Note 8)	11.6	183.2
	1,052.9	1,070.8
Long-term Obligations (Note 8)	836.1	634.2
Long-term Deferred Income Taxes	75.9	80.3
	1,964.9	1,785.3
Shareholders' Equity		
Capital Stock (Note 9)	450.9	448.3
Retained Earnings	591.5	500.4
	1,042.4	948.7
	$ 3,007.3	$ 2,734.0

Approved by the Board:

P.S. Walters
Director

J.M. Tory
Director

Consolidated Statements of Earnings

(in millions, except per share amounts)	For the 53 weeks ended January 3, 1998	For the 52 weeks ended December 28, 1996
Total revenues	$ 4,583.5	$ 3,955.9
Deduct:		
Cost of merchandise sold, operating, administrative and selling expenses	4,204.1	3,712.1
Depreciation	78.1	77.5
Interest	86.1	96.3
	4,368.3	3,885.9
Earnings from operations before unusual items and income taxes	215.2	70.0
Unusual items (Note 10)	0.0	(45.0)
Earnings from operations before income taxes	215.2	25.0
Income taxes (Note 11)		
Current	105.0	9.4
Deferred	(6.3)	6.8
	98.7	16.2
Net earnings	$ 116.5	$ 8.8
Earnings per share	$ 1.10	$ 0.09

Consolidated Statements of Retained Earnings

(in millions, except per share amounts)	For the 53 weeks ended January 3, 1998	For the 52 weeks ended December 28, 1996
Opening balance	$ 500.4	$ 514.4
Net earnings	116.5	8.8
	616.9	523.2
Dividends declared	25.4	22.8
Closing balance	$ 591.5	$ 500.4

Consolidated Statements of Changes in Financial Position

SEARS ♦ CANADA

(in millions)	For the 53 weeks ended January 3, 1998	For the 52 weeks ended December 28, 1996
Cash Generated From (Used For) Operations		
Net earnings	$ 116.5	$ 8.8
Non-cash items included in net earnings, principally depreciation	88.9	86.2
Funds from operations	205.4	95.0
Changes in working capital (Note 12)	(106.5)	183.2
	98.9	278.2
Cash Generated From (Used For) Investment Activities		
Purchases of capital assets	(160.4)	(63.2)
Proceeds from sale of capital assets	1.1	8.9
Charge account receivables	(82.8)	(189.3)
Deferred charges	(1.9)	(2.4)
Investments and other assets	6.8	(14.4)
	(237.2)	(260.4)
Cash Generated From (Used For) Financing Activities		
Issue of long-term obligations	134.9	100.0
Repayment of long-term obligations	(104.6)	(71.3)
Net proceeds from issue of capital stock	2.6	106.3
	32.9	135.0
Cash (Used For) Dividends	(25.4)	(22.8)
Increase (decrease) in cash net of bank advances and short-term notes at end of year	(130.8)	130.0
Cash, net of bank advances and short-term notes at end of year	$ 68.3	$ 199.1

Notes to Consolidated Financial Statements

1 SUMMARY OF ACCOUNTING POLICIES

Principles of Consolidation

The consolidated financial statements include the accounts of Sears Canada Inc. and its subsidiaries together with its proportionate share of the assets, liabilities, revenues and expenses of real estate joint ventures ("the Company").

Fiscal Year

The fiscal year of the Company consists of a 52 or 53 week period ending on the Saturday closest to December 31. The 1997 fiscal year for the consolidated statements presented is the 53 weeks ending January 3, 1998 and the comparable period is the 52 weeks ending December 28, 1996.

Inventories

Inventories are valued at the lower of cost or net realizable value. Cost is determined for retail store inventories by the retail inventory method and for catalogue order and miscellaneous inventories by the average cost method, based on individual items.

Prepaid Advertising Expense

Catalogue production costs are deferred and amortized over the life of each catalogue on the basis of the estimated sales from that catalogue.

Deferred Receivables

Deferred receivables are charge account receivables that have not yet been billed to the customers' accounts. Service charges are not accrued on these accounts over the deferral period which generally ranges from six to thirteen months.

Capital Assets

Capital assets are stated at cost. Depreciation and amortization provisions are generally computed by the straight-line method based on estimated useful lives of 2 to 10 years for equipment and fixtures, and of 10 to 40 years for buildings and improvements.

The Company's proportionate share of buildings held in joint ventures is generally depreciated by the sinking fund method over 20 to 40 years.

The Company capitalizes interest charges for major construction projects and depreciates these charges over the life of the related assets.

Deferred Charges

The cumulative excess of contributions to the Company's pension plan over the amounts expensed is included in deferred charges.

Debt issuance costs are deferred and amortized by the straight-line method to the due dates of the respective debt issues. Securitization set up costs are amortized on a straight-line basis over a maximum of five years.

Consulting fees for major projects are amortized by the straight-line method over the period of future benefit ranging from three to five years.

Certain other costs are deferred and amortized by the straight-line method over the remaining life of the related asset.

Deferred Income Taxes

The Company follows the comprehensive method for accounting for deferred taxes. Deferred income taxes arise from timing differences between tax and financial reporting. Short-term deferred income taxes relate principally to the reporting of such items as reserves for returns and allowances, and insurance provisions. Long-term deferred income taxes relate principally to the reporting of such items as depreciation and pension expense.

Foreign Currency Translation

Obligations payable in U.S. dollars are translated at the exchange rate in effect at the balance sheet date or at the rates fixed by forward exchange contracts.

Transactions in foreign currencies are translated into Canadian dollars at the rate in effect on the date of the transaction.

Pensions

The Company maintains a defined benefit, final average pension plan which covers substantially all of its regular full-time associates as well as some of its part-time associates. The plan provides pensions based on length of service and final average earnings.

SEARS✦CANADA

Current service costs under the Company's pension plan are charged to operations as they accrue. The excess of the market value of pension fund assets over the actuarial present value of the accrued pension obligations as at January 1, 1986 and any surpluses or deficits arising since that date are amortized over the expected average remaining service life of the associate group covered by the plan. Actuarial valuations are calculated using the projected benefit method pro-rated on services, based on management's best estimate of the effect of future events (Refer to Note 7).

The Company provides life insurance, medical and dental benefits to eligible retired associates. These benefits are accrued in the year that an associate retires. The accumulated obligation as at January 1, 1989, for previously retired associates, is being amortized over 10 years beginning January 1, 1989.

Earnings per Share

Earnings per share is calculated based on the weighted average number of shares outstanding during the fiscal year.

2. CHARGE ACCOUNT RECEIVABLES

Details of charge account receivables are as follows:

(in millions)	1997	1996
Charge account receivables	$ 1,655.7	$ 1,568.5
Less: amounts securitized	(965.6)	(961.2)
Net charge account receivables	$ 690.1	$ 607.3

3. OTHER RECEIVABLES

Other receivables consist of the following:

(in millions)	1997	1996
Deferred receivables	$ 497.4	$ 456.1
Less: amounts securitized	(24.4)	(97.6)
Net deferred receivables	473.0	358.5
Miscellaneous receivables	61.5	67.2
Total	$ 534.5	$ 425.7

4. INVESTMENTS AND OTHER ASSETS

(in millions)	1997	1996
Unsecured debentures	$ 20.1	$ 20.1
Subordinated loans	2.2	9.0
Other	0.5	0.5
Total	$ 22.8	$ 29.6

Unsecured debentures in the amount of $14.1 million and $6.0 million are due in 2010 and 2011 respectively. Subordinated loans are due in 2006. All bear interest at floating rates.

5. NET CAPITAL ASSETS

Capital assets are summarized as follows:

(in millions)	1997	1996
Land	$ 68.1	$ 65.8
Buildings and improvements	561.3	524.5
– held by joint ventures	266.6	256.2
Equipment and fixtures	694.7	598.2
Gross capital assets	$ 1,590.7	$ 1,444.7
Accumulated depreciation		
Buildings and improvements	276.6	261.8
– held by joint ventures	41.5	36.3
Equipment and fixtures	447.5	402.2
Total accumulated depreciation	765.6	700.3
Net capital assets	$ 825.1	$ 744.4

The carrying values of land and buildings are evaluated by management on an ongoing basis as to their net recoverable amounts. This is a function of their average remaining useful lives, market valuations, cash flows and capitalization rate models. Situations giving rise to a shortfall in the net recoverable amounts are assessed as either temporary or permanent declines in the carrying values; permanent declines are adjusted. Management does not foresee adjustments in the near term.

Notes to Consolidated Financial Statements *continued*

6. DEFERRED CHARGES

(in millions)	1997	1996
Excess of pension contributions over amounts expensed, including contributions for post retirement benefits of $3.1 million ($4.8 million – 1996)	$ 107.5	$ 117.0
Deferred consulting fees	0.7	4.4
Tenant allowances for proportionate interests in joint ventures	9.4	8.5
Debt issuance and securitization set up costs	6.2	6.6
Other deferred charges	11.6	11.7
Total deferred charges	$ 135.4	$ 148.2

7. PENSION PLAN

Selected financial information relating to the Company's pension plan is summarized as follows:

(in millions)	1997	1996
Pension plan assets at market value	$ 1,137.8	$ 1,015.0
Present value of accrued pension obligations	$ 697.1	$ 701.0

8. LONG-TERM OBLIGATIONS

(in millions)	1997	1996
Unsecured Debentures:		
9.25% due February 26, 1997	$ -	$ 100.0
11.00% due May 18, 1999	150.0	150.0
11.70% due July 10, 2000	100.0	100.0
8.25% due December 11, 2000	125.0	125.0
7.80% due March 1, 2001	100.0	100.0
6.55% due November 5, 2007	125.0	-
Proportionate share of long-term debt of joint ventures with a weighted average interest rate of 9.0% due 1998 to 2013	229.8	223.2
Capital lease obligations: interest rates from 8.0 % to 17.0%	17.9	19.2
	847.7	817.4
Less principal payments due within one year included in current liabilities	11.6	183.2
Total long-term obligations	$ 836.1	$ 634.2

The Company's proportionate share of the long-term debt of joint ventures is secured by the shopping malls owned by the joint ventures and, in some cases, guaranteed by the Company. The Company's total principal payments due within one year include $10.5 million ($81.8 million – 1996) of the proportionate share of the current debt obligations of joint ventures.

Principal Payments

For fiscal years subsequent to the fiscal year ended January 3, 1998, principal payments required on the Company's total long-term obligations are as follows:

(in millions)		
1998	$	11.6
1999		158.7
2000		253.7
2001		134.3
2002		33.4
Subsequent years		256.0
Total debt outstanding	$	847.7

Significant Financing Transactions

On January 5, 1996, Sears Canada Inc. issued $100.0 million of 7.8% unsecured debentures due March 1, 2001.

On April 1, 1996, the outstanding 15.125% Series V secured debentures of Sears Acceptance Company Inc. ("Acceptance"), a wholly owned subsidiary of Sears Canada Inc., in the amount of $66.4 million matured.

On October 22, 1996, Sears Canada Receivables Trust – 1996 (Trust 3) was created. This new financing vehicle allows the Company to securitize charge account receivables, including deferred receivables.

On February 26, 1997, the outstanding 9.25% unsecured debentures of Sears Canada Inc. in the amount of $100.0 million matured.

On November 5, 1997, Sears Canada Inc. issued $125.0 million of 6.55% unsecured debentures, due November 5, 2007.

During 1997, long-term financing for new capital projects of real estate joint ventures was obtained in the amount of $9.9 million. In addition, $81.8 million of joint venture debt matured in 1997, of which $78.5 million was refinanced.

9. CAPITAL STOCK

An unlimited number of common shares are authorized. Changes in the number of outstanding common shares and their stated values since December 31, 1995 are as follows:

	1997		1996	
	Number of shares	Stated value (millions)	Number of shares	Stated value (millions)
Beginning Balance	105,610,910	$ 448.3	94,946,372	$ 342.0
Issued pursuant to stock options	348,594	2.6	340,728	2.4
Issuance of shares	–	–	10,323,810	103.9
Ending Balance	105,959,504	$ 450.9	105,610,910	$ 448.3

As at January 3, 1998, details of stock option transactions under stock option plans are as follows.

Options granted and accepted	Option price	Expiry date	Options exercised	Options outstanding
213,125	$ 9.07	Mar. 1997	183,185	–
175,975	$ 5.69	Feb. 1998	148,498	27,477
142,150	$ 7.53	Feb. 1999	97,100	45,050
195,200	$ 7.49	Feb. 2000	135,642	59,558
232,301	$ 5.58	Feb. 2001	174,479	57,822
275,375	$ 5.58	Feb. 2006	30,243	245,132
60,000	$ 9.72	Nov. 2006	–	60,000
286,750	$ 10.65	Jan. 2007	–	286,750
30,000	$ 10.82	Feb. 2007	–	30,000

Options to purchase up to 322,000 common shares have been authorized to be granted under stock option plans in 1998.

The Company is authorized to issue an unlimited number of non-voting, redeemable and retractable Class 1 Preferred Shares in one or more series. As at January 3, 1998, the only shares outstanding were the common shares of the Company.

Notes to Consolidated Financial Statements *continued*

10. UNUSUAL ITEMS

(in millions)	1997	1996
Costs related to the restructuring of business units and processes, including severance	$ -	$ (42.2)
Loss incurred on closure of buildings as a result of operational efficiencies	-	(6.2)
Gain on sale of two service centres	-	3.4
Unusual items	$ -	$ (45.0)

11. INCOME TAXES

The average combined federal and provincial statutory income tax rate, excluding Large Corporations Tax, applicable to the Company was 43.5% for 1997 and 43.2% for 1996.

A reconciliation of income taxes at the average statutory tax rate to actual income taxes is as follows:

(in millions)	1997	1996
Earnings from operations before income taxes	$ 215.2	$ 25.0
Income taxes at average statutory tax rate	93.6	10.8
Increase (decrease) in income taxes resulting from:		
Non-taxable portion of capital gains	(0.1)	(0.1)
Non-deductible items	0.4	0.5
Large Corporations Tax	4.8	5.0
Income taxes	$ 98.7	$ 16.2
Effective tax rate	45.9%	64.8%

12. CHANGES IN WORKING CAPITAL

The cash generated from (used for) working capital is made up of changes in the following accounts:

(in millions)	1997	1996
Other receivables	$ (108.8)	$ 81.9
Short-term deferred income taxes	(1.9)	6.7
Inventories	(149.2)	16.0
Prepaid expenses and other assets	(2.4)	8.6
Accounts payable	87.3	22.9
Accrued liabilities	(6.5)	24.0
Income and other taxes payable	75.0	23.1
Cash generated from (used for) working capital	$ (106.5)	$ 183.2

13. COMMITMENTS

Minimum capital and operating lease payments, exclusive of property taxes, insurance and other expenses payable directly by the Company having an initial term of more than one year as at January 3, 1998 are as follows:

(in millions)	Capital leases	Operating leases
1998	2.9	66.1
1999	2.7	66.8
2000	2.7	63.9
2001	2.7	62.6
2002	2.7	59.8
Subsequent years	16.9	421.6
Minimum lease payments	$ 30.6	$ 740.8
Less imputed interest	12.7	
Total capital lease obligations	$ 17.9	

Total rentals charged to earnings under all operating leases for the year ended January 3, 1998 amounted to $79.4 million ($75.0 million – 1996).

14. SEGMENTED INFORMATION

Segmented Statements of Earnings for the 53 weeks ended January 3, 1998 and the 52 weeks ended December 28, 1996

(in millions)	1997				1996			
			Real Estate Joint				Real Estate Joint	
	Mdse.	Credit	Ventures[2]	Total	Mdse.	Credit	Ventures	Total
Total revenues[1]	$ 4,210.6	$ 310.6	$ 62.3	$ 4,583.5	$ 3,605.7	$ 292.4	$ 57.8	$ 3,955.9
Segment operating profit	141.7	127.5	32.1	301.3	27.0	109.1	30.2	166.3
Interest expense				86.1				96.3
Unusual items				-				45.0
Income taxes				98.7				16.2
Net earnings				$ 116.5				$ 8.8

Segmented Statements of Financial Position as at January 3, 1998 and December 28, 1996

(in millions)	1997				1996			
			Real Estate Joint				Real Estate Joint	
	Mdse.	Credit	Ventures[2]	Total	Mdse.	Credit	Ventures	Total
Assets								
Cash	$ 64.9	$ -	$ 3.4	$ 68.3	$ 199.4	$ -	$ 1.8	$ 201.2
Total receivables	90.9	1,130.3	3.4	1,224.6	83.0	946.5	3.5	1,033.0
Inventories	640.3	-	-	640.3	491.1	-	-	491.1
Net capital assets	568.4	-	256.7	825.1	495.3	-	249.1	744.4
Other	230.5	14.0	4.5	249.0	235.1	22.3	6.9	264.3
Total assets	$ 1,595.0	$ 1,144.3	$ 268.0	$ 3,007.3	$ 1,503.9	$ 968.8	$ 261.3	$ 2,734.0
Liabilities								
Accounts payable	$ 555.2	$ -	$ 5.0	$ 560.2	$ 464.1	$ 1.7	$ 7.1	$ 472.9
Accrued liabilities	294.5	21.8	2.1	318.4	302.2	22.2	0.5	324.9
Other	191.7	31.7	15.2	238.6	151.8	1.3	14.9	168.0
Total liabilities excluding debt	$ 1,041.4	$ 53.5	$ 22.3	$ 1,117.2	$ 918.1	$ 25.2	$ 22.5	$ 965.8
Capital employed	$ 553.6	$ 1,090.8	$ 245.7	$ 1,890.1	$ 585.8	$ 943.6	$ 238.8	$ 1,768.2
Capital expenditures	$ 147.3	$ -	$ 13.1	$ 160.4	$ 62.2	$ -	$ 1.0	$ 63.2
Depreciation and amortization	$ 72.6	$ -	$ 5.5	$ 78.1	$ 71.6	$ -	$ 5.9	$ 77.5

1 The real estate joint venture revenues are net of $3.7 million ($3.6 million – 1996) representing the elimination of rental revenues earned from retail stores. Rental expense of the real estate joint venture segment has been decreased by the same amount having no effect on segment operating profit.

2 The real estate joint ventures had cash generated from operations of $8.7 million ($7.2 million – 1996), cash used for investment activities of $13.9 million ($4.4 million – 1996), and cash used for financing activities of $6.8 million ($3.6 million – 1996).

Notes to Consolidated Financial Statements *continued*

15. RELATED PARTY TRANSACTIONS

Sears, Roebuck and Co. is the beneficial holder of the majority of the outstanding common shares of Sears Canada Inc.

During the year, Sears, Roebuck and Co. charged the Company $5.5 million ($2.6 million – 1996) in the ordinary course of business for shared merchandise purchasing services. These amounts are included in the cost of merchandise sold, operating, administrative and selling expenses.

Sears, Roebuck and Co. charged the Company $18.4 million ($19.2 million – 1996) and the Company charged Sears, Roebuck and Co. $4.6 million ($4.8 million – 1996) for other reimbursements. These reimbursements were primarily in respect of customer cross-border purchases made on the Sears Card, and the Sears, Roebuck and Co. charge card, as well as software and support services.

There were no significant commitments, receivables or payables between the companies at the end of 1997 or 1996.

16. FINANCIAL INSTRUMENTS

In the ordinary course of business, the Company enters into financial agreements with banks and other financial institutions to reduce underlying risks associated with interest rates and foreign currency. The Company does not hold or issue derivative financial instruments for trading or speculative purposes and controls are in place to prevent and detect these activities. The financial instruments do not require the payment of premiums or cash margins prior to settlement. These financial instruments can be summarized as follows:

Foreign Exchange Risk

From time to time the Company enters into foreign exchange contracts to reduce the foreign exchange risk with respect to U.S. dollar denominated goods purchased for resale. There were no such contracts outstanding at the end of 1997 or 1996.

Securitization of Charge Account Receivables

Securitization is an important financial vehicle which provides the Company with access to funds at a low cost. Acceptance sells undivided co-ownership interests in its portfolio of charge account receivables and deferred receivables to independent trusts, collectively referred to as SCRT. Acceptance retains the income generated by the undivided co-ownership interests sold to SCRT in excess of SCRT's stipulated share of service charge revenues (Refer to Notes 2 and 3).

Interest Rate Risk

To manage the Company's exposure to interest rate risks, the Company has entered into interest rate swap contracts with Schedule "A" Banks. Neither the notional principal amounts nor the current replacement value of these financial instruments are carried on the consolidated balance sheet.

As at January 3, 1998, the Company had two interest rate swap contracts in place to reduce the risk associated with variable interest rates associated with the commercial paper issued by Trust 1. For the year ended January 3, 1998, a net interest differential of $13.2 million ($12.8 million – 1996) was paid on the floating-to-fixed interest rate swap contracts and was recorded as an increase of interest expense of the Company.

Credit Risk

The Company's exposure to concentration of credit risk is limited. Accounts receivable are primarily from Sears Card customers, a large and diverse group.

Interest Rate Sensitivity Position

Interest rate risk reflects the sensitivity of the Company's financial condition to movements in interest rates.

The table below identifies the Company's financial assets and liabilities which are sensitive to interest rate movements and those which are non-interest rate sensitive. Financial assets and liabilities which do not bear interest or bear interest at fixed rates are classified as non-interest rate sensitive.

SEARS ♦ CANADA

(in millions)	1997		1996	
	Interest Sensitive	Non-Interest Sensitive	Interest Sensitive	Non-Interest Sensitive
Cash net of bank advances and short-term notes	$ 68.3	$ -	$ 199.1	$ -
Investments and other assets	$ 22.8	$ -	$ 29.6	$ -
Total receivables	$ -	$ 1,224.6	$ -	$ 1,033.0
Long-term obligations (including current portion)³	$ (33.7)	$ (814.0)	$ (179.9)	$ (637.5)
Net balance sheet interest rate sensitivity position	$ 57.4	$ 410.6	$ 48.8	$ 395.5

3 Interest sensitive portion includes long-term prime-rate based debt and current portion of long-term debt due to be renegotiated.

In addition to the net balance sheet interest rate sensitivity position, the Company is also affected by interest rate sensitive debt outstanding in SCRT. Any change in short-term interest rates will impact floating rate debt and debt with maturities of less than one year held by SCRT, which totaled $811.1 million at January 3, 1998 ($726.6 million at December 28, 1996). An increase in the cost of this off-balance sheet debt will result in a decrease in the Company's share of service charge revenues. This interest rate exposure is offset by interest rate swap contracts held by the Company in the notional amount of $200 million ($250 million – 1996).

Fair Value of Financial Instruments

The estimated fair values of financial instruments as at January 3, 1998 and December 28, 1996 are based on relevant market prices and information available at that time. As a significant number of the Company's assets and liabilities, including inventory and capital assets, do not meet the definition of financial instruments, the fair value estimates below do not reflect the fair value of the Company as a whole.

Carrying value approximates fair value for financial instruments which are short-term in nature. These include cash and short-term investments, charge account receivables, other receivables, prepaid expenses and other assets, bank advances and short-term notes, accounts payable, income and other taxes payable, and principal payments on long-term obligations due within one year. For financial instruments which are long-term in nature, fair value estimates are as follows:

(in millions)	1997		1996	
	Carrying or Notional Amount	Fair Value	Carrying or Notional Amount	Fair Value
Financial Assets and Liabilities				
Investments and other assets	$ 22.8	$ 22.8	$ 29.6	$ 29.6
Long-term obligations	$ (836.1)	$ (895.7)	$ (634.2)	$ (713.9)
Off-Balance Sheet Interest Rate Swaps				
9.32%, expiring April 1997	$ -	$ -	$ 50.0	$ (1.5)
9.40%, expiring April 1999	$ 100.0	$ (6.4)	$ 100.0	$ (12.1)
9.54%, expiring April 2002	$ 100.0	$ (16.5)	$ 100.0	$ (19.1)
	$ 200.0	$ (22.9)	$ 250.0	$ (32.7)

The fair value of investments and other assets and long-term obligations was estimated based on quoted market prices, when available, or discounted cash flows using discount rates based on market interest rates and the Company's credit rating. As long-term debt coupon rates are higher than current market interest rates, the fair value of the Company's long-term debt exceeds its carrying value.

The fair value of the interest rate swap contracts was estimated by referring to the appropriate yield curves with matching terms of maturity. A negative fair value reflects the estimated amount that the Company would pay to terminate the contracts at the reporting date.

Corporate Governance

In December, 1994, the Report of The Toronto Stock Exchange Committee on Corporate Governance in Canada recommended 14 guidelines for improved corporate governance which were adopted by the Montreal Exchange and The Toronto Stock Exchange.

The Corporation has considered the TSE Report and these guidelines in developing and formalizing its corporate governance practices. A Statement of Corporate Governance Practices has been prepared in accordance with the requirements of the Exchanges and is contained in the Management Proxy Circular of the Corporation.

The Board of Directors is responsible to oversee the business and affairs of the Corporation and to act with a view to the best interests of the Corporation, providing guidance and direction to the management of the Corporation in order to attain corporate objectives and maximize shareholder value.

The Board of Directors and the Audit and Corporate Governance, Compensation, and Nominating Committees of the Board are each responsible for certain corporate governance functions in accordance with their respective mandates. The Audit and Corporate Governance Committee is responsible for monitoring and guiding the corporate governance approach and practices of the Corporation.

Directors and Officers (as at January 3, 1998)

SEARS ♦ CANADA

Board of Directors

Jalynn H. Bennett ♦
President, Jalynn H. Bennett and Associates Ltd.

James R. Clifford ♦
President and Chief Operating Officer, Sears Canada Inc.

Gary L. Crittenden ♦
Executive Vice President and Chief Financial Officer,
Sears, Roebuck and Co.

William A. Dimma ♦●
Corporate Director

Jeanne E. Lougheed ■
Corporate Director

Arthur C. Martinez ■
Chairman of the Board, President and Chief Executive Officer,
Sears, Roebuck and Co.

James W. Moir, Jr. ●
President and Chief Executive Officer,
Maritime Medical Care Inc.

Alfred Powis ♦■●
Corporate Director

Anthony J. Rucci ■
Executive Vice President, Administration,
Sears, Roebuck and Co.

James M. Tory ♦■
Partner, Tory Tory DesLauriers & Binnington,
Barristers & Solicitors

Paul S. Walters ■●
Chairman of the Board and Chief Executive Officer,
Sears Canada Inc.

Committees

■ Compensation   ♦ Audit and Corporate Governance   ● Nominating
J.R. Clifford and P.S. Walters are ex officio members of the Nominating Committee.

Honorary Directors

James W. Button
Former Senior Executive Vice President
of Merchandising, Sears, Roebuck and Co.

C. Richard Sharpe
Former Chairman of the Board and Chief Executive Officer,
Sears Canada Inc.

Officers

Paul S. Walters
Chairman of the Board and Chief Executive Officer

James R. Clifford
President and Chief Operating Officer

Patricia E. Beaudoin
Senior Vice-President, Human Resources

H. Ray Bird
Senior Vice-President, Credit

John T. Butcher
Senior Vice-President and Chief Financial Officer

Brent V. Hollister
Executive Vice-President, Sales and Service

Richard W. Sorby
Executive Vice-President, Marketing

William R. Turner
Executive Vice-President, Merchandising and Logistics

Rudolph R. Vezér
Senior Vice-President, Secretary and General Counsel

Corporate Information

Head Office
Sears Canada Inc.
222 Jarvis Street
Toronto, Ontario
Canada M5B 2B8

Transfer Agent and Registrar
CIBC Mellon Trust Company
Toronto, Ontario
Montreal, Quebec

Answerline: (416) 643-5500 or 1-800-387-0825

Internet Address: www.cibcmellon.ca (website) or
inquiries@cibcmellon.ca (e-mail)

Listings
The Montreal Exchange
The Toronto Stock Exchange

Trading Symbol
SCC

Annual and Special Meeting
The Annual and Special Meeting of Shareholders of
Sears Canada Inc. will be held on Monday, April 20, 1998 at
10:00 a.m. in the Burton-Wood Auditorium
Main Floor
222 Jarvis Street
Toronto, Ontario, Canada

Édition française du Rapport annuel
On peut se procurer l'édition française de ce
rapport en écrivant au:

S/703, Relations publiques
Sears Canada Inc.
222 Jarvis Street
Toronto, Ontario
Canada M5B 2B8

Pour de plus amples renseignements au sujet de la
Société, veuillez écrire au Service des relations
publiques, ou composer le (416) 941-4425

For More Information
Additional copies of the Annual Report can be obtained through the
Public Affairs Department at the Head Office of Sears Canada Inc.

For more information about the Company, write to
Public Affairs, or call (416) 941-4425

Internet Address: www.sears.ca (website) or enquiries:
home@sears.ca

Produced by Sears Canada Inc.
Public Affairs

Design by Compendium Design International Inc.

Photography of Chairman of the Board by Christopher Campbell,
Publication: Canadian Retailer.

Printed in Canada by Kempenfelt Graphics Group Inc.

Front cover: Fashions by Jones Studio
Back cover: Fashions by Nygard Collection

Certain brands mentioned in this report are the trademarks of Sears
Canada Inc., Sears, Roebuck and Co., or used under license. Others are
the property of their owner.

Appendix D: The Basics

1. Accounting Equation:

Assets = Liabilities + Owner's Equity

2. T Account:

Account Title	
Left Side debit	Right Side credit

3 Rules of Debit and Credit:

Balance Sheet Accounts

ASSETS		LIABILITIES	
Asset Accounts		Liability Accounts	
Debit for increases	Credit for decreases	Debit for decreases	Credit for increases

OWNER'S EQUITY

Owner's Equity Accounts

Debit for decreases	Credit for increases

Income Statement Accounts

Debit for decreases in owner's equity Expense Accounts		Credit for increases in owner's equity Revenue Accounts	
Debit for increases	Credit for decreases	Debit for decreases	Credit for increases

Normal Balance

4. To Analyze a Transaction:

1. Determine whether an asset, a liability, owner's equity, revenue, or expense account is affected by the transaction.
2. For each account affected by the transaction, determine whether the account increases or decreases.
3. Determine whether each increase or decrease should be recorded as a debit or a credit.

5. Financial Statements:

INCOME STATEMENT
   A summary of the revenue and the expenses of a business entity for a specific period of time, such as a month or a year.

STATEMENT OF OWNER'S EQUITY
   A summary of the changes in the owner's equity of a business entity that have occurred during a specific period of time, such as a month or a year.

BALANCE SHEET
   A list of the assets, liabilities, and owner's equity of a business entity as of a specific date, usually at the close of the last day of a month or a year.

STATEMENT OF CASH FLOWS
   A summary of the cash receipts and cash payments of a business entity for a specific period of time, such as a month or a year.

6. Accounting Cycle:

1. Analyze and record transactions in journal.
2. Post transactions to ledger.
3. Prepare trial balance, assemble adjustment data, and complete work sheet.
4. Prepare financial statements.
5. Journalize and post adjusting entries.
6. Journalize and post closing entries.
7. Prepare post-closing trial balance.

7. Types of Adjusting Entries:

1. Deferred expense (prepaid expense)
2. Deferred revenue (unearned revenue)
3. Accrued expense (accrued liability)
4. Accrued revenue (accrued asset)
5. Amortization expense

Each entry will always affect both a balance sheet and an income statement account.

8. Closing Entries:

1. Transfer revenue account balances to Income Summary.
2. Transfer expense account balances to Income Summary.
3. Transfer Income Summary balance to Capital.
4. Transfer withdrawals account balance to Capital.

9. Special Journals:

Rendering of services
   on account ⟶ recorded in ⟶ Revenue (sales) journal
Receipt of cash from
   any source ⟶ recorded in ⟶ Cash receipts journal
Purchase of items
   on account ⟶ recorded in ⟶ Purchases journal
Payments of cash for
   any purpose ⟶ recorded in ⟶ Cash disbursements journal

10. Shipping Terms:

	FOB Shipping Point	FOB Destination
Ownership (title) passes to buyer when inventory is	delivered to freight carrier	delivered to buyer
Transportation costs are paid by	buyer	seller

11. Format for Bank Reconciliation:

Cash balance according to bank statement		$xxx
Add: Additions by depositor not on bank		
statement	$xx	
Bank errors	xx	xx
		$xxx
Deduct: Deductions by depositor not on bank		
statement	$xx	
Bank errors	xx	xx
Adjusted balance		$xxx
Cash balance according to depositor's records		$xxx
Add: Additions by bank not recorded by depositor ..	$xx	
Depositor errors...	xx	xx
		$xxx
Deduct: Deductions by bank not recorded		
by depositor	$xx	
Depositor errors...	xx	xx
Adjusted balance...		$xxx

12. Inventory Costing Methods:

1. First-in, First-out (FIFO)
2. Last-in, First-out (LIFO)
3. Average Cost

13. Interest Payment Computations:

$$\text{Interest Payment} =$$
$$\text{Face Amount (or Principal)} \times \text{Stated Rate} \times \text{Time}$$

14. Effective Interest Method:

$$\text{Interest Expense} =$$
$$\text{Carrying Value (present value)} \times \text{Effective Rate} \times \text{Time}$$

15. Methods of Determining Annual Amortization:

STRAIGHT-LINE: $\dfrac{\text{Cost} - \text{Estimated Residual Value}}{\text{Estimated Life}}$

DECLINING-BALANCE: Rate* × Book Value at Beginning of Period

*Double-declining rate is twice the straight-line rate (1 ÷ Estimated Life).

16. Cash Provided by Operations on Statement of Cash Flows (indirect method):

Net income, per income statement			$xx
Add: Amortization of capital assets		$xx	
Decreases in current assets (receivables,			
inventories, prepaid expenses)..............		xx	
Increases in current liabilities (accounts			
and notes payable, accrued liabilities) ..		xx	
Losses on disposal of assets and retirement			
of debt		xx	xx
Deduct: Increases in current assets (receivables,			
inventories, prepaid expenses)..............		$xx	
Decreases in current liabilities			
(accounts and notes payable,			
accrued liabilities)		xx	
Gains on disposal of assets and			
retirement of debt		xx	xx
Net cash flow from operating activities.................			$xx

Appendix E: Abbreviations and Acronyms Commonly Used in Business and Accounting

ASB	Accounting Standards Board
CA	Chartered Accountant
CAAA	Canadian Academic Accounting Association
CBCA	Canada Business Corporations Act
CCA	Capital cost allowance
CEO	Chief Executive Officer
CGAAC	Certified General Accountants Association of Canada
CGA	Certified General Accountant
CIA	Certified Internal Auditor
CICA	Canadian Institute of Chartered Accountants
CMA	Certified Management Accountant
CPP	Canada Pension Plan
Cr.	Credit
Dr.	Debit
EFT	Electronic funds transfer
EHT	Employment Health Tax
EI	Employment Insurance
EPS	Earnings per share
FASB	Financial Accounting Standards Board
FIFO	First-in, first-out
FOB	Free on board
GAAP	Generally accepted accounting principles
GST	Goods and Services Tax
HST	Harmonized Sales Tax
IASC	International Accounting Standards Committee
IIA	Institute of Internal Auditors
LIFO	Last-in, first-out
LCM	Lower of cost and market
n/30	Net 30
n/eom	Net, end-of-month
NBV	Net book value
NSF	Not sufficient funds
P/E Ratio	Price-earnings ratio
POS	Point of sale
PST	Provincial Sales Tax
ROI	Return on investment
SMAC	Society of Management Accountants of Canada
UCC	Undepreciated capital cost
WC	Workers' Compensation

Appendix F: Classification of Accounts

Account Title	Account Classification	Normal Balance	Financial Statement
Accounts Payable	Current liability	Credit	Balance sheet
Accounts Receivable	Current asset	Debit	Balance sheet
Accumulated Amortization	Capital asset	Credit	Balance sheet
Accumulated Depletion	Capital asset	Credit	Balance sheet
Advertising Expense	Operating expense	Debit	Income statement
Allowance for Doubtful Accounts	Current asset	Credit	Balance sheet
Amortization Expense	Operating expense	Debit	Income statement
Appropriation for _____	Shareholders' equity	Credit	Retained earnings statement/ Balance sheet
Bonds Payable	Long-term liability	Credit	Balance sheet
Building	Capital asset	Debit	Balance sheet
Canada Pension Plan Payable	Current liability	Credit	Balance sheet
_____ Capital	Owners' equity	Credit	Statement of owner's equity/ Balance sheet
Capital Stock	Shareholders' equity	Credit	Balance sheet
Cash	Current asset	Debit	Balance sheet
Common Shares	Shareholders' equity	Credit	Balance sheet
Cost of Goods Sold	Cost of goods sold	Debit	Income statement
Depletion Expense	Operating expense	Debit	Income statement
Discount on Bonds Payable	Long-term liability	Debit	Balance sheet
Dividend Income	Other income	Credit	Income statement
Dividends	Shareholders' equity	Debit	Retained earnings statement
Dividends Payable	Current liability	Credit	Balance sheet
Donated Capital	Shareholders' equity	Credit	Balance sheet
Employees Income Tax Payable	Current liability	Credit	Balance sheet
Employment Health Tax Payable	Current liability	Credit	Balance sheet
Employment Insurance Payable	Current liability	Credit	Balance sheet
Equipment	Capital asset	Debit	Balance sheet
Future tax asset	Current asset/Long-term asset	Debit	Balance sheet
Future tax liability	Current liability/Long-term liability	Credit	Balance sheet
Gain on Disposal of Capital Assets	Other income	Credit	Income statement
Gain on Sale of Investments	Other income	Credit	Income statement
Goodwill	Intangible capital asset	Debit	Balance sheet
GST Payable	Current liability	Credit	Balance sheet
HST Payable	Current liability	Credit	Balance sheet
Income Tax Expense	Income tax	Debit	Income statement
Income Tax Payable	Current liability	Credit	Balance sheet
Insurance Expense	Operating expense	Debit	Income statement
Interest Expense	Other expense	Debit	Income statement
Interest Income	Other income	Credit	Income statement
Interest Payable	Current liability	Credit	Balance sheet
Interest Receivable	Current asset	Debit	Balance sheet
Inventory	Current asset	Debit	Balance sheet
Investment in Bonds	Long-term asset	Debit	Balance sheet
Investment in Shares	Long-term asset	Debit	Balance sheet
Land	Capital asset	Debit	Balance sheet
Lease Liability	Current liability/Long-term liability	Credit	Balance sheet
Leased Asset	Capital asset	Debit	Balance sheet
Loss on Disposal of Capital Assets	Other expense	Debit	Income statement
Loss on Sale of Investments	Other expense	Debit	Income statement
Marketable Securities	Current asset	Debit	Balance sheet
Notes Payable	Current liability/Long-term liability	Credit	Balance sheet
Notes Receivable	Current asset/Long-term asset	Debit	Balance sheet

Account Title	Account Classification	Normal Balance	Financial Statement
Organization Costs	Intangible capital asset	Debit	Balance sheet
Patents	Intangible capital asset	Debit	Balance sheet
Payroll Tax Expense	Operating expense	Debit	Income statement
Pension Expense	Operating expense	Debit	Income statement
Pension Liability	Long-term liability	Credit	Balance sheet
Petty Cash	Current asset	Debit	Balance sheet
Preferred Shares	Shareholders' equity	Credit	Balance sheet
Premium on Bonds Payable	Long-term liability	Credit	Balance sheet
Prepaid Insurance	Current asset	Debit	Balance sheet
Prepaid Rent	Current asset	Debit	Balance sheet
Prepaid Pension Cost	Long-term (other) asset	Debit	Balance sheet
PST Payable	Current liability	Credit	Balance sheet
Purchases	Cost of goods sold	Debit	Income statement
Purchases Discounts	Cost of goods sold	Credit	Income statement
Purchases Returns and Allowances	Cost of goods sold	Credit	Income statement
Rent Expense	Operating expense	Debit	Income statement
Rent Income	Other income	Credit	Income statement
Retained Earnings	Shareholders' equity	Credit	Balance sheet/Retained earnings statement
Salaries Expense	Operating expense	Debit	Income statement
Salaries Payable	Current liability	Credit	Balance sheet
Sales	Revenue from sales	Credit	Income statement
Sales Discounts	Revenue from sales	Debit	Income statement
Sales Returns and Allowances	Revenue from sales	Debit	Income statement
Sales Tax Payable	Current liability	Credit	Balance sheet
Sinking Fund Cash	Long-term asset	Debit	Balance sheet
Sinking Fund Investments	Long-term asset	Debit	Balance sheet
Stock Dividends	Shareholders' equity	Debit	Retained earnings statement
Stock Dividends Distributable	Shareholders' equity	Credit	Balance sheet
Supplies	Current asset	Debit	Balance sheet
Supplies Expense	Operating expense	Debit	Income statement
Transportation In	Cost of goods sold	Debit	Income statement
Transportation Out	Operating expense	Debit	Income statement
Uncollectible Accounts Expense	Operating expense	Debit	Income statement
Unearned Rent	Current liability	Credit	Balance sheet
Utilities Expense	Operating expense	Debit	Income statement
Utilities Payable	Current liability	Credit	Balance sheet
Vacation Pay Expense	Operating expense	Debit	Income statement
Vacation Pay Payable	Current liability/Long-term liability	Credit	Balance sheet
Workers' Compensation Payable	Current liability	Credit	Balance sheet

Glossary

Accounts receivable turnover. Net credit sales divided by average accounts receivable. (677)

Acid-test (quick) ratio. Quick assets divided by current liabilities. (677)

Adverse audit opinion. Audit report indicating that the auditor believes that the financial statements are not presented fairly in accordance with generally accepted accounting principles. (688)

Annuity. A series of equal cash flows at fixed intervals. (565)

Appropriation. The amount of a corporation's retained earnings that has been restricted and therefore is not available for distribution to shareholders as dividends. (533)

Bearer bond. Bond that is unregistered and payable to whomever is holding the bond. (563)

Bond. A form of note employed by corporations to borrow on a long-term basis. (560)

Bond indenture. The contract between a corporation issuing bonds and the bondholders. (562)

Callable bond. Bond that may be redeemed before maturity at the option of the issuer in accordance with the conditions specified in the bond indenture. (563)

Capital transaction. Transaction involving the firm's own shares. (521)

Carrying value. The amount at which a long-term investment or a long-term liability is reported on the balance sheet (face value less any unamortized discount or plus any unamortized premium); also called basis or book value. (570)

Cash. Cash on hand and demand deposits, coins, currency (paper money), cheques, traveller's cheques, money orders, and money on deposit that is available for unrestricted withdrawal from banks or other financial institutions. (613)

Cash dividend. A cash distribution of earnings by a corporation to its shareholders. (523)

Cash equivalents. Short-term, highly liquid non-equity investments that are readily convertible to cash and subject to an insignificant risk of changes in value. (613)

Cash flows from financing activities. The section of the statement of cash flows that reports cash flows from transactions affecting the equity and long-term debt of the entity. (613)

Cash flows from investing activities. The section of the statement of cash flows that reports cash flows from transactions affecting investments in noncurrent assets. (613)

Cash flows from operating activities. The section of the statement of cash flows that reports the cash transactions derived from the principal revenue-generating activities of the firm. (613)

Common shares. The basic ownership class of a corporation. (517)

Common-size statement. Financial statement in which all items are expressed in percentages. (674)

Contract rate. The interest rate specified on a bond that determines the interest payments each period; also called the coupon rate, stated rate, or nominal rate. (566)

Contributed surplus. Account(s) where we record contributions to equity arising from capital transactions other than the issuance of shares. (515)

Convertible bond. Bond that can be exchanged for shares at the option of the investor in accordance with the conditions specified in the bond indenture. (563)

Cumulative preferred shares. Preferred shares entitled to current and past dividends before dividends may be paid on common shares. (518)

Current position analysis. Analysis to assess the ability of a business to pay its current liabilities. (675)

Current (working capital) ratio. Current assets divided by current liabilities. (676)

Debenture. Unsecured bond backed only by the general creditworthiness of the issuing company. (563)

Deficiency. The debit balance in the owner's equity account of a partner. (494)

Deficit. A debit balance in the retained earnings account. (515)

Defined benefit pension plan. Pension plan that specifies either the benefits to be received by retired employees or the formula for determining those benefits. (584)

Defined contribution pension plan. Pension plan that specifies the amount that an employer must contribute to the pension plan during the employee's working life, but does not specify pension benefits to be paid during the employee's retirement. (584)

Denial of opinion. Audit report indicating that the auditor has been unable to gather sufficient appropriate evidence to form an opinion as to whether the financial statements are presented fairly and in accordance with generally accepted accounting principles. (688)

Direct method. A method of reporting the cash flows from operating activities as the difference between the operating cash receipts and the operating cash payments. (614)

Discontinued operations. The operations of a business segment that has been sold, abandoned, spun off, or otherwise disposed of, or is the subject of a formal plan for disposal. (528)

Discount on bonds payable. The excess of the face amount of bonds over their issue price. (566)

Dividend yield. Dividends per share divided by market price per share. (684)

Dividends per common share. Common dividends divided by average number of common shares outstanding during the period. (684)

Earnings per share. The net income available to common shareholders divided by the weighted average number of common shares outstanding during the year. (531)

Effective interest rate method. Method that calculates interest each period by multiplying the historical market rate times the carrying value of the long-term liability or long-term investment. (569)

Extraordinary item. A significant gain or loss that has all of the following characteristics: occurs infrequently, does not arise from normal business operations, and is not the result of management decisions or determinations. (528)

Fully diluted earnings per share. Earnings per share figure showing maximum dilution of current earnings if potential conversions had taken place during the period. (532)

Future tax asset. Future income tax deduction, arising from temporary differences that caused an excess of taxable income over pretax accounting income in an earlier period. (586)

Future tax liability. Future income taxes that will have to be paid, arising from temporary differences that caused an excess of pretax accounting income over taxable income in an earlier period. (585)

Historical summary. Section usually included in the annual report disclosing selected financial and operating data of past periods. (689)

Horizontal analysis. Percentage analysis of increases and decreases in related terms in comparative financial statements of two or more years. (670)

Indirect method. A method of reporting the cash flows from operating activities as the net income from operations adjusted for all deferrals of past cash receipts and payments and all accruals of expected future cash receipts and payments. (614)

Inventory turnover. Cost of goods sold divided by average inventory. (678)

Leverage. Difference between the rate earned on shareholders' equity and the rate earned on total assets. (682)

Liquidating dividend. A distribution out of paid-in capital when a corporation permanently reduces its operations or winds up its affairs completely. (527)

Liquidation of a partnership. The winding-up process when a partnership goes out of business. (491)

Management report. Statement by management usually included in the annual report accepting responsibility for preparation of the financial statements and commenting on internal control and other related matters. (687)

Market rate. The rate of interest which investors use to compute the present value of an investment such as a bond or note; also called the effective or yield rate. (566)

No par value share. Share with no monetary amount stated on the share certificate. (516)

Nonparticipating preferred shares. Preferred shares with a limited dividend preference. (517)

Number of days' sales in inventory. Inventory divided by average daily cost of sales. (679)

Number of days' sales in receivables. Accounts receivable divided by average daily credit sales. (678)

Number of times interest charges earned. Income before tax and interest expense divided by interest expense. (680)

Outstanding shares. The shares that are in the hands of shareholders. (516)

Owner's equity. The rights of the owner to the residual assets in a business left over after creditors have been paid. (11)

Paid-in capital. Share capital plus contributed surplus. (516)

Par value share. Share with a monetary amount stated on the share certificate. (516)

Partnership. An unincorporated business wherein two or more persons carry on a business together for profit. (481)

Partnership agreement. The formal written contract creating a partnership. (482)

Preemptive right. The right of each shareholder to maintain the same fractional interest in the corporation by purchasing shares of any additional issuances. (516)

Preferred shares. A class of shares with preferential rights over common shares. (517)

Premium. The excess of the issue price of bonds over the face amount. (569)

Present value. The estimated present worth of an amount of cash to be received (or paid) in the future. (564)

Present value of an annuity. The sum of the present values of a series of equal cash flows to be received at fixed intervals. (566)

Price-earnings ratio. Market price per share divided by earnings per share. (684)

Profitability. Ability of a firm to earn income. (675)

Qualified audit opinion. Audit report that is qualified because the financial statements do not conform with generally acceptable accounting principles or because the auditor has been unable to carry out all the tests necessary in the circumstances. (688)

Quick assets. Cash and other current assets (such as marketable securities and receivables) that can be readily converted to cash. (677)

Rate earned on common shareholders' equity. Income available to common shareholders divided by average number of common shares outstanding during the period. (683)

Rate earned on shareholders' equity. Net income divided by average total shareholders' equity. (682)

Rate earned on total assets. Net income plus interest expense (net of tax) divided by average total assets. (681)

Ratio of capital assets to long-term liabilities. Net capital assets divided by long-term liabilities. (679)

Ratio of liabilities to shareholders' equity. Total liabilities divided by total shareholders' equity. (687)

Ratio of net sales to assets. Net sales divided by total assets excluding long-term investments. (681)

Realization (in a parternship). The sale of assets when a partnership is being liquidated. (491)

Refundable deposits. Security or container deposits that the business intends to return to customers in the future. (438)

Registered bond. Bond whose owner is recorded in a registry kept by the issuing company, so that the issuer makes payments of interest and principal only to that party. (563)

Related party transaction. Transaction in which one of the parties involved has the ability to significantly influence the action of the other party. (691)

Retained earnings. Net income retained in a corporation. (515)

Retroactive adjustment. An adjustment to the opening balance of retained earnings reflecting the cumulative effect on prior years' income of a current change in an accounting policy. (535)

Secured bond. Bond backed by specific assets pledged as collateral by the issuing company. (563)

Segmented information. Data, often presented in the notes to the financial statements, which discloses information about the operating activities and assets of various segments of a business. (693)

Serial bonds. An issue of bonds whose maturities are spread over several dates. (563)

Share capital. Account where we record the amount assigned to shares when they are issued. (515)

Shareholders. The owners of a corporation. (513)

Shareholders' equity. The equity of the shareholders in a corporation. (515)

Sinking fund. Assets set aside in a special fund to be used for a specific purpose. (577)

Solvency. Ability of a business to meet its financial obligations as they come due. (675)

Statement of cash flows. A summary of the major cash receipts and cash payments for a period. (612)

Stock dividend. Distribution of a company's own shares as a dividend to its shareholders. (524)

Stock split. The issuance of a proportionate number of additional shares to existing shareholders in order to reduce the market value per share. (522)

Stock (shares). Shares of ownership of a corporation. (513)

Straight-line amortization method. A method that provides for equal periodic amortization expense over the estimated life of an asset. (569)

Subsequent events. Events, which occur or become known after the close of the fiscal period, that could have a significant effect on the financial statements. (694)

Taxable income. Income calculated in accordance with the rules of the Income Tax Act and used as the basis for computing taxes payable. (585)

Temporary differences. Differences between taxable income and pretax accounting income because some items of revenue and/or expense are recognized in a different period for computing taxable income than they are recognized in the income statement. (585)

Term bonds. An issue of bonds that all mature at the same date. (563)

Treasury shares. Shares repurchased by a company and held for resale. (521)

Underwriter. Securities firm that sells bonds on behalf on an issuing company. (560)

Unqualified (clean) audit opinion. Auditor's report that concludes that financial statements are presented fairly and in accordance with generally acceptable accounting principles. (688)

Unusual item. Material, atypical and infrequent gain or loss, which meets some, but not all of the criteria to be classified as an extraordinary item. (529)

Vertical analysis. Percentage analysis to show the relationship of each component to the total in a single statement. States each item on the balance sheet as a percentage of total assets and each item on the income statement as a percentage of sales. (673)

Working capital. Excess of current assets over current liabilities. (676)

Index

INDEX OF REAL COMPANIES

Photo Credits

Check Figures for Selected Problems

Problem	Check Figure
12–1A	3. Ending capital, Tsao, $40,000
12–2A	Plan e (1) Haddox, $87,000
12–3A	2. Total capital, $205,000
12–4A	3. Total assets, $232,600
12–5A	Receipt of deficiency—Crowder, $4,600
12–1B	2. Total assets, $116,000
12–2B	Plan f (1) Driscoe, $54,000
12–3B	2. Total capital, $162,000
12–4B	3. May 1, 20—, Denny capital, $90,060
12–5B	Receipt of deficiency, Owen, $5,100
13–1A	1. 1995 Preferred $84,000, Common 0
13–2A	Total shareholders' equity, $3,145,000
13–3A	2. Common shares, June 30, 1999, $692,800
13–4A	3. Total shareholders' equity, $2,784,840
13–6A	Unappropriated retained earnings, $575,000
13–1B	1. 1998 Preferred: $21,000, Common, $54,000
13–2B	2. Total shareholders' equity, $3,871,000
13–3B	3. Unappropriated retained earnings, $2,046,500
13–4B	3. Total paid-in capital, $1,242,600
13–6B	July 23 stock dividend, $3,618
CP13–1	Opening common shares, $4,961,000
14–1A	1. EPS Plan 2, $3.60
14–2A	1. Issue price of bonds, $8,297,750
14–5A	1. April 1 total cash proceeds, $1,011,667
14–6A	October 31, 2004—loss on sale, $2,304
14–7A	1. Lease liability January 1, $132,484
14–1B	1. EPS Plan 3, $5.12
14–2B	2a. Interest expense, $416,018
14–3B	3b. Carrying value June 30, 2000, $13,968,883

Problem	Check Figure
14–4B	December 31, 2001 interest expense, $78,298
14–5B	March 31, 2000—conversion rights, $85,000
14–6B	July 31, 2006, loss on recall of bonds, $2,534
14–7B	Amortization expense December 31, $23,062
CP14–2	g. Interest expense, $27,937
Comp. Prob.	2c. Total assets, $8,993,845
15–1A	Net cash flows from operations, $87,900
15–2A	Net cash flows from investing, ($120,100)
15–3A	Net cash flows from financing, ($81,300)
15–4A	Net cash flows from operations, ($32,900)
15–5A	Cash received from customers, $944,000
15–6A	Cash paid for merchandise, $1,091,600
15–1B	Net cash flow from operations, $103,000
15–2B	Net cash flow used in financing, ($32,000)
15–3B	Net cash flow used for investing, ($90,000)
15–4B	Net cash flow from operating activities, $65,000
15–5B	Cash payments for merchandise, $526,200
15–6B	Cash received from customers, $2,434,600
CP15–1	Net cash flow used in investing, ($214,200)
CP15–2	Cash payments for merchandise, $996,150
CP15–3	Net income, $42,000
16–1A	Decrease in net income 33.3%
16–2A	2000 net income as % of sales 8.5
16–3A	1c. Acid test ratio 1.4 (1.4:1)
16–4A	5—39.7, 14—18.2%, 19—0.6%
16–1B	Net sales increase 20.1%
16–2B	2000 net income as % of sales 5.4%
16–3B	1b. Current ratio 2.9 (2.9:1)
16–4B	4—14.0, 13—12.13, 16—$2.16

To the owner of this book

We hope that you have enjoyed *Accounting, Volume 2,* and we would like to know as much about your experiences with this text as you would care to offer. Only through your comments and those of others can we learn how to make this a better text for future readers.

School _____ Your instructor's name _____

Course _____ Was the text required? _____ Recommended? _____

1. What did you like the most about *Accounting, Volume 2?*

_____

_____

_____

2. How useful was this text for your course?

_____

_____

_____

3. Do you have any recommendations for ways to improve the next edition of this text?

_____

_____

_____

4. In the space below or in a separate letter, please write any other comments you have about the book. (For example, please feel free to comment on reading level, writing style, terminology, design features, and learning aids.)

_____

_____

_____

_____

Optional

Your name _____ Date _____

May ITP Nelson quote you, either in promotion for *Accounting, Volume 2* or in future publishing ventures?

Yes _____   No _____

Thanks!

PLEASE TAPE SHUT. DO NOT STAPLE.

TAPE SHUT

TAPE SHUT

- - - FOLD HERE - - -

MAIL ▷ POSTE
Canada Post Corporation
Société canadienne des postes

Postage paid	Port payé
if mailed in Canada	si posté au Canada
Business Reply	**Réponse d'affaires**

0066102399   **01**

Nelson

TAPE SHUT

TAPE SHUT

0066102399-M1K5G4-BR01

ITP NELSON
MARKET AND PRODUCT DEVELOPMENT
PO BOX 60225 STN BRM B
TORONTO ON M7Y 2H1